BRITAIN AND THE BOLSHEVIK REVOLUTION

By the same author

THE USSR: Portrait of a Super Power
POLITICAL CULTURE AND SOVIET POLITICS

BRITAIN AND THE BOLSHEVIK REVOLUTION

A Study in the Politics of Diplomacy,
1920 – 1924

Stephen White

Lecturer in Politics
University of Glasgow

© Stephen White 1979

First published 1979 by
THE MACMILLAN PRESS LTD
London and Basingstoke
Associated companies in Delhi
Dublin Hong Kong Johannesburg Lagos
Melbourne New York Singapore Tokyo

Filmset in Great Britain by
Vantage Photosetting Co., Ltd,
Southampton and London
Printed by Redwood Burn Ltd,
Trowbridge and Esher

British Library Cataloguing in Publication Data

White, Stephen, *b. 1945*
    Britain and the Bolshevik Revolution
    1. Great Britain—Foreign relations—Russia
    2. Russia—Foreign relations—Great Britain
    3. Great Britain—Foreign relations—1910–1936
    4. Russia—Foreign relations—1917–1945
    I. Title
    327.41'047   DA47.65

    ISBN 0–333–25671–9

For my parents

Contents

Preface

This study deals with the development of Anglo-Soviet relations from the revolution of 1917, when they began, to the recognition of the Soviet by the British government in 1924, when they reached an at least provisional *terminus ad quem*. As the immediate post-revolutionary years have been considered reasonably fully elsewhere I have preferred to concentrate upon the latter part of this period, and the bulk of the volume is accordingly devoted to an account of the short but turbulent years between the conclusion of the Anglo-Soviet Trade Agreement of March 1921 and the formal act of recognition of February 1924. So far from establishing fully 'normal' relations between the two countries, I shall argue, the trade agreement in fact gave rise to a series of diplomatic manoeuvres designed to undermine the Soviet government or otherwise commit it to Allied purposes which in political terms represented a continuation of the military intervention of the immediate post-revolutionary period. The first part of this volume deals with the attempt of the British government under Lloyd George to achieve this objective by direct negotiation; the second considers the attempt of the Conservative administration which succeeded it to achieve the same objective by more openly 'confrontationist' tactics. The third part, 'Recognition', deals with the change in business opinion regarding the desirability of closer relations with Russia in the latter part of 1923, a change which, it will be argued, is crucial to an understanding of the recognition of the Soviet government at the beginning of the following year by the first Labour government.

The treatment which follows, accordingly, ranges somewhat more widely than diplomatic history as conventionally understood. In particular, I have tried to relate the development of formal inter-state relations to three broad themes: first, the politics of the labour movement towards revolutionary Russia, a variable factor which (though I shall argue it is somewhat sentimentally described as 'solidarity') did play a part in first limiting

British military involvement in Russia and then bringing about the recognition of the Soviet government at the beginning of 1924; second, the influence upon government of business and financial opinion; and third, the impact upon formal inter-state relations of the developing competition for hegemony in the colonial world, especially in Asia, where British imperial rule faced an assertive and increasingly radical nationalist opposition with which Soviet foreign policy appeared to have a close and pernicious association. To integrate these themes coherently within the overall argument has been a difficult task, but a necessary one; for it is the thesis of this study that to confine the study of British-Soviet relations to the exchange of communications between governments would be profoundly to misunderstand the nature of the relationship between what were essentially two rival and mutually incompatible conceptions of world order. This, then, is a study in the sociology of international politics rather than a record of diplomatic interchange; it deals, in the last resort, with relations between classes rather than with those between states.

The plan of the book is briefly as follows. The first part, 'Negotiation', considers the evolution of Anglo-Soviet relations under the Premiership of Lloyd George. Successive chapters discuss the negotiation of the trade agreement of 1921; Labour 'solidarity' with Soviet Russia during this period; and the diplomatic conferences of Genoa and The Hague of 1922, which both summed up and completed this phase of relations between the two governments. The second part, 'Imperial Confrontation', examines the international dimension of British-Soviet relations under the more imperially-minded administration of Bonar Law. The new government's more traditional perception of the manner in which British interests might best be defended led to a series of sharply-worded communications to the Soviet government, culminating in the 'Curzon Note' of May 1923. Its greater preoccupation with imperial and colonial affairs, it is argued, reflected the temporary predominance of an 'agrarian-colonial-finance' section within British governing circles, although the threat to their interests which Soviet colonial intrigue in fact presented seems in retrospect to have been greatly exaggerated. The third part, 'Recognition', returns to the European context and considers the evidence of a growing conviction among merchants and manufacturers that their interests might more adequately be served by a policy of closer commercial relations with Russia, for which the diplomatic recognition of its government appeared to be a necessary prerequisite. It was this *entente commerciale*, it is argued, rather than a hypothetical community of socialist sentiment, which had most to do with the recognition of the Soviet government by the first Labour government at the beginning of the following year. The Conclusion considers the interaction of class, party and foreign policy more generally over the period as a whole.

This study has been some time in gestation, and many people have helped to make it better than it would otherwise have been. In Glasgow, Alec Nove, the supervisor of the thesis upon which this study is based, commented most helpfully upon the earlier manuscript and offered a characteristic mixture of advice, encouragement and stimulation at all times. My colleagues in the Department of Politics and the Institute of Soviet and East European Studies have similarly been generous with their time, attention and assistance. Seminar audiences in Glasgow and Oxford heard parts of the manuscript at various times and in various guises, and I have benefited from the discussions which followed. The British Council made it possible for me to spend an academic year at Moscow State University and every effort was made there to facilitate my studies. Elsewhere, Walter Kendall was kind enough to read and discuss a number of chapters with me; Mary McAuley read and commented constructively upon an earlier version of the manuscript as a whole; Marcel Liebman, Kenneth Young and the late Barry Hollingsworth corresponded with me and sent useful material and advice; and Rajani Palme Dutt and Morgan Phillips Price (both now, alas, deceased) were good enough to discuss their recollections of the period with me. Grants in aid of research were provided by the University of Glasgow and by the Carnegie Trust of the Universities of Scotland.

I am indebted to the librarians of the following institutions for permission to consult manuscript materials in their possession: Birmingham Public Library; Birmingham University Library; Bodleian Library, Oxford; British Library, London; British Library of Political and Economic Science, London; Cambridge University Library; Communist Party, London; Confederation of British Industry, London; Conservative Party Research Department, London; Council of Foreign Bondholders, London; Edinburgh Trades Council; Engineering Employers' Federation, London; Glasgow University Library; Guildhall Library, London; Hoover Institution, Stanford, California; House of Lords Record Office, London; India Office Library, London; Internationaal Instituut voor Sociale Geschiedenis, Amsterdam; Labour Party, London; Leeds University Library; Liverpool Public Library; Manchester University Library; Mitchell Library, Glasgow; National Library of Scotland, Edinburgh; Newcastle University Library; Nuffield College, Oxford; Russo-British Chamber of Commerce, London; Scottish Public Record Office, Edinburgh; Scottish Trades Union Congress, Glasgow; Sheepscar Library, Leeds; Sheffield Public Library; Sheffield Trades and Labour Council; Society for Cultural Relations with the USSR, London; Trades Union Congress, London; and Warwick University Library, Coventry. Mr David Marquand permitted me to consult the MacDonald Papers while still in his possession, and Viscount Bridgeman and Lord Ponsonby of Shulbrede were kind enough to lend me manuscript material. Transcripts from Crown Copyright records in the Public Record Office appear by permission of the Controller of H.M. Stationery Office.

Finally, I must thank the departmental secretaries, Jean Beverly, Hazel Falconer, Elspeth Shaw and Celia Wallace, for coping swiftly and efficiently with various drafts of this volume, and my wife, Ishbel, for her patience, advice and encouragement. In this, as in so many ways, she makes it all worthwhile.

Glasgow   Stephen White
                                              July 1979

List of Abbreviations

The following abbreviations have been employed in this study:

BSP	British Socialist Party
Cab	Cabinet Papers in the Public Record Office, London
DBFP	*Documents on British Foreign Policy*, First Series, ed. E. L. Woodward and R. Butler, vol. 1– (London 1947–)
DVP	*Dokumenty Vneshnei Politiki SSSR* (Documents on the Foreign Policy of the USSR), ed. A. A. Gromyko et al., vol. 1– (Moscow 1957–)
FBI	Federation of British Industries
F.O.	Foreign Office Papers in the Public Record Office, London
H. C. Debs	*Parliamentary Debates*, 5th series, House of Commons
ILP	Independent Labour Party
NEP	New Economic Policy
NKID	Narodnyi Komissariat po Inostrannym Delam (People's Commissariat for Foreign Affairs)
NKVT	Narodnyi Komissariat Vneshnei Torgovli (People's Commissariat of Foreign Trade)
Prem.	Prime Minister's Papers in the Public Record Office, London
PSS	V. I. Lenin, *Polnoe Sobranie Sochinenii* (Complete Works), 55 vols (Moscow 1957–65)
RKP(B)	Rossiiskaya Kommunisticheskaya Partiya (Bol'shevikov) (Russian Communist Party (Bolsheviks))
TUC	Trades Union Congress
UDC	Union of Democratic Control

Part I

NEGOTIATION

1 The Trade Agreement

On 16 January 1920 the Allied Supreme Council, meeting in Paris, declared the blockade of Soviet Russia at an end. 'The Allies now understand the impossibility of fighting the Bolsheviks in Russia', Lord Riddell noted in his diary. 'No nation is prepared to supply troops or money.'[1] The Supreme Council went on to adopt a resolution providing for an 'exchange of goods on the basis of reciprocity between the Russian people and Allied and neutral countries'. It was insisted that this did 'not mean a change in the policy of the Allied governments towards the Soviet government';[2] but it was difficult, on the face of it, to regard the Allies' decision as anything other than a complete reversal of the policy which they had previously pursued towards the Bolshevik authorities. A policy of peace and commerce, it appeared, was now to succeed the hostile confrontation of the immediate post-revolutionary years.[3]

Other than formally, in fact, there had been little change in British or Allied policy; for what the Supreme Council's decisions represented was not so much the adoption of a new and no longer anti-Bolshevik strategy but rather the selection of a new and, it appeared, more promising tactic by which that strategy might be pursued. This new tactic, in the words of a Foreign Office memorandum, was designed to provide an 'opportunity of testing the theory frequently advanced of late that the lifting of the blockade would do more to oust or modify Bolshevism than armed intervention ever accomplished'.[4] 'Commerce', Lloyd George, the British Prime Minister, explained to the House of Commons, 'has a sobering influence in its operations. The simple sums in addition and subtraction which it inculcates soon dispose of wild theories.' The 'moment trade was established with Russia', he told the Allied meeting, 'Communism would go'.[5]

The implications of the Allies' strategy were spelt out more fully in the *Daily Chronicle*, a journal normally close to the Premier's thinking. So far from the reopening of trade representing a first step towards an understanding with the Bolshevik government, the paper noted on 19 January 1920, 'its intention, apart from economic reasons, lies in an exactly contrary direction'. The co-operative societies, through which the trade was to be conducted, were known to be far from Bolshevik in sympathy. If the peasantry could be supplied through them with boots and clothing this would have a 'greater effect in combating Bolshevik belief and tendencies than a prolonged estrangement could possibly have'; while if the Soviet government, on the other hand, attempted to impede the establishment of relations of this kind, there would probably be an 'immediate and violent uprising on the part of the twenty-five million members of the co-operative societies'. As Lord Hardinge noted in a telegram to Paris on 20 January, the Soviet government appeared, at least in the recently conquered areas of Siberia and southern Russia, to have abandoned its plans to absorb the co-operatives. If this were so, it constituted a 'notable victory for individualism as opposed to Communism'. It would lead, he thought, either to formal relations with the Soviet government, or to an 'attempt to use the Co-operatives as a substitute for Kolchak and Denikin in the struggle with the Soviet government'.[6] It was the latter strategy which the Supreme Council had evidently adopted.

The possibility of utilising the Soviet co-operatives in this manner clearly required at least the acquiescence of the Soviet authorities; and it appeared at first as if this might be forthcoming. In a telegram to Paris on 2 February 1920, however, Tsentrosoyuz, the central co-operative organisation, rejected the Allies' proposals and suggested instead that it send its own representatives abroad 'in possession of all the necessary information and with all the necessary broad powers'. The delegates would leave as soon as a route and visas had been arranged, and they would be invested with the authority to conduct negotiations and to conclude binding agreements.[7] The chairman of the delegation, it was subsequently announced, would be Maxim Litvinov, the Soviet Deputy Commissar for Foreign Affairs; another member would be Leonid Krasin, the Commissar for Foreign Trade; and few of its remaining members had previously had more than a peripheral connection with the work of the co-operatives.[8] The Bolsheviks, in fact, had neatly inverted the Allies' stratagem: they were sending abroad, ostensibly as a Tsentrosoyuz delegation, a group of 'prominent Soviet workers and communists headed by the People's Commissar'. The governments of western Europe 'right from the start regarded it not as a representative body of co-operators, but as a body with full powers representing the Russian Soviet Government'.[9] Lord Riddell enquired of Lloyd George on 6 March whether the Russian delegation could be considered to represent the co-operatives or the Bolshevik government. 'The Soviet', he replied, 'undoubtedly'.[10]

A number of difficulties remained, in particular the question of the acceptability of Litvinov as a member of the delegation; but an accommodation was eventually reached and the group left Moscow at the end of March for Copenhagen, where further talks were to take place with Allied representatives. The talks failed to achieve a satisfactory resolution of the problem of the restoration of trade with Russia; and accordingly the Supreme Council, meeting at San Remo on 26 April, agreed that negotiations with the Russian trading delegation should be resumed in London 'at the earliest date convenient to them'.[11] Negotiations began there at the end of May 1920. The Russian delegation had already succeeded in negotiating a major agreement with a consortium of Swedish firms in the course of its journey to London. An agreement with Britain, however, Krasin wrote, was of 'decisive importance' for the Bolsheviks. Britain was the most powerful country in Europe, and a British decision in this respect might be expected to influence other governments. An agreement, however limited, could be expanded and augmented; failure, however, might lead to failure elsewhere as well. Thus 'from the end of May 1920', recalled Krasin, 'all the efforts of the Soviet foreign delegation were concentrated upon the achievement of an agreement with England'.[12]

British policy remained equivocal. Lloyd George had sponsored the Allied change of front, and he was deeply committed to the success of the negotiations. Curzon, however, though Foreign Secretary, declined at first to enter into relations of any kind with the Soviet representatives, and at the opening of the talks he refused even to shake hands with Krasin until Lloyd George (who recounted the story some years later to Maisky) appealed to him to 'be a gentleman'.[13] Churchill, who was at this time at the War Office, regarded the impending negotiations with no greater enthusiasm. In a memorandum addressed to the Supreme Council meeting at San Remo, he declared that they must 'decide which of two factors is most (*sic*) dangerous to the existing order of society in Europe and to the security of the United Kingdom, namely . . . recognition of the Soviet Government or starvation and disease in Europe on an unprecedented scale'. He was not present at the meeting with Krasin; and was reported afterwards to have asked, 'did you shake hands with the hairy baboon?'[14] Differences within the Cabinet, in fact, remained hardly less significant than they had been throughout the course of the previous year; and this was among the factors responsible for the fact that the negotiations lasted almost ten months, from the end of May 1920 until 16 March 1921, when the trade agreement was finally concluded.

The first meeting between the two sides was devoted to a preliminary exchange of views on measures essential for the renewal of trade relations.[15] It soon became apparent that the British negotiators attached particular importance to a limited number of more specific issues. One was the question of British prisoners of war who were still detained in Russia in conditions which were thought to leave a great deal to be desired. Of greater importance were the issues of propaganda and the question of Russian debts and obligations, the acknowledgment of which, if not their repayment in full, was regarded as a matter which must be satisfactorily resolved before an agreement could be contemplated. Krasin suggested in reply that contentious points of this kind should be reserved for consideration at a bilateral conference to be convened expressly for this purpose, allowing trade to develop in the meantime. This, however, was to misunderstand the motives of the British government in entering into ostensibly 'trading' negotiations. For many members of the Cabinet saw no great virtue simply in providing for the renewal of trade between the two countries; they regarded any such agreement, rather, as an inducement to the Soviet government in return for which it might make concessions upon matters of greater relevance to British interests. It was precisely these matters which Krasin, perhaps disingenuously, now proposed to postpone.

At the meeting between the two sides which was held on 29 June 1920, Lloyd George complained that this amounted to a 'practical refusal to accept the only conditions which made possible the resumption of trade relations'. The matters to which the British negotiators had drawn attention, he insisted, were 'fundamental questions'.[16] A memorandum which was handed to

Krasin the following day, shortly before his departure for Moscow, accordingly sought a 'categorical answer: yes or no' as to whether the Soviet government was prepared to enter into a trade agreement upon certain specified conditions. These were: that each side should 'refrain from hostile actions or measures directed against the other side, and from the conducting of any kind of official propaganda' (this was the British government's 'basic condition'); that British and Russian citizens detained by either side should be free to return to their homeland; that both governments should agree in principle to pay compensation to private citizens who had rendered goods or services to the other side for which they had not been paid; and finally, that the measures suggested by the Soviet representatives to facilitate trade relations and communications should be implemented. If these principles were accepted as the basis of an agreement the details could swiftly be settled by negotiation; but if a positive reply had not been received after seven days, the negotiations would be considered at an end.[17]

Georgy Chicherin, the People's Commissar for Foreign Affairs, did not fail to protest in his reply of 7 July 1920 against 'accusations, contrary to the real state of affairs, that Soviet Russia is carrying out attacks on the British Empire'. In the 'interests of a swift conclusion of peace between Russia and Great Britain', however, the principles set out in the British memorandum were accepted as the 'basis for an agreement'. A more fully elaborated text might be worked out in detailed negotiations between the two governments, which should begin without delay.[18] An 'understanding had, therefore, been reached', Bonar Law, Lord Privy Seal, told the House of Commons on the government's behalf, 'as to the principles on which a trade agreement would be negotiated'.[19] The armed conflict which broke out at this point between Russia and Poland halted further moves. The connection between that conflict and the development of Russo-British trade was not an obvious one. Trade, however, had been only the ostensible subject of the negotiations; their real substance had remained pre-eminently political throughout.

A Polish offensive had been launched on 25 April 1920. The Polish forces had enjoyed considerable initial success, and on 8 May they had succeeded in capturing Kiev. The Polish offensive received no direct support from the British government; but there was satisfaction in some quarters at the prospect of the Poles achieving at least a part of what the Allies had so recently failed to accomplish, and a telegram of congratulations from King George V on 3 May 1920, the anniversary of the foundation of the Polish state, was widely regarded as implying rather more than it expressly conveyed. The Polish advance, however, was checked, and on 25 June the Bolsheviks re-captured Kiev and began to institute a vigorous counter-attack. On 11 July they captured Minsk, and on 27 July they took Pinsk and moved for the first time into ethnographic Poland, meeting very little resistance. The capture of Warsaw and the 'sovietisation of Poland', it appeared, could not long be delayed.

The implications of this advance were far-reaching. Once the Polish line of defence was breached, the British minister in Warsaw had noted, the barrier against Bolshevism would be shifted much farther west, and an opportunity would be given to 'latent Bolshevism in Czechoslovakia to join hands with Russian Bolshevism, thereby creating a very serious state of things for Central Europe and the Western Powers'.[20] A meeting of Allied representatives at Spa on 10 July was told that Hungary would undoubtedly 'become Bolshevik' within two weeks of the occupation of Poland. Nor was it likely that Germany would remain unaffected. The Bolsheviks might link up with German radicals; and an Independent Socialist government might well be formed, which might then refuse to carry out the peace treaty. And then 'where', asked Lloyd George, 'would the Allies be?' The Allies must secure an independent Poland, he warned, 'otherwise all their work could be undone'.[21]

Curzon accordingly wrote to Chicherin to propose an armistice between the two contending parties, to be followed by a peace conference in London. While the British government could not assist Poland in any actions hostile to Russia, it was noted, the government was nevertheless obliged by the terms of the League of Nations agreement to 'defend the inviolability and independence of Poland within its legal ethnographic frontiers'. The Allies would do so, if necessary, by all the means in their power.[22] Nor could negotiations for a trade agreement be resumed if Russian forces were invading Poland; and Krasin and Lev Kamenev, a member of the Bolshevik Politburo who had joined the trade delegation at this point, were instructed to remain in Reval until an armistice had been concluded.[23]

Polish-Soviet negotiations, however, broke down, and the Red Army continued its apparently irresistible advance. Krasin and Kamenev, who had meanwhile been allowed to proceed to London, were summoned to meet Lloyd George on 4 August 1920. No armistice had yet been concluded, the Prime Minister pointed out, and Russian forces were now invading ethnographic Poland. The Polish government had been urged to accept any reasonable peace terms it was offered; but the reality, the Premier went on, was that no armistice had been concluded and 'the army is moving on Warsaw'. A further meeting took place two days later. Unless there was a stoppage within the following forty-eight hours, Lloyd George warned, 'the conference, trade and everything else went'.[24] The Soviet delegates' reply did not satisfy him. If this was the Soviet government's final word on the matter, he wrote to Kamenev, the British government could regard it only as a refusal of the conditions for an armistice which had been outlined at their meeting on 6 August. The meeting of the Allies at Hythe, which was shortly to take place, would proceed upon this assumption.[25]

The situation was certainly grave, Lloyd George told the Allied meeting. The Poles were 'quite demoralised and . . . incapable of either civil or military direction'. But there was little that the Allies could do. They could blockade the Russian ports; and they could provide assistance to General Wrangel in South Russia, whose performance against the Bolsheviks had so far been superior to that of his predecessors. The only supplies which Britain could provide to the Poles, however, were a 'certain amount of pack saddlery, sets of equipment, boots, clothing and so on'. Apart from these supplies, Britain could give support from the sea; but that was all. Lloyd George summed up the measures which could be taken to 'secure the real independence' of Poland as follows: '(i) Internally, by helping with officers, technical advisors, munitions and material; (ii) By a reimposition of the blockade'; on the assumption '(a) That a state of war did not exist with the Soviet Government; (b) That neither France nor England could send troops; (c) That the amount of money that each of the Allied countries would be able to subscribe must be strictly limited'. If terms were imposed upon the Polish government which were not acceptable to that government and which infringed Polish independence then common action along these lines would be taken: naval manoeuvres, the blocking of communications, the provision of war material and advice to Poland, the support of Wrangel and of the border states, counter-propaganda, and the expulsion of Kamenev and Krasin. Crucially, however, no Allied forces were to be provided.[26]

The situation eased considerably upon receipt from Kamenev of the terms of armistice and peace preliminaries which the Russian delegates proposed to submit to their Polish counterparts at Minsk. The terms, it was noted, 'might be supplemented by details of secondary moment'. As they stood, however, they were agreed to be as good as could reasonably have been expected; in particular it was a 'great cause of satisfaction' that they 'secured the independence of Poland'. The Poles were, of course, at liberty to attempt to improve upon them through negotiation; but the Polish government was to be informed that the British government could not assume the responsibility of taking hostile action against Russia if the conditions now offered in their general substance were refused.[27] If an agreement were made, the House of Commons was informed, or if Polish independence, at least, were conceded, then the Russian delegation would be allowed to remain in the country to continue the negotiation of a trade agreement, and the government would make no attempt to intervene in the further development of Russo-Polish relations. The government undertook, in any case, to take no action until the House of Commons had met and its approval had been obtained for any proposed course of action.[28]

It subsequently emerged that the terms as communicated to the Polish negotiators included at least one provision not to the taste of the Cabinet, the formation of a working-class 'civil militia' in Poland. Lloyd George and Giolitti, the Italian Prime Minister, met at Lucerne on 22 August 1920 and agreed in deploring such a proposal. What might happen if Poland collapsed and the Bolsheviks succeeded in reaching the German border? The Germans, Lloyd George noted, 'were an orderly people whose natural tendency was anti-Bolshevik. But if they were driven too hard they might be forced into Bolshevism.' Undoubtedly, he added, there were revolutionary elements in Germany, and if the guns and rifles were still there the position would be dangerous. The Premiers accordingly agreed to urge the Soviet government, 'in the interests of peace', not to insist upon 'conditions inconsistent with Polish independence' such as 'some special form of government' or a requirement that the army or militia be 'drawn from or placed under the control of any particular class of people'.[29] A communique to this effect was sent to Kamenev and published in *The Times* on 24 August 1920. Curzon, in a telegram to Chicherin, reiterated the point.[30]

Chicherin's reply expressed surprise that the matter should be regarded in such a light; the British government's belief that workers by their very nature must be imbued with Bolshevik doctrines, he thought, could 'only be welcomed by those who expected the extension of Bolshevism to Britain'. In the interests of securing agreement, however, the Soviet government was prepared to concede the point. Balfour, Lord President of the Council, regarded this change in policy with 'satisfaction'.[31] Kamenev's failure to mention this part of the draft agreement, however, was regarded by the British government as a 'crude infringement of trust', making further negotiations with the government he represented 'more difficult, if not impossible'.[32] His imminent departure for Moscow allowed the Cabinet to adopt a more considered attitude to the developments with which he had been associated.

A refusal to allow Kamenev to return, it was noted, would probably lead to the termination of the trade negotiations, 'which at present held out some prospect of useful results'. It was agreed that the Prime Minister should nevertheless see Kamenev before his departure and give him a warning about his recent conduct.[33] The interview took place later the same day. Kamenev, Lloyd George charged, had taken 'steps of an active character to subsidize a newspaper (the *Daily Herald*) not merely hostile to the Government . . . [but] a newspaper whose object is to attach the institutions of this country, which every day is trying to sow strife between classes, to create unrest, to spread discord'. Kamenev, in addition, had communicated the Soviet terms for peace with Poland to the British government but had omitted provisions 'quite incompatible with the independence of Poland'. His trustworthiness as a representative was thereby impugned; and if he had not in any case been leaving the following day it would have been necessary to have asked him to do so.[34]

Kamenev's conduct of his responsibilities was not the only point which hindered the resumption of negotiations. The position of British prisoners in Russia, especially those detained in Baku, was also a source of some concern. There were about a hundred and fifty of them, a Conference of Ministers was told on 15 September 1920; and there was 'evidence that they were very indifferently fed'. No further negotiations, it was agreed, could take place until they had been released.[35] There was also the question of propaganda. Curzon drew attention to this issue in two communications to the Soviet government on 1 and 9 October 1920. Kamenev, he charged, had engaged in 'practically open propaganda'; and the Third Congress of the Communist International, over which Lenin had presided, had 'openly announced that the Communist Party, and thus also the Soviet government, intended to use all means to overthrow existing institutions throughout the world'. These actions, and others, were 'clearly directed against British interests'.[36] A 'real hurricane of propaganda, intrigue and conspiracy against British interests and British power in Asia' had also been initiated. Such a situation, Curzon insisted, 'must be ended if the trade negotiations, to which both sides attach so much importance, are to be concluded'.[37]

The question of the prisoners of war presented few intrinsic difficulties; and the Soviet government in turn suggested a means of making the exchange.[38] Further correspondence followed; and a protocol was signed on 1 November 1920 providing for the release of all British subjects detained in Baku.[39] Bonar Law, speaking in the House of Commons, explained that the delay in resuming the trading negotiations with Soviet Russia was 'not difficult to explain. The arrangement was contingent upon some agreements by the Soviet government, among which was the return of prisoners. When that is done, the negotiations will be resumed.'[40] An agreement on this point had now been reached, and this objection, presumably, no longer applied. There were other factors, however, which also contributed to the decision to resume negotiations.

The first of these was the degree of relative stability which had been reached upon the battlefield. To the surprise and, no doubt, greatly to the relief of the Cabinet, the Poles had checked the advance of the Red Army and then, on 16 August, with Soviet forces within sight of the Polish capital, they had reversed it and instituted a successful counter-attack. The two sides eventually concluded an armistice on 12 October; and on 18 March 1921, just two days after the trade agreement with Britain, a formal peace treaty was signed.[41] The Allies need no longer concern themselves for the fate of this 'bulwark against Bolshevism';

equally, they must for the foreseeable future rule out the prospect of a military offensive against the Soviet government from this quarter.

Nothing, moreover, could now be hoped for from Wrangel's forces in the south of Russia. His declining fortunes were reported to the Cabinet on 11 November; and agreement was reached that British policy (which had throughout been more circumspect than that of the French) 'should be that of strict neutrality which should on no account be compromised'.[42] Wrangel's final defeat came in the same month when the Bolsheviks invaded his last stronghold and, on 14 November 1920, took Sebastopol. No alternative to the Soviet regime could now reasonably be foreseen by even its bitterest opponents in the government ('so many prophecies of the impending fall of the Bolshevik Government had been confidently made, and as surely falsified', wrote Lord Curzon, that he had himself 'long since ceased to attach much importance to these political predictions');[43] there was accordingly every reason to seek to achieve by negotiation what could not now be achieved by force of arms.

It was of importance also that another view of the nature and stability of the Soviet government, one sharply at variance with the picture painted by official sources, was becoming available through the reports of individuals and groups who had visited Soviet Russia and assessed the situation at first hand. George Lansbury, who visited Russia early in 1920, was so impressed by his experiences that he addressed a telegram to the Prime Minister from Moscow, assuring him that he was making the 'mistake of [his] life' with regard to the Bolshevik leaders, who were in fact 'first-rate clear-headed honest humane men'. He concluded his message, somewhat optimistically, by urging Lloyd George to 'come here [and] join in [a] conference with Lenin. [I] am certain [that] your eyes would be opened [as] soon as you cross [the] frontier.' The Bolsheviks, he wrote, were 'doing what Christians call the Lord's work'; Lenin's devotion to the cause of humanity made his whole life like 'that of one of the saints of old.'[44]

Professor William Goode, a *Manchester Guardian* correspondent who had visited Russia the previous summer, produced an account of his visit entitled 'Bolshevism at Work' at about the same time. Goode was granted interviews with Lenin and Chicherin, and he recorded that the leaders were 'profoundly simple in their dress, food [and] life' despite the 'slanderous descriptions of them circulated in the West of Europe'. He had 'not found the millennium—far from it—but the reality is far otherwise than the stories circulated at home would make one believe'. He believed in particular that the Soviet government was supported by the 'mass of the workers solidly' and, actively or passively, by as many as two thirds of the peasants.[45] H. G. Wells, who visited Russia the following year, concurred in this verdict: the Bolshevik government, he thought, was 'as securely established as any government in Europe'. He pressed this view personally upon Curzon.[46]

Perhaps the greatest impact of all, however, was made by the visit of the Trades Union Congress and Labour Party delegation to Russia in the summer of 1920. The delegation found that British press reports were 'perversions of the facts'; the revolution, in their view, had 'not had a fair chance'. They recommended that the entire British labour movement should 'demand the removal of the last vestige of blockade and intervention, and the complete destruction of the barrier which Imperialists have erected between our own people and our brothers and sisters of Russia'. Many notions which had enjoyed wide currency in the press were refuted: nobody had been seen falling dead of starvation in the street; there was no evidence of interference with religious observance; no Chinese soldiers had been found; neither women nor children appeared to have been nationalised; and the leading Commissars did not lead a life of luxury. The delegates concluded by urging that the new Soviet government be 'unconditionally recognized'.[47]

The delegates were far from unanimous in their admiration of the new regime. Most of them, however, would have agreed with Ben Turner, the delegation's chairman, who told the Labour press on his return that the stories of attempts to hoodwink the delegates were 'nonsense' and that those which reported the country to be in a condition of anarchy were 'totally untrue'. There was some evidence of hunger, but for this the intervention and the Allied blockade were chiefly responsible. The public health arrangements of the Soviet authorities, indeed, were 'marvellous'. Turner had no doubt that the Bolshevik government enjoyed the support of the bulk of the Russian people; and all the delegates were agreed upon the 'urgent necessity of an immediate peace'.[49] Five of them, in fact, went so far as to appeal to trade unionists to take direct action in an attempt to influence the British government in this sense.[50]

The government, evidently concerned to redress the balance, established a Committee to Collect Information on Russia in May 1920 under the chairmanship of Lord Emmott. It issued an Interim Report the following December, dealing with the treatment of British prisoners in Russia. Their suffering, the report conceded, appeared to have been not nearly as severe as that of the Russians themselves. One man, for instance, had been placed in an overcrowded cell; but he had been accommodated at all only by the somewhat desperate expedient of removing the nearest occupant, taking him outside, and shooting him. The prisoners' living conditions, nevertheless, were far from satisfactory (one man, for instance, had been given a bowl of soup with a horse's eye floating in it); and on the whole the Soviet authorities were adjudged 'incapable of discharging their responsibilities towards British subjects detained in Russia'.[51] Such reports notwithstanding, however, the government was less than completely successful in its attempt to counter the picture of Soviet Russia which Labour and Liberal commentators were now providing, and a better-informed and more determined public opinion became another of the factors which was helping to impel the government towards the conclusion of an agreement with its Soviet counterpart.

Not less important in bringing about a change in the government's policy was the collapse of the post-war boom in the autumn of 1920. In June 1920 the proportion of the insured population out of work had been a relatively modest 2.6 per cent; but by September the proportion had increased to 3.8 per cent, and by December it had more than doubled to 7.9 per cent.[52] Special reports on unemployment began to be circulated to government ministers in October 1920, and a Cabinet committee on unemployment was set up two months later. By January 1921, the Minister of Labour told a Conference of Ministers, the problem was 'becoming increasingly serious' (unemployment had meanwhile increased still further to 11.2 per cent of the insured workforce).[53] Unemployment benefit was a serious burden upon the public purse at a time of stringent economies; the unemployed, besides, were notoriously the most disaffected section of the workforce. The decline in the value of foreign trade appeared to have a particularly close connection with the rise in unemployment; and to many ministers there were now compelling economic arguments for the continuation and successful conclusion of the trade negotiations with Russia.[54]

It appeared, moreover, that the development of trade with Russia might be particularly well calculated to alleviate the problems which the government confronted. Orders of up to one hundred million pounds, the *Observer* predicted on 5 November 1920, would be obtained in the first year after trading relations had been restored. Dealing with the future of the negotiations ten days later in the House of Commons, Bonar Law (himself a businessman) declared that trade with Russia was 'still more desirable now, when there is a state of unemployment in this country. We shall certainly do nothing to prevent these relations being resumed as far as we can . . . Trade relations have been renewed by other governments, and this country must do its best to get its share of the trade.'[55] Nearly two million pounds' worth of wheat, it was reported, had been imported from Russia in 1913, together with four and three-quarters of a million pounds' worth of eggs. Almost 70 per cent of British flax imports had come from Russia, together with 52 per cent of hewn and sawn fir, and 45 per cent of pit props. The absence of these imports was believed in many cases to be holding back the development of important industries and causing short time working and redundancies, while the absence of traditional sources of supply of food was held to be largely responsible for the high cost of living.[56]

The Soviet trading delegation was well aware of the interest in business and governmental circles in developing this trade, and it attempted—not without success—to stimulate it further. The All-Russian Co-operative Society, or 'Arcos', a private British company but under ultimate Russian control, was registered on 11 June 1920; it entered into negotiations with various firms and some contracts were signed for the eventual supply of goods.[57] A particularly great impression was created by an order which was placed with five Yorkshire firms for the supply of broadcloth to a total value of nearly a million pounds sterling, payable in cash, which was concluded in the middle of September on receipt of an urgent order from Moscow. The news, Krasin recalled, had a 'most striking effect' on the London stock exchange, and it 'caused a sensation in the City. . . . We were inundated with inquiries'. There followed a 'whole series of newspaper articles in influential papers, and interest in trade deals with Soviet Russia increased markedly'.[58] *The Times*, on the basis of enquiries made among business circles, admitted that there was a 'growing volume of opinion in favour of trade being resumed'. Interviews appeared in the press in October 1920 with A. G. Marshall, the managing director of 'Becos', a federation of engineering firms, and with the chairman of the professional association of the rubber industry, both of whom urged the establishment—in Britain's interests—of the closest possible trading relations with Russia. The *Daily News* the following month printed a series of leading articles by Arthur Cummings which reported that business opinion generally shared these views.[59]

Writing to Lloyd George on 4 October 1920, Krasin dwelt upon the importance of the resumption of relations between the two countries from this point of view. A whole series of deals and contracts, he noted, could be 'made forthwith following the conclusion of a trade agreement'. Preliminary negotiations had confirmed the possibility of exporting railway locomotives to Russia, and of arranging for the repair in Britain of Soviet engines, a contract in which 'several railway and machine-engineering firms in Britain were interested'. The annual value of orders from Soviet Russia for railway equipment would be in excess of ten million pounds, and they could be placed largely in British factories, which were otherwise short of orders and far from fully employed. Other substantial orders were being held up only because of a lack of transport facilities and because of the 'impossibility of establishing normal trading relations until an agreement was concluded between the two states on these questions'.[60] Negotiations, Krasin recalled, were initiated with a 'whole range of major firms': with the Slough Trading Company for the supply of five hundred automobiles, with Marconi, with Armstrong-Whitworth and Co., and for the formation of a British-Russian trading society. The delegation gave no binding promises; but 'all the same several industrial groups began to exert pressure upon the Foreign Office and upon Lloyd George'. By the time the question of the prisoners of war had been settled and the negotiations renewed, the trade delegation 'had a fairly powerful group in the City behind it'.[61]

This current of opinion did not pass unnoticed in the Foreign Office. On 20 December an article from the previous day's *Sunday Times* was placed on file. The article's headline read: 'Why we must Trade with Russia: Orders British Firms Require: An End to Depression'. It went on to note that if Britain did not enter into trading relations with Russia 'other countries will capture the market'. British manufacturers were reported to be 'unanimous' in the belief that settled trade conditions could not be restored until trade relations with Russia had been resumed. The representatives of at least one Midland engineering firm, it added, had already made contact with Krasin.[62] On 6 December a letter arrived at the Foreign Office from the Indian Tea Association bearing a similar message. 'Every effort', it urged, should be made to bring about closer trading relations with Russia.[63] Later in December the information was circulated that two mills in Yorkshire, Fenton Textiles Ltd. and C. and J. Hurst Ltd., had signed contracts with the Russian trading delegation. According to a letter to the Prime Minister which the *Yorkshire Post* published on 11 December, these were the only two mills in Yorkshire which were working on a full-time basis. The 'leading commercial associations and business men', noted a Foreign Office minute, now favoured the resumption of trade with Russia. A further minute added that disappointment if the negotiations broke down 'would not be limited to labour only'. There had been a 'good many indications lately of a change of mind in commercial and industrial circles'.[64]

There were, then, some grounds for thinking that the negotiations might proceed further when Krasin again communicated with the British government on 9 November 1920. A further note drew attention to the 'most unsatisfactory position' in which the negotiations had been left. Ten months had passed since the Supreme Council had proposed their initiation, and four months had passed since the basis of an agreement had been reached. A 'swift and direct answer' was now sought as to whether the British government was ready to enter into negotiations in order to establish normal relations.[65]

A speech by Lloyd George at the Guildhall, and a speech by Sir Robert Horne, President of the Board of Trade, in which he had argued the necessity of resumption of trade between the West and Russia, gave some indication of the trend of Cabinet thinking.[66] Curzon, Churchill and that section of business whose interests had suffered as a result of the Soviet government's nationalisation, however, appeared still to oppose any sort of agreement, or even negotiations, with the Soviet authorities.[67] Curzon certainly expressed a desire to 'have nothing to do with the agreement'; and the Foreign Office as a whole undertook 'no responsibility for the drafting of the Trade Agreement', preferring that matters of this kind remain the responsibility of the Department of Overseas Trade.[68] Some evidence of the concessions which it might be necessary to make to this group was provided by the draft text of a trade agreement which *The Times* made public on 5 October 1920 (it was subsequently repudiated). Compared with the basis of agreement reached in the June–July exchange of notes it contained a number of alterations in the British interest, in particular a requirement that the Soviet government recognise the whole of the Russian state debt.[69]

Issue was joined at a meeting of the Cabinet on 17 November 1920. Sir Robert Horne began by putting the case for the conclusion of the treaty. The Russians, he argued, were prepared to place large orders in the country, and many of the contracts were at an 'advanced state'. They were of the 'greatest importance . . . from the commercial point of view and because of the menace of unemployment, of the likelihood that during this winter the slump will last for a considerable time'. If Britain did not engage in this trade it would be lost to other countries, and the debts would never be paid. The trading community as a whole, he believed, wanted to resume the trade, although there would be protests from some concessionaries. He felt strongly, moreover, that the 'only way [they would] fight Bolshevism is by trade. It thrives best in uncivilised conditions.'

Curzon objected. He did not attempt to dispute the economic arguments; his concern was with the conditions of the agreement. With regard to the repatriation of prisoners, he thought, the Russians had been 'trying to trick us'; while as concerned propaganda, the other fundamental condition which the government had made, the evidence was that 'from Moscow to Tashkent conspiracies worked by Bolshevik agents and paid for by Bolshevik gold' were proceeding uninterrupted. The Bolsheviks, moreover, did 'not intend to desist from propaganda. The purpose and pith of their government is propaganda throughout the world. You conclude an agreement with them. The same business will go on at Teheran, Baku, Enzeli, Bokhara etc. . . .' The government, he thought, should be 'very cautious at signing the trade agreement because the two conditions have not been loyally acted upon'. Austen Chamberlain remarked that he 'agreed generally' with these views.

Lloyd George, however, pointed out that had the conditions of agreement already been binding, then there were some things which the British government itself ought not to have done: such as unloading rifles at Danzig with British troops, sending a military mission to Poland, and so on. Bonar Law agreed with Horne's initial arguments. They had been 'playing with this Russian situation too long. You cannot go on talking and not conclude an agreement.' Furthermore, the country was 'in for bad unemployment. There is some business to be got in this way'; whereas if no agreement were made the 'effect on the public mind of the imaginary volume of trade . . . would be very bad', and they would have 'no leverage against the political hostility of Russia'. In sum, they would 'lose the chance of political leverage and do it at the expense of losing some trade'. He agreed with Horne, moreover, that Bolshevism would 'come to an end under civilized conditions'.

The Prime Minister concurred. He had seen a good many businessmen, he reported, and they had 'rather frightened him about the next eighteen months'. He and Bonar Law had met the chairman of the Federation of British Industries and had found that no orders were coming in. They might have the 'worst period of unemployment any of us have known. The Russians are prepared to pay in gold and you won't buy.' Their refusal to do so, moreover, would certainly be discovered, and this would 'add to the public discontent'. The manufacturers were in favour. The financiers naturally wanted their bonds, and he didn't blame them; but 'the pressure from the Midlands is all the other way'. They had been hearing predictions of the fall of the Soviet government for the previous two years. It had been their opponents, in fact, who had all collapsed, whereas the Prime Minister could 'not see any immediate prospect of the collapse of the Soviet government'.[70]

The debate was continued the following day. Churchill contended that the government were not yet committed. The scale of the proposed transactions was petty compared with the bulk of British trade as a whole; and it would 'only bolster up the Bolshevik government and their military organization'. He 'objected to helping them out of the difficulties which they had made for themselves by their Communism'. He accepted (somewhat inconsistently) that they 'should not turn [the agreement] down', but the government ought to make sure that the Bolsheviks had 'given evidence of goodwill and ceased hostilities in the East'.

Lloyd George pointed out that they could stipulate that hencefor-
ward there must be no hostile action. 'You can name all the places
... Meanwhile trade is going from bad to worse.' He spoke not as
an advocate of Bolshevism: on the contrary, he was 'trying to
prevent Bolshevism in this country'. Churchill, unabashed, retorted that the Premier was 'on the high road to embrace Bolshevism. I am going to keep off that and denounce them on all possible
occasions.' He, Curzon, Montagu and Long were convinced that
conditions must be specified and observed before, and not following, the conclusion of an agreement.

It was eventually decided to authorise the President of the
Board of Trade to conclude a trade agreement with Russia on the
general lines of the exchange of notes of June and July 1920; but it
was to be signed on the understanding that the conditions
specified in that exchange should be 'definitely re-stated in the
Trade Agreement' and regarded as fundamental to it. A provision
should also be included whereby in the event of either party failing
to fulfil its obligations under the terms of the agreement the other
would be entitled to denounce it. The attention of the Russian
government was additionally to be drawn 'either in the Agreement itself or in a covering communication to the Russian representatives, to any specially important respects in which, in
accordance with the terms of the Agreement, the Bolsheviks must
alter their present procedure or policy'. The Prime Minister was
authorised to announce that a draft agreement was in preparation
upon this basis. It was agreed, however, that the conclusion of a
trade agreement 'would not be assumed to hamper the discretion
of Ministers in public statements regarding the Bolshevist system
of Government'.[71]

The draft agreement was considered at a meeting of the
Cabinet eight days later. The proposed text was adopted after a
number of amendments had been made, prohibiting hostile
action and propaganda against the institutions of the United
Kingdom and Dominions more explicitly in the preamble and
referring back for further consideration the draft letter which was
to be handed to Krasin as a statement of the government's
interpretation of the agreement. It was agreed that, should the
agreement be concluded, the Russian government would 'not be
allowed to escape responsibility for hostile propaganda by shelter-
ing itself behind the activities of the "Third International"'.[72] On
29 November the draft trade agreement was handed to Krasin.[73]

The final phase of negotiations, which began at this point and lasted until the following March, revolved around three main issues. The British draft, in the first place, provided for the annulment of the agreement three months after either side had given notice to this effect. Krasin, in a preliminary comment, objected that this was a question of 'cardinal importance'. The period suggested was 'completely insufficient'; it would simply discredit the trade agreement in the eyes of the world and 'above all ... in the eyes of business people'. Contracts for railway locomotives, turbines, railway materials and so on required a period of from two to five years to fulfil. 'At least twelve months', he thought, must be provided for in the agreement; and each side should agree to assist in attempting to secure the fulfilment of contracts based on a longer period.[74] The question of the import and sale of Russian gold was also in dispute. When sold to the Bank of England it realised rather less than its price on the world market; and the question of granting such imports the privileges of 'most favoured nation' status was accordingly considered. The Soviet title to the gold, however, had to be left to the courts to determine, and it was agreed that no definitive ruling on this question could be included in the text of the agreement.[75]

On the British side the major point of contention concerned propaganda. The government, Lloyd George informed Krasin, had no objection at all to the specification by the Soviet government, as the British government had done, of particular countries within which propaganda directed against its interests must cease. The British government had made explicit reference to a number of countries because 'undoubtedly a good deal of hostile propaganda had been carried on in those particular areas against British interests'. This must be brought to an end. It would, the Premier pointed out, be 'almost impossible' for him to secure acceptance of the agreement by the government unless 'those who were specially interested in those countries were satisfied that hostile propaganda would cease'. He proposed that both governments expressly renounce 'encouragement or assistance to any propaganda conducted outside its own territories'. Such a formulation, Krasin thought, 'might be acceptable' so far as the Soviet government was concerned.[76]

It appeared for a time possible that the sceptics within the Cabinet might be encouraged by the rising at the naval base of Kronstadt, which broke out in March 1921, to resume their formerly uncompromising attitude. Cecil Harmsworth, Under-Secretary of State at the Foreign Office, informed the House of Commons on 9 March that the base was 'completely in the power of the revolutionary sailors', adding that the position in the capital was 'obscure' and that the loyalty of the Red Army appeared 'uncertain'. Press reports dealing with the rising in Petrograd and Moscow, describing the flight of Lenin and Trotsky and the hoisting of the white flag over the Kremlin, were officially confirmed; and a statement was issued on 8 March to the effect that almost all of Petrograd was in the hands of the mutineers. The Soviet government protested vigorously: the statement, it declared, was 'undoubtedly intended to harm further negotiations between Russia and England concerning the Trade Agreement'.[77]

It was represented to the Cabinet on 14 March, in the light of these developments, that the Soviet government's position was in fact 'by no means stable'. There were advantages, it was urged, in 'not hastening the conclusion of an Agreement which was desired by the Bolsheviks mainly in order to enhance their prestige'. Intelligence reports, however, suggested that it would be prudent not to take the anti-socialist character and viability of the mutiny for granted;[78] and the Cabinet decided that they had 'already suffered delay in this matter' and that the issue should 'now be forced to a conclusion'. Subject to the detailed amendments which had been suggested, Horne was authorised to proceed with the conclusion of the agreement.[79]

The economic arguments for doing so remained compelling. As Horne reminded the House of Commons, Russia was 'one of the great producing countries of the world', providing Britain before the war with one-eighth of her grain, one-seventh of her butter, one-half of her eggs and timber, and four-fifths of her flax. The shortage of these commodities had led to increased prices, and to unrest amongst the mass of working people. Although it would be 'years and years' before these pre-war levels would be attained, the government was 'anxious to see Russia producing again'. Exports to Russia, moreover, had been substantial before the war, and Russian purchases of machinery had been exceeded only by those from India. It was 'of the greatest possible moment', Horne concluded, 'that we should have opportunities of selling that machinery to Russia, of selling all the manufactures which our people work into fabrics by their hands—that we should especially at the present time be able to give increased employment to our people'.[80] To love one's neighbour, Lloyd George remarked, was 'not only good sound Christianity: it is good business'.[81]

These arguments were reinforced by the news that the negotiations which the Russian trade delegation had been conducting with the engineering firm of Armstrong Whitworth and Company had resulted in the conclusion of a preliminary agreement, providing for the repair of three hundred Soviet locomotives over a period of five years. The agreement was conditional upon the conclusion of a satisfactory trade agreement with the British government.[82] The existence of a contract to this effect was acknowledged in the House of Commons; and it was noted that it would provide work for some three thousand unemployed men on Tyneside. The trade delegation, moreover, was conducting negotiations for the purchase of agricultural machinery with a series of Swedish and German firms;[83] and a major order for some six hundred locomotives had just been placed with a German concern. Such orders, it appeared, could readily have been placed with British firms had the trade agreement been in existence. Krasin himself believed that it was the order for German locomotives which at this point precipitated the government's decision to proceed with the signature of the agreement.[84] On 16 March 1921 Horne and Krasin signed the document and the extended negotiations came to a close.

The agreement itself, in its final form, was described as 'preliminary' in character, pending the 'conclusion of a formal general Peace Treaty between the governments of these countries by which their economic and political realtions shall be regulated in the future'. The document was concerned simply with the 're-sumption of trade and commerce between the [two] countries'.[85] Under the terms of the agreement trade was to be facilitated by the removal of any form of blockade or other obstacle, by the extension of foreign merchant marine status to the ships, crews and cargoes of either party, by the clearance of sea mines, and by the exchange of officials and official agents with rights and facilities and protection for the purposes of official dealings. Private postal and telegraphic communication was to be restored, and documents and official papers concerned with trade were to be treated as if issued by a recognised foreign government. The British government undertook not to attempt to seize gold, money or goods rendered by the Soviet government in the course of trading relations; and the funds and other property of the late Imperial and Provisional Russian governments in Britain and of the British government in Russia were placed under guarantee, pending a decision upon their ownership in a subsequent general treaty.

The agreement was to come into force immediately, and both parties were bound 'at once to take all necessary measures to give effect to it'. After an initial twelve-month period had elapsed the treaty could be terminated six months after receipt from either side of notice to this effect. The contravention by either party of any of the provisions of the treaty, however, or of any of the conditions relating to propaganda contained in its preamble, would immediately free the other party of its obligations. A special declaration was also signed, providing for the 'just settlement in the formal Treaty, envisaged in the Preamble', of the claims of either party or of its citizens towards the other, concerning either property or rights or the obligations incurred by previous or existing governments in either country.[86]

It nevertheless remained an agreement of a strictly provisional character, and no attempt was made by the British government to convene the general conference which was to make a more comprehensive settlement. The government considered, Lloyd George told the House of Commons, that the 'first step' was to 'bring the Trade Agreement into practical working'; they were 'not prepared to make proposals for a general conference until [they had] gained experience of the working of this agreement'.[87] A favourable legal judgment, moreover, had not yet been secured.[88] While the agreement recognised the Soviet government as the *de facto* government of Russia—which, Lloyd George pointed out, 'undoubtedly it is'—the agents appointed by that government were not to be recognised as diplomatic representatives.[89] Claims were to be reserved for discussion until a general settlement was made of all the matters in dispute between the two governments, when, the Prime Minister added, the government 'meant to insist upon them'. It was, he insisted, 'purely a trading agreement'.[90]

The agreement was in fact more readily intelligible in a rather different sense. Speaking in the House of Commons, Sir Robert Horne explained his belief that 'nothing will so upset the Communist system there as to resume trade'. The Russian people would 'very soon become ready to adopt individual effort to produce goods which can be exchanged for our commodities'. 'The only way in which you will succeed in killing Bolshevism', he noted, 'will be by bringing Russia and the Russian people under the civilizing influence of the rest of the world, and you cannot do that in any better way than by beginning to enter into trade and commerce with them.' Even if only a small amount of trade could be done, they could 'look forward to . . . a better system in Russia'.[91] If the development of trade did in fact take place, a Foreign Office memorandum noted, the Soviet government would have to 'modify its economic practice', leading to a 'very modified and much less dangerous Soviet'. It was, indeed, 'more than probable that the days of the Communist Government as such will be numbered'.[92]

This perspective was articulated most clearly, perhaps, by the Prime Minister himself. There was already a change in Russia, he told the House of Commons, from the 'wild extravagant communism of a year or two years ago'. It was becoming accepted that that system was an 'impossible one'. All the time, he believed, 'we are simply converting them' through a 'gentlemanly process of instruction'. An opponent of the agreement, he assured the House, would find that Lenin was 'a man after his own heart if he has only a little patience, if he does a little business with him, a little trading, a little exchange of commodities. The moment they begin to realize they cannot run their country except upon the same principles which have brought prosperity to other countries, they will begin to realize that the only way to bring prosperity to Russia is to put an end to their wild schemes.'[93] It was Lloyd George's hope, commented Karl Radek, a secretary of the Comintern and one of the Bolsheviks' most skilled polemicists, that Manchester trousers and shirts would 'make the Bolsheviks a bit more reasonable', and that Sheffield razors might 'if not cut their throats, at least turn them into gentlemen'.[94] The Prime Minister had always believed the fundamental attempts to modify the social order must necessarily be futile and short-lived; and it was this belief which informed the efforts which were made under his guidance in the course of the following year towards a more definitive solution of the 'Russian problem'.

2 Labour and Soviet Russia

In addressing the House of Commons in November 1919, Churchill was asked by the Cabinet to 'make it clear that the British government were not out to destroy a revolutionary Government in Russia'.[1] Government policy had indeed encountered persistent and often bitter opposition from that quarter. Churchill's statement, however, was intended primarily for the benefit of the government's critics outside Parliament, in particular those in Labour and working-class circles. There was indeed 'no doubt', George Barnes, a former Labour MP, informed the Cabinet, 'that the feeling among Socialists and Labour men was that the Government were pursuing a capitalist policy'.[2] Opposition from such sources, as this chapter will be concerned to demonstrate, was not generally inspired by the radical sentiments to which Barnes had drawn attention. It did, however, play a part in first limiting and then bringing to an end the government's direct involvement in Russian affairs; and an account of the change in policy which this represented—not to speak of the impact of the Russian Revolution on British political life more generally—would not be complete without some attention to it.

This is not necessarily to accept the much larger claim, that (as the *New Leader* put it on 13 October 1922) Labour had 'compelled the abandonment of Mr. Churchill's campaign of intervention . . . brought the blockade to an end, [and] stopped the plans for interference in the Polish war' in 1920. The Cabinet's decision to withdraw British troops from Russia, it has already been noted, may in fact be accounted for in terms quite independent of working-class pressure: cost, and the failure of the anti-Bolshevik armies in the field, were altogether more salient considerations. It will be suggested further that, while a degree of suspicion attached to the government's conduct during the Russo-Polish war of 1920, there was in fact little substantive difference between its policy and that of Labour: for both supported Polish independence, but wished to avoid direct military involvement in the conflict.

Labour opposition, in other words, reflected a widespread determination to avoid the financial burden and loss of life attendant
upon war; it did not, other than exceptionally, represent an
identification with the Bolshevik and proletarian cause.

It should first be noted that Labour opposition of any kind to the
government's Russian policy had scarcely begun to develop
before the signature of the armistice and the Labour Party's
withdrawal from the Coalition in November 1918: that is to say,
not until some time after intervention on a major scale had been
initiated. The rumour of an imminent Japanese incursion into
Siberia with the blessing of the Allies led H. B. Lees-Smith to raise
the question in the House of Commons on 14 March 1918. The
venture, if it were seriously contemplated, would, he thought,
demonstrate the 'moral bankruptcy of the Alliance'.³ Writing in
the *Labour Leader* on the same day, Philip Snowden charged that
ministers, despite their 'hypocritical platitudes about this being a
war for democracy', were secretly encouraging the 'most militar-
ist and imperialist country in the world to attack, and to
endeavour to overthrow, the newly established democracy of
Russia'. Colonel Wedgwood later suggested the establishment of
a committee to consider 'how best relations between this country
and Russia can be improved'. Intervention in Russia, against the
will of the Russians, he thought 'absolutely futile and damaging to
the whole of the Allied cause'. The Bolsheviks, added Joseph
King, a Liberal member, 'may not have been our choice, but they
are at the present time undoubtedly the choice of the people of
Russia'.⁴

At the Labour Party conference which opened two days after
these remarks had been delivered, however, there was little
discussion of Russian affairs. Attention centred rather upon the
surprise appearance of a 'strange man with a yellow face',⁵
Alexander Kerensky, who was introduced to the conference by
Arthur Henderson. Henderson, who declared that he had a 'very
high appreciation of the work he was endeavouring to do on behalf
of that great people he represented', introduced Kerensky as 'one
whose name had been closely associated with their work during
the past year' and managed to secure the conference's agreement
that he should be heard. Kerensky's address, in which he declared
that the 'Russian people and the Russian democracy' were 'fighting against tyranny' and would do so 'to the end', appears to have

been less than completely successful. Kerensky apart, however, the only direct reference to intervention was made by Sylvia Pankhurst, who commented briefly upon 'the Japanese business'. 'Even an honest Liberal', H. N. Brailsford wrote in the *Herald*, 'would have said "Let Russians settle their own affairs". An honest Socialist would have withstood with double stubbornness a patently capitalist intervention.' The 'damning record' would relate that British Labour 'looked on as dumb spectators' at the destruction of the Soviet Republic.[6]

The subsequent landing of troops in Siberia was described by the ILP National Council as a 'challenge to democracy and Socialism' in a manifesto published in the *Labour Leader* on 1 August 1918. It represented an attempt to overthrow the social revolution and to re-establish the rule and power of capitalism. Socialists in Britain and in other Allied countries could 'not remain silent and indifferent under the challenge and menace of this act of imperialist aggression. We appeal therefore to British organized Labour to express the strongest condemnation of the participation of the British government in an act which constitutes a crime against national independence and against the Russian Revolution . . . a crime which if persisted in will prove not only disastrous to Russia but to the cause of freedom and democracy throughout the world'. Snowden talked of a 'departure of momentous significance', a 'second Belgium'; while Sylvia Pankhurst, Walton Newbold and others urged 'Save the Revolution'.[7]

The response of official Labour was rather less forthcoming. An Inter-Allied Conference of Labour and Socialist parties, which met in London from 17 to 20 September 1918, confined itself to an expression of the 'deepest sympathy' to the labour and socialist organisations of Russia which were continuing the struggle against German imperialism, and went on to condemn the treaty of Brest-Litovsk.[8] The resolution which was finally adopted not merely failed to point out, as a minority draft had done, that intervention 'under the pretext of fighting Bolshevism, would serve the reaction against Socialism and Democracy': it managed to avoid any direct reference to intervention whatsoever. Henderson, whose influence had been directed towards the adoption of this latter formulation, had been instructed by his party executive neither to 'approve or condemn Allied intervention, but [to accept] intervention as an accomplished fact'.[9] A national conference of shop stewards, meeting on 7 and 8 September 1918 in

Birmingham, did adopt a resolution 'requiring' the government to withdraw its troops from Russia. Almost one-third of the delegates opposed the motion, however, on grounds of 'expediency', and on the whole shop stewards were 'still a long way from committing themselves to action against the war'. The workers, complained *Call*, 'should intervene. Why do they accept the word of Kerensky in preference to that of the representatives of organized Russian labour?'[10]

Brailsford, writing in November, talked of Labour's 'failure to stand by the Russian Revolution'. The *Call* asked why official Labour was 'dumb' in regard to intervention. 'Do not let it be said', it appealed, 'that it was the apathy if not the hostility of the workers of Britain that delayed the complete triumph of the workers of the world'.[11] It was not until the war had finally ended, however, that (as the *New Statesman* put it) the time came to break the 'self-imposed silence which we have observed with regard to the British government's attitude towards Russia'. The journal had hitherto 'shrunk from the responsibility of taking a strong line'; and so long as the need had existed in Russia of repelling German advances, it had been willing to support 'precautionary measures'.[12] Now, however, Labour began more openly to take issue with government policy in Russia. Opposition to the Bolsheviks, Basil Thomson, Director of Intelligence at the Home Office, reported to the Cabinet, which had been 'so marked in the early days of the revolution', was disappearing. People were now 'asking whether Allied intervention was really necessary'.[13]

The Labour Party manifesto issued for the 1918 general election contained a call for the 'immediate withdrawal of the Allied forces from Russia'.[14] Following the election the party and the TUC, 'concerned at the reports respecting the Government's policy with regard to Russia', addressed a letter to the Prime Minister, seeking an assurance that there was 'no intention on the part of the British government to interfere with the right of the Russian people to decide for themselves their own form of government' and asking that the armed forces be withdrawn at the 'earliest possible moment'. A reply was received two days later; but nothing followed, and a subsequent letter, sent on 3 January 1919, was not even acknowledged. 'Up to May 1919', the executive complained, 'it had not been possible . . . to secure any official indication of the objects sought to be achieved by the Allies in their Russian policy.'[15]

The industrial side of the movement did not require such extended consideration of the matter. Shortly after the general election, the Birmingham Trades Council adopted a resolution calling for a conference to consider action to 'compel the Government to withdraw all troops from Russia, in order that the Russian Democracy be allowed to establish whatever form of internal government they require'. Other local labour bodies were coming to similar conclusions.[16] By the spring of 1919, Basil Thomson reported to the Cabinet, 'every section of the workers' appeared to be against conscription and intervention in Russia. 'Even mild trade unionists are said to be strongly moved over these matters.'[17]

On 26 March 1919 the national conference of the Miners' Federation unanimously adopted an executive resolution calling on the government immediately to 'withdraw all British troops from Russia, and to take the necessary steps to induce the Allied Powers to do likewise'.[18] A week later a special conference was convened by the Labour Party executive and by the Parliamentary Committee of the TUC to define their attitude to the proposed Covenant of the League of Nations. An emergency resolution was put forward by the miners calling for the withdrawal of British troops from Russia, the raising of the blockade against Germany, the release of conscientious objectors and the withdrawal of the conscription bill then before Parliament. Speaking for the resolution, Bob Smillie, the President of the Miners' Federation, urged that a special conference be held with the object of determining what form of industrial action could be taken to achieve these objects. The chairman of the Parliamentary Committee, J. H. Stuart-Bunning, who presided, refused to accept the second part of the miners' resolution since it implied industrial action, a course to which the political section of the movement could not be committed. This ruling was accepted; the first part of the resolution, however, was adopted without opposition.[19]

The Labour Party executive issued a manifesto to the press after the meeting, expressing 'grave concern regarding the long drawn-out delay of the Paris Conference to agree upon the terms of peace, thus entailing a continuation of the blockade and a paralysis in industrial and political order which have led inevitably to the spread of anarchy in certain European states, so that democratic government there and elsewhere is now seriously threatened'. The policy of military interference in Russia, it

urged, should be 'stopped forthwith'. British soldiers, it noted
with particular indignation, had been 'left practically isolated in
Murmansk and Archangel, and exposed to attack'. It was agreed
to send a deputation to the Prime Minister to present the terms of
the resolution which the miners had proposed; but an attempt to
defeat the government's policy by industrial action, the party
warned, would be a 'new precedent in our industrial history'. As
Smillie later remarked, 'nothing effective was done'.[20]

The Council of the Triple Alliance, meeting at Southport on 16
April 1919, now endorsed the miners' initiative and proposed that
the Parliamentary Committee of the TUC be called upon to
summon a special national conference to decide what form of
action might appropriately be undertaken.[21] A deputation from
the Council met the Parliamentary Committee on 15 May 'in
order to urge upon them the absolute necessity of calling a
Conference immediately'. The Committee decided in the first
instance to seek a meeting with the Prime Minister; and an
interview took place on 22 May. On 28 May, following the
interview, the Parliamentary Committee decided not to proceed
with the call for a conference, as the Triple Alliance had urged.[22]
The *Herald* found the decision 'amazing'; and it had, admittedly,
been taken by a small majority vote. It was not intervention in
Russia, however, which appeared to account for the dissatisfaction of the minority: they were more concerned with the questions
of conscription and a secret military circular issued by Winston
Churchill which had been published in the *Herald*. No answer had
yet been found to the *Herald*'s question: 'Resolutions and pious
protests are not enough. The war must be stopped. What will
Labour *do*, not *say*, to stop it?' 'We have been treated to resolutions
from the Triple Alliance, trade union executives, and political and
industrial demonstrations', commented the *Worker*, 'and yet nothing is done'.[23]

The Labour Party annual conference took place in Stockport at
the end of June 1919. In his presidential address the chairman,
John McGurk, told delegates that there could be 'no peace so long
as we continue to indulge in military adventures in Russia'.
Russia, he urged, 'must be left free to work out its own political
salvation'. He was less enthusiastic about a proposal to employ
the strike weapon for political purposes, an 'innovation in this
country' which was being 'canvassed with much energy'. It was
advocated at the conference itself by Frank Hodges of the miners'

union, Robert Williams of the transport workers' union and a number of others. Bob Smillie, who proposed the resolution to this effect, pointed out that the government itself might not have acted entirely constitutionally in sending the troops to Russia in the first place; and more generally he thought it 'rather strange that the Executive Committee of the Labour Party should have taken up exactly the position of every exploiter and capitalist and politician in this country' on the issue. Such were the feelings of delegates that, despite the appeals of J. R. Clynes, a motion was carried by a 2–1 majority demanding the 'immediate cessation' of intervention and instructing the executive to consult with the Parliamentary Committee of the TUC with a 'view to effective action being taken to enforce these demands by the unreserved use of their political and industrial power'.[24]

The *Fortnightly Review* thought the proposal the work of 'firebrands who are bent on destroying the Constitution'. The labour movement, it declared, had been 'captured by extremists'. Hodges, however, had pointed out that the resolution was no more than an 'expression of opinion'. It simply proposed that the Parliamentary Committee of the TUC be invited to call a conference to consider a resolution on the lines of that which the Labour Party conference had just adopted. It was not in itself a decision in favour of 'direct action', for the Labour Party could not commit the industrial action of the movement to action of this (or any other) kind. As the *Times* noted, the resolution in fact 'committed nobody to anything'.[25]

Discussions also took place at the Labour conference regarding a proposal which had been made more than a month earlier that a general strike be called in Italy, France and Britain in order to bring about the end of intervention. The Labour representatives secured the adoption of a statement providing simply for demonstrations of protest (rather than industrial action) by the workers of each country 'in the form best adapted to their circumstances and to their method of operation'. It was agreed that the British labour movement should stage demonstrations throughout Britain on 20 July 1919, a Sunday; while French and Italian workers were prepared to stage a twenty-four hour general strike on 21 July, a working day. 'The importance of this strike must be pressed upon the workers', ran a Comintern resolution on the subject, 'in order to convince them that their interests are those of Soviet Russia and to build up a strong feeling of revolutionary international solidarity among them.'[26] The British leaders, however, made little effort to implement the decision; and the resulting series of demonstrations was widely regarded as a fiasco.[27]

Nor could responsibility for the failure be ascribed entirely to an irresolute leadership. A relatively militant labour body, for instance, the Glasgow Trades Council, complained to Labour headquarters that the proposed dates were unsuitable since the annual Glasgow holiday would begin shortly beforehand (it was decided to hold a demonstration on 3 August instead, but both the speakers proposed, Smillie and MacDonald, were unable to attend, and the meeting appears not to have taken place). 'Listen, Brother Pollitt. I can see through your game', a trade union activist told Harry Pollitt. 'This strike is to help Russia, not Poplar.'[28] Only among the dockers, the Norwich boot and shoe operatives and the Merthyr miners did industrial movements of any significance take place. The demonstrations were reported to have been poorly attended, both of those held in London meeting opposition from counter-demonstrations and those in other towns simply endorsing the official resolution.[29] A number of resolutions reached the Foreign Office; but as a minute drily observed, 'No action seems necessary. We frequently receive such protests.'[30] A. A. Watts, in an 'Appeal to the Working Class' in the *Call* on 19 June, admitted that 'to the average man, Russia is a long way off'. How much longer, he asked, would they continue 'tamely [to] look on and allow our capitalistic gang to continue its efforts to strangle [the Revolution]?' A 'Manifesto to British Labour' appeared in the paper the following week, calling upon British workers to 'retrieve the already tarnished reputation of our movement'. The 'frightful murder of a nation', charged the *Worker* on 25 October, was being engineered by the government and 'acquiesced in by the British working class'.

The Parliamentary Committee of the TUC, in the event, decided not to act upon the Labour Party conference resolution, and a meeting of the Triple Alliance on 23 July 1919 decided that action should be taken on their own initiative. It was agreed to circulate a ballot paper in order to obtain members' opinions on the question of the withdrawal of their labour to secure, among other objects, the end of the intervention in Russia.[31] This was an opportunity, *Call* pointed out, for British labour to clear itself of 'all suspicion of having betrayed the cause of the Russian Revolution'. Churchill announced on the same day in the House of

Commons that the troops in Murmansk and Archangel were to be
evacuated before the winter, however, and a decision was taken to
postpone the ballot until after the TUC had met.[32] The TUC in its
turn decided on 12 September that the Parliamentary Committee
should again present the movement's demands to the government, and that only if it were not satisfied should a special meeting
be convened. Robert Williams expressed his exasperation in
Forward: 'With 5¼ millions of organized workers', he commented,
British labour was 'helpless and impotent' on Russian policy.
'Marx had once called the British workers the advance guard of
the international proletariat, but now they had become the
Chinese of Europe'.[33] Indeed by the autumn of 1919, Basil Thomson reported to the Cabinet, feeling with regard to intervention
had 'practically died out'.[34]

The Labour Party executive, meeting on 7 October 1919,
decided that further inquiries should be made of the Foreign
Office regarding British intervention in Russia. A letter was
accordingly addressed to Balfour by the party's Secretary 'with a
view to eliciting information as to the present position of affairs'.
The questions dealt with restrictions still obtaining with regard to
trade with Russia via the Baltic, and asked when it was proposed
that military action in Russia should cease. The party was
informed, however, that it was 'impossible to fix such a date'.[35] A
further resolution reached the Foreign Office from Herbert Morrison, on behalf of the London Labour Party, who was content to
'ask that the points dealt with will receive your careful attention'.[36]
As the *Call* pointed out on 23 October, people grumbled, they
were discontented, they adopted resolutions protesting against
intervention, sometimes they even threatened, 'but they do nothing which could really frighten the bandits in office'. People
would 'have to do something more than pass resolutions of
protest'.

The special conference of the TUC met at the Central Hall,
Westminster, on 9 and 10 December 1919. Its agenda included
the nationalisation of the mines, the cost of living and trade union
co-ordination as well as conscription and British policy towards
Russia, on which a deputation had just been to see the Prime
Minister. A resolution was adopted expressing the conference's
'profound dissatisfaction' with the Prime Minister's responses
and calling for the government to respond to the Soviet government's peace overtures, to raise the blockade and to facilitate

trade between the two countries. No more effective means of
enforcing these proposals was envisaged, however, than that a
delegation should be sent to Russia to conduct an 'independent
and impartial inquiry into the political, industrial and economic
conditions' in that country which should be considered at a
special conference the following year. The proceedings, *The Times*
commented editorially, were on the whole a tribute to the 'so-
briety of the trade union movement in the mass'; they would give
'little encouragement to the red revolutionaries in Russia and
elsewhere who are continually led to believe that this country is on
the verge of a terrific upheaval which will reduce it to the same
condition as their own unhappy land'.[37]

The resolution adopted at the TUC special conference fell conspicuously short of the policy pressed upon the movement by the
National 'Hands off Russia' Committee. In a circular of 18
September 1919 the Committee had called not only for the
withdrawal of troops but also for the suspension of supplies to
Denikin and Kolchak and the establishment of full diplomatic
relations with the Soviet government.[38] The Committee was
certainly the most prominent body engaged in promoting opposition to the government's Russian policy at this time within the
labour movement. It is difficult to accept its organisers' claim,
however, that the Committee was a 'powerful force' in the agitation, much less that Labour opposition had a considerable influence upon the government policy or that its inspiration was, to a
significant degree, an identification with the Bolshevik and proletarian cause.[39]

The Committee was established at a meeting in London on 18
January 1919. Three hundred and fifty delegates were reported to
have been in attendance, representing the major socialist societies
and organisations as varied as the West London League for the
Blind. A fifteen-man committee was elected, and a resolution was
adopted which called for an 'active agitation upon every field of
activity to solidify the Labour Movement in Great Britain for the
purpose of declaring at a further conference, to be convened for
that purpose, a general strike, unless before the date of that
conference the unconditional cessation of Allied intervention in
Russia . . . shall have been announced'. The delegates failed to
achieve unanimity, some believing that the workers would 'only
strike on economic questions immediately affecting them'; but it

was agreed that 'Hands off Russia', or even a call for the British revolution, could subsequently be added to these initial demands. The bodies represented were invited to form 'Hands off Russia' committees in their own localities.[40]

A further meeting was held in London on 8 February, presided over by E. C. Fairchild of the BSP and addressed by Lansbury, John Maclean, R. C. Wallhead and others. According to a report received by the government, however, while there had been a 'distinct advance in audacity of statement and general bearing' and an increase in the waving of red flags, rather less than one-third of the proceedings of the meeting had in fact been devoted to the Russian question.[41] The *Call* reported on 13 February that the meeting had been 'memorable'; but it noted that the difficulties of transport had been 'without a parallel in recent years', limiting, presumably, the size of the audience. The grounds on which the paper chose to criticise the government's policy, moreover, were simply that it constituted a 'flat denial of their own announcements in support of the principle of self-determination', on which basis, it noted, the organisers of the demonstration had received the 'active assistance and support of a legion of people in the country who do not ordinarily, as yet, find themselves in alliance with the BSP'.

Messages of support, indeed, were received from figures as diverse as E. D. Morel, Bertrand Russell, Arthur Ponsonby and Bernard Shaw. Such was the nature of the Committee's opposition to intervention, recalled a Liberal MP who had been a member of its executive, that while its support came mainly from Labour and trade union politicians it attracted also a 'sprinkling of Liberals, Quakers, Pacifists, and even some Conservatives'. There was no reason why it should not do so: for, as a manifesto issued by the local committee in Woolwich pointed out, the body 'stood for no more and no less than "Hands off Russia"'. The Woolwich committee in itself regarded Soviet Russia as a workers' state, and as deserving of support on that ground; but the National 'Hands off Russia' Committee, it pointed out, had avoided 'expressing any definite opinion on this point'.[42]

A further meeting took place in Manchester on 21 June 1919. Intervention in Russia was again condemned, together with military and industrial conscription. There was indeed a danger, Smillie told the delegates, of the 'perpetuation of militarism and conscription for all time'.[43] Following the conference it was agreed to establish a national 'Hands off Russia' movement 'which accepted the broad principle of non-interference in Russia'. The conference appointed a committee, of which A. A. Purcell became chairman; W. P. Coates, the BSP national organiser, was loaned to the body as secretary; and offices were established in Manchester.[44] A national organiser was subsequently appointed. Only by this date, August 1919, could a national 'Hands off Russia' Committee be said to have come into being (the Committee, Coates told an interviewer in Tiflis four years later, had been 'inaugurated in August 1919').[45]

Already by this time, however, the Cabinet had decided upon the evacuation of northern Russia, and a decision had been taken (on 12 August) that a 'final' contribution should be made to assist General Denikin. The Cabinet, in fact, had reversed its policy before a national 'Hands off Russia' organisation had even come into existence. Pollitt recalled, moreover, that while 'every effort was made to intensify all the work connected with the Hands off Russia Movement', they were 'not able to develop the mass movement to the point where the trade unions were prepared to take strike action'.[46] The Committee had no greater success, as has already been noted, in persuading the TUC to endorse its four-point programme; and the attempt to organise among trade unionists led somewhat later to the publication of an acrimonious correspondence in which the National Transport Workers' Federation had accused the Committee of 'attempting to induce its members to strike without the authority of their Unions'.[47] A good deal of the Committee's apparent vitality in any case derived less from working-class support than from the financial subsidies which it was receiving from Moscow.[48]

The Labour Party in Parliament offered no more resistance to intervention than the labour movement outside it. The party's spokesmen did oppose intervention, arguing that it constituted a denial of the right of nations to self-determination; and they also pointed out that, if it were to be successful, it would have to be carried out on a scale which lay far beyond the bounds of feasibility.[49] But few Labour members pressed the point with any urgency, and in general there was a marked reluctance to give even the impression of a degree of sympathy towards the professedly workers' government which now existed in Moscow. Indeed it was in many ways precisely this antipathy towards Bolshevism, rather than any degree of fellow feeling, which accounted for the party's opposition to intervention: for intervention, it appeared, so far from undermining the Bolsheviks, might actually be strengthening them by allowing them to represent themselves as good Russian patriots rather than as the unscrupulous fanatics they really were. It would be 'better to try and kill Bolshevism by feeding it', Clynes suggested to the House of Commons, 'rather than by fighting it'. The raising of the blockade, the *New Statesman* thought, might in fact be the 'severest blow that Great Britain is capable of dealing to the Bolshevik regime'.[50]

The raising of the blockade and the establishment of a complete peace with Russia were the two main elements of 'Labour's Russian Policy', a statement of party objectives which was published at the beginning of 1920. To act in this manner, the statement pointed out, would 'no more imply moral support of [the Bolshevik government] than did our former recognition of the Tsar's government'.[57] It was not perhaps surprising that Balfour should have found it possible to speak of the 'extraordinary measure of agreement' between Labour and the government on this issue.[52] More generally, Snowden charged, the 'full story of the apathy and weakness of British Labour towards the policy of the Allied governments in their determined efforts to overthrow the Socialist Revolution and to re-establish the monarchical and capitalist regime' was one which should 'make every democrat feel hot with shame and humiliation'. Only rank-and-file pressure, he noted, had secured the adoption of the resolution on Russia at the party conference in June 1919; and it had been the non-Coalition Liberals, rather than the Labour members, who had raised the question of Russian policy most frequently in the House of Commons. The indifference and complacency of official Labour, he charged, amounted to 'practical support of the government's policy'. If the Allied adventure failed, as it seemed likely to do, it would 'not be due to the opposition of the British Labour Movement ... a determined attitude against this policy by British Labour would have brought intervention to an end long ago'.[53]

The charge was a harsh, but not an entirely unmerited one. Nor is it sufficient to attribute responsibility for Labour's attitude simply to the party's temporising leadership, as Soviet scholars, for instance, have typically attempted to do.[54] The Labour executive, certainly, had no love for the Bolshevik cause, or for militant or extra-constitutional action in general; yet where rank-and-file pressure was strong and determined it could make itself effective. This, evidently, was not the case with regard to Russia. Basil Thomson, whose regular reports to the Cabinet on 'Revolutionary Organisations in the United Kingdom' tended if anything to exaggerate the revolutionary threat and the influence of Bolshevism, was certainly of this opinion. The objection of trade unionists to intervention, he reported, was that they did 'not see any necessity for it. They say that Russia has never been any good to us as an Ally, and should be left to settle her own affairs. No British lives ought to be lost for her sake.' It was not likely, he thought, that anything 'drastic' would be done in connection with the conscription and intervention issues, for 'drastic action means the loss of wages for themselves'. Despite the 'sound and fury' of resolutions on Russian policy, he added, the rank and file 'refuse to be interested in anything Russian'.[55] Even the extremists, he noted, had 'realised that it would be useless to call a national strike on such a question'.[56]

Harry Pollitt, probably one of the 'extremists' whom Thomson had in mind, admitted the essential truth of this charge on at least one occasion. The working class, he was reported to have told a meeting in Liverpool, 'cared only for beer, tobacco and horse-racing, and it would take twenty years to educate them'.[57] J. T. Murphy, who was probably another, agreed that the British labour movement 'rejected the principles of the Soviet Revolution so far as its own development was concerned'.[58] Sylvia Pankhurst, observing from the top of a bus a crowd of workers reading the stop-press news, recalled returning eagerly to the spot to 'discover from a sheet thrown down on the wet pavement that what the people were reading is "Becket beat McGoorty"', a prize fight result. There was 'little genuinely revolutionary feeling in [the] country', she noted; the masses were 'in the main untouched by the Soviet struggle'.[59] Neither nationally, nor even locally, in fact, did there appear to be a significant degree of opinion in favour of proceeding beyond merely verbal opposition to the government's Russian policy.[60] At least until the end of 1919, by which time intervention had effectively ended, it is difficult to find a single instance in which an important section of the labour movement called for an end to military intervention in Russia in terms which clearly extended beyond a desire simply to avoid the loss of working-class lives and unnecessary expenditure. There was no 'fight to save the Soviet Republic'.

The Polish military advance into Soviet Russia in the spring of 1920 seemed to most sections of the labour movement an intolerable act of aggression which could not have taken place without the active connivance of the Allies. 'The marionettes are in Warsaw, but the strings are being pulled from London and Paris', declared the *Herald* on 30 April. The Polish army was 'very well-equipped—largely with British aeroplanes, guns and munitions', added the *New Statesman* on 8 May. It was an 'Imperialist venture pure and simple'.[61] A ship called the 'Jolly George' was at this time being loaded at the East India dock in London. Some of the cargo which arrived for it was packed in crates labelled 'OHMS Munitions for Poland'. The dockers, believing that this indicated that the stores were destined for the Polish armed forces, sent a deputation to Ernest Bevin and Fred Thompson of the Dockers' Union and received assurances that the union would support them if they refused to load or coal the ship. The crates had to be disembarked. The dockers, it appeared, had frustrated a government attempt to assist the Polish offensive; their action was widely applauded both within and outside the labour movement.[62]

It by no means followed, however, that the dockers' action was 'indicative of the intense feeling aroused among Trade Unionists', or that the British workers were now 'ready for any action to defend workers' Russia'.[63] Pollitt, who had been actively involved in the dockside agitation, confessed himself 'greatly disappointed' by an earlier failure to secure a stoppage of work on two Belgian barges which were being converted for the transport of munitions to Poland. On 1 May, moreover, the Danish steamer, 'Neptune', had been allowed to leave the East India Dock upon a similar mission, despite the efforts of Pollitt and his associates. Although the extremists had been 'much elated' by their success with the 'Jolly George', Basil Thomson reported to the Cabinet, most of the agitation would 'end in talk, for there is no real support for the cause of the Russian Soviets among the working classes'.[64]

The affair of the 'Jolly George' was reviewed a few days later at the triennial conference of the Dockers' Union. Bevin, who moved an emergency resolution on the matter, made it clear that the union's support for the London dockers' action implied no view, whether favourable or unfavourable, of the principles of the Soviet social order. 'Whatever may be the merits or demerits of the theory of government of Russia', he told the delegates, 'that is a matter for Russia, and we have no right to determine their form of government, any more than we would tolerate Russia determining our form of government'. The speech displayed a grasp of the classic principles of British foreign policy, his biographer has commented, 'which neither Canning nor Cobden could have bettered'.[65]

The 'Hands off Russia' Committee, attempting to capitalise on the success of the 'Jolly George' incident, now urged that a national conference be held in order to declare a strike to force the government to bring about peace between Russia and Poland and halt the successful Polish advance. 'Mere pious resolutions won't force the hands of the Government', the manifesto pointed out, 'but resolutions backed by industrial action will'. A week later an appeal was issued under the signature of a number of prominent trade unionists, calling for a conference 'in order to declare a National "down-tools" policy of 24 hours to make peace with Russia'. Peace, they argued, was 'to the interest of the organized workers of Great Britain'. The King, moreover, had 'created a precedent [for] a down-tools policy by advocating a general cessation of work on November 11 as a reminder of Armistice Day'. The Parliamentary Committee of the TUC and the Labour Party were urged to follow this exalted precedent.[66]

The Labour Party conference, which met at Scarborough from 22–25 June 1920, duly adopted a resolution declaring that the economic restoration of Europe was the 'only secure foundation for the peace and prosperity of the world' and calling upon the Allies to recognise the Russian government and to end all direct or indirect attacks upon it. No more forceful means of promoting the policy was envisaged, however, than that the Prime Minister should be 'requested to receive a deputation' on the subject. An addendum to the resolution was proposed by Hodgson, a BSP representative, calling for the summoning of a national conference to organise a general strike to end the government's direct and indirect support of attacks upon Soviet Russia. In the twelve months since the last resolution had been adopted, he told the delegates, 'no serious attempt has been made to act upon it'. 'For Heaven's sake let us have a sting in the thing', he urged, 'even if it is only at the tail'.[67] More effective steps might indeed have been taken had it in fact been the case that a 'powerful movement to halt intervention stirred the British working class ... under the leadership of the militants and revolutionaries'. The proposal, in the event, was 'heavily defeated'.[68]

It was similarly the fear that British forces might again become entangled in a military hostilities on the Continent, rather than hypothetical sentiments of class solidarity, which lay mainly behind the most notable single example of labour opposition to government policy in Russia throughout this period, the formation of the Councils of Action in August 1920. The Polish offensive, after some striking initial successes, had been checked and then reversed by the Red Army, which had thereupon instituted a vigorous counter-attack. Armistice negotiations broke down at the beginning of August, and the Red Army continued its apparently irresistible advance.[69] British forces, it appeared, might now be compelled to intervene in order to preserve Polish independence and the Versailles settlement as a whole. *The Times* on 6 and 7 August warned that the situation was as grave as that of August 1914; and the *Herald* for once agreed. The country was 'again in urgent danger of a great war', the paper warned on 5 August. Unless Labour wanted the return of militarism and conscription, it urged, '*act now* . . . Let the Prime Minister know that you will not have this war—that you will down tools from one end of the country to the other rather than fight a wanton war or allow it to be fought'.

It was difficult to know how seriously the threat should be regarded; but previous experience of the government's relations with Russia, and of Churchill's conduct in particular, suggested that it would be prudent to allow the government as little latitude as possible. Arthur Henderson, as Secretary of the Labour Party, accordingly sent a telegram to local party branches on 4 August declaring that the possibility of an extension of the war was 'extremely menacing', and urging that they organise demonstrations against intervention and the supply of men and munitions to Poland.[70] The Parliamentary Labour Party, the Labour executive and the Parliamentary Committee of the TUC met on 9 August and warned that war was 'being engineered between the Allied Powers and Soviet Russia on the issue of Poland'. Such a war, it declared, would be an 'intolerable crime against humanity'. It was agreed that the movement's whole industrial power should be used to prevent it, and a fifteen-man Council of Action was set up to carry these decisions into effect. A national conference of local trade union and Labour Party branches was also to be held at the earliest possible opportunity. The Council held its first meeting the following day, 10 August, and agreed that the conference should be held the following Friday, 13 August, 'whether the threatened war with Poland was averted or not'.[71]

Before the conference met, the Council had undertaken a series of interviews or otherwise communicated with the main protagonists. The representatives of the Russian and Polish governments were sent copies of the 9 August resolution;[72] and the Council sought and obtained an interview with Lloyd George on 10 August, the record of which was published the following day in the *Herald*. The paper also made public the text of the official Soviet peace terms, which conceded the independence of Poland and offered a more generous boundary to the Poles than the 'Curzon line' which the Allies had originally proposed. The Council wrote accordingly to Lloyd George on 11 August, presuming from their interview the previous day that 'in view of your declaration of non-interference ... further interference by the Allies with Russia on behalf of Poland or General Wrangel ... will not be proceeded with'. They hoped also that the government's peace terms with Russia would now be published.[73] Further interviews with Lloyd George and with the Russian mission in London took place on 12 August. The Council was asked by Lloyd George to use its influence with the Russian government to 'keep to the published Peace Terms rather than stiffen them, in view of the military successes then being achieved by the Red Army'.[74]

By the time the conference assembled in the Central Hall, Westminster, on 13 August, in fact, peace appeared effectively to have been secured, provided only that no significant changes were introduced into the published Soviet peace terms. William Adamson, Chairman of the Parliamentary Party, who presided, declared that the Council had 'focussed the practically unanimous opinion of this country against any more war or armed intervention in the affairs of other countries'. Indeed so effectively had it done so, he believed, that 'up to the present the government has been kept back from the slippery slope that would lead to another European conflagration (Cheers)'. He appealed to the conference to 'demonstrate the deep and united feeling existing against any action on the part of our government which would drag our people into war and abolish any prospect of peace in Europe for a long time to come'. They were not concerned, he emphasised, with the merits or demerits of the present rulers of Russia, or with the vices and virtues of the Bolshevik form of government; 'the issue is far greater than that'.[75]

Bevin presented a report to the conference on behalf of the

Council of Action. The Council, he declared, was 'as strong on Polish independence as anyone else'. It was convinced, however, that that independence was not at stake, and indeed 'had never been at stake'. It was also determined that a general peace should be achieved and maintained in the world. No amendments were allowed; and the conference proceeded forthwith to adopt a resolution approving the formation of the Council of Action and another which welcomed the Russian declaration on the independence of Poland and pledged the conference to 'resist any and every form of military and naval intervention against the Soviet Government of Russia'. The Council was to remain in being until the blockade had been ended, the Soviet government had been recognised, and unrestricted trading and commercial relations between the two countries had been restored. A final resolution authorised the Council to take such steps as might be necessary to give effect to the decisions of the conference and to the policy of the labour movement, and empowered it to impose a levy of a halfpenny per member upon affiliated organisations to meet its special requirements. 'It may not be possible to let you have any active work to do', the resolution's seconder pointed out, 'but you can all pay, and that is the way in which everyone will be able to play a part in this great Movement'.

The Council, in the event, did not call for the withdrawal of labour, as it had been empowered to do; but 'Peace with Russia' demonstrations were held on Sunday 22 August, and a set of propaganda leaflets was issued.[76] A manifesto entitled 'Peace with Soviet Russia. [A] Manifesto to the workers of Great Britain' demanded 'peace at once, a full peace, with recognition and trading rights and commercial relationships'. Some six thousand were persuaded to demonstrate in London; the numbers elsewhere, however, according to *The Times* report of the following day, were rather less (at Bradford, for instance, where there had been a downpour of rain, only three hundred appeared). Further demonstrations were organised on 17 October to draw attention to the relationship between trade with Soviet Russia and unemployment.[77] The heading of a printed handbill issued by the Council indicated the manner in which the 'Russian question' was now regarded. 'Peace with Russia', it read, 'would mean for British workers Cheaper Food, Cheaper Clothes, Cheaper Fuel, Cheaper Building, and more Employment'.[78]

The Council continued to meet; but it did so less and less

frequently. Indeed a good many people, the *Manchester Guardian* remarked on 13 November 1920, had 'probably almost forgotten by this time the existence of the Council of Action established some time ago to deal with the question of peace with Russia'. The Council, it reported, had not met regularly of late, but it was still meeting from time to time as required, and it was 'now preparing to take a hand should any further complication arise in the negotiations for the re-opening of trade with Russia'. The Council itself explained, in a leaflet issued at this time, that 'after a necessary suspension of activities due to the Miners' Strike and other causes' it had 'decided to reopen the fight with the Government to secure Peace and Trade with Russia'. Leaflets were now available from its offices on the subject of 'Trade with Russia in relation to Unemployment and the Cost of Living'.[79] A further and, it appears, final meeting was held on 23 December. According to *The Times* report of the following day, a statement dealing with the Irish question was prepared for discussion at the forthcoming Labour Party conference.

The National Council had also authorised the formation of local Councils of Action, some three or four hundred of which came ultimately into existence. *The Times* reported on 16 August that the proposal had been 'adopted without delay in industrial areas'. Councils had been set up in Sheffield, Plymouth, Gateshead, Northampton and Leicester; and some had appointed subcommittees. The National Council was informed four days later that 135 local Councils had so far been formed, 25 in London and 110 in the provinces.[80] By the time the National Council issued its second 'Report to the Local Councils of Action' on 10 September 'more than three hundred' were in existence, covering the most important industrial centres. Altogether 'about 350 Councils' were established.[81]

   The response to the Council's appeal was by no means uniformly enthusiastic. In most cases, however, the Councils were swiftly formed through the action of the local Trades Council or Labour Party, and in a few places a local organisation of some vigour and comprehensiveness resulted. The local Council at Merthyr Tydfil was probably the most elaborate of those which sprang into existence at this time. The Council was expressly designed to provide the 'necessary guidance to commence the development of a new order of society', and its constitution was drafted with some care since it was intended to 'outlast the mere occasion that is upon us'. A Central Council was established, to be composed of representatives of local labour organisations appointed at public mass meetings; and representatives would be replaced if they failed to attend meetings regularly. The *Pioneer*'s editorial declared that the new Council was 'destined to be an important instrument for the emancipation of the workers'.[82] The Council co-operated with the local Trades Council and with the Irish Self-Determination League in holding a meeting on the Irish question, reported in the *Pioneer* on 4 December. A circular was also issued to other local Councils in September, emphasising that Russia, Ireland and unemployment were all part of the same problem. Taken together, it was suggested, these problems threatened the 'existence of the capitalist system of production'.[83]

These initiatives were paralleled at Birmingham, where a local Council was established on 17 August 1920 at a special conference convened by the Trades Council.[84] It was decided initially to rely upon the local Labour Party organisation, but some sub-committees were eventually appointed, and the Council (on which there was some Communist representation) took an increasingly radical line. On 8 September a resolution was adopted calling for a date to be fixed on which a strike would be called if peace had not by then been concluded with Russia. On 18 November W. P. Coates, of the 'Hands off Russia' Committee, addressed the Council executive, and it was agreed to attempt to convene a meeting of all local Councils 'to consider what steps shall be taken to enforce Peace and Trade with Russia'. An appeal to this effect was approved and circulated.[85] Little came of the proposal, however, and there was no support for moves the following 11 February and 5 March to form a Council of Action to call a general strike to bring about peace with Russia and to protest against unemployment. The Trades Council's Annual Report noted that the Council 'more or less soon became moribund'. The treasurer, in fact, had been left five pounds out of pocket; donations 'however small' were invited.[86]

Birmingham was not the only Council to urge an extension of the scope of the Councils and a convention of local Councils. Some sixty local Councils, for instance, called for the inclusion of the Irish question in the Council's mandate.[87] After Ireland, however, the most widely canvassed proposal was the convocation of a national conference of local Councils of Action, as the Birmingham Council had suggested. Its most persistent advocate was the North-East District Council of Action at Newcastle. On 5 September the Council addressed a telegram to the National Council calling for another national conference to be held to keep the Council in session and to extend its mandate to Ireland and the withdrawal of British troops overseas.[88] Dissatisfied with the National Council's response, the North-East Council despatched a circular to every other local Council urging that such a conference be held. More than seventy local Councils were reported to have replied to the circular and to have endorsed it;[89] and some wrote directly to the National Council urging that a conference be called.[90]

The National Council, in its reply, professed to see 'no good purpose' in undertaking action of this kind. A House of Commons debate was forthcoming; thereafter, it thought, the situation could be reviewed.[91] Yet it was not simply the backing of the moderately-inclined National Council which the proposals lacked: crucially, they failed to evoke a significant degree of rank and file support. Indeed, with the exception of occasional local initiatives, the Councils uniformly failed to realise the hopes of those who saw them as embryonic Soviets.[92] Indicative of the manner in which the Councils movement was in fact regarded by those who had brought it into being was an 'Appeal to the British Nation' published by the *Herald* on 7 August 1920 under the signature of seven prominent trade unionists. The statement laid particular emphasis upon the fact that 'at the present time we can ill afford to spare even a few thousand men or a few million pounds from our depleted financial resources ... Houses are lamentably short and the prime necessities of life becoming increasingly difficult to obtain.' People in every country wanted only to devote themselves more and more to rational and peaceful construction, urged the signatories; 'we want peace—a real peace, a lasting peace, rather than endless wars and threats of wars'. The appeal was endorsed by Lansbury, Purcell and Williams as well as by more moderate figures such as Clynes, Henderson and Bevin. However much Labour might be divided on the question of domestic policy, commented the Birmingham *Town Crier* on 20 August, there was 'complete unity on the question of peace'.

As Rajani Palme Dutt warned in the *Communist*, the issue before them was 'not essentially a revolutionary class-issue but simply an expression of war-weariness and horror at the prospect of being dragged into another war'. The final outcome, he warned, might be 'disappointing to those who have built high hopes upon it'.[93] There was in fact no evidence, wrote two well-placed contemporaries, that the desire to bring intervention to an end was 'accompanied by any desire to set up in Great Britain the constitution which is believed to obtain in Moscow and Petrograd'.[94] The Councils owed their existence, rather, on the evidence of the Home Office's Intelligence Reports, to the 'general fear of war that exists in the lower middle and working classes, and not to any tenderness for Russia'. If there had been no question of conscription there would have been a 'very feeble response to a strike-call to enforce recognition of the Soviet Government'; local reports indicated that 'although the men would refuse to respond to calling up notices', they would in fact 'support the Government in countering Bolshevik action'.[95] As Walton Newbold, shortly to become a Communist MP, recorded, the workers and the armed forces were intensely hostile to the prospect of an extension of the war to Russia; against this they were 'ready to protest in word and deed. They were tired of the whole business of the war'. But there was 'no desire to follow Russia. That plain, blunt fact we had to face'.[96]

The Councils, in addition, were 'generally ... shy of Communists'.[97] The Communist Party, which had just been formally constituted, immediately sought to obtain representation upon the National Council of Action, and it submitted a proposal for action, 'Labour's Five Points', to the Council for its consideration. But the request for representation was refused, both on the National Council and at the conference of 13 August 1920, and the party's proposal for action appears not even to have been considered.[98] Local party branches, moreover, experienced 'considerable difficulty in securing representation on the local Councils of Action'.[99] The party attempted to exert such influence as it did command by supporting a number of more militant local initiatives, such as the call to establish a Federation of London Councils of Action. 'The rank and file are with us', the *Communist* declared on 14 October 1920; 'the revolt against this apathy is everywhere'. But nothing more was heard of the proposals, and other suggestions, such as the call to 'Fix a Date' for the conclusion of peace with Russia, met with a largely indifferent response. Many non-Labour elements, Beatrice Webb noted in her diary, 'all the middle class pacifists and many middle class taxpayers', were grateful for the Labour Party's intervention. Even the City, reported the *New Statesman*, supported Labour on this issue; 'everyone in England wants a settlement and peace'.[100] It was less clear that support existed for the Communist Party's more radical perspectives.

Nor was it even clear that the Councils had prevented British military involvement in the Russo-Polish conflict. There had been no prospect of a substantial British involvement at any time, Churchill's presence in the Cabinet notwithstanding,[101] and the Council failed in addition to prevent the movement of British military supplies to Poland, a task with which it had been entrusted by the 13 August conference. The National Council explained in its third 'Report to Local Councils' of 1 October 1920 that it had collected a great deal of information, 'some of it very conclusive', about such movements. The Council felt, however, that it would be 'unfair to throw upon the transport workers the responsibility for stopping these supplies, whilst acquiescing in other workers continuing to manufacture them. Then the difficulty arose of ascertaining the ultimate destination of munitions in the process of manufacture.' These problems, moreover, had been 'accentuated by the threatened stoppage in the mining industry, which has during the last few weeks from the public point of view thrown the question of Russia into the background', as well as by the 'prevailing hope that the negotiations at Riga would result in an early settlement of the Russo-Polish question'.[102] Nothing, it appeared, was going to be done.

The Council's response provoked dismay in some quarters. 'Frankly', wrote the *Communist* on 7 October, 'the National Council of Action has failed.' The Council had been supposed to prevent supplies and munitions being sent in support of the attack on Soviet Russia; but this it was 'quite obviously not doing. Somehow, and from somewhere in this country, those supplies are being sent.' Despite the efforts of the railway and transport workers in the various countries, the Birmingham *Town Crier* added on 8 October, 'great quantities of ammunition and guns continue to reach Poland'. Ships 'laden with war material' were being 'allowed without hindrance to leave the ports of Western Europe and Great Britain'. The problem remained, however, as the National Council explained to the local Council in Newcastle, that the 'facts and circumstances which called the Council into being, and which made its action effective with regard to the threats of war-like measures against Russia, are altered considerably, and it is no use acting as though those facts were unchanged'.[103] The labour movement had indeed been able to prevent open war with Russia, Methil Council was told, but it was 'very doubtful whether the Labour Movement is at all as unanimous in the taking of similarly drastic steps to achieve peace with Russia' or to prevent all exports of munitions to Poland.[104] War had been prevented; thereafter, however, public interest had 'waned considerably'.[105]

Brailsford was still ready the following year to urge that the work of the Councils of Action was 'far from being completed'. Labour could 'not be satisfied with this negative result. Peace is not concluded. The Soviet government is not recognized.'[106] But there was no serious prospect of the Council again assuming the initiative in such matters. As J. C. Wedgwood, a member of the National Council, pointed out, the Council 'must use the machinery of general consent; and general consent is only rarely available'. Only extraordinary circumstances had created the Council and persuaded the labour movement to entrust it with extensive powers: war and the threat of war had 'made this a special case'.[107] The subsidiary objectives which the Council was also pledged to achieve, including the improvement of relations with Soviet Russia, aroused no similar enthusiasm or unanimity at either the local or the national level. The Council's role accordingly become a purely propagandist and an increasing marginal one. British workers, commented the *Worker*, had formed a Council of Action, and then, 'as if that were enough work for a year, have gone to sleep again'. While they gloried in the prowess of the Bolsheviks, commented *International*, a journal of the ILP left, 'our own Socialist movement is the most weak, helpless, confused and backward of any country in Europe'.[108]

The approach to the 'Russian question' with which the Council of Action had come increasingly to associate itself, one which emphasised the importance of the resumption of trading relations with Russia for the British domestic situation, became increasingly influential within the labour movement as the post-war boom came to an end in the autumn of 1920. As early as the previous spring Neil Maclean had pointed out to the House of Commons that Russia was willing to take locomotives, railway rolling-stock and engineering products from Britain, and was willing to send in return oil, grain, timber and the goods which were needed to restore pre-war levels of production in Britain. The prospect was one which 'must appeal to the commercial instincts of business men, to say nothing of the practical needs of the very people themselves'.[109] Labour and independent Liberals had urged the opening up of trade with Russia 'time and time again', declared another Labour member. If they were to 'save this country, if [they were] to effect the security and happiness of the people, to remove unrest and discontent and prevent the social revolution', he continued, 'then that trade must be restored, allowing prices to be reduced'.[110]

Britain imported nearly one hundred million pounds worth of goods from Russia in 1913, William Adamson, the party's leader, reminded the House on 22 December 1920, and had exported goods to Russia to a value of some fifty million pounds. Those imports, he argued, could make a considerable contribution to the reduction of prices in Britain; and taken together with British exports, they demonstrated the 'importance of renewing trade relations with the Russian people at the earliest possible moment, from the point of view of the cost of living, and as a means of finding a market for our goods'. An even more substantial trade might be done than in 1913, he thought, for the Russians were in need of a great many goods which Britain was in a position to supply. The notion that trade with Russia could relieve unemployment, Adamson concluded, had 'taken hold of the imagination of a great section of our people'; and both he, and the Labour Party in general, were in 'complete agreement' with it.[111]

Many Labour members were influenced by the situation in their own constituencies. Many manufacturers in the part of Leeds he represented, James O'Grady told the House, were 'on the verge of bankruptcy'. The Colne Valley, a major textile manufacturing centre, had 'nearly closed down', although Russia could take all it was capable of producing. Local manufacturers, even 'large industrial firms', had approached him with regard to the possibility of obtaining orders in that country, and local trade unionists had 'flooded' him with resolutions on the subject. The problem was simply that the trade agreement had not yet been signed. Within a month of its conclusion, he predicted, 'large numbers of men and women would find re-employment, the wheels of industry would be set going busily, and firms would be prevented from bankruptcy'.[112] Other speakers drew attention to the effect which the decline of the Russian trade was having upon the dockyards, the Scottish herring business and the tea industry. Orders that might have been placed in Britain, it was thought, were now being placed in Germany, or held up indefinitely.[113]

The prospects of trade with Russia received a more detailed examination in the press. In 1913, *Forward* reported on 6 November 1920, nearly half of Britain's imports of coniferous timber and pitwood had come from Russia, as well as huge quantities of wheat, eggs and butter, the domestic prices of which were going up 'because the British profiteers won't make peace with Russia'. Exports to Russia had been of major significance for the engineering, boot and shoe, textile and other industries, and the passage of time had if anything increased the opportunities which were available. Government policy was 'not only strangling and starving Russia', the paper concluded; 'it is strangling and starving us'. What more congenial employment could British workers have under capitalism, wrote G. D. H. Cole, 'than to work, even as the wage-slaves of capitalist employers, in order to supply the needs of the world's only Socialist Republic?'[114]

A party statement, 'Unemployment: a Labour Policy', was issued in January 1921. It contained the report of a Joint Labour Party-TUC committee which had investigated the problem of unemployment, together with the resolutions adopted at a special conference on the subject held on 27 January 1921. The statement called for the maintenance of unemployed and under-employed wage-earners and their families, the commissioning of works of social utility and the 'financing of schemes for the revival of British industry and the restoration of industry and commerce abroad'. The report concluded, in particular, that there must be an 'immediate resumption of trade with Russia' and that the trade agreement, still being negotiated by the two sides, must be concluded and brought into operation forthwith. 'Almost immediately', the report promised, 'employment would be provided in some of our staple industries and the process of slowing down production would be retarded and perhaps reversed.'[115]

The eventual signature of the trade agreement in March 1921 was warmly welcomed in labour circles.[116] It would facilitate the development of trade and the reduction of unemployment; and at the same time, some Labour MPs noted, it would 'remove one of the strongest props that support the present system in Russia'.

Government policy, complained Myers, had hitherto succeeded only in uniting the Russian people behind the Soviet government. A trade agreement, however, promised to prove one of the shortest cuts towards breaking down the 'impossible theories' which the Bolsheviks were believed to hold and assisting in the formation of a 'stable Government' in their place. Neither Churchill nor the French government had been able to crush Bolshevism by military force, Clynes pointed out; perhaps it would be better after their experiences to 'try some other method'.[117] To expand British trade with Russia, then, seemed likely to reduce the level of unemployment, lower prices, and at the same time to undermine the political theories with which the Soviet government was associated. Such was the political inspiration of 'Labour's Russian Policy'.

3 Conferences

The strategy of 'peaceful penetration'[1] appeared to have got off to an auspicious start when the New Economic Policy (NEP), effectively de-nationalising small-scale industry and retail trade and returning to more orthodox principles of public finance and law, was endorsed by the Tenth Congress of the Russian Communist Party in March 1921. Its decisions, the *Review of Reviews* declared, had been 'in favour of the abandonment of Communism'. The 'Communistic experiment had failed', commented the *New Statesman*; Lenin was now 'driving the Russian State furiously back on the road to capitalism . . . All in Russia acknowledge this save a handful of desperate doctrinaires'.[2] Lenin, added the *Spectator*, the author and head of the organisation which had administered Communism by means of the Soviets, had 'admitted the economic collapse of his system'. It was now conceded that the abolition of private enterprise and private commerce had been a 'disastrous fiasco', wrote the *Economist*; the Soviet leaders themselves admitted that the 'attempt to force Communism on the nation had failed'. From a business point of view, the paper added, there were 'undoubtedly big possibilities'.[3]

Indeed many at this time believed, as Krasin's wife recalled, that it would 'not be long before foreign capital would reassume, under modified conditions, its former prominent place in Russia'. In well-informed quarters, added *The Times*, it was believed that Lenin was persuaded of the failure of Bolshevism and that it was 'only a matter of hitting on a suitable formula to re-introduce the capitalistic system into Russia'.[4] The advice which the Foreign Office received from its representatives in Russia was largely in accord with these impressions. The two previous months, wrote William Peters, Assistant Agent at the British Mission in Moscow, at the end of May, had been marked by a 'complete change in the Soviet internal economic situation'. The Soviet government, he reported, was now 'consciously encouraging the growth of capitalism'. The head of the British Mission, R. M. Hodgson, attended a meeting in London in April 1921 organised by the London Chamber of Commerce. He expressed himself fully in agreement with a speech made by Bernard Pares, Professor of Russian at Liverpool University and a former Foreign Office adviser on Russian affairs, in which Pares had declared that in five years' time Bolshevism would be 'off the books' and they would be 'dealing with the ruins left by Bolshevism'.[5] An attempt to persuade the Soviet authorities to return to the economic and political arrangements which had earlier prevailed, it appeared, might not now meet with an entirely indifferent response.

Lloyd George was particularly impressed by a speech made by Lenin on 1 November 1921, in which the Soviet leader was reported to have said that there was 'no doubt among Communists that we have suffered a heavy defeat on the economic front', and to have conceded that the New Economic Policy involved a 'transition to the re-establishment of capitalism to a certain extent'.[6] Lenin, the Prime Minister told the House of Commons, 'admits they have been wrong, he admits they have been beaten'. His speech, Lloyd George declared, was a 'condemnation of the doctrines of Socialism', an 'admission of the complete failure of the Communist system': a 'very remarkable condemnation and exposure of the doctrines of Karl Marx by . . . its greatest exponent, the only man who has ever tried honestly to put these doctrines into operation'.[7] Lenin, he informed the Cabinet, was 'moving away from communism'; the government's duty must now be to 'support the anti-communistic elements in Russia'.[8] The remainder of his Premiership was associated with a number of attempts to do so.

A first opportunity was provided by the famine which occurred in the Volga area of Russia in 1921–2. The famine followed an exceptional period of drought, compounded by the loss of stock and equipment which had taken place during the civil war period. About fifteen million people were reportedly threatened with starvation. Agreements for assistance were signed with the American Relief Administration and with Frijhof Nansen, representing the Red Cross, in August 1921, and a number of smaller initiatives were undertaken by organisations such as the Imperial War Relief Fund, the Save the Children Fund, and the Friends' Emergency and War Victims Relief Committee.[9] The official British response was somewhat less accommodating. The Soviet government, Gregory noted in a Foreign Office minute on 12 September, despite 'insidious and indirect pro-Bolshevik propaganda' in 'fairly reputable sections of the press', was not an acceptable agency for the distribution of relief. The Soviet government was 'virtually ·anarchy itself'; its disappearance would therefore 'alter little from that point of view, whilst from every other it would relieve Europe of a nightmare'.[10] To provide relief, *The Times* explained on 25 August, would mean 'maintaining the Bolshevists in power at the moment when their misdeeds have wrought themselves out in their inevitable consequences and are threatening the collapse of the whole hateful and criminal system'. To any such attempt, the paper declared, it would be 'most emphatically and resolutely opposed'. Winston Churchill shared these doubts. He had the 'gravest objections' to giving help and countenance to the 'tyrannic Government of these Jew Commissars', he wrote to Curzon; 'we want to nourish the dog, not the tapeworm which is killing the dog'.[11]

There was an alternative view of British policy, however, and not necessarily one which rested on a greater degree of cordiality towards the Soviet government and its political objectives: for the Bolsheviks' great need of outside assistance and support, it began to be realised, might well compel them to make the political reforms and concessions about which they had previously proved obdurate. This was not a strategy which the government cared publicly to embrace. Indeed the famine in Russia, Lloyd George told the House of Commons, was 'so appalling a disaster that it ought to sweep every prejudice out of one's mind and only appeal to one emotion—pity and human sympathy'. But he went on to add a number of conditions which substantially qualified these admirable sentiments. In the first place, he pointed out, the administration of relief must be controlled by those who were providing it (in this case the Allied powers); and in addition, he thought, the Soviet government should be required, as a condition of that assistance, to recognise all its financial obligations towards foreign governments and their nationals. He had no wish to take advantage of this 'dire calamity' to seek the recognition of Soviet debts and obligations, he insisted; 'merely to use the famine for that purpose would be diabolical'. But if the Soviet government wished to create confidence and obtain the support of the western trading community, 'they must say they will recognise all these obligations'.[12] Lloyd George raised these points at a meeting with

Berzin and Klishko of the Russian Trading Mission on 5 August 1921. The meeting had been called at Berzin's request to discuss the possible provision of famine relief; now, it appeared, the essence of such negotiations would be debts and propaganda.[13]

The question was examined shortly afterwards at an Allied conference in Paris. It would be 'abominable', Briand, the French Prime Minister, declared, to treat the Russian famine from 'any other than a humanitarian point of view'. Lloyd George agreed. Relief, he thought, was an 'extremely difficult, very urgent and very terrible problem'; it would 'require the miracle of the loaves and fishes over again'. He proposed that an international committee be established 'solely for this humanitarian purpose'. Were this done, he thought, the Russian people would not be ungrateful; he was confident, moreover, that this would be the 'best way of saving Russia from something almost as bad as the plague—the Bolshevist system'. A Commission was appointed accordingly; its precise composition was established at a meeting three days later.[14] The Commission agreed that its first task must be to despatch a 'committee of experts' to Russia to examine the situation at first hand, and permission was sought from the Soviet government to enable it to do so. Chicherin, however, rejected the idea indignantly: it was attempting to substitute a long and complex investigation, which neither the American nor Nansen's relief organisations had found necessary, for the direct and immediate assistance which was so urgently required. The proposal was a 'mockery of the millions who were starving and dying'.[15]

Further discussions were held in Brussels between 6 and 8 October 1921. The furnishing of credits, it was agreed, should be made conditional upon the admission into Russia of the Committee of Inquiry, and upon the recognition by the Soviet government of the debts and other obligations of its predecessors. It must also provide guarantees for future credits.[16] The British government did agree independently to provide assistance to the Red Cross; but the medical goods, clothing and food supplies were valued at only one hundred thousand pounds. Beyond this, explained Philip Lloyd-Greame, Director of the Department of Overseas Trade, the 'only way' in which the necessary confidence could be created was by 'establishing those conditions upon which alone credit can be given and maintained in all civilized commercial communities'.[17]

This strategem was almost successful. Chicherin, at least, in view of what he regarded as an unfavourable international situation, appears to have been willing at this point to concede the Allies' demand that the Tsarist debts be recognised. Lenin, however, disagreed with both his proposal and his assessment of the overall situation, and he introduced a number of amendments into a statement on the question of debts, originally drafted by Chicherin, which was adopted by the Politburo of the Russian Communist Party on 27 October 1921.[18] It formed the basis of a communication to the Allies the following day. No people, the note began by declaring, could be expected to pay the price of 'chains fastened upon it for centuries' by a political system it had succeeded in replacing. The note went on, however, to outline what were described as a number of 'highly important concessions'. The Soviet government, in the first place, would now be willing to meet the claims of holders of small numbers of Russian bonds, for whom the recognition of debts was a matter of 'vital importance'; and it was also prepared to recognise the obligations towards other states and their citizens which arose from state loans concluded by the Tsarist government before 1914, provided that 'special conditions and facilities' were devised to enable it to do so. The western powers, for their part, must conclude a 'definite and general peace' with the Soviet government, and must extend to it their full diplomatic recognition. Any other questions which remained at issue should be settled by an international conference called for this purpose.[19]

The British reply, L. S. O'Malley suggested in a Foreign Office minute, should be 'as little contentious as possible and should not discourage the Soviet government from making further concessions'. Gregory added that a swift response would prevent the issue being 'diverted from the famine towards the dangerous question of recognition'. Curzon wrote to Chicherin on the following day, accordingly, 1 November 1921, seeking 'further information' regarding the loans which had been made to the Tsarist government after 1914, and raising the question of compensation for foreign citizens whose property in Russia had been nationalised.[20] The Soviet reply, however, considered these questions 'so complicated, and to such an extent interconnected' with the problem of the economic recovery of Russia and of Europe more generally, that they could be resolved only at the international conference which had earlier been proposed.[21] On this the discussion effectively concluded.

Another approach to the 'Russian problem' began to emerge towards the end of the year. This was the notion that a consortium should be formed of financiers and industrialists from France, Britain, America and Germany, whose task it should be to bring about the economic recovery of central and eastern Europe.[22] Lloyd George broached the subject at a meeting with Krasin, called at the Prime Minister's request, on 16 December 1921. Lloyd George, who was joined by Sir Robert Horne, the Chancellor of the Exchequer, suggested to Krasin that the restoration of Russian railways, agriculture and industry 'might most effectively be accomplished by a syndicate of private financiers from Britain, France and Germany'. It would be their job to develop the machinery of trade, including transport, and to undertake direct investment in a number of appropriate cases. The German partners to the arrangement, in view of their 'greater acquaintance with Russia', would undertake the major part of the work; and the control of some Russian railways, it was thought, might serve as a suitable guarantee of their investment (Lloyd George told the Cabinet the same day that foreign control of the Soviet customs was also being considered for this purpose).[23]

Krasin replied that foreign entrepreneurs might find it difficult to cope with the 'peculiar conditions' under which the railway system operated in Russia; and in any case the Soviet government could not possibly consider surrendering control of the railway system to an outside syndicate. The main obstacle to the further development of trade, he thought, was the lack of diplomatic recognition of the Soviet government by the western powers and of a comprehensive peace treaty, not the lack of incentives for private commerce and investment. Indeed there was a distinct possibility, in the absence of stable diplomatic relations of the kind he had indicated, that control of the railways by a foreign syndicate might simply be used to organise opposition to the Soviet government. The scale of the investment required, moreover, was such as to require the participation of the western governments themselves (and especially that of the United Kingdom); the efforts of the financiers alone, he thought, would not be sufficient.[24]

The proposal was considered further at a series of meetings between Lloyd George and M. Briand, the French Prime Minister, in London,[25] and at a conference of bankers, financiers and government ministers from Britain, France, Italy and Belgium which was held in Paris at the end of December 1921. It was agreed to accept a British proposal that an international private consortium be set up, charged with assisting the recovery of the railways, ports and commerce of eastern Europe, and especially of Austria, Poland and Russia. The initial capital of twenty million pounds would be provided by the member states, and the profits accruing to the German participants would be devoted to the repayment of reparations.[26] The proposal was endorsed by a meeting of the Allied Supreme Council at Cannes on 10 January 1922. A resolution was adopted providing for the establishment of an 'international corporation with affiliated national corporations for the purpose of the economic reconstruction of Europe and the co-operation of all nations in the restoration of normal prosperity'. A committee was set up to examine the project in greater detail, and to proceed with the organisation of the corporation 'with a view to its beginning operation at the earliest possible moment'.[27]

The committee, which met in London from 21 to 25 February 1922, decided upon the establishment of a central corporation with a capital of two million pounds and of associated national corporations with a capital of twenty million pounds, in which not only the founder-states should participate, but also America, Japan, Denmark and Czechoslovakia. The earlier proposal had declared that no prosperity was possible unless economic principles were observed which were 'essential to the development and even the existence of private enterprise',[28] a provision which, it was noted, applied above all to Soviet Russia. The committee agreed that the proposed consortium should have no dealings with states which did not recognise all their previous debts and obligations and compensate all foreign nationals for their loss of property, and which did not establish a legal system which would 'comprehensively guarantee and encourage commercial activity'.[29]

The proposal, however, scarcely advanced beyond this point. American participation was not forthcoming; and more important, the project met with considerable resistance from precisely those industrial and governmental circles in Germany itself which were supposed to be mainly responsible for its implementation. It was argued that the more or less 'colonial' character of the agreement would arouse opposition within Soviet Russia; and that it might be more advantageous to attempt to develop relations on a bilateral basis.[30] The consortium proposals did, however, bear a close relation to the attempts which were made later in the year at conferences in Genoa and The Hague to 'solve the Russian problem'.

The Supreme Council, at its meeting in Cannes, had also given its approval to a motion proposed by Lloyd George calling for an international economic and financial conference in February or early March to which all the European powers, including Russia, should be invited to send representatives. The conference, the resolution declared, would represent an 'urgent and essential step towards the economic reconstruction of Central and Eastern Europe' and towards alleviating the 'paralysis of the European system' more generally. No nation, the resolution conceded, could dictate to another the 'principles on which they are to regulate their system of ownership, internal economy and government'. But if foreign investors were to be persuaded to assist in the process of economic reconstruction they would have to be assured that their property and rights would be respected and the fruits of their enterprise secured to them. All public debts and obligations would therefore have to be acknowledged, private property would have to be restored or satisfactory compensation provided, and a legal system would have to be established which would 'sanction and enforce commercial and other contracts with impartiality'. Financial and currency reforms would also be required, and the states concerned would also have to agree to refrain from propaganda and aggressive actions towards outside parties. If these conditions were accepted by the Soviet government, the resolution concluded, the Allies would be prepared to grant it 'official', or *de jure* recognition.[31]

The resolution was well received in business and financial quarters. There had been some commercial dealings with central Europe, the chairman of the National Provincial Bank told its annual meeting in January 1922, but the situation was still far from satisfactory. He expressed the hope that the proposed conference would provide for the 'regeneration and reorganization of that part of the world and the subsequent resumption of trade on a more normal basis'. The chairman of Martins Bank also welcomed the conference; while the chairman of the Westminster Bank added that until the country's export trade was regained, the outlook 'must remain far from cheering'. What was needed most, he thought, was the restoration of the markets of central Europe and Russia.[32] 'Most far-seeing financiers and industrialists', commented the *Economist*, realised in addition that the co-operation of the present Soviet government was 'essential to the solution of Russia's economic problems'. The diplomatic recognition of that government, it thought, was clearly an 'essential preliminary to any programme of economic reconstruction'.[33]

Opinion in governmental circles was by no means so enthusiastic. Curzon was particularly concerned at the possibility that the Soviet government might be given full diplomatic recognition. This was a matter for the Foreign Office as well as for the Cabinet, he pointed out to Tom Jones, Deputy Secretary to the Cabinet, although the Foreign Office had not in fact been approached for its advice. The Soviet government's sole objective in seeking recognition, he wrote to Churchill, was to fortify their position; thereafter they would 'revert to type'. 'What impresses one most', he wrote, 'is that the Soviet propaganda (to which Lenin is privy—we can prove his responsibility) still continues unabated. I hope therefore we shall be cautious before we give the final leg up to Lenin, Trotsky and Co.'[34] Curzon expressed the same sentiments to Austen Chamberlain. The trade agreement had proved a 'farce', he wrote, and Soviet propaganda seemed scarcely to have been affected by it.[35] Churchill was also concerned about 'this Genoa business'. Lloyd George's greatest objective, it seemed to him, was Moscow: to make Britain the county 'in the closest possible relations with the Bolsheviks, and to be their protectors and sponsors before Europe'. He was 'unable to discern any British advantage, however slight, in this'.[36]

Churchill, Chamberlain noted in a letter to Lloyd George on 21 March 1922, was in fact the person who had 'taken the strongest line on this subject': he had, indeed, made it clear that he could not remain a member of the government if *de jure* recognition were extended to the Soviet government. Such an eventuality, Chamberlain noted, would place Conservative members of the Coalition government in an 'impossible' position: for Churchill would then appear 'more Tory than the Tory Ministers'. He might have made the difference that existed in the Cabinet appear greater than it actually was, Chamberlain remarked in a further letter two days later; but he begged the Premier to 'take trouble with Winston'. Bonar Law also, he added, was 'restless about Genoa'.[37] Lloyd George, for his part, retorted that he would not go to Genoa unless he was free to recognise the Bolsheviks upon the conditions which the Allies had agreed at Cannes, and that the Cabinet would have to decide between himself and Churchill. If the Conservatives took Churchill's view, he wrote to his secretary, 'I go without any hesitation'.[38]

Issue was joined at a Conference of Ministers on 27 March 1922. Lloyd George began by emphasising the need to revive European trade and commerce. It was essential that not simply experts, but 'political representatives of Governments should meet and endeavour to arrange something to re-establish the trade of Europe'. Some members of the Cabinet, Lloyd George had pointed out to Chamberlain three days earlier, did not realise how grave the trade situation was. The replies he had received from men whose judgement and knowledge of business he trusted in response to questions on this subject had been 'invariably not merely gloomy, but seriously pessimistic'.[39] The conference would accordingly deal with the restoration of transport and commercial networks throughout Europe, especially in Austria and Russia, and with the economic reconstruction of the Continent more generally.

Russia, in fact, was the most difficult question with which the conference would have to concern itself. The Prime Minister suggested that the Allies should take their decision regarding the possible diplomatic recognition of the Soviet government upon the basis of their impression 'as to whether [the Soviet government] had practically abandoned Communistic principles in dealing with foreign Powers, or not'. There were two parties in Russia, the Premier believed, 'one entirely communistic, and the other prepared to abandon Communism in dealing with foreign countries'. He did not known which of the two was in the ascendant; but if it were the latter, he thought it would be a 'mistake to send them away with a refusal to do business'. As he put it to Chamberlain, if the Communist Party were in a dominant position in Moscow there could be no question of recognition. If, however, the 'party that is prepared to surrender its Bolshevism and to make terms with the Western capitalists has captured the Soviet authority, then it would be folly not to help Russia to return to the community of civilized nations'.[40]

The Prime Minister was opposed, once again, by Churchill, who had the gravest doubts about coming to an agreement of any sort with the Soviet government. He refused, he declared, to take 'sides against Russia as a whole in favour of a band of dastardly criminals'.[41] Curzon, at a Conference of Ministers the following day, expressed a similar opinion. His 'main idea', he said, was that 'on no account should the British government act alone in this matter'. The Prime Minister agreed. He read out an extract from a letter sent to him by the Home Secretary, however, 'indicating that M. Lenin was abandoning his Communistic principles. If this were the case, by recognizing him we should be supporting those in Russia who were in favour of moderation.'[42] He had, in fact, already told the Czech Prime Minister Beneš that European assistance was 'absolutely essential to the Bolsheviks and that they could not do without it. For this reason he thought that the Bolshevists would give any terms that the Western Powers asked. If Lenin came back from Genoa with nothing in his hands, he would be overthrown.'[43]

There were two questions to be considered, Lloyd George told a meeting of the Cabinet later the same day. The first concerned the economic conditions under which British traders could be persuaded to resume business with Russia; the second was the 'larger question at the base of our economic troubles, the unrest in Eastern Europe, which disturbed the trader and made him suspicious'. There was a state of 'something like menace along the Russian frontier'. Half of Europe, in fact, was 'living under a condition of menace of war'. The first objective of the Genoa Conference, he thought, should be to establish a pact among all the nations of Europe against aggression, guaranteeing in particular that Russia would not attack Roumania, Latvia, Lithuania, Poland or Finland, or vice versa. Trade was then standing at a very low ebb, owing in part to the international situation. 'Until some such condition of peace was established', he insisted, there 'would not be an effective revival'.

As far as Russia was concerned, the Premier went on, efforts to restore trading relations had been 'only partially successful'. The Soviet government had failed to carry out its obligations as strictly as they had a right to expect; but the fact remained that Russia was still outside the comity of nations, and 'until that fact was changed the full restoration of trade would be difficult'. Lenin, however, was believed to have been personally responsible for most of the recent economic legislation, which had amounted to the 'abandonment of communism'; and the Russian delegates might well come to Genoa having 'practically surrendered their

Communistic principles and willing to enter into negotiations
with the Capitalistic communities'. If this were the case, he urged,
the Allies ought to give 'all necessary support to the anti-
Communistic elements in Russia' and declare that if Communist
principles were abolished they would be ready to assist in the
economic development of that country. Full diplomatic recognition, however, would not be granted until the powers had been
able to satisfy themselves that the agreements made at Genoa
were being respected and implemented.

Curzon thought the question of recognition premature; and he
attached 'more importance to acting with Europe than to any
other point'. Churchill found even this hard to stomach. The
terms of the trade agreement had been 'repeatedly broken'; yet
now the Cabinet was being asked to go still further to meet the
Soviet government, whose only aim in attending the conference,
he thought, was to gain prestige in order to 'rivet their shackles
even more closely on the ignorant peasants'. He was concerned
that at a time of a strong Conservative majority—'in a country',
moreover, 'deeply devoted to the monarchy'—it was proposed to
accord them this favour. Chamberlain intervened at this point,
and upon his formulation of the consensus of opinion a precarious
compromise was reached. British representatives at Genoa, it was
agreed, were not to act in isolation. Should it emerge that the
Soviet representatives were willing, in good faith, to accept the
Allies' conditions, 'full ceremonial recognition' should be accorded to them only to the extent implied by the appointment of a
Chargé d'Affaires.[44]

Lloyd George outlined the government's policy to the House of
Commons on 3 April 1922. The Soviet government, he insisted,
must 'recognize all the conditions imposed and accepted by
civilized communities, as the test of fitness for entering into the
comity of nations'. Debts, for instance, must be recognised, if not
settled immediately: 'a country that repudiates her obligations
because she changes her government is a country you cannot deal
with—certainly not in these days when governments change so
often'. The property of foreign nationals, where it had not been
destroyed, must be restored and due compensation paid. Judicial
tribunals must be set up which were not the 'creatures of the
Executive'; and attacks upon the institutions of other countries
must cease. Lenin, he believed, had made an 'admission of the
complete failure of the Communist system'. If this represented a

genuine determination on the part of the Soviet government to honour the principles of respect for private property, respect for the rights of individuals, fair play to those who made investments there, and acknowledgement of honourable debts, then there was a 'real basis upon which we can treat'. Access to the courts, and some form of recognition, would follow; but not full recognition until the Soviet government had given 'actual proof' of its *bona fides*.[45]

The Allies had agreed at Cannes upon an invitation to the Soviet government couched in terms similar to those which the Premier had adumbrated,[46] and it was thought highly desirable that the Soviet government should be induced to accept them, at least in principle, before the conference began its work. Lloyd George accordingly raised the matter at a meeting with Krasin on 10 February 1922. Krasin, however, who was about to return to Moscow, informed the Premier that the Soviet government could not accept the Cannes conditions nor undertake to abide by them since they were one-sided in their application and the formulation of many paragraphs was unacceptable for a variety of reasons.[47] Lloyd George replied that the agreement of the Soviet government to participate in the Genoa conference would be regarded in itself as evidence of its willingness to abide by the Cannes conditions. If the Soviet government refused to accept them, he warned Krasin, the conference itself might be prejudiced; certainly, at least, it would be easier for the French—who in any case regarded the conference with some scepticism—to refuse to take part. The Soviet government, he urged, should announce its acceptance in principle of the Cannes resolutions—they were, after all, 'only the conditions on which every civilized government conducted its affairs'—and should then argue its case in detail when it came to consider their practical application. Until the Russian government acknowledged (but not necessarily paid) its debts, he feared that the business community could not be brought whole-heartedly to accept any arrangements with that country. He hoped for an unqualified answer.

Krasin, however, who was aware that the Premier was seeking to restore his political fortunes by a successful initiative in the field of foreign policy, continued to object to being required to accept conditions before the negotiations with which they were associated had begun. This amounted, he argued, to the signature of a contract without a guarantee of reciprocity.[48] Lloyd George was

therefore able to give the House of Commons no greater reassurance on this point than simply to inform them that the Soviet
government had accepted the invitation to attend the conference,
in which special attention had been drawn to several of the
paragraphs of the resolutions which had been agreed upon at
Cannes. The Soviet government's acceptance, he noted, had been
'without any protest or qualification in respect of those
paragraphs'.[49]

The Soviet government, for its part, was resolved (as Chicherin
put it) to 'struggle against economic co-operation taking the form
of the economic domination of Russia'.[50] Lenin urged the delegation to quote 'particularly often' the first point of the Cannes
resolutions (the final part of which had been omitted from the text
communicated by the Italian Foreign Minister), which provided
for the right of a state to regulate its own economic order, form of
government, and system of property.[51] A detailed estimate was
also prepared, based upon two years' work by a special commission under the auspices of the Commissariat of Finance, of the
damages suffered during the war of intervention and the civil war.
For this sum, some thirty-nine million gold roubles, the Allies
were to be held responsible.[52]

The Bolsheviks, however, were not compelled to rely alone
upon the logical force of their arguments: the development of
relations with Germany provided additional, and more substantial, grounds for optimism. A proposal put forward by Krupps to
establish an armaments factory in Russia was endorsed by Lenin
in January 1922. Its acceptance was necessary, he thought, 'right
now, before the Genoa Conference. For us it would be infinitely
important to conclude at least one, and preferably several concession contracts with German firms in particular.'[53] Relations with
the German government and with German industrialists developed so rapidly that a draft treaty, on the lines of that subsequently concluded at Rapallo, was ready for signature when the
Soviet delegates stopped over in Berlin in the course of their
journey to the conference.[54] The Bolsheviks' position, in fact, was
an altogether less precarious one than the British government had
supposed; and this misconception had much to do with the failure
of the Genoa Conference to achieve the definitive resolution of the
Russian question for which its promoters had hoped.

The Genoa Conference was officially designated an 'international
economic conference'.[55] This, however, did 'not prevent its

organisers from forming a political combination and raising political questions', as the secretary to the Soviet delegation, Boris Stein, recorded.[56] Notwithstanding the Conference's wide mandate, formally embracing financial, commercial and transport as well as political matters, it soon became clear that the 'main, if not the only question at Genoa' was the 'Russian one'.[57] The Political Commission, one of the four upon which the work of the Conference was devolved, was the arena within which issue was joined: it was in effect 'entirely devoted to the Russian question', the other Commissions, as Chicherin described them, being 'only decoration'.[58] An attempt was made throughout, consistent with the ostensible purpose of the Conference itself, to represent the political differences which divided the two sides as simply 'technical questions' which men of goodwill should have no difficulty in resolving. This convenient fiction notwithstanding, however, it was precisely upon such pre-eminently political issues as the nationalisation of private property, forms of government and the administration of justice that the Conference eventually foundered.

The extent of the Allies' demands became evident when a memorandum was published which had been discussed and approved at a preliminary meeting held in London from 20–28 March 1922 and which was used by the five inviting powers as the basis of their proposed resolutions. This document, the Experts' Memorandum, was designed, in the words of the secretary of the Soviet delegation, to ensure that foreign capital should 'feel at home' in Soviet Russia.[59] Foreign businessmen, the memorandum noted, would require a 'considerable transformation in prevailing conditions' if they were to provide the assistance upon which Russia's economic revival was held to depend. Fundamental was the inviolability of the ownership of land and the sale of the produce it yielded. So far as industry was concerned, 'active measures' must be undertaken to provide for the freedom of activity of the foreign entrepreneur and his staff, the security of their industrial operations and fixed capital, their right to import such goods as they required, to distribute their manufactured produce, to hire and fire labour and to earn a 'normal profit'. The Soviet government, moreover, must accept all the financial obligations of its predecessors, and accept responsibility for all the losses suffered by foreign nationals. Considerable changes were also required in the legal system.[60]

The Experts' Memorandum, the Soviet delegation replied,

despite its expressed concern for 'justice' and the economic
recovery of Russia, amounted to a proposal for 'not simply the
exploitation, but the absolute enslavement of the working population of Russia by foreign capital'. It avoided at the same time the
basic question—as they saw it—of bringing about the recovery of
the Russian economy.[61] Lloyd George, however, had no wish to
appear as determinedly uncompromising as the memorandum
suggested; and on 14 April, four days after the Conference had
begun, he arranged a series of more informal discussions in his
headquarters at the Villa d'Albertis. These, Chicherin is reported
to have said, were the 'only thing that happened at Genoa'.[62]

The proceedings were opened by Lloyd George. British public
opinion, he assured Chicherin, was now prepared to accept that
the system of government in Russia should be a matter for the
Russians themselves. But when it came to the establishment of
trading relations, 'certain conditions were indispensable'. One of
these was the recognition of debts to individuals: the House of
Commons would accept nothing less, and private investment in
Russian industry and agriculture would not otherwise be forthcoming. Another was the restoration of private property, perhaps
on a lease-hold basis; and another was the cancellation of the
claim for damages suffered during the civil war which the Russian
delegation had put forward, a demand which was 'rather like
putting the Western countries in the position of paying an
indemnity'. Chicherin explained, in reply, that while Russian
political leaders had some differences of opinion, there was also
the 'great elemental force of mass ideas upon fundamental questions which involved the whole mass of workers and peasants and
could not be set aside'. Russian workers, for instance, would not
accept the restoration of private property, or the recognition of
debts without reciprocity. Arrangements had been made, however, for foreign businessmen to acquire concerns in Russia upon
a lease-hold basis for a fixed number of years, which might
provide a form of compensation; and pre-war debts might also be
acknowledged, upon certain conditions. The 'Alabama' case of
1862, moreover, appeared to provide a legal precedent for the
Russian counter-claims to which Lloyd George had referred.
Further exchanges followed concerning particular features of the
Russian economic and political system; but pleasant as it was for
the delegates to get to know each other, M. Barthou, the French
representative, observed, they were 'playing hide-and-seek. It
was essential to come to some understanding.'

A further meeting took place the following day, 15 April 1922. Lloyd George began by remarking that the Russian counter-claims, a detailed statement of which had just been received, were 'startling beyond conception'. It was a question for a country which made a revolution to decide whether or not it had been worthwhile; it could not 'send in the bill to other countries'. Nor could the private debts of individuals be ignored: the transactions involved had been negotiated not by governments but by the claimants themselves, and no reduction in their rights could be considered. A satisfactory settlement on this point, Lloyd George declared, was a 'test of whether it was possible to proceed at all with the Russian question'. Inter-government debts, on the other hand, could be written down, arrears of interest disregarded, and future payments of interest postponed. Chicherin, in reply, de-fended the Russian counter-claims: the counter-revolutionary armies, he insisted, had been 'wholly created' by the Allies, and the damage they had wrought had been enormous. The restora-tion of factories *in natura* was also an 'impossibility', since for the most part such factories had been absorbed by other and larger concerns, and in any case there were a 'certain number of separate factories which could not be restored to private ownership owing to the resistance of the workers'. The two sides were evidently still separated by differences of principle, and it was accordingly decided that the Soviet delegates should be invited to refer back to Moscow for further instructions. 'If Russia gave an unfavourable reply', Lloyd George made clear, 'there would be an end of the Russian question. If the reply was favourable they could go on to discuss the other questions.'[63]

The Premier's initiative had been shrewdly judged; and five days later Chicherin, who had been in communication with his government, wrote to him in an altogether more accommodating vein. Russia's economic position, Chicherin pointed out in his letter, was such that the country could not undertake to repay in full all foreign debts and obligations. The delegation was nevertheless prepared, in the interests of an agreement, to accept the Allied terms on all points other than that which required the restitution to foreign nationals of their former possessions, pro-vided that the Russian war debts and interest payments were written down in return, and that 'adequate financial help' was provided to enable the country to emerge as quickly as possible from its existing economic situation. In the absence of assistance of this kind there could be no point in accepting financial obligations which could not be discharged; nor could the Soviet government reasonably be expected to repay the debts of its predecessors while it remained without diplomatic recognition. Former owners would also be given either the use of their property, or where that was not possible an agreed amount of compensation.[64]

This final concession, however, had been opposed by some members of the Soviet delegation, and the Politburo ruled in their favour.[65] The reply to the Experts' Memorandum which the Soviet delegation issued on 24 April accordingly reiterated Chicherin's offer to acknowledge pre-war debts, but the right of foreign nationals to the use of property which they had formerly owned and which had not been nationalised was conceded only 'where this was possible having regard to the socio-economic system and basic laws of the Russian republic'. All arrears of interest were also to be annulled.[66] The Russian delegates, the Cabinet was told, were 'proving very intractable and unreasonable'.[67] The French and Belgian delegations, indeed, were not prepared to endorse the official Allied reply to the Russian memorandum of 24 April, although it largely recapitulated the Experts' Memorandum to which they had earlier given their assent.[68] The reply, together with a covering note from the Italian Foreign Minister, was transmitted to the Russian delegation on 2 May 1922.

Russian prosperity, the note began by declaring, could not be revived without the capital and commercial experience of the West. That capital and experience would not in turn be made available until a 'feeling of security' had been restored: that was to say, until foreign nationals had guarantees that they could resume their former undertakings in Russia, and start new ones, with the 'certainty that their property and their rights will be respected and the fruits of their enterprise assured to them'. Foreign governments could make an additional contribution to Russian economic recovery, either through the proposed international corporation or through export credit legislation. The Soviet government, for its part, would be required to 'refrain from any action which might disturb the territorial and political *status quo* in other States' and to take measures to prevent any activities of this kind which might originate from within its territory. It would also have to acknowledge all the debts and obligations of its predecessors (although their immediate repayment would not be demanded, and the amount of war debt might be reduced), and it would have to acknowledge the right of private claimants to either restitution of their property or a satisfactory form of compensation. A number of changes would also be required in the Soviet legal system.[69] As a Foreign Office minute commented, the memorandum asked 'everything—or practically everything—and offers nothing in return'. The Russians could not possibly accept it without endangering their government in the eyes of its supporters; the object of their reply would simply be to 'make it appear that they are not primarily responsible for the failure of Genoa'.[70]

The possibility of reaching agreement upon this or any other basis had in any case already been prejudiced by the conclusion of a German–Soviet treaty at Rapallo on 16 April 1922. The treaty, which was published two days later, 'disturbed the whole Conference for several days'.[71] The British delegation, Gregory wrote, was 'very much disturbed . . . It was at once realised that the whole situation was transformed'. The existence of a secret military convention was also suspected.[72] The French delegation immediately withdrew from the Committee of Experts, and the German delegation was denied the right to participate further in the Conference. All Commission meetings for that day were cancelled.[73] The continuation of the Conference itself, indeed, appeared in doubt: French participation became even more grudging, and the Soviet government, having secured under Article 2 of the Rapallo treaty the recognition of its nationalisation of the property of foreign nationals as well as a diplomatic and tactical *coup*, became even less concerned to satisfy the claims of Allied nationals. The Conference, Gregory recalled, was left to discuss secondary questions of no great importance, 'or at least, none that would have justified the continuous session in foreign parts of so many of the leading politicians of Europe'. Gregory and Litvinov, indeed, were agreed in finding the Rapallo treaty the 'only concrete achievement' of the Conference.[74]

It was not upon the Rapallo treaty, however, that the Conference eventually foundered. Altogether more crucial was the fact that it had proved impossible to overcome or represent as 'technical' the 'basic root difference' (in Stein's words) which separated the two sides and which was reflected in their social systems, their world-outlooks and their attitudes to the revolution in Russia. To the Soviet side, the abolition of the private ownership of the means of production was the very essence of that revolution; to the Allies, on the other hand, it was precisely the most basic of the changes they required.[75] Indeed the conference had been not so much a meeting of practical businessmen, commented *Mezhdunarodnaya Zhizn'*, as a clash between two world-outlooks, a 'struggle between proletarian socialism and bourgeois individualism'. It had been a continuation of the struggle against native and foreign capital to secure the achievements of the revolution; it was one of many steps to the new social order, an order which would be established 'not by the agreements of diplomatists but by the movement of the working class'.[76]

British disappointment was summed up by the *Economist*. The 'extremist section' in Russia, it concluded, held 'more power . . . than was assumed'. The moderates, accordingly, had been unable to carry the 'whole-hearted recognition of private property rights', the '*sine qua non* of restored commercial intercourse' on anything other than a gold or barter basis.[77] 'Extreme theorists', Lloyd George explained to the House of Commons, had overawed the 'practical statesmen of the Soviet system'. Theorists, he complained, could 'not realize the difference between a logical proposition and a business one'. Most of the Bolsheviks' gold, however, had been exhausted, and they had offered major concessions. The whole question of relations between Soviet Russia and the western powers was to be examined again at a meeting in The Hague. The Premier was 'very hopeful' that when they came to an 'examination of the practical details, something may be achieved'.[78]

The augury for the Hague Conference was not quite so favourable as the Prime Minister had indicated. The German government had not been invited; and the American government, which had, decided not to participate.[79] The representatives of the states which did attend, moreover, had powers only *ad referendum*: they were 'experts' rather than plenipotentiaries, with the power not to take decisions but only to refer back proposals to their respective governments. Nor could it be overlooked that many of the Allied representatives had an interest in the proceedings which was hardly likely to incline them towards compromise. The chairman of the French delegation, Alphand, was the director of the Department of Private Property and Interests in France and of the bureau for the defence of the property of French citizens in Russia; and another member of the delegation had formerly owned a rubber factory in Russia.[80] The chairman of the Belgian delegation was the head of the Belgian bank which held the largest number of Russian bonds, and another member of the delegation was represented upon the committee for the defence of Belgian interests in Russia. Andersen and Petersen, who represented Denmark, were the director and secretary respectively of the Danish society for the defence of claims in Russia; and the British delegation included Leslie Urquhart, the President of the Association of British Creditors of Russia, who was present, the government explained, in order to represent the interests of British bondholders.[81]

It was not surprising in the circumstances that the Conference concerned itself with something other than the 'practical solution to the Russian question apart from political considerations' of which the House of Commons was subsequently informed.[82] It was rather the case, Stein remarked, that questions which had been considered 'political' at Genoa and had been discussed in the Political Commission were now, in a 'miraculous transformation', declared exclusively 'technical' in character. It was 'not in the least' the case that no political questions were discussed: the aim was rather to be able to 'remove any awkward points from the agenda, "deeming" them "political"'.[83] The Hague Conference, accordingly, was no more successful in providing a solution to the 'Russian problem' than its predecessor at Genoa had been: for at neither Conference could the western powers persuade the Russian delegation to accept their ostensibly 'practical' and 'businesslike' proposals, involving as they did major changes in the Soviet social order which the latter were at no time prepared to accept.

The Conference was divided into two Commissions, the Russian and the Non-Russian. The second Commission began its deliberations on 16 June 1922, ten days before the Russian delegation arrived. Proceedings were subsequently devolved upon three sub-commissions, which dealt respectively with the questions of private property, debts and credits. The sub-commission on credits, however, soon decided that the loan which the Soviet delegates sought was 'impossible in the current economic and political situation of Europe'. All that could be done was to encourage the provision of loans by private capitalists, who in turn would require some assurance that their investments would be secure; and no further details were provided of the extent to which western governments would be prepared to assist in this development. The Russian delegation received nothing more substantial, Litvinov complained, than a series of 'very interesting lectures on the meaning of confidence'.[84] The delegation itself observed, in its subsequent report to the Soviet government, that the absence of government or government-guaranteed private credits was in itself sufficient to preclude the possibility of a successful outcome to the Conference as a whole.[85]

The sub-commission on debts opened with the standard disclaimer that those present were there as 'experts, men of business, who consider real facts, not devoting their attention to any political questions'. It was informed by Litvinov at the outset, however, that the Soviet government could accept no obligations unless it could be certain of its ability to fulfil them; and that it did not consider that the recognition of debts was an action to be performed unilaterally. The chairman, M. Alphand, replied by observing that circumstances might force the Soviet government to 'submit to the general law which governs relations between civilized states, and to recognize the obligations accepted by preceding governments'. Andersen, the Danish representative, added that the most acceptable form of guarantee from the private claimants' point of view might be the 'transfer of the administration of all the income of the Russian government to an International Commission'. This might possibly be regarded as an infringement of sovereignty; but states which were bankrupt, he informed Litvinov, could 'not allow themselves the luxury of pride'.[86] The sub-commission on debts was accordingly able to come no closer to agreement than that which had dealt with credits.

The most important issues of all were reserved for the sub-commission on private property. Indeed the 'whole history of the Hague Conference', Stein noted, was 'essentially the history of the negotiations on private property'.[87] Sir Philip Lloyd-Greame, Director of the Department of Overseas Trade, who chaired the meetings of this sub-commission, began in familiar fashion by urging that their discussions should be of a 'practical and businesslike character', avoiding what he called 'general questions'. The members of the Non-Russian Commission, he pointed out, were 'practical business people' whose concern was simply to establish whether conditions could be guaranteed which were 'capable of engaging the confidence of those who would have to invest their money in Russia', a question outside the control of their respective governments. The Soviet delegation's announcement of a list of concessions which would be offered to foreign nationals appeared to him altogether insufficient. The list included only an 'insignificant part' of formerly foreign-owned property; it did not indicate what compensation would be offered; and it was not clear to what extent such essential principles as the 'non-interference of trade unions in the running of enterprises' would be observed.[88]

The gap which separated the two sides, in fact, was too wide to be bridged. The Russian delegation, Krasin noted in reply, while seeking to involve foreign capital in the recovery of the economy, based its proposals upon the economic needs of the country. Concessions were being offered because they might be of benefit to the country's economy, not because the property had previously been owned by foreigners. The restoration of private property, in any case, was a Utopian notion: transport had been nationalised, and there had been many other changes. The western powers, for their part, found the list presented limited and unsatisfactory; there was no guarantee of restitution; and there was not even an assurance that all former owners would automatically receive concessions. In his opinion, Lloyd-Greame observed, the 'only form of real compensation which the Russian government could give at the present time' was 'restitution of property in all cases where that is possible'.[89] It was equally clear that no agreement was likely to be reached on such a basis.

A final plenary meeting between the Russian and the Non-Russian Commissions took place on 19 July 1922. Litvinov, in his address, indicated that it might be possible to inquire of the Soviet government as to whether the debts of previous governments in respect of private citizens might be recognised, even though credits might not immediately be forthcoming. Lloyd-Greame, in reply, thought this an 'extraordinarily important' statement, signifying a 'new stage in [their] negotiations'. The Belgian delegate who followed him, however, M. Cattier, professed to understand the declaration somewhat differently: Litvinov had offered to submit a number of questions to his government, but nothing more than this. Litvinov had, indeed, made it clear that he could give no guarantee regarding the possible response of the government he represented.[90] The Non-Russian Commission, accordingly, while welcoming the tone of Litvinov's declaration, agreed that it could 'not find the basis of an agreement' within its terms.[91]

Defending the Conference in the House of Commons, Lloyd-Greame declared that it represented a 'long step forward on the path towards a Russian settlement'. The 'sole hope' of Russian industry, he thought, lay in 'bringing back the skill and experience of those who have done so much to build them up in the past'. In this respect the Russian delegation had suffered from a 'complete misconception of facts and actual possibilities'. The final phase of the Conference, however, had offered 'real hope of concrete results'; the Russian delegation's proposal, in particular, represented a 'very distinct, indeed a remarkable advance' on their previous position.[92] Nothing would get better in Russia, Lloyd George added sternly, and it was 'no use pretending' that it would, until Russia fell 'in with the civilized world'. Getting the western capitalist to return was 'essential to Russia, to enable her to run her manufactures'. The Soviet government, where it was possible, must therefore restore the owners of property to their former positions, and provide inducements for investors. This, he insisted, was a 'purely business proposition'; Soviet experience had shown 'how impossible it is to govern a country on these disastrous principles'.[93]

The Hague Conference, Lloyd George's optimism notwithstanding, in fact brought to an end the concerted attempts of the western powers to 'transplant again the exotic plant of capital upon Russian soil'.[94] Any such development, it was clear, must secure the agreement of the Soviet government, no prospect of whose forcible overthrow could now be seriously entertained; yet at virtually no time did it appear likely that such consent would be forthcoming. The Prime Minister had proceeded throughout, in fact, upon the engaging but fallacious assumption that the attempt to construct society upon principles different from those which prevailed in the West could be only, as he put it, a 'passing phase'[95]: a short and ultimately unavailing attempt to suspend the operation of economic laws which were universal in their application and inexorable in their logic. The experience of Genoa and The Hague revealed, much to his chagrin, that this apparently elementary truth had not yet been grasped by the Soviet government; his appeal for a 'practical businesslike settlement', accordingly, fell upon stony ground. Lloyd George's domestic political position, as well as the attempt which he had largely sponsored to settle the 'Russian problem' through conference diplomacy, was a casualty of this misapprehension.

Part II

IMPERIAL CONFRONTATION

4 Imperial Crisis and Soviet Russia

The difficulties which Lloyd George experienced in obtaining support for his policy towards Russia at the Genoa and Hague conferences showed how serious the rifts within the Cabinet had become by the summer of 1922. The Premier's eagerness to placate the Russians, at the expense, it appeared, of fundamental and more long-standing British interests, was one of the issues on which Cabinet differences ran deepest; but there were others, including the settlement in Ireland, the reputed sale of political honours, and developments in the Near East. Overcome by these divisions, the Coalition government collapsed in October 1922, and at a general election the following month the Conservatives were returned to power. The perspectives in foreign affairs with which Lloyd George had been so closely associated — agreement through negotiation, Europe as the principal arena of policy, and an emphasis upon the stimulation of foreign trade—would now, it appeared, be succeeded by a more orthodox interpretation of British foreign policy within which imperial considerations, and the interests of British possessions in the East more particularly, might be expected to assume an altogether more prominent place.

There was, of course, a good deal which was traditional about this interpretation of British foreign policy, and there was a good deal which was traditional also about the increasing degree of attention which began to be devoted in this connection to the activities of the Russian government in Asia. But although the struggle for influence between the two powers in that continent was of relatively long standing, there was something new about the form which that rivalry now assumed: for the expansion of Russian influence was associated after 1917, as it had not been before, with the propagation of a revolutionary and anti-imperialist ideology which appealed directly to disaffected radicals throughout the colonial world. Western civilisation, in Lord d'Abernon's portentous words, was now 'menaced by an external danger which . . . threatened a cataclysm equalled only by the fall of the Roman Empire'. Britain's 'stupendous and vital interests in Asia', in particular, were threatened by a 'grave danger than any which existed in the time of the old imperialistic regime in Russia'.[1] British policy towards the Soviet government and the defence of imperial interests in the East, accordingly, became more closely related; and it is this 'imperial confrontation' which forms the subject of the present chapter and of the two which follow it.

During the immediate post-revolutionary years, with only a part of the former Russian Empire as yet under the control of the Bolshevik government, developments in Asia had tended generally to take second place to those in the European continent. Imperial considerations nevertheless played a by no means negligible part in the government's decision to intervene militarily in Russian affairs, and the same considerations helped to determine government policy with regard to the objects of that intervention. He was 'personally very much afraid', Lloyd George told the Cabinet on 25 July 1919, 'that a united Russia would be a great menace to us in the East'.[2] Two months later the Prime Minister again raised the question of the 'ultimate aim of British policy in connection with Russia'. It might, he thought, be 'in the interests of the British Empire to aim at a limited Russia under any government, whether it was Bolshevik or non-Bolshevik'. Quoting Lord Beaconsfield on the Russian threat, he declared that 'the future of the British Empire might depend on how the Russian situation developed, and he personally did not view with equanimity the thought of a powerful Russia of 130 million inhabitants'.[3]

Not all members of the Cabinet were persuaded that it should be the object of British policy to secure a divided or 'federal' Russia, however, and with the advance of the Bolshevik forces a threat to British interests of a rather different kind began to materialise. 'Bolshevist activity in Persia and Central Asia', a Conference of Ministers agreed on 12 November 1919, 'was one of the most troublesome problems which the British Empire had to face'.[4] Alarming reports began to reach the Foreign Office from its representatives in the field. Chicherin's assistant, Dr Narimanov, a native of Baku, was reported to have written to the Azerbaidzhani goverment urging it to join a 'great movement against England'; and the Tashkent Soviet had apparently written to the Georgian Prime Minister to the same effect.[5] From Tiflis Wardrop reported that the Bolsheviks were 'sending numerous agents to [the] Caucasus and Persia with large funds'. Fifteen hundred Bolsheviks were known to have left Baku for India. The Foreign Office agreed that the development was a 'highly dangerous' one.[6]

Unless some 'speedy action' were taken, Wardrop added shortly afterwards, there was a 'grave risk of the crushing of Transcaucasia by [the] Bolsheviks, who will then work their will in Persia and Transcaspia and beyond'. Entreaties were also received from the Persian government for assistance lest the country be 'overrun by Bolshevism'.[7] The Cabinet agreed that arms, munitions and (if possible) food should be sent to the Transcaucasian states. Transcaucasia, the Cabinet was told, was the 'bridge which must be defended by the Allies' to prevent the union of Bolsheviks and Moslems and a 'Bolshevik invasion of the East'.[8] The Allies might abandon Russia, Churchill pointed out, but Russia would 'not abandon them'. The Russian bear ranged 'widely over the enormous countries which lead to the frontiers of India, disturbing Afghanistan, disturbing Persia, and creating far to the southward great agitation and unrest among the millions, hundreds of millions, of our Indian population, who have hitherto dwelt in peace and tranquillity under British rule'.[9] The government accordingly became anxious (as Lord Hardinge put it in a letter to Paris) to 'stabilize the political and economic situation in the Caucasus, in order that it may serve as a barrier against a possible Bolshevik military advance instead of becoming a free passage for communications between the Bolsheviks and pan-Islamic forces and possibly necessitating our abandoning the greater part of Asia and concentrating on the defence of India'.[10]

How such a barrier was to be constructed, however, was by no means clear. Henry Wilson told a meeting at the Foreign Office that it would in fact be impossible to provide for the military defence of Georgia and Azerbaidzhan, although there was no doubt that in its absence they would both 'go Bolshevik'.[11] Wilson attended a meeting of ministers in Paris on 16 and 18 January 1920 at which the problems raised by the retreat of Denikin and the consequent threat to the Caucasus and the Caspian were discussed. The Caspian, Churchill represented to the meeting, was the 'pivot of our whole strategic position in the East'. Its capture by the Bolsheviks would 'bring about the final downfall of Denikin, turn the frontier of the Caucasus, expose North Persia to attack, and immediately increase the resources of Bolshevism by giving them control of the oil and other produce of these regions'. Some line of defence against a Bolshevik advance had clearly to be constructed, and Churchill at least was inclined to doubt whether it was right to establish such a line at a point no more advanced than the Caucasus, thereby leaving the Denikin country 'outside the ring fence and inside the Russian bearpit'.[12] Walter Long, First Lord of the Admiralty and a former Colonial Secretary, added at a Conference of Ministers two days later that the danger to the Eastern Empire was 'greater than it had ever been before. If we did not take immediate steps we might in the near future be fighting desperately for the retention of our Eastern Empire.' Lloyd George had some doubts on this score; but Curzon agreed that if command of the Caspian were lost, they might 'find that before long our whole Eastern Empire was rocking'. If they could dominate it, on the other hand, this might 'alter the whole position in the East'.[13]

The Allied Supreme Council, in the event, agreed to grant *de facto* recognition to Armenia, and did so also for Georgia and Azerbaidzhan. No power, however, the Foreign Office was told, had been prepared to supply the three divisions which the Inter-Allied Military Council considered necessary if their independence were successfully to be maintained,[14] and entreaties for more tangible evidence of British support had regretfully to be declined. The Treasury, Curzon informed the British representative in Tiflis, was not prepared to provide a loan to the Caucasian republics; the Armenian and Georgian governments were advised to direct their attention instead to the City of London.[15] Curzon added the following month that there could be 'no question of our giving Georgia and Azerbaidzhan active military support in the case of an attack upon them by Soviet forces'.[16] Azerbaidzhan, in the absence of such support, came under Soviet rule in April 1920, and in November 1920 the same fate befell Armenia. The British government, Curzon wrote to its representative in Tiflis, was 'not indifferent to the fate of Georgia', the only Caucasian republic which now remained outside Soviet control; the Cabinet, indeed, was 'strongly in favour of her independence'. Other burdens, however, were such that they could 'not say what practical form their sympathy is likely to take'.[17] The question became an academic one when in Febuary 1921 Georgia came under Soviet control and was declared a Soviet Republic. Curzon was informed on 20 April that the British mission there had been successfully withdrawn; all that remained was a typewriter and a Sunbeam car.[18]

The opening of negotiations with the Russian trading delegation appeared to offer a more promising line of approach. If it were not feasible militarily to defend the Eastern Empire against Bolshevik advances, it might at least prove possible to limit the Bolshevik danger by requiring from them, in return for an agreement to enter into trading relations, an undertaking to refrain from agitation and propaganda inimical to British interests. The Cabinet, accordingly, reviewing the withdrawal of British forces from northern Persia and the vulnerable position in which this placed Persia and Mesopotamia, found the question 'closely connected with our general policy towards Soviet Russia', a policy which was 'at present indefinite and somewhat paradoxical'. The Bolsheviks, on the one hand, were making difficulties for the government all over the East, in Turkey, the Caucasus, Persia, Turkestan and Afghanistan, and they had 'not concealed their intention to create trouble for us in India'. On the other hand, trade negotiations with the Soviet government were shortly to be initiated and Krasin, when he arrived, would be received by the Prime Minister and by the Foreign Office. It was 'generally felt ... that advantage should be taken of the forthcoming conversations with M. Krasin, if possible, as a condition of entering into trade relations, to effect an all-round settlement which would include the East'.[19]

Curzon expanded upon this theme at a Conference of Ministers on 28 May 1920. Any agreement in regard to trade, he thought, would be 'impossible unless a general agreement on the political questions at issue with the Soviet government were arrived at. It was most desirable that a comprehensive arrangement should be reached. The Conference was asked to remember that the recent political situation gave H. M. G. an opportunity for driving a good bargain'.[20] The Russian government, Curzon argued in a memorandum, was 'threatened with complete economic disaster', and he believed it would 'pay almost any price for the assistance which we—more than anyone else—are in a position to give'. The British government, for its part, could hardly consider coming to the rescue of the Bolsheviks without exacting a price for it; and that price, he thought, could 'far better be paid in a cessation of Bolshevik hostility in parts of the world of importance to us than in the ostensible interchange of commodities, the existence of which on any considerable scale in Russia there is grave reason to doubt'. The cases which the Foreign Secretary quoted in which the Soviet government was either 'openly at war with peoples or States in whom we are concerned, or are engaged in propaganda, plots and alliances directed against British interests in the British Empire in the East' included Afghanistan, Persia and the Caucasus.[21]

The question of Soviet propaganda in the East accordingly attracted a good deal of attention in the course of the trade negotiations, which began at this point and lasted until the following spring.[22] Four conditions were specified by the British government in its note of 30 June 1920, upon whose acceptance by the Soviet government the continuation of the negotiations was stated to be dependent. Apart from the return of detainees, compensation to private citizens and the facilitation of trade, the first, and most important, was that each side should 'refrain from hostile actions or measures directed against the other, and from the conducting of any kind of official propaganda, direct or indirect, against the institutions of the other side', and that the Soviet government should in particular 'refrain from any kind of attempt by means of military action or propaganda to urge the peoples of Asia to any kind of hostile actions directed against British interests or against the British Empire'. This, in the opinion of the British government, was the 'basic condition of any kind of a trade agreement between Russia and any of the western powers'.[23]

Similar requirements were made of the Soviet government in the autumn of 1920. The conditions which had to be met if the trade negotiations were to be resumed, Curzon pointed out in a note on 1 October, had been broken and were 'being continually broken'. Radio and press commentaries, together with the 'revolutionary Conference of Asiatic peoples in Baku', were 'clearly directed against British interests'. The same applied to Soviet actions in Caucasus, Persia, Central Asia and Afghanistan.[24] Soviet forces had entered Persia, Curzon added on 9 October; a military agreement with Turkish nationalist forces, 'obviously aimed against British interests', had been concluded; a body had been established at Tashkent, whose object was the organisation of the forces of Central Asia with a view to an attack upon British interests; and at congresses in Moscow and elsewhere a 'real hurricane of propaganda, intrigue and conspiracy against British interests and British power in Asia' had been unleashed. Such activities must cease forthwith if the negotiations were to proceed further.[25]

The two governments eventually agreed to resume the talks; and on 18 November 1920 the Cabinet decided that the President of the Board of Trade should conclude a trade agreement with the Russian delegations upon the lines of the exchange of notes of the previous June and July. The conditions specified in that exchange were to constitute the basis of such an agreement, and they were to be 'definitely re-stated in the [text of the] Trade Agreement'. Either party should be free to terminate the agreement in the event of the other party failing to fulfil the obligations placed upon it; and the attention of the Russian government was to be drawn, 'either in the agreement itself or in a covering communication to the Russian representatives, to any specially important respects in which, in accordance with the terms of the Agreement, the Bolsheviks must alter their present procedure or policy, e. g. to annul their treaty with Afghanistan to desist from co-operation with Mustapha Kemal, and from hostilities or propaganda in Persia, India etc.'.[26] If the Soviet government were to continue hostile propaganda in Persia, Afghanistan, or India, Horne warned the Russian negotiators, 'that would be a fact that would lead [the British government] at once to cease to carry out the agreement'.[27] A 'most active propaganda' had been going on in that part of the world, he told the House of Commons, and it was of a character 'most hostile to British interests' and 'avowedly for the purpose of upsetting British institutions in India'. The government had made it clear to the Soviet representatives that such propaganda should 'cease at once . . . if this agreement is to be carried out'.[28]

The preamble to the trade agreement accordingly stated that it was a condition of the agreement that each party should refrain from 'hostile action or undertakings against the other and from conducting outside of its own borders any offical propaganda direct or indirect against the institutions of the British Empire or the Russian Soviet Republic respectively'. The Russian Soviet Government was required, more particularly, to refrain from 'any attempt by military or diplomatic or any other form of action or propaganda to encourage any of the peoples of Asia in any form of hostile action against British interests or the British Empire, especially in India and in the Independent State of Afghanistan'.The British government made a similar undertaking in respect of the countries which formed part of the former Russian Empire and which had now become independent. The contravention by either side of any of the provisions of the agreement or of its preamble, it was agreed, would immediately free the other side of its obligations.[29]

A more detailed statement of the British government's requirements was contained in a letter which was handed to the Soviet negotiators at the time of the signature of the agreement. The letter, Chamberlain explained to the House of Commons, stated the 'action required to be taken by the Soviet government as an essential corollary of the Trade Agreement'.[30] It was justly remarked that it did 'not appear to have anything to do with trade'.[31] It contained, rather, a recital of 'facts ... characterising the activity of the Soviet Government in India and in Afghanistan, not conforming to the requirements of the Treaty and requiring immediate cessation if this Agreement is to be observed in good faith'.[32]

The letter began by pointing out that the Soviet government, in its declarations and in the offical press, had made no secret of the fact that the main aim of its policy in recent years had been the overthrow of British rule in India. The British government had for some time been aware of 'intrigues, which are being carried on by various means and in various directions by the Soviet government, by its agents, by people acting under its instructions and by its supporters for the achievement of this aim'. Indian rebels were working in Bolshevik institutions and with Bolshevik money 'in order to sow unrest in India and to encourage anti-British feeling in the countries bordering India, mainly in Afghanistan'; and M. N. Roy, the Indian Communist, had established a 'forward base for work in India' at Tashkent, whence it was proposed to transfer activities, as soon as circumstances permitted, to the more propitous location of Kabul. Emissaries had already been sent to India 'for the study on the spot of the possibility of revolutionary work, in the army or in the peasant or industrial population, or by means of the organization of extremist political schools on a basis favourable to Bolshevik and revolutionary plans'.

Soviet relations with Afghanistan had similarly been directed towards securing a 'means of disturbing the peace in India'. The right of unimpeded transit had been sought in order to bring rifles and ammunition to the tribes which inhabited the British side of the border; and relations had been established with the tribal leaders most hostile to Britain. The British government did not object to a Soviet-Afghan agreement which concerned the normal form of neighbourly and commercial relations. The proposals to provide the Afghan government with money, ammunition and aeroplanes and to establish Soviet consulates on the eastern border of the country, however, were measures 'exclusively . . . hostile to British interests'. The Red Army, also, was believed to have been instructed to raise the red flag upon the Pamir plateau, as an 'indication to the Indian peoples that their liberation is near', and there was reason to believe that a plan of action for the area had been drafted. Enough had been said, it was considered, to 'indicate the general character of the activity of the Soviet government on the cessation of which HMG must insist as an essential condition of the conclusion of any kind of agreement between the two governments'.

These were uncompromising words; but only upon this basis had Curzon and his associates been persuaded to suspend—even temporarily—their rooted objection to the conclusion of this, or any other agreement with the 'deplorable government at Moscow'. If they cared about anything in the agreement, wrote a Foreign Office official in a minute which received the endorsement of the Foreign Secretary, it was the 'possibility that it may stop Bolshevik propaganda against us in the East or elsewhere'.[33] The Horne letter, in fact, made it clear that the signature of the trade agreement, so far at least as the British government was concerned, was in no sense a compromise upon issues of political principle, still less a definitive resolution of matters in dispute between the two governments. It established no more than a provisional and highly conditional *modus vivendi* between an embattled imperial power, whose interests were concentrated above all in Asia, and state which was dedicated to the revolutionary overthrow of that edifice at what was considered to be its weakest point. The trade agreement did not resolve this basic political antagonism: it re-stated it.

Bolshevik propaganda in the colonial world had become a problem to the Cabinet almost as soon as the Bolshevik revolution itself had taken place. In December 1917 the Intelligence Bureau of the Department of Information circulated a memorandum dealing with the manifesto which the Soviet government had issued 'to all the toiling Moslems of Russia and the Orient'. The manifesto, the Bureau considered, was 'another indication of the ultimate Bolshevik policy, which is a campaign . . . designed to overthrow the existing order all over the world, as it has already been overthrown in Russia'. The Viceroy was advised by the Secretary of State for India that it should be 'suppressed for as long as possible'.[34] A 'Blue Book' was issued in Moscow the following year under the auspices of the NKID. Its title page read 'India to the Indians: Down with Imperialists: Long Live the International'. Two copies were forwarded to the Foreign Office by Wardrop, who commented that the introduction was a 'malicious attack on British rule in India by a person who is obviously ignorant of the rudiments of the subject'. Translations were being prepared into European and Asiatic languages.[35]

In March 1919 it was reported that The Hague had become the chief centre for Bolshevik propaganda in the East. 'Very large sums' were being spent upon propaganda directed at India, Persia and Egypt (recent troubles in that country, indeed, had been 'almost certainly originated by them').[36] The Bolsheviks were devoting increased attention to the East, *The Times* noted on 12 December 1919. Afghanistan was 'regarded as a propaganda centre'; classes being arranged to train emissaries to go to India and elsewhere; and 'immense sums of money' for propaganda were being sent from Moscow to Tashkent.[37] Paul Dukes, who had been active in British intelligence work in Russia, explained to the paper's readers that 'for a year after the Bolshevik revolution little attention was paid to the East, the Bolsheviks being so confident of an immediate Western revolution. But in proportion as their expectations sank in the West their hopes in the East rose, and they are now concentrated entirely on Asia'.[38] The Bolsheviks, Churchill told a Dundee audience, would indeed 'do their utmost to stir up rebellion and sedition and fan the flames of class hatred in every other land, and especially in the Eastern world, where we in Britain have such great interests'.[39]

Evidence of such activity began to accumulate in the Foreign Office, especially following the Second Congress of the Communist International in the summer of 1920. A communication from Copenhagen stated that the International had been 'making huge preparations to develop revolutionary propaganda in the Near and Far East', and that a 'general revolt in the East next autumn' was planned to 'hurry up the World Revolution, for which the chiefs of Soviet Russia have still great hopes'.[40] A secret Bolshevik-Turkish Nationalist agreement was reportedly signed at Trebizond in October 1920. A further report stated that a secret treaty had been signed at the Foreign Ministry in Moscow by representatives from Turkey, Persia, Afghanistan, India and other Eastern countries, whose main points were that England was to be 'attacked through India' and that the national movement in India was to be assisted by all parties. [41]

Not all such reports were taken seriously in government circles. A Foreign Office comment upon a report of Lenin's speech to the Second Comintern Congress, for instance, in which he had claimed the support of 70 per cent of the world's population for the Bolshevik cause, noted drily that 'if Lenin really represented 70 per cent of the population of the world, his speech would be magnificent'.[42] Rex Leeper minuted on 6 July 1920, however, that the reports of 'huge preparations' for propaganda and of a 'general revolt' planned for the East that autumn appeared to him 'reliable'. They confirmed several other reports which had recently been received from Moscow, and demonstrated that such initiatives were an 'essential part of the Bolshevik programme'. Their overall object, it appeared, was to 'foment trouble throughout the East for the "capitalistic" powers, particularly Great Britain, trouble that will ultimately lead to their downfall in these regions'.[43]

The situation in Afghanistan was particularly closely connected with the defence of the British position in India, the issue around which discussions of Eastern affairs tended to revolve. Following the death of the Amir in February 1919, his son Amanullah succeeded to the throne. British recognition of his accession was not, however, immediately forthcoming; and Amanullah responded by opening relations with Soviet Russia, and declaring Afghanistan independent of British suzerainty.[44] The Cabinet considered the 'disquieting situation' in the country on 6 May 1919. The new Amir, Curzon reported, had recently been adopting a 'truculent attitude'. He had published a proclamation of a 'most outrageous nature, stating that both Moslems and Hindus in India were being subjected to abominable treatment by the British administration', and had issued a statement which had been 'tantamount to a declaration of complete independence'. The atmosphere was 'electrical'. The month-long Third Anglo-Afghan war ensued; on its conclusion the independence of Afghanistan was recognised and the British annual subsidy was discontinued.[45]

The fourth clause of the peace agreement provided for the subsequent conclusion of a treaty of friendship between the two countries; and in October 1920 the Amir invited a British delegation to Kabul for negotiations towards this end. It had in the meantime been discovered, however, that the Amir had concluded a treaty with the Soviet government, containing clauses which appeared to the Cabinet 'clearly directed against ourselves'. Soviet consulates near the Indian border, in particular, could have 'no other object than the promotion of propaganda in India'. The Amir had assured the British authorities that Soviet diplomatic representatives would be required to observe the protocol appropriate to their position; but he had not, as requested, provided the text of the agreement. The danger consequently arose that British delegates might simply be played off against the Bolsheviks, and a subsidy secured from both sides. It was decided that a decision with regard to the despatch of delegates should be left to the Viceroy of India and his associates. Advantage was taken of the conclusion of the trade agreement, however, to draw the Soviet government's attention to the unfavourable view which the British government took of these developments.[46]

It subsequently became known that the Soviet-Afghan treaty, which had been signed on 28 February 1921, contained provision for an annual subsidy and for the supply of military munitions and materials. The Cabinet laid the 'utmost emphasis' upon the undesirability of permitting the Afghan government to receive a subsidy from the Soviet government, directed against Indian interests, as well as from the British authorities. It was true that, in view of military obligations elsewhere, it might be preferable to tolerate a Soviet subsidy for the present than risk the heavy expense of a further frontier war. The Viceroy should nevertheless be advised that the Cabinet still strongly held the view that a 'Bolshevik subsidy would in itself be the strongest *prima facie* evidence of arrangements directed against the British Empire'.[47]

The Cabinet failed to prevent the ratification of the Soviet

Afghan treaty, however, and attention turned instead to the possibility of offering the Afghan government 'sufficent induce-ment in money and arms to make her throw over the Bolshevist treaty entirely'. The Viceroy was informed that the British rep-resentative now present in Kabul for the purposes of negotiation should 'naturally regulate his offer of money etc., according to the completeness of Bolshevik elimination'; for the Bolsheviks had a known hostility to the British Empire', and a 'known desire to wound what they describe as a capitalist government throughout the East'. [48] But the prospect of concluding an agreement of this kind, which had at one time appeared good, thereafter receded, and the Viceroy and his associates, who had hoped to secure the 'exclusion and discomfiture of the Bolsheviks', were compelled in the end to fall back upon a treaty which would leave the Afghans free to receive a subsidy and munitions from this quarter. The outcome was regarded by the Cabinet with 'intense dislike'.[49]

The British position in Persia, another crucial element in the defence of India, appeared to have been more securely established with the conclusion of an Anglo-Persian treaty on 9 August 1919. The British government accepted an undertaking to 'respect absolutely the independence and integrity of Persia'; but a series of clauses followed which provided, among other things, for the secondment of British 'expert advisers' with 'adequate powers' to the Persian administration, and for the appointment of British officers and men in order to secure the 'establishment and preser-vation of order in the country and on its frontiers'.[50] Advances of cash were to be made to the Persian government under the terms of the agreement, Harmsworth told the House of Commons, 'with a view to the establishment in Persia of a Government able to withstand pressure from any quarter'. An additional safeguard was that the South Persian Rifles, a force instituted in the middle of the war 'for the purpose of maintaining British interests', were to remain under British control.[51]

The hope that the agreement might be ratified, however, was based upon the loyalty of the then Prime Minister, Mushir-el-Dowleh. On 3 November 1920 the Cabinet received with dismay the information that 'he had failed us and resigned'. While the Bolsheviks were then engaged in operations against Wrangel's forces, moreover, once they had achieved success the Red Army could be 'let loose in Persia', involving British forces there in 'great danger'.[52] The treaty, in the event, was not ratified; and the following spring it was announced that the last British forces were 'in process of being withdrawn'. More than two years later *The Times* commented that it was an 'unfortunate but undeniable fact' that the British were not popular in Persia.[53]

Egypt had a less obvious contribution to make to the defence of India; but from the point of view of the Empire as a whole its place was no less important. Egypt, Lloyd George pointed out to the House of Commons, was 'not in the position of other nations to which complete self-determination can be afforded, without reference to any external conditions'; for the country was 'abnormally placed in reference to the world, and especially in reference to the British Empire', more than three hundred million of whose four hundred million inhabitants lived to the east of the Suez Canal.[54] Britain had declared a protectorate over the country in 1914. Unrest, however, persisted subsequently, and a mission was despatched to Egypt at the end of 1919 to study the causes of disorder and make recommendations with regard to the political future of the country. Many of the middle and semi-educated classes had supported British rule in the past, Lord Milner, who had headed the enquiry, reported to a Conference of Ministers the following November. It had therefore been a great shock to him to discover what a change had taken place in this regard. If they were to keep control of the country other than by martial law, he believed, it was essential to 'break up the 10% of the more educated classes and get some of them on our side, even if, in order to do so, it was necessary to make some considerable sacrifices'. In particular, the Egyptians, 'who for forty years we had professed to be training to govern themselves', must be given an opportunity of doing so. The government was dealing, he reminded them, with Orientals, who were essentially 'very clever and potentially very naughty children'. Once convinced of British goodwill, however, they would become 'very manageable'.[55]

Negotiations took place with Adly Pasha, the Egyptian Prime Minister, during the summer of 1921. The negotiations, however, proved fruitless, and the situation deteriorated further. On 17 November Field-Marshal Allenby, who had assumed control of British forces in the country, sent a telegram to London warning that the decision to refuse national independence 'must entail serious risk of revolution throughout the country', and would in any case result in 'complete administrative chaos' and 'serious injury to financial and economic interests'.[56] A Conference of

Ministers considered the question the following day. There was a danger, Curzon reported, of the creation of a very serious situation in Egypt; the government was probably on the verge of a 'serious new emergency' which would 'strain our available resources to the utmost'.[57] The intractability of the situation eventually convinced most ministers of the need to accept at least some of the nationalists' demands; and on 28 February 1922 a British Declaration was issued. It offered to recognise Egypt as an independent sovereign state, provided the vital importance of the relations between Britain and Egypt to the British Empire were acknowledged. Four points, in particular, were to be reserved to the discretion of the British government. These included the security of imperial communications in Egypt; the defence of Egypt against all foreign aggression; and the protection of foreign interests and minorities in Egypt. The nationalists, however, had secured their principal objective.[58]

Recent events in Egypt, declared the journal *Near East*, bore 'too close a resemblance to the German-encouraged Bolshevism of the continent of Europe to escape the conclusion that they are closely related both in inception and organization'. The forms of local opposition, indeed, were, all exact replicas of different phases of Bolshevism. There existed a 'diabolical plot', the journal was convinced, 'which, if it succeeds, will make Egypt a second Russia'. *United Empire* retained an open mind as to whether Bolshevism was responsible for the recent unrest in Egypt and India. It noted, however, that 'well-meaning theorists', such as Gandhi and Zaghlul Pasha, the Egyptian nationalist leader, had 'called forces into play which they are no more capable of controlling than was M. Kerensky able to control the excesses of the Russian Revolution'.[59]

The danger could easily be exaggerated. The Foreign Office, however, found it worthwhile to collect reports dealing with the possible connection between Bolshevism and domestic unrest in Egypt, and the appointment of an officer, whose particular responsibility it should be to watch and control Bolshevik activities, was actively considered.[60] Allenby wrote to the Foreign Office at the beginning of 1920, following a discussion with the officials responsible for advising on matters of public security and the organisation of intelligence in Egypt, regarding 'measures necessary to deal with Bolshevism and cognate problems'. The appointment of a junior officer attached to Intelligence was, he thought, 'essential'.[61] A member of the Alexandria Police Secret Service was eventually recommended; and the Foreign Office informed Allenby that arrangements could be made in Britain for him to 'receive training in anti-Bolshevik methods'.[62] The British government, through its Moscow representatives, also informed the Soviet government that, while the protectorate was being ended, Britain was continuing to maintain her special rights in Egypt and would regard any interference in the internal affairs of that country as a hostile act against Great Britain. A number of leaders of the Egyptian Communist Party were subsequently arrested, and the penal code was altered so as to allow the Egyptian government to act effectively against 'subversive, anarchist, communist and anti-constitutional ideas'.[63]

Developments in Ireland could hardly be related to the military defence of India; yet there was no need to go further than Marx to conclude that the possession of that country might lie at the very foundation of the imperial edifice. Churchill, indeed, echoed this view when he declared to the House of Commons in December 1920 that Ireland was the 'heart's centre of the British Empire. Any disturbance or movement there produces vibrations, almost convulsions, throughout the whole of our system of society.'[64] For some years past and at that time, the Chief Secretary for Ireland added two months later, 'Sinn Fein extremists and their Soviet colleagues in Ireland—there is Sovietism in a marked degree in Ireland—have conspired to smash the Empire'. Sinn Fein policy was 'watched by sinister eyes in Great Britain, in Egypt, in India and throughout the world'; its success would mean the 'break-up of the Empire and of our civilization'.[65] The Irish Labour Party, the House of Commons was told, was 'affiliated with the Third International in Moscow'; and the Transport Workers' Union in that country was closely associated with the Industrial Workers of the World, a most dangerous body which sought to 'foment revolutions in every country with a view to getting a sort of Soviet Republic established'.[66] Churchill told the Cabinet that he had, in fact, found the Labour Party in Ireland 'not unhelpful'. There was 'some Sovietism among them', however, and some even feared, he told the House of Commons, that the present Irish Government, which was administering the treaty settlement of December 1921, might be 'overturned by a coup d'etat and that a red Soviet Republic may be set up'.[67]

There was no confirmation of a report that four million roubles had been raised in Soviet Russia to be sent to Sinn Fein in Ireland, thus 'assisting a conspiracy to subvert the Government and institutions of this country'; but the Prime Minister assured the Commons that the government was 'keeping a close watch on the matter'.[68] In March 1921 a report reached London of a meeting of Communists from European countries which had resolved that the British Communists should get in touch with Sinn Fein and arrange a programme of common action; and the following month it became known that Litvinov, from Reval, had established contact with Irish dissidents through the intermediacy of Krasin and had arranged to set up 'germ cells' among them with the aid of fifty thousand pounds which Krasin had been remitted for this purpose.[69] The same month the government informed the House of Commons that evidence had been found of a connection between the Bolshevik government and Sinn Fein; and shortly thereafter a White Paper on the subject was published.[70]

The Paper, entitled 'Intercourse between Bolshevism and Sinn Fein', contained the text of a draft treaty between the Soviet Russian government and the Irish Republican government, together with a number of commentaries upon it. The treaty, which had been drawn up in June 1920, was in fact a fairly unremarkable document. It provided for no more than the diplomatic recognition of each state by the other, the development of economic co-operation between them, and the prevention of the transport of military supplies intended for use against either state through the territory of the other. It entrusted the Irish representative in Russia, among other things, with responsibility for representing the interests of the Roman Catholic Church within the territory of the RSFSR. The Republican government, moreover, appeared to have agreed to no more than that the treaty should be 'very carefully considered'.

The preamble to the document, however, did include as an agreed object the 'liberation of all people from imperialistic exploitation and aggression'; and a memorandum written by a Sinn Fein MP, Dr Patrick McCartan, which was published together with the treaty, clearly envisaged the despatch of a Republican mission to Russia under his leadership.[71] McCartan appeared also to hold the view that the treaty might be regarded as providing for the training of Irish Republican naval and military forces in Soviet Russia. Subsequent intelligence reports indicated that the Irish Communist Party had received financial assistance from the Comintern (it appeared nevertheless to be heavily in debt and operating upon a bank overdraft);[72] and that radical forces opposed to the treaty settlement with Britain had been attempting to buy guns and ammunition in Russia.[73]

It was developments in India, however, which gave the greatest cause for concern. The government was already committed, in the words of the Secretary of State's announcement to the House of Commons of 20 August 1917, to the gradual development of self-governing institutions in India 'with a view to the progressive realization of responsible government in India as an integral part of the British Empire'; and this proposition formed the basis of the Montagu-Chelmsford Report on Indian Constitutional Reform which was published the following year. The Government of India Act of 1919, however, disappointed many Indians: the elective assembly which it established had no control over the Viceroy and his executive, who could pass ('certify') legislation on their own authority; and the imperial government alone was to judge the 'time and the measure of each advance' towards more fully responsible government.[74] The Act was compromised, moreover, by the adoption at the same time of legislation permitting trial without jury and arbitrary arrest (the Rowlatt Acts of 1919), and above all by the action of General Dyer in firing upon an unarmed crowd at Amritsar in April 1919, resulting in the death of 379 and the wounding of a further twelve hundred Indians.[75]

Montagu's original undertaking, its modest terms notwithstanding, had in fact been sanctioned by the Cabinet with some reluctance. 'Constant harping on the theme that we are fighting for liberty and justice and the rights of peoples to direct their own destinies', the Secretary of State observed in May 1917, together with the influence of the Russian Revolution and the position which India had assumed in the councils of the Empire, had strengthened the reform movement and 'created a ferment of ideas by which the Government of India are evidently somewhat alarmed'. To refuse to review existing constitutional arrangements would, in the circumstances, be a decision fraught with 'grave danger'.[76] Balfour was still inclined to deprecate any 'hasty decision to concede to an Oriental country a system of self-government which was . . . quite unsuitable to the Dependency'. Curzon, however, pointed out that action of some kind was unavoidable, for 'the situation was serious: the revolutionary propagandists of the genre of Tilak and Mrs Besant were dangerous, and in the East things were apt to move with the startling rapidity of a prairie fire'. Austen Chamberlain added that the mood in India was one of 'alert expectancy'; unless the government made a 'timely and satisfactory pronouncement' the situation was fraught with the 'gravest of possibilities'.[77] The government's declaration, in particular, must contain the formula 'ultimate self-government within the Empire', which, Montagu explained, 'had become a shibboleth' and could not safely be omitted.[78] His statement, couched in these terms, was made six days later.

The government was nevertheless concerned to counter the 'idea, which was prevalent among many people both in India and at home, that the British raj was doomed, that [they] were fighting a rearguard action in India, and that India would gradually be handed over to the Indians'. On the contrary, Churchill told a Conference of Ministers in February 1922, the British position in India must be strengthened; and, although he had supported the Indian reforms at the time, he expressed some doubt regarding the 'expediency of granting democratic institutions to backward races'.[79] The 'false impression should at once be dissipated', Lloyd George told a group of ministers later the same month, that government policy was ultimately to end British rule and hand over India to the Indians. The government had in fact 'no intention of leaving India or of allowing British supremacy there to be challenged . . . There must be a master in India . . . We were now masters in India, and we should let it be understood that we meant to remain so'.[80] An ultimate move to Indian self-government could not be excluded; but the Cabinet, remarked Curzon, 'probably contemplated an intervening period that might extend to 500 years'.[81]

This agreeable perspective was clouded not simply by the growing strength of the non-cooperation movement. For as the war ended, a government publication noted, 'to the menace of German arms there succeeded the more formidable menace of Bolshevik ideas'.[82] India, Montagu told the House of Commons, was 'notoriously the object of Bolshevik propaganda'. He had no reason to think, he informed the House in December 1919, that the well-known desire of the Bolsheviks to spread their doctrines had in fact met with any success in that country.[83] The War Office,

however, in a statement released at the beginning of 1920, reported the progress of a party of Bolsheviks and Turks with
aeroplane parts, petrol and a wireless set in the direction of
Kabul. A 'large number of propaganda schools' had been opened
in Tashkent, where Oriental languages would be taught and
whence agents would be despatched to India, China and the
Muslim countries. The Tashkent Soviet, at a recent meeting, was
believed to have determined to concentrate efforts first on India,
and it was intended to open up propaganda schools there
shortly.[84] A writer in the *Review of Reviews*, discussing the 'Bolshevist menace to India', could 'confidently state that the disruptive
influences at present to be observed in the countries of the Middle
East assuredly have their origins in Bolshevist Russia'. The
headquarters from which such activities were directed was
located in Afghanistan; their object was to bring about 'the destruction of the last barrier which divides the Bolshevik power
from the invasion of India'.[85]

The government was evidently disposed to take these warnings
seriously. The Russian thousand-rouble note, the House of Commons was told, which had the slogan 'Workers of the world, unite'
printed on its face in nine languages, had been declared illegal in
India. The restriction would be lifted if there were evidence of a
cessation of Bolshevik propaganda in India.[86] Rouble notes to a
total value of some two and a half million pounds were surrendered, a sum which *The Times* found 'both surprising and significant'. Other attempts to promote Bolshevik propaganda in the
Dependency, the paper thought, might well be expected. A
number of other devices were in fact reported: Bolshevik leaflets
were found concealed in copies of the Gospels (printed, cunning-
ly, in Chinese), and a news service was provided for Indian
newspapers, the response to which was stated to have been
'remarkable'. It could not be established that Bolshevik finance
lay behind the venture, the paper commented, but it was 'certain
that Red propagandists take every advantage of Indian
susceptibilities'.[87]

Writing to the Under-Secretary of State in the Foreign Office in
February 1920, Curzon expressed his full awareness of the
'danger of subversive doctrines being spread by Bolshevik agents'
and his strong conviction that 'no efforts should be spared to
check them by all the means at the disposal of HMG'. The
Viceroy had, in fact, already informed him of the appointment of

officers whose duties included counter-propaganda, the organisation of internal and external intelligence, and the undertaking of appropriate measures to prevent the entry of Bolshevik emissaries.[88] A more detailed statement of the 'Bolshevik situation . . . and of the precautionary measures taken by the Government of India up to the end of January 1920' was received the following March. A Special Bureau of Information had been set up under Lt Col W. F. T. O'Connor, with a staff of two. O'Connor knew Russian, Chinese and Persian, and had served with the Allied forces in Vladivostok. The Bureau's first action was to prohibit the circulation of rouble notes, and it also maintained surveillance at frontiers and ports. The Bureau issued a 'Weekly Report' from the beginning of 1920, copies of which were placed on file in the Foreign Office.[89]

No 'actual avowed Bolshevik agents' had been discovered by the following October, the Viceroy informed London; but a number of people known to be sympathetic to Bolshevism were under observation. The number of such people was 'constantly increasing'. Many of them were connected with other forms of agitation, the Viceroy explained, such as strikes, peasants' movements and so on, since the Bolshevik movement in the East was 'not for the moment mainly Communist but uses for its purpose every form of anti-British agitation'. Precautionary measures included extra vigilance on the part of frontier officials, the appointment of officers to investigate, report upon and hinder the spread of Bolshevism, and the proscription of 'undesirable papers' such as the *Herald*. The surveillance and the detention of refugees had also been undertaken, together with a regular examination of the press and other written propaganda.[90] An outline of 'precautionary measures' which was compiled towards the end of 1920 added further details: the movement of jewels was being closely watched, and anti-Bolshevik fictional writing had been encouraged. The production of films of a suitable character was also under consideration, but over-energetic measures, it was thought, might arouse an 'unhealthy interest in the question in quarters where little or nothing may be known regarding it'.[91]

The Special Bureau of Information was disbanded at the end of 1920. This did 'not, however, involve any relaxation of the watch on Bolshevik movements in India', the Indian authorities informed London: an officer in the Foreign and Political Department had been appointed to carry on the work which the Bureau had hitherto undertaken.[92] A special organisation had been set up, Montagu assured the House of Commons in March 1921, to deal with Bolshevik activities in India. It would not be prudent to disclose details of the arrangements which had been made; but 'every step necessary to checkmate them' had been taken, he trusted successfully. A year later he informed the House that Bolshevik propaganda had 'contributed something' to the unrest in India. A 'splendid organization', however, had been developed to counter this menace, to whose efficiency the Bolsheviks themselves had rendered tribute by recalling some of their agents.[93]

An Inter-Departmental Committee on 'Bolshevism as a Menace to the British Empire' met at the Foreign Office in July 1921. Its final report concluded that there was 'no doubt of the essential hostility of the Soviet government towards the British Empire'.[94] A paper on 'Bolshevik Intrigue', circulated to the Cabinet by Montagu, noted that India still represented the 'main objective of Bolshevik foreign policy'. Every effort was being made to damage British interests in India and throughout the East, and to bring about a 'combined effort converging on India'. The general effect of these activities, the paper concluded, had been to bring about a situation 'actually dangerous to the safety of the Empire'. 'Serious steps' must be taken to counter their 'hostile influence'.[95] Too much was put down to non-cooperation, Montagu wrote to Lord Reading, which was 'really due to undiscovered ramifications of international revolutionaries in Geneva, America and Russia'.[96]

A careful record was kept of apparent violations of the terms of the trade agreement;[97] and further measures of an anti-Bolshevik character were undertaken towards the end of 1922, following the Fourth Comintern Congress in the autumn of that year. At the Congress, it was reported from Zurich, a decision had been taken to 'institute immediately a reinforced communistic activity and propaganda in the Far East, especially in India'. Some one hundred and twenty thousand pounds, the Secret Intelligence Service reported, had been allocated to M. N. Roy, the Indian revolutionary, to further these objectives.[98] The *Workers' Weekly*, accordingly, was banned, since it had 'contained writings of an Indian revolutionary [i.e. Roy] which are seditious in India'; and a trial was instituted in the summer of 1923 at which a number of Indians who had received training in Soviet Russia were charged with conspiracy.[99] In line with efforts to strengthen imperial institutions generally, moreover, an attempt was made to submit the question of Bolshevism to the collective discussion and decision of the member countries of the Empire themselves.

A first opportunity to do so was provided by the 1921 Imperial Conference. The Conference, a Cabinet Committee agreed on the recommendation of the Indian authorities, should consider 'united action against Communist propaganda'.[100] The matter came up at the sixth session of the Conference, on 24 June 1921. William Hughes, the Australian Prime Minister, agreed with Curzon's opening remarks to the effect that Bolshevism was the 'very negation of all the British Empire stands for'. It was 'no use shutting our eyes to the fact that against the British Empire there is a world-wide conspiracy . . . We cannot, we dare not, ignore its sinister purpose, its menacing effects'. He believed that it was time 'some deliberate and systematized effort was made to counteract this propaganda and to tell the world the things for which the British and the Empire stand'. The evidence was accumulating, Montagu added, that the Bolshevik government was 'pursuing by propaganda, and even, indeed, by preparation for warlike operations, determined action against British interest in the East'. He drew attention to the Soviet government's 'sinister purpose'.[101]

The question of action against the spread of Communist propaganda was omitted from the agenda of the next Imperial Conference in 1923; but the Cabinet agreed that the matter might be raised after the Foreign Secretary's statement, which 'must necessarily include a reference to our policy towards the Russian Soviet Government'.[102] There was in fact 'ample evidence', Curzon considered, in a memorandum prepared for a speech to the Conference, that the Soviet government would lose no opportunity by bribes, intrigue and propaganda to destroy the United Kingdom, the British Empire and indeed 'the existing organization of society'. The weight of their attack, for geographic and traditional reasons, was directed against India and against the position of the British government in Turkey and the Near East. Imperial considerations required that it be 'resolutely met'.[103]

The question was discussed further at the fifth session of the Conference. Lord Peel, the Secretary of State for India, noted that the 'Bolshevik menace' had 'not gone very far at present in India, but it is a thing which always had to be watched'. Tej Bahadur Sapru, for the Indian government, added that unrest could not in every instance be identified with Bolshevism; but there was 'every need for being alive to the danger and for taking active steps to prevent the poison spreading, and we must be forearmed'. There was no country which required more or greater development of publicity or propaganda on 'sounder lines', he thought, than India, in order to let the people know what the dangers of Bolshevism really were.[104]

It appeared to some, indeed, as if the member countries of the Empire faced a common and indivisible problem: 'one scheme', as Sir Edward Carson put it in the House of Commons, 'openly stated to be to reduce these islands, this Great Britain, to the single territory which she occupies here, and by these operations [to] take away from her all the keys of our great Empire'. The Bolsheviks, added another Conservative member, 'deliberately support the disaffected elements of the British Empire in Ireland ... In India, Afghanistan, and Egypt it is the same'.[105] The international revolutionary movement, in the even more alarmist view of the Duke of Northumberland, was responsible for a 'conspiracy to destroy the social and economic structure of the British Empire', together with 'all religion, all moral laws, all property, and all forms of government throughout the United Kingdom, India, our Colonies, France and America'. The rebellion in Ireland was 'only part of the movement', he insisted; equally serious was the outlook in India and Egypt. In fact the anti-colonial movements in India, Egypt and Ireland were part of a 'much greater world-wide Movement', the *National Review* declared. It 'has its centre in Moscow and is, in fact, the Revolutionary Government of the World'.[106]

Responsibility for the initiation of appropriate action rested ultimately with the government which stood at the base of this threatened imperial edifice. On 5 August 1921, accordingly, the Cabinet concluded that sufficient use had not been made of the terms of the Russian trade agreement to 'prevent Russian hostility and anti-British propaganda in Afghanistan and elsewhere'. It was agreed that the Prime Minister should make representations to the head of the Russian Trade Delegation; and he was to be supplied by the Secretary of State with details of breaches of the agreement.[107] There was 'strong evidence of bad faith on the part of the Bolsheviks', the Cabinet was told, 'in carrying out the conditions of the Trade Agreement'.[108] Two days later the Cabinet was informed that the material could shortly be made available; and on 19 August a draft note to the Soviet government was circulated by the Secretary of State for India, setting forth 'numerous breaches of the Russian Trade Agreement by the Soviet Government'. It was agreed that the draft should be used as the basis of a despatch to be prepared by the Foreign Secretary, to be approved beforehand by the Prime Minister. It should contain instances of breaches of the agreement and press for an explanation, demanding at the same time that such infringements of the agreement should cease. The note should 'stop short', however, 'of an actual threat of cancellation of the Trade Agreement, which should at this stage be held in reserve'.[109]

The British note of 7 September was handed to Chicherin on 15 September 1921.[110] The Soviet government, it charged, had failed to give effect to the obligations laid upon it by the trade agreement which had been signed the previous March. The note professed to include only the 'more flagrant' of these violations, based upon 'irrefutable evidence' in the government's possession. It sought a reply 'without delay' to these and other, more specific charges. Hostile activities, the note pointed out, still continued unabated, although the successful working of the trade agreement depended upon their cessation. The Communist International was prominently associated with activities of this kind; and one of its foremost aims appeared to be to 'undermine British institutions, particularly in the East'. The essentially subversive character of those aims was clear, as was the 'close association' between its activities and those of the Soviet government.

The Soviet government, the note went on, had been engaged in 'continued intrigue with Indian revolutionaries in Europe'; and it had been 'trying to persuade a well-known Indian anarchist, Dr Hafiz, who has been studying the manufacture of bombs in Vienna, to proceed to Afghanistan to supervise a bomb depot on the borders of India in order to facilitate their importation into India'. He was now engaged in the manufacture of smokeless powder in Kabul. Rothstein, the Soviet representative in Teheran, was believed to be attempting to influence Persian Members of Parliament and 'other Persians of good standing' against the British government; and the 'obnoxious work' of the Tashkent propaganda centre had not ceased. In Turkey, the government thought itself in possession of the 'real motives' for the military assistance which the Soviet government had been providing to the Kemalist forces.

The 'most serious charge of all', however, related to Afghanistan. The recently-concluded Russo-Afghan treaty, it was noted, provided for a subsidy and a telegraph line, and for consulates whose location was justified upon commercial grounds but which appeared to be intended rather as 'prospective centres of propaganda'. The underlying Soviet aim, it was thought, was to secure the formation of a 'powerful united Moslem movement which would deal the final blow against the power of capital' by destroying the colonial base upon which it was believed to rest. The government asked for an assurance that the 'constant flow of inflammatory invective' and 'actual hostile activities by Soviet agents', both of which contravened the provisions of the trade agreement, would cease forthwith.

The Soviet reply to what Lloyd George rightly termed a 'very stern message' was less than forthcoming. Berzin, the Soviet representative in Britain, submitted an 'interim reply' on 26 September, in which he noted that many of the charges in the British note would 'not bear the most superficial examination'.[111] Litvinov's formal reply was handed to Hodgson in Moscow the following day, and forwarded by him to London. It was at once apparent, Litvinov began, that the accusations contained in the British note were either groundless, or else based upon false information or forged documents. The identification of the Third International with the Soviet government, for instance, could not be sustained. The International happened to be located in Moscow, where alone there was freedom to propagate communist ideas, and its executive happened to include some people who were also members of the Soviet government; but the Second International, which was located in Brussels, similarly included on its executive two former members of the Belgian and the British governments. There only five Russians among the thirty-one members of the Third International's executive; and of these five, three were not members of the Soviet government.

Stalin and Eliava, Litvinov continued, had no connection with the International; and neither they nor Karakhan had delivered the reports which had been ascribed to them in the British note. M. Nourteva, described in the note as 'Director of Propaganda under the Third International', had similarly nothing to do with the International; and in June 1921, when he was supposed to have been giving a speech, he had in fact been in prison, where he had been throughout that, and the three preceding months. Lenin had not made a speech on 8 June as stated; nor were the phrases attributed to him to be found in his speeches to the International at other times, which had dealt with entirely different topics. No school of revolutionary propaganda for the training of Indian emissaries existed in Tashkent; and no relations existed with Dr Hafiz and his smokeless powder factory. Strict instructions had, on the contrary, been sent to the Soviet diplomatic representatives in the East, ordering them to refrain from anti-British propaganda as required by the terms of the trade agreement (a copy of the instructions which had been sent to the Soviet representative in Kabul had in fact been communicated to the Prime Minister by the Soviet representative in Britain and circulated to the Cabinet).[112] In what way, Litvinov asked, could the assistance given openly to the Afghan government, in accordance with a treaty the terms of which had been communicated to the British government, be considered an anti-British action? The Soviet government, on the contrary, had throughout made clear its respect for the independence of those Eastern governments with which it had established relations; and such assistance as had been offered to them was simply intended to compensate them for the inequity of their former relationship with the Tsarist administration.[113]

The facts upon which the British note had been based, Montagu assured the Cabinet, had been collected by his staff at the India Office, and could be 'fully substantiated'.[114] Hodgson, however, wrote from Moscow to point out a number of weaknesses in the British case. The Third Congress of the Communist International, he noted, had opened on 22 June, and Lenin could not therefore have addressed it, as the British note had indicated, on 8 June (the speech which he had made on 5 July did however contain passages which were at least 'reminiscent' of those which had been quoted). The reports supposedly delivered to the Congress on 1, 5 and 20 June were open to the same objection. Nourteva had indeed been in prison since March of that year, and it was therefore impossible for him to have made the speech attributed to him.[115] Hodgson added, in a letter to J. D. Gregory, that there was in fact 'no evidence to the effect that the [Soviet] Government is wilfully evading its obligations'. Even those who were unfavourably disposed towards it had been surprised by the terms of the British note. Lenin's utterances, he thought, however indiscreet, were considerably less exceptionable than, for instance, Churchill's declaration that Lenin and Trotsky were 'living on the jewels they stole from the women they murdered'.[116]

Curzon, moreover, now learned to his consternation that the Foreign Office could substantiate only two or possibly three of the charges which had been made, and that there existed no independent evidence—and certainly none which could be made public—in support of the rest of the government's case. He was advised to reply briefly, 'reasserting the truth of our charges, without however producing any evidence (because we have not got it)'. Curzon declared himself 'positively appalled at these suggestions and indeed at the entire history of this case'. A departmental committee had been collecting and assessing evidence for months, and a document had been issued asserting the 'irrefutable and indisputable' authenticity of the government's charges; yet now it appeared impossible to substantiate them. He had 'grave doubts', in fact, if any reply at all was now possible; in which case there would be 'nothing left for me but to bear the odium of having made public charges which I cannot sustain'. Those who had led him thus far, he thought, should now attempt to extricate him as best they could. He regarded the general position 'with dismay'.[117]

Silence in response to such a challenge, however, would be 'held to imply acceptance of the charge, or at least inability to meet it';[118] and the terms of a reply were eventually devised. The British note, which was communicated to Hodgson on 2 November 1921, began by maintaining that the charges in the earlier note had been made only after a 'prolonged and careful investigation in each case'. It declined, however, to specify in every instance the source from which the information had been derived. The speech by Lenin to which reference had been made had in fact been delivered on 5 June; and Litvinov's attempt to dissociate the Soviet government from the Third International had 'ceased to beguile'. The British government had no doubt as to the authenticity of the reported statements of Stalin and Eliava; nor did it accept the Soviet government's denial of any connection with Indian revolutionaries, or of Rothstein's propagandist activities in Teheran. The Soviet government, moreover, had continued to print propaganda in the languages of the East. The British government, the note concluded, had 'consistently and faithfully' conformed to the conditions of the trade agreement; a similar degree of loyalty was demanded on the part of its Soviet counterpart.[119]

Radek subjected the British charges to a searching examination in a series of articles in *Pravda*. He concluded that the documents upon which the British government's accusations were based were 'not only forgeries, idiotic forgeries, but the forgeries of the German counter-intelligence, which are sold to all who wish to buy them'. They had been communicated to Basil Thomson, the Head of British Intelligence, by the Security Head in Germany, Weisman. Part of the material had already appeared in the émigré press; and he recommended Curzon to subscribe directly to their journal, *Ostinformation*, whose elementary errors had been reproduced in the British note, rather than proceed through the intermediacy of Weisman. The journal's address was thoughtfully appended.[120] It seemed unlikely, Radek went on, that Nourteva, although accused of treason, should be released and allowed to address meetings. Curzon, he thought, must be working upon the analogy of 'some countries where people involved in speculation in Marconi shares can remain members of the Government' (a reference to the pre-war shares scandal, in which Lloyd George, among others, had been implicated). The despatch of agitational trains to the eastern parts of Soviet Russia was a matter for that country alone. As for reports that such trains had been despatched to Persia and Afghanistan, 'no trains have been seen by anyone . . . for the simple reason that neither country has any railway line.'[121]

Radek's articles, translations of which were forwarded to London by Hodgson, were an effective debating reply to the accusations of colonial intrigue which the British notes had contained. They were less successful in disposing of the British government's essential charge, however, which was that the Soviet government, together with the Communist International, had been providing moral and sometimes more substantial assistance to opponents of British imperial rule, particularly in the East. It would indeed have been surprising if an avowedly revolutionary regime had not been engaged in some activities of this kind, and the British government was not alone in finding Soviet protestations of innocence on this score somewhat difficult to accept. The consistent refusal to accept responsibility for the activities of the Communist International was considered particularly unconvincing. The Soviet government's response on this point, however, was more than a diplomatic tactic, convenient though it undoubtedly was; it also reflected the very real dilemma inherent in the conduct of foreign relations by a revolutionary socialist government with the surrounding capitalist states with which it was, at least for the time being, obliged to coexist. To this we now turn our attention.

5 Soviet Russia and Revolution

Early Soviet foreign policy was based upon the assumption that two social orders representing the interests of different and antagonistic classes could not long coexist, and that in the struggle between them socialism would be triumphant. Soviet diplomatic activity, accordingly, devoted rather more attention to appeals to the 'working class of all countries' than to the governments which, at least formally, represented them.[1] There was indeed some doubt as to whether it was proper to speak at all of a 'Soviet foreign policy' as distinct from the revolutionary policy of a socialist party in power. 'What? Are we going to have foreign relations?', Lenin is reported to have remarked. Trotsky, on his appointment as the first People's Commissar for Foreign Affairs, announced simply that he would 'issue some revolutionary proclamations to the peoples and then close up shop'.[2]

The gradual accumulation of international commitments, however, the most notable early instance of which was the trade agreement with Britain, together with an apparent stabilisation in the European political situation, brought with them a growing realisation that 'state' and 'revolutionary' policies might not always readily be reconciled. It would be wrong to suggest that a definitive endorsement of either perspective was made by the Soviet leadership within the period we are considering: the question remained an open one until the failure of the German insurrection of 1923, and probably beyond. But the 'revolutionary' perspective, in the European context at least, become an increasingly hypothetical and long-term one; and the Bolsheviks, from about the end of 1920, increasingly devoted their attention to the real if more modest advances which it appeared possible to achieve in the East.

It was clear that their main adversary in this regard must be the British government, whose colonial possessions and areas of interest were similarly located. 'The very fact of the existence of Soviet Russia', a contemporary Soviet pamphlet pointed out, 'places a question mark over the centuries-old possessions of the British bourgeoisie, over all the British colonial empire'. British statesmen understood perfectly that the 'revolution, having succeeded in Russia, cannot remain within its boundaries, that the establishment of the power of the Soviets in Russia will give a powerful impetus to the liberation of the peoples of the East'. The Soviet government's 'main and most dangerous enemy from the moment of the October Revolution', noted M. N. Pavlovich, the prominent Soviet Orientologist, 'was the most powerful imperialist power of today—Britain, always seeing in a strong and united Russia a threat to the hegemony of Great Britain in Persia, Afghanistan and especially in India'. For the British Empire this was, as Bystriansky put it, 'in a real sense a question of to be or not to be'.[3]

The British government, as we have seen, took this threat very seriously. No directly offensive measures against the Soviet government could be undertaken, following the conclusion of the trade agreement; but it was still possible, as the exchange of diplomatic correspondence in the autumn of 1921 had shown, to use the agreement as a bargaining counter, offering continued and perhaps even increased access to the British market in return for the cessation of revolutionary propaganda. Counter-intelligence was a second, and sometimes a more effective means of defending what were regarded as essential British interests. It was not only defensive tactics of this kind, however, which frustrated the achievement of Soviet objectives: the strength of indigenous traditions and the resource of local rulers, it became increasingly clear, were obstacles of a not less substantial character. The Soviet government's optimism, in retrospect, seems to have had no more substantial foundation than the British government's corresponding but equally misplaced pessimism.

'For several years' recalled M. N. Roy, 'Soviet diplomacy and communist propaganda could be hardly distinguished'.[4] Even the agencies by which these respective policies were advanced appeared indissolubly linked. A 'most important historical fact, influencing the whole of our foreign policy during 1919', noted Chicherin, the People's Commissar for Foreign Affairs, was the 'foundation of the Third International'. One could 'not exist',

Kamenev declared, 'without the other'. The 'mutual solidarity of the Soviet republic and of the Communist International', commented *Izvestiya*, 'is an accomplished fact. The spiritual, moral and material bond between them is based on a complete solidarity of interests.'[5] Both the International and Narkomindel came ultimately under the control of the Politburo of the Russian Communist Party, a body which—in Lenin's words—resolved 'all questions of foreign and domestic policy';[6] and Comintern representatives were normally included in the staff of Soviet diplomatic missions abroad.[7]

Of the two bodies, however, it was clearly the Communist International whose leading personnel carried the greater political weight. Zinoviev, its chairman, was a close associate of Lenin's and a figure of considerable eminence in his own right within the Bolshevik party. Chicherin, in contrast, had a compromising aristocratic background and had formerly served within the Tsarist Ministry of Foreign Affairs. He was a learned man, a talented musician and an outstanding linguist; but he had been a Menshevik until 1918, joining the Bolsheviks only upon his return to Russia in that year.[8] He was 'very industrious, conscientious and has the great advantage—in a Government of which so many members are Jews—of being of good Russian stock', noted a 'Who's Who in Soviet Russia' produced under the auspices of the Foreign Office. But he was 'shy and nervous and lacks the qualities of a leader', and was 'not in the inner councils of the Communist Party—it is, indeed, certain that in his case nationalism comes before communism—and is not a member of the "Politbureau", which decides the main issues of foreign policy'.[9]

It appeared at first, indeed, as if the Communist International might subordinate to itself not simply the Foreign Affairs Commissariat but the Soviet party and state as a whole. In 1922 the Workers' Opposition group within the Russian Communist Party appealed to the International over the head of the party's Central Committee. Those who had signed the appeal, the RKP's Congress acknowledged, 'in no sense violated party discipline simply by virtue of having sent this appeal to the supreme organ of our class communist organization—the Comintern . . .'.[10] The appeal was considered by a commission of the International, under the chairmanship of Klara Zetkin. It was eventually rejected; but the submission, a contemporary recalled, 'appeared in the eyes of Western Communists to be fully justified', and they were 'surprised' by its failure.[11] Their reaction may have been a naïve one: Russia, Zinoviev had noted the previous year, had already become the 'main country of the Third International', as France had been within the First International; and 'upon the voice of our party', he told the RKP's Congress in 1922, 'very much depends in the Comintern'.[12] But at least until 1924 the Comintern's proceedings were conducted in German, the 'language of international socialism', rather than Russian; and its executive, Zinoviev promised, would be transferred to Britain or France, so soon as the proletarian revolution had triumphed in either country.[13]

These international perspectives, moreover, were written into in the state institutions of the young Soviet republic. The Council of People's Commissars styled itself simply a 'workers' and peasants' government', not the government of a particular nation-state; and steps were taken in early agreements—notably in the treaty with Finland of 1 March 1918—to make provision for supra-national economic organs and planning.[14] The Constitution of the RSFSR, adopted on 10 July of the same year, accorded the political rights enjoyed by Russian citizens equally to foreigners employed within the territory of the RSFSR and 'belonging to the working class or to the non-exploiting peasantry'. Local Soviets were empowered to grant Russian citizenship to such people 'without troublesome formalities'; and they enjoyed the right to elect and be elected to the Soviets and to their executive committees. As new nations joined the proletarian revolution and united with the RSFSR, P.I. Stuchka, a noted jurist and member of the NKID collegium, pointed out, it was likely that the title of the Constitution would in due course have to be changed to that of the 'European Soviet Federated Socialist Republic'.[15]

The October Revolution had been carried through on the assumption that if the Russian workers—a minority in their own country—broke the chain of imperialism at its weakest link, the workers in the advanced industrial countries would carry it through to completion. The revolution in Russia, Lenin declared, was 'only the beginning of the world socialist revolution'. There was no doubt that the socialist revolution in Europe 'must and will begin. All our hopes for a *final* victory of socialism are founded on that certainty'. They had never deluded themselves, he added, that they would be able to complete the transition to socialism without the help of the international proletariat. The Russians had begun the revolution; the French, Germans and British would complete it, and socialism would be victorious.[16] They were fighting not only against Russian capitalism, Lenin added in January 1919; they were 'fighting against the capitalism of all countries, against world capitalism, for the freedom of all workers'.[17]

It was a struggle, moreover, in which the Bolsheviks were bound to be successful. 'No force on earth', Lenin declared in March 1919, could 'hold back the progress of the world communist revolution towards the world Soviet republic'. They would put up with any hardship in order to achieve complete victory, and in order that the Russian and the newly-established Hungarian Soviet Republics should be 'joined by—and we will see them join—the International Soviet Republic'.[18] The victory of the world proletarian revolution was certain, he told the First Congress of the Communist International in the same month, and the formation was imminent of the international Soviet republic. All those present who had seen the formation of the Communist International and of the Soviet republic would, he assured them, see the formation of the World Federal Republic of Soviets. That July, he declared in the summer of 1919, was the 'last difficult July'. The following July would be met by the 'victory of the international Soviet republic—and that victory will be complete and final'.[19]

The first issue of the Comintern's new journal, *Communist International*, appeared on 1 May 1919. 'In 1919 the great Communist International was born', wrote its executive committee in an appeal entitled 'Long Live the First of May'; in 1920, it promised, 'the great international Soviet republic will be born'. Zinoviev, writing on 'perspectives of proletarian revolution', noted that 'while these lines are being written, the Third International has as its main base already three Soviet republics—in Russia, in Hungary and in Bavaria'. Nobody would be surprised, however, if by the time his lines appeared in print there were 'not three, but six or more Soviet republics'. In a year, he forecast, they would 'already be beginning to forget that in Europe there was a struggle for communism, for in a year all Europe will be communist'. Capitalism might survive a further year in Britain and in America; but this would be 'beside a wholly communist European continent'.[20]

The Soviet republics in Hungary and Bavaria, however, soon foundered; and by the end of the year Lenin, while expressing his 'firm belief' in victory, drew attention to the 'difficulties and sacrifices' which had been experienced.[21] Zinoviev admitted to the Second Congress of the Comintern in the summer of 1920 that they had been 'over-enthusiastic'; 'two or even three years', he conceded, might now be required before Europe became Soviet. The victory of the Communist International, he wrote, was nevertheless 'unconditionally guaranteed'; in the 'shortest possible time' they would see the 'international Soviet socialist republic'.[22] The year 1920, admitted *Communist International*, in fact turned out to be a 'year of difficult struggles' in which a considerable number of heavy defeats had been suffered.[23] It was impossible to disguise the fact, Zinoviev conceded, that at the foundation of the International they had all counted upon a very much quicker tempo of international revolution than had in fact occurred. 'Not only us, but our worse enemies were at that time convinced that socialist revolution on a world scale was going to develop at a mad gallop'. In the event, the development of the international proletarian revolution had proceeded and was proceeding more slowly than they had expected.[24] On the whole, he told the Thirteenth Congress of the Russian Communist Party, they had estimated the objective tendencies of development correctly. 'But the factor "time"', he admitted, 'we did not assess altogether accurately'. At the time of the signature of the Brest-Litovsk peace, even Lenin had been convinced that the victory of the revolution in most of the advanced capitalist countries was a matter of two or three months. It was now clear that such a revolution would be a matter not of 'three months, but of a far longer period'.[25]

The possibility that the period of stability in western Europe might prove short-lived could not be discounted.[26] But the Third Congress of the International, which met in June and July of 1921, had to reckon with the failure of the ill-judged 'March action' in Germany and with the introduction of the New Economic Policy in Russia. This, Zinoviev admitted, was a 'political setback for the whole workers' movement . . . that slowed down the tempo of the proletarian revolution'; and the converse was also true: the setback which the proletariat of the western European countries had suffered between 1919 and 1921 had also influenced the policy of the first proletarian state, and slowed down the tempo of development in Russia. The Third Congress, he pointed out, had to 'reckon with a slower tempo of international proletarian revolution than the First Congress had done'.[27] It was realised, Trotsky observed, that the postwar revolutionary ferment was over. It was time to turn to winning the masses with a united front tactic, that was, 'organising the masses on a programme of transitional demands'.[28] No fixed time or tempo could now be forecast for the development of the revolutionary movement.[29] It was perhaps understandable that, as Zinoviev complained, 'some of our friends and enemies' should have interpreted the 'new tactic of the Comintern—the tactic of the united front—as a denial of the hope of world revolution'.[30]

One consequence of this new situation was that the distinction between the International and Narkomindel, and between 're-volutionary' and 'state' policy generally, began to receive a greater degree of emphasis. The Communist Party, Chicherin explained, stood at the head of a great state. As a government, it entered into relations with all other governments, and established firm and friendly relations with them; and it conducted a state policy, defined by the interests of the workers. The policy of the state and the policy of the party, however, must be 'clearly distinguished. Speaking on behalf of government bodies, we place the second on the side. The fate of the communist movement, the successes and trials of Communist parties are the concern of other bodies. Our concern must rather be with the fortunes of the Soviet state'.[31] This distinction was not always consistently observed (a *Pravda* cartoon of 13 January 1922 summed up the ambiguity of the situation by depicting a fiery Zinoviev delivering a harangue to the workers while behind him Chicherin held his head in his hands); but from the early 1920s, at least, it became an increasingly standard feature of Soviet diplomatic discourse.

A second consequence was the attention which the Bolsheviks now began to give to the possibility that events in the colonial world might compensate for a period of what appeared to be relative stability in Europe. Lenin had in fact been pre-eminent among contemporary socialists in the extent to which he had appreciated the revolutionary significance of the East. In an article written as early as 1908, entitled 'Inflammatory Material in World Politics', he noted the 'sharpening of the revolutionary-democratic movement in Asia', which gave the Russian Revolution a 'great international ally both in Europe and in Asia', and gave it, at the same time, 'not only a national, Russian enemy, but also an international enemy'. In 'Backward Europe and Advanced Asia', he wrote that 'throughout Asia, a mighty democratic movement is growing, spreading and gaining in strength . . . Hundreds of millions of people are awakening into life, light and freedom'. They had a loyal ally in the proletariat of the western countries, whose victory would liberate both the peoples of Europe and the peoples of Asia.[32] Socialists, Lenin argued, should demand not only the unconditional and immediate liberation of the colonies: they must also give 'resolute support to the more revolutionary elements in the bourgeois-democratic movements of national liberation in these countries'. There was no doubt that the victory of the Russian proletariat would create 'unusually favourable conditions for the development of revolution in both Asia and Europe'.[33]

Among the first legislative acts of the Soviet government was a 'Declaration of the Rights of the Peoples of Russia', which provided for the self-determination and free cultural expression of the peoples of Russia, and an appeal 'To the Moslem Toilers of Russia and the East', which noted that 'even far-off India' had 'raised the standard of revolt' and was 'calling the peoples of the East to the struggle for liberation'. Moslem customs, beliefs and institutions were declared inviolate; and the new government formally renounced the agreements with the Allied powers providing for the annexation of Constantinople, the division of Persia and the partition of Turkey. On their banners, they declared, the Bolsheviks carried the cause of the liberation of the oppressed peoples of the world; their sympathy and support in return was invited.[34]

By no means all the Bolshevik leaders were as yet convinced of the importance of the colonial revolution. Trotsky, for instance, was reportedly 'not much interested in colonies'.[35] Bukharin acknowledged that colonial risings were associated with the decline of capitalism; but risings in 'Ireland, India, China and like', he argued, could have 'absolutely no *direct* relation to the developing proletarian revolution'. In these countries the working class was usually very weak, and there could accordingly be no prospect of the establishment of a dictatorship of the proletariat.[36] Zinoviev himself, in his report to the Eighth Congress of the RKP in March 1919, gave no attention to the East until his attention was called to it, in the course of his concluding remarks, by an interjection from the floor. His lengthy account of the work of the International to the Seventh All-Russian Congress of Soviets in

December 1919 concentrated exclusively upon developments in Europe and America. He did not wish to dwell upon the situation in other countries, he explained, 'in order not to make [his] report too lengthy'. As late as June 1920 he held that only the 'first tongues of flame' of the revolutionary fire were appearing in the East; only a 'weak beginning' had been made.[37]

With the extension of the bounds of Soviet-ruled Russia and the failure of the advance of the Red Army into Poland to precipitate a popular rising, however, the East began to claim both more general attention and a more exalted place in Bolshevik revolutionary strategy. Some, indeed, claiming the authority of Marx, went so far as to hold that the socialist revolution in the West must actually be 'preceded by a number of national revolutions of the oppressed peoples and first of all of India and the peoples of the East'. 'India must be freed by the Muslim proletariat with the help of Soviet Russia', wrote a group of Soviet workers in the East to Lenin on 12 June 1920, 'and definitely before the revolution takes place in London'.[38] Whatever the relative importance to be attached to the colonial revolution, however, it remained to elaborate a strategy by which it might be effected. This task was taken up at the Second Congress of the Comintern in the summer of 1920. That Congress, urged *Communist International*, must 'direct its attention to the East—for whoever is able to approach the subject nations of the East and then make them his allies . . . will emerge victorious in the final struggle between labour and capitalism'.[39]

The main object of the Congress, Lenin explained, was to 'work out or to outline a practical starting point so that the work which hitherto has been conducted among hundreds of millions of people [in the East] in a disorganized manner, should be conducted in an organized manner, unitedly, systematically'. Both in his opening address and in his report on behalf of the commission on the colonial and national question, Lenin emphasised the importance of the formation of Soviets in the non-capitalist countries. 'Soviets are possible there', he insisted; 'they will be not workers', but peasant Soviets or Soviets of the toilers'.[40] The principle of the Soviet organisation was a simple one, and it could be applied not only to proletarian but also to peasant, feudal and semi-feudal relations. On this basis it would be possible to unite the revolutionary workers of the Communist, developed countries

with the 'revolutionary masses of those countries where there is
no, or almost no proletariat, with the oppressed masses of colonial, eastern countries'. Given assistance from the Russian workers, the colonial countries might indeed be able altogether to
by-pass the capitalist stage of development.

The commission which discussed the national and colonial
question in more detail found it difficult to agree with Lenin's
view that support should be given to the bourgeois-democratic
movement in the backward countries, and it was eventually
agreed to designate such movements 'national-revolutionary'
rather than 'bourgeois-democratic'. To Lenin, however, there
was 'no doubt that any nationalist movement can only be
bourgeois-democratic, since the main mass of the population in
the backward countries consists of peasants, the representatives of
bourgeois-capitalist relations'. Although openly reactionary leaders should not be supported, Communist parties in the East could
not operate other than through the support of such movements.
More generally, Lenin concluded, revolutionary work in the
national and colonial question must now constitute their 'main
task'.[41]

Not all delegates were convinced by these propositions. M. N.
Roy, in particular, emphasised the changes which had occurred
during the war in British India, Dutch India, China and elsewhere. In these countries, he noted, a mass movement was
developing, which would make it less necessary to offer concessions to non-proletarian elements. The first and essential task, in
his view, was the foundation of a Communist party, which would
'organize peasants and workers and lead them to revolution and
to the establishment of Soviet republics'.[42] Serrati, the Italian
Socialist, who intervened later in the debate, went even further
and opposed the provision of any aid whatsoever to bourgeois
'national-revolutionary' parties. The theses, he declared (to the
vocal indignation of many delegates), might even be described as
counter-revolutionary. These objections notwithstanding, the
theses were adopted, with three abstentions.[43]

The theses called, among other things, for a 'closer union
between the proletarians and the toiling masses of all nations and
countries for joint revolutionary struggle to overthrow the land-
lords and bourgeoisie' (this was to be made the 'cornerstone of the
Communist International's policy on the national and colonial
questions'). All Communist parties were required to render 'di-

rect assistance . . . to the revolutionary movements in dependent or unequal countries (for instance, in Ireland, and among the negroes of America and so on) and in the colonies'. The conditions for admission to the International, adopted on 6 August 1920, included a requirement that affiliated parties in countries with colonial possessions adopt a 'particularly explicit and clear attitude' on this question. Colonial liberation movements must be supported 'not merely in words but in deeds'; and a 'genuinely fraternal attitude' should be inculcated towards the working people of the colonial and oppressed nations. Moscow and Petrograd, it was urged at the Congress, should become a 'new Mecca for the East'.[44]

Concluding the proceedings, Zinoviev dwelt upon the 'gigantic importance' of the fact that among the delegates there had been several representatives of the workers and poor peasants of the East. The national movements of the East, he declared, would 'unite with the European and American movement and will deal a final blow to capitalism'. British capitalism, Radek stated, could not be overcome only in London, Sheffield, Manchester and Glasgow; 'it must be broken in the colonies. There is its Achilles heel . . .'.[45] The people of the Near and Far East, added Pavlovich, represented a 'source of new strength for the Communist International'. All Communists had now 'become Asians, i.e. simply allies of the whole struggling colonial and semi-colonial world'.[46]

The Bolsheviks now spoke, Lenin remarked, 'not only as the representatives of the proletarians, but also as the representatives of the oppressed peoples'. The slogan 'proletarians of all countries and oppressed peoples, unite', strictly speaking, was a departure from the *Communist Manifesto*; but the *Manifesto*, he pointed out, had been written under 'completely different circumstances', and from the point of view of contemporary conditions the slogan was in fact a correct one. All Asia was in ferment, and in India a revolutionary movement was forming. The Entente had made Russia the 'direct representative of the whole mass of the oppressed population of the world . . . We speak as the representatives of 70% of the people of the world'. On the introduction to political life of the working masses of the East, Lenin argued, now depended 'to an enormous degree' the fate of the whole western civilisation. The West was 'digging its grave in the East'.[47]

It remained to bring the International's policy to the attention of those for whose benefit it had been formulated; and this was the task to which the Congress of the Peoples of the East, which

assembled at Baku in September 1920, now addressed itself. The
decision to hold the Congress was taken at the end of June at a
meeting of the Comintern executive together with some of the
delegates who had attended the Second Congress.[48] An invitation
was issued 'to the enslaved masses of Persia, Armenia and
Turkey', not forgetting 'more distant peoples' in India and the
Moslem lands. 'Spare no effort to be present in the greatest
possible numbers', ran the circular. The Congress, it was hoped,
would 'give strength to millions and millions of the enslaved
throughout the world', and 'bring closer the day of final victory
and liberation'; it was to be the 'supplement, the second part' of
the proceedings of the Second Comintern Congress.[49] Its debates
marked a further step towards the elaboration of an adequate
revolutionary strategy on the national and colonial question; and
they made perfectly clear against whom that strategy would
principally be directed.

Almost two thousand delegates from twenty-nine eastern
nationalities were present to hear the opening addresses.[50]
Zinoviev began by outlining the work of the Second Comintern
Congress and recapitulating its conclusions. They aimed at Baku,
he noted, to secure a more complete representation of the toilers of
the whole of the East than had been possible in Moscow. He
pronounced the Congress a 'most important historical event';
now 'not individuals, but tens, hundreds of thousands, millions of
the toiling peoples of the East are rising up, who represent the
majority of the world's population and who, thus, are alone
capable of resolving finally the struggle between labour and
capital'. Before them there now stood the 'task of igniting a
general holy war against the English and French capitalists'.
'Comrades! brothers!', he concluded, 'we call you to a holy war
above all against English imperialism!'. His appeal was greeted
with 'stormy applause' and 'repeated cries of "hurrah"'; the
delegates stood, brandished their weapons, and replied 'we vow
it'. Might their declaration be heard in London, Paris and all the
cities where capitalists still remained in power, urged Zinoviev;
'Long live the fraternal alliance of the peoples of the East with the
Communist International! May capitalism perish! Long live the
empire of labour!' Stormy applause broke out; and the delegates
replied in their turn 'Long live the Third International, long live
the unifiers of the East—our respected leaders, our beloved Red
Army'.[51]

This, not surprisingly, was the most dramatic point of the

proceedings; and the address as a whole occupied the entire first session. Radek followed with a report on the 'international situation and the tasks of the toiling masses in the East'. 'We are united with you by fate', he told the delegates. 'Either we unite with the peoples of the East and speed up the victory of the western European proletariat, or we will perish, and you will be enslaved'.[52] A Council of Action and Propaganda was elected at the final session of the Congress. It was mandated to conduct propaganda, to publish a journal and pamphlets, to organise a university of social sciences for the East, and to offer assistance to revolutionary movements. The Council, which was to function as a subordinate organ of the International, had a membership of forty-eight; and in turn it was to elect a presidium of seven, two of whom, with the right of veto, were to represent the Comintern executive.[53] The work of the Congress concluded with the adoption of a series of resolutions, and of a manifesto to the eastern peoples which called for the 'liberation of mankind from the yoke of capitalist and imperialist slavery . . . In this holy war all the revolutionary workers and oppressed peasants of the West will be with you . . . Long live the unity of all peasants and workers of the East and West, the unity of all the workers, all the oppressed and exploited'.[54]

Reactions to the Congress in Russia varied only in their degree of enthusiasm. *Pravda* on 8 September hailed the Congress as a 'major event in the history not only of the East, but in the history of world revolution'. The development of a powerful revolutionary movement in the East, it considered, heralded the 'fall of imperialism and the triumph of the world socialist revolution'. Pavlovich, who had attended the Congress and was one of the Comintern representatives upon the presidium of the Council of Action and Propaganda, declared that the Congress had 'made the first breach in the Chinese wall which hitherto separated the peoples of the East, firstly, from each other, and secondly, from the revolutionary West'. In all these countries, he believed, the pre-requisites existed for social revolution. There could be 'no doubt that the Congress of the Peoples of the East will play a major historical role in the speeding up of the process of separation of the "colonies" from the metropolitan countries . . . and of the communist order throughout the world'. If the outcome of the Congress had been the establishment of the Council of Action, declared an editorial in the Baku paper *Kommunist*, the 'offspring of the Council will be the formation of a federation of Soviet peoples in the East.'[55]

The Times professed editorial amusement at what it termed the 'spectacle of two Jews, one of them a convicted pickpocket, summoning the world of Islam to a new Jehad'. Baku, explained another journal, was an 'amazing city', a 'place where life is so constantly unsafe that people regard barbarism and bloodshed as part of the ordinary routine of existence'; its working people were 'as picturesque and villainous a set of ruffians as ever made up a riot'.[56] The Cabinet, however, was evidently disposed to regard the matter more seriously. Curzon, in his notes to Chicherin of 1 and 9 October 1920, took particular exception to Soviet activity in the Caucasus, Central Asia, Persia and Afghanistan, and to the 'revolutionary Conferences of Asiatic peoples in Baku';[57] and every effort was made to prevent the delegates from reaching their destination. A maritime patrol was maintained along the northern Turkish coast, and the Turkish representatives were able to proceed only when a storm blew up and the patrol vessels were forced to put into Constantinople. 'Almost half-dead', it was reported, the Turkish delegates eventually reached Baku.[58] The delegates from Persia were less fortunate; some were arrested by the local police, acting at the instigation of British officers, while those who reached the Caspian Sea and began to cross it were bombarded by a British aeroplane, killing two delegates and wounding several others.[59]

The conduct of propaganda in the colonies was clearly one of the ways in which the Soviet government could most effectively pressurise its British counterpart; and there is some evidence that the Bolshevik leaders in fact regarded the support of radical movements in the East as no more than a useful tactical gambit in its negotiations towards a trade agreement. This essentially manipulative line of thinking emerged reasonably clearly on a number of occasions. Trotsky, for instance, in a letter to Chicherin in June 1920, expressed the opinion that a Soviet revolution in the East would be of advantage 'mainly as a most important item of diplomatic exchange with Britain'. Every means should be employed, he urged, to 'underline our readiness to do a deal with England regarding the East'.[60] Krasin reported to Litvinov in an intercepted letter that the British government was 'very well-informed regarding the secret negotiations between Moscow and the Oriental countries . . .' and were in 'great fear of a Bolshevik offensive in Persia'. This possibility, together with domestic labour unrest, had 'forced Lloyd George to enter into negotiations with Russia'.[61] Pavlovich also observed that the 'decisive course' of Soviet action in the East, reflected particularly in the establishment of the Council of Action and Propaganda of the Peoples of the East, had compelled British ruling circles to accelerate the changing of their policy towards Soviet Russia. The Baku Congress had met in September; and *'already in December'*, he pointed out, the British government had prepared the draft of a trade agreement.[62]

The final text of the trade agreement, making specific provision for the curtailment of colonial propaganda, was signed in London in March 1921; and the Soviet government appears generally to have abided by the undertakings to which it was thus committed, often to the dismay of more vigorously-inclined local radicals. The Tashkent propaganda school was closed down (Roy recalled that the students' political consciousness had in any case been a low one; there was a 'general craze' to learn aviation, those who were not selected complaining that their more fortunate colleagues owed their success to the fact that they had 'turned against the faith of their forefathers and accepted the atheistic cult of communism');[63] and instructions were issued to the Soviet representatives in Afghanistan and Persia that they should observe the provisions of the trade agreement and refrain from 'artificial attempts to introduce communism'.[64] Indeed the trade agreement, two members of the Council of Action and Propaganda based at Baku complained in an (intercepted) letter to its chairman, had dealt a 'fatal blow' to their work. Hitherto the 'main basis of our agitation was our struggle with England. This was the most convincing argument in our work and the cornerstone of our propaganda'. The conclusion of the agreement, which prohibited such activity, had now placed the eastern Communists in a very awkward position and 'entirely ruined the work which they had built up with such difficulty'. In the circumstances, they wrote, 'what possible sense can there be in continuing our work in the East?'[65]

It appeared, then, that the work of agitation and propaganda among the eastern peoples which had been initiated at Baku had now been sacrificed to Soviet state interests. To an extent, at least, it seems difficult to resist the conclusion that the Soviet leaders simply had 'no desire to endanger the hope of a provisional *modus vivendi* with the western powers'; a conclusion which appears to have been shared at the time by a number of colonial radicals.[66] This, however, is only part of the explanation we require. For it was at least as important that the Baku Congress and its aftermath had demonstrated that the organisation of the colonial revolution was by no means so straightforward a matter as seems originally to have been supposed, and that the attempt to introduce directly communist measures in the eastern countries might be altogether premature. To refrain from 'artificial attempts to introduce communism' represented as much the lesson of the Bolsheviks' disenchanting experience as it did a conscious decision to subordinate the eastern revolution to the maintenance of the trade agreement with Britain.

Among the more notable problems with which Soviet policy found itself confronted was the strength of indigenous social and cultural tradition. The Baku Congress provided some evidence of its importance. 'Many violent speeches were made', according to one report, 'but the general effect was in many cases spoiled by large numbers of the Moslem representatives going outside to say their prayers'. 'Not the faintest notice was taken of the numerous speeches made', it appeared, 'the delegates being far more interested in each others' swords and revolvers'. Some, indeed, had brought local produce with them, and 'with this they proceeded to trade and from all accounts manged to do considerable business during their stay in Baku'.[67] Many speeches directed loudly applauded attacks at British and French imperialism; but the dominant theme was an uncomplicated nationalism, and the delegates not infrequently expressed a desire to do without outside 'interference' in their political and cultural affairs.[68]

The 'Ghilan episode' demonstrated some of the difficulties which might be encountered in eastern countries in which radical parties attempted to proceed directly to the construction of a socialist order.[69] The port of Enzeli on the Caspian Sea was occupied by Soviet forces on 18 May 1920, and the nearby town of Resht, in Ghilan province, was taken when its Anglo-Indian garrison fled. A republic was declared there on 4 June, and a Provisional Revolutionary Government was formed under the leadership of the Persian democrat Kutchuk Khan. Its members bore the title of Commissar, and a message of cordial support was despatched to the Soviet government. The attempt to introduce communism in the province, however, reported Narkomindel, 'did not lead to successful results'. Anti-religious propaganda was widely resented, and the peasants refused to respond to an invitation to take over the land.[70]

A new Central Committee was subsequently elected by the Persian Communist Party; and 'after clarification of the failure of communist policy in Ghilan' it 'adopted a resolution on the necessity for the revolution in Persia to pass through a bourgeois stage'.[71] In January 1921 a set of 'theses on the social-economic situation and the tasks of the Iranian Communist Party "Adalyat"' spelt out the implications of the new policy in some detail. The theses insisted that the party must refrain from the 'immediate introduction of purely communist measures' and admitted the 'impossibility of the early appearance of communism in Persia', acknowledging the strength of religious and cultural attitudes and institutions. The Ghilan episode, moreover, had 'again raised the threat of Russian domination and this weakened the anti-English movement'. Any further armed intervention from the same quarter, it was thought, would only harm the revolutionary movement. The party should concentrate rather upon securing the support of all classes from the proletariat to the middle bourgeoisie, and it should seek the co-operation of parties representing the interests of the petty bourgeoisie and the intelligentsia.[72]

The support of Kutchuk Khan, commented Georgy Safarov, a member of the NKID collegium, had been the result of an 'over-estimation of the real relation of forces', the outcome of which had been exclusively to the benefit of world imperialism. Where the working-class organisation was weak, there was a need to avoid 'revolutionary adventurism'. A long transitional or NEP period was necessary for the eastern countries, where religious, ethnic and cultural prejudices remained strong, as well as for Soviet Russia itself.[73] Stalin, writing in *Pravda* on 10 October 1920, warned communists in backward areas against pursuing policies which would alienate the local population—'cavalry raids', as he put it, 'with the object of "immediately communizing" the backward masses'. Bazaars, which had been closed during the civil war, were now permitted to re-open; private trading was encouraged; and property rights, even those of the rich, were scrupulously respected. Mosques which had been seized by the state were returned to their congregations; and Moslem judicial processes were permitted to re-establish themselves. In order to carry out the 'difficult, but by no means impossible task' of achieving a transition to socialism, Stalin noted, it was 'essential to take into consideration all the peculiarities of the economic condition, even the historical past, way of life and culture of these peoples'.[74]

A greater degree of emphasis began henceforth to be placed upon the development of the working-class movement and of indigenous Communist parties in the eastern countries; and at the Third Comintern Congress, which met in 1921, this task was given priority over the development of the national-democratic movement. The strength of cultural tradition operated even here, however, to frustrate the achievement of this new and apparently more 'realistic' objective. The suspicion existed, in the first place, that the Soviet leaders intended simply to utilise the eastern peoples for their own tactical ends, and that they continued to regard them, in however unconscious a manner, as the Tsarist colonisers who preceded them had done. 'We, the people of Turkestan', declared a delegate to the Baku Congress, 'have never seen comrade Zinoviev, we have never seen comrade Radek, we have never seen the other leaders of the revolution'. They should come and see what was being done by their local agents, who were alienating the masses from Soviet power. 'Take away your counter-revolutionaries . . . take away your colonisers, now working under the mask of communism', he demanded, to the 'stormy applause' of delegates.[75]

A delegate at the First Conference of Muslim Communists of Central Asia complained similarly that they were 'still obliged to endure a contemptuous attitude on the part of the former privileged classes towards the indigenous masses. This attitude is that of the communists, who retain a mentality of oppressors and regard the Muslims as their subjects'. Very many Russian Communists were to be found, Safarov told the RKP's Tenth Congress in 1921, who were altogether in favour of the dictatorship of the proletariat but held that, since such peoples as the Kirgiz and the Uzbeks lacked an industrial proletariat, the direction of the agencies of that dictatorship must be exclusively in the hands of Russians.[76] 'What's new with you?' Bukharin had asked a delegate to the party's Twelfth Congress from an outlying region. 'Nothing much. We're throttling the nationals', the man had replied.[77] There were many such comrades in the localities, Safarov commented, who were 'under the power of an ideology which is alien to us'; The result was that the traditional mistrust of great powers, 'sometimes unintentionally, half-consciously', was being applied to relations with the new Soviet state.[78]

Colonial radicals themselves, moreover, consistently failed to draw a revolutionary, as distinct from a nationalist, moral from developments in Russia. The concession of institutions of self-government to the formerly subject peoples of the minority republics attracted a good deal of favourable comment, and the rapid progress of the backward areas of Central Asia impressed many both within and outside the socialist movement.[79] Even the most militant sections of Indian youth, however, had 'no clear conception of the ideals of the Russian Revolution, nor of the principles of Marxism . . . They were first attracted to the Revolution on purely national grounds'. Indian socialists, indeed, have themselves attested to the superficiality of their acquaintance with marxism at this time.[80] The Indian delegates to the Third Congress of the Comintern, Roy recalled, were unable to explain how the liberation of the colonial peoples was to be brought about, or what sort of regime might succeed the colonial administration. No marxist literature was available; the Bolsheviks were associated simply with 'uncompromising anti-imperialism'. The public trials of Indian Communists which took place some years later, ironically, served to clarify for at least one radical the nature of the doctrine to which nominally he subscribed.[81]

A number of communist-aligned groups existed in India at this time; and Roy, the most prominent radical in exile, published a socialist paper (originally entitled 'Vanguard of Indian Independence'), copies of which, together with his book 'India in Transition', were soon reaching India.[82] Attempts to build up an Indian Communist Party, however, continued to be frustrated by personal jealousies and antagonisms; and attempts to win over the nationalist movement met with little success. 'One must . . . see things as they are', Radek told the Fourth Congress of the Comintern. In India, in the 'great trade union movement . . ., in this great wave of strikes, we play no role as yet'; and they had 'not yet taken the first step as a real workers' party'. No socialist political movement had indeed as yet come formally into existence in that country.[83]

The Times continued to regard the political orientation of the non-co-operation movement with some suspicion. A secret Bolshevik circular which the paper printed on 1 January 1923, however, revealed a 'very unsatisfactory state of affairs'. Their propaganda schools were 'practically useless', the circular stated, and 'no results whatever' had attended their agents' work. At least one large sum of money for party work, recalled an emissary from the British Communist Party, had successfully been smuggled into India by one of the graduates of the former Tashkent propaganda school. But the man in question had used it all to build himself a house; and much of the Bolsheviks' early financial support had suffered a similar fate. As late as 1923 Communists existed only in isolated groups in Calcutta, Bombay, Madras and Lahore, and there appeared to be little contact between them. Three years later, Philip Spratt, the emissary, recalled, the party had only fifteen or twenty members, and of these some were entirely nominal. The party's members in Lahore, for instance, were 'all very charming fellows, but disinclined to do anything'.[84]

Government intelligence, moreover, remained throughout in control of the situation. In 1923 censorship was tightened, copies of the *Vanguard* were seized, and surveillance was increased. The movement was left 'crippled and disorganized'.[85] A large proportion of Roy's despatches, Intelligence sources later reported, were intercepted and read, providing an 'unfailing source of information of proved accuracy as to the movement of men, money and literature'. The knowledge derived from it had been 'used more than once to the discomfiture of our enemies'.[86] A conspiracy trial was held at Peshawar in May 1923, and a further trial took place at Cawnpore the following year. The defendants received four-year prison sentences; but the appeal court judges found the notion of a conspiracy 'absurd and unbelievable'. At no time, they concluded, had the movement represented a serious threat to state security.[87]

Comintern spokesmen continued to profess optimism in regard to the prospects of the revolutionary movement in the colonies. 'Significant results', Zinoviev maintained in his report to the Fourth Congress, had been achieved in India, where the work of their comrades had 'met with success'. In addition, 'more or less powerful nuclei' had been formed in Turkey, China and Egypt.[88] An unmistakably greater emphasis, however, began to be placed upon approaching the eastern question 'not only theoretically, as during the Second Congress, but practically'. There was a need for a 'practical approach', it was urged, to questions which the Second Comintern Congress had considered 'in a general and

purely theoretical way'; it was essential to 'shift from declarations
to actions'.[89] The Fifth Comintern Congress was accordingly
invited by Manuilsky to consider the 'better application in the
given concrete circumstances' of the general principles formulated at the Second Congress. That Congress, he noted, had been
'unable to indicate concrete means by which a united working-
class front between proletarians and colonies might be established'. This omission must be repaired forthwith.[90]

The strength of affiliated parties in the East had certainly
remained at an unsatisfactory level. The relevant figures were
published in 1923. Two thousand members were reported in
Persia, with one press organ; in Egypt there were fifteen hundred
members, but no journal; while in China and Korea there appeared to be neither members nor publications, and no reference
at all was made to India or Afghanistan, for in neither country did
an affiliated party yet exist.[91] The Persian Communist Party
subsequently admitted a fall in membership to no more than one
thousand members; and by 1924 membership had declined still
further. The party's delegate to the Fourth Comintern Congress
could take refuge only in the hope that with the growth of an
industrial proletariat its prospects would improve.[92] Zinoviev,
commenting upon the first five years' existence of the International, admitted that 'only a beginning' had been made to serious
revolutionary work in the colonies and semi-colonies. The following five years, he suggested, should be devoted above all to work in
this area. There was a need for 'more, far more attention to the
East, to the colonial and semi-colonial countries'.[93]

The attempt to establish influential Communist parties in the
East and to develop a radical perspective within the nationalist
movement had evidently had little success. An effort was being
made at the same time, however (such activity was, indeed, alone
consistent with the trade agreement), to develop close and friendly diplomatic relations with progressive and 'anti-imperialist'
governments in the colonial world, above all with those of Afghanistan, Persia and Turkey. Their common opposition to the
imperial powers, it appeared, might provide a basis for co-
operation and united action; while activity of this kind promised
to undermine the imperial edifice at a particularly sensitive point.
Britain was only an Empire, Narkomindel's journal pointed out,
'so long as she holds India. Take India away from her, and she

becomes a small island kingdom'. India was the 'foundation stone of the British Empire'; if revolution broke out there it would bring· with it 'enormous changes in the history of mankind'.[94] Such, at least, were the objectives of Bolshevik diplomatic policy. As relations developed with colonial governments, however, it became clear that that policy was confronted by difficulties and dilemmas no less substantial than those which had hindered more overtly revolutionary initiatives.

The governments of independent and professedly 'anti-imperialist' Asian states, in the first place, proved scarcely less anxious than the British government had been to specify, as a condition of entering into an agreement with the Soviet authorities, that agitation and propaganda calculated to disturb political stability in their countries be terminated. Soviet diplomatic overtures towards the East began as early as January 1918; but for various reasons, not all of which were technical, formal agreements with the governments of Persia, Turkey and Afghanistan were not concluded until the spring of 1921.[95] The treaties, and the negotiations which preceded them, were generally accompanied by expressions of cordial friendship and solidarity as against a common enemy, British imperialism; but the eastern envoys studiously avoided committing themselves to the principles of the Soviet order so far as their own countries were concerned. Indeed the agreements, on the contrary, generally bound both parties to respect the 'freedom of the peoples of the East on the basis of independence and in accordance with the general wishes of their populations'; the 'right of each nation to the free and unrestricted choice of its political destiny', both parties undertaking 'strictly to refrain from interference in the internal affairs of the other party'; and the 'right to freedom and independence' of the peoples of the East and of the Russian people and their 'right to choose a form of rule in accordance with their wishes', to quote articles from the treaties with Afghanistan, Persia and Turkey respectively.

These were by no means ritual assurances. Soviet representatives in Afghanistan and Persia, on the contrary, were instructed by Chicherin to refrain from 'artificial attempts to introduce communism' and to maintain the 'strictest non-interference in the internal affairs' of the states to whose governments they were accredited.[96] Soviet policy, in the words of one such envoy, was one of respect for local norms and customs and recognition of the right of nations to self-determination. He deplored the attempts of 'foreign enemies of our friendship' to put about malicious rumours of a Soviet-inspired 'red peril'; the Soviet government, he insisted, had no intention of inciting social or political revolution, believing that differences in forms of rule should not preclude agreement in respect of general questions of foreign policy.[97] The eastern governments, which followed the movements of Soviet representatives with some attention, made it abundantly clear that their maintenance of diplomatic relations with Soviet Russia was dependent precisely upon the observance of such principles.

Soviet spokesmen argued that, notwithstanding this renunciation of the means by which the revolutionary cause had traditionally been advanced, such agreements (in this case with Turkey) could 'only accelerate the process of maturation of the social revolution both throughout the Moslem East and in Turkey itself'. The influence of Soviet Russia upon the East, held another writer, even if socialist and anti-British propaganda were suspended, was 'nevertheless constantly growing', as a result of Soviet Russia's refusal to act as an imperialist power and the enlightened character of her foreign policy. This was evident, it was thought, in a number of expressions of general sentiment contained in the treaties which had been concluded with Turkey and with Persia.[98]

Soviet optimism had its root in the discussions at the Second Congress of the Comintern on the problem of the formation of class alliances in the colonial world, and above all on the question of the 'national bourgeoisie'. Lenin, as we have noted, had originally proposed that the International lend its support to 'bourgeois-democratic' elements, being convinced that the nationalist movement in predominantly peasant colonial countries could be of no other character. He was persuaded, however, to adopt the designation 'national-revolutionary' for these groups; and all agreed to rule out the support of openly reactionary elements. There remained some ambiguity, nevertheless, in the formula proposed, which now became the basic document of Comintern strategy. It extended so far as to the adoption of both Lenin's theses and of additional theses proposed by M. N. Roy, which took an altogether more sceptical view of the national bourgeoisie and emphasised rather that the 'first and essential task' must be the formation of Communist parties in the eastern countries.[99]

This precariously-balanced formula did not long remain unchallenged. By the end of the year the Persian Communist Sultan-Zade was prepared to argue, at a meeting of the Comintern executive, that the bourgeoisie of the backward countries was not in fact capable of fighting on the side of the national-democratic revolution as their colonial strategy required. Speaking with the disappointing events in Ghilan province especially in mind, he argued that the nationalists would either 'pass over into the counter-revolutionary camp' or 'at the first opportunity reach an agreement with capitalist Europe'. Eastern communists, he thought, should direct their efforts against the indigenous as well as against the international bourgeoisie.[100] Sokol'nikov more tactfully pointed out that their 'allies' in the East were 'concluding agreements with our military enemy—the Entente'. It was necessary, he argued, for communists to 'take carefully into consideration all the peculiarities of each individual country and avoid any routine'.[101]

The official view, as expressed by Zinoviev, continued to be that the liberation struggle, 'despite all the efforts of the imperialist governments', was 'developing more and more'. There could be no argument, he thought, that this struggle, 'although it does not have a socialist and communist character, nevertheless objectively remains a struggle against the capitalist regime'. Stalin, characteristically, put the point even more baldly. The struggle of the Amir of Afghanistan for independence, he wrote, was 'objectively a *revolutionary* struggle', since it weakened and undermined imperialism. The same was true of the attempts to secure national independence of the Egyptian merchants and intellectuals, notwithstanding the 'bourgeois origin and bourgeois title of the leaders of the Egyptian national movement [and] the fact that they are opposed to socialism'.[102] A movement, evidently, might be 'objectively revolutionary' even if it lacked a proletarian base, a working-class or radical leadership, and a revolutionary or even a reformist programme. Experience was soon to demonstrate the limitations of such an accommodating theory.

India, for instance, was held by a writer in the journal of the Socialist Academy to be the 'closest to revolution' of all the countries of the East in 1922. That country, in the view of another writer, had 'definitely entered the phase of social struggle with the participation of the broad working-class and peasant masses'. National independence already did 'not reflect the tendencies of her development', which was from the stage of the bourgeois to that of the social revolution. The Indian revolution was pronounced 'on the agenda'.[103] Gandhi, who led this promising movement, was admittedly an incorrigible pacifist with a reactionary world-outlook; but he was held nevertheless to represent the 'necessity of the unity and solidarity of the Indian people against English domination', which was a 'major stage in the course of the liberation struggle of the Indian people'.[104] There was 'no doubt', Sultan-Zade declared in the Moscow theoretical journal *Pod Znamenem Marksizma*, that the national bourgeoisie of India, together with the workers, peasants and craftsmen of that country who shared an equal interest in the ending of foreign servitude, would 'in the end achieve a complete liberation from the yoke of English tyranny'.[105]

These opinions had to be revised when Gandhi called off the civil disobedience campaign in February 1922 following an incident at Chari Chaura in which twenty-two policemen were murdered by an irate mob. Roy warned at the Fourth Comintern Congress that in those eastern countries, such as India, which had seen a greater degree of capitalist development, the upper levels of the bourgeoisie had accumulated a considerable investment in the existing system. They now found that it might be 'more advantageous for them to remain under the protection of the imperialists, since if the great social unrest which took place at the end of the war acquired a revolutionary character, it would remove not only the foreign imperialists but also the native bourgeoisie'. In no eastern country, in fact, did the native bourgeoisie consider itself capable of assuming responsibility for public order after the departure of the imperialists; they feared, rather, that a period of anarchy, chaos and civil war would supervene which would clearly conflict with their interests, and they were willing, for this reason, to reach an accommodation with the imperial overlord. The 'great revolutionary movement' in Egypt and India, therefore, which had formerly represented a serious threat to imperialism, was now 'unable significantly to harm it'. There came a time, Roy warned, when such people 'inevitably betray the revolution and become a counter-revolutionary force'.[106]

In states which possessed a formally independent government the position was scarcely more satisfactory. In Egypt, the Fifth Comintern Congress was told, Zaghlul Pasha had uttered some 'revolutionary phrases' and had been 'accepted as leader of the

Egyptian people'. But once he had taken power the whole of the central committee of the Egyptian Communist Party had been placed in jail, where they had been 'horribly maltreated'.[107] In Persia an emerging middle class was in contention with a feudal aristocracy. Despite their economic weakness, reported Narkomindel, these 'national-democratic elements' were 'beginning to exert a decisive influence upon Persian policy'. On the whole, they represented a 'progressive factor'; and together with other 'national democratic elements' such as the intelligentsia, merchants and professional organisations, they were playing a 'significant role in the strengthening of friendly relations between Russia and Persia and in the success of our policy in Persia'.[108] The Persian Communist Party, however, was banned, and its members forced into an underground existence. The Persian government, for its part, prepared to enter into agreements which, as the Soviet diplomatic representative pointed out, clearly contravened the terms of its treaty obligations towards the Soviet government.[109]

Indeed it could not escape attention that the Soviet cause enjoyed a degree of success among merchants and traders—interested in improving their access to the Russian market but scarcely in the promotion of radical social change—to an extent generally greatly in excess of that attained by local socialist forces. The opening of a Russian bank in Persia, reported Narkomindel, was 'welcomed by the Persian population and merchants'. They welcomed the Soviet trade representative also; and participated in a series of trade fairs and exhibitions in Soviet Russia.[110] A major Persian merchant, influential at this time in government circles, later recalled that not one Persian merchant could be found who had not been in favour of the restoration of regular trading relations with Russia, even if the organisation of Russian foreign trade remained entirely in the hands of the state. Merchants, he thought, were 'one of the most active social forces in our country which put pressure upon our government in 1921', compelling it unconditionally to recognise the Soviet government and to conclude the Persian-Soviet treaty.[111] This situation was in many respects similar to that in Afghanistan, where the 'most heterogeneous social circles', including those connected with the ruling family, welcomed the conclusion of the Soviet-Afghan agreement.[112]

The most conspicuous disjunction between the overall anti-imperialist strategy and the interest of local radicals, however, occurred in the case of Soviet relations with Turkey, where Kemal Ataturk's forces were at this time conducting an offensive against Greek occupying forces. They were the friends of Russia, Kemal told the Turkish National Assembly, because the Russians earlier than anyone else had acknowledged their national rights and had begun to respect them. Russia, in such circumstances, could be 'assured of our friendship today, tomorrow, and for ever'.[113] But communist principles, he made clear, were 'irreconcilable with our way of life', and the government would be 'absolutely right in taking measures against those who would wish to apply those theories to practice'. The question of the principles of capitalism and communism, he insisted, was in no sense involved in the development of their relations with Soviet Russia.[114]

Kemal was as good as his word. The Turkish Communist leader Subhi, who had returned to the country at the end of 1920, was seized at Trabzon along with fourteen associates and drowned, in circumstances which appeared to indicate the connivance of the authorities.[115] The Turkish government was certainly directly responsible for the formation of a spurious non-revolutionary 'Communist party', which simply served, Safarov noted, as a 'pretext for the persecution of genuine Communists, who did not possess official "recognition"'.[116] While the Ankara government was fighting the Entente for the independence of Turkey, a Turkish delegate pointed out to the Third Comintern Congress, it was also fighting against the communist movement. The Communist party which Kemal had founded clearly had the 'provocative aim' of attempting to end any communist influence in Turkey; and he was simultaneously conducting a 'vigorous struggle against Communists'.[117]

It was imperative, Radek wrote in *Izvestiya* on 27 July 1922, for the Ankara government to understand that it could 'save Turkey only if it realized that there is no policy for Turkey to pursue other than a policy of unification with the proletarian revolution'. A 'true liberation' was possible, he insisted, 'only in a union with Soviet Russia'. The following October, however, an armistice was negotiated in the war between Greece and Turkey, and Kemal had no need to continue to temper his policies in order to secure further Soviet diplomatic support. The Congress of the Turkish Communist Party, accordingly, despite 'exhaustive guarantees of loyalty', was broken up by police; the party's activity was banned;

and more than three hundred Communists were arrested throughout the country.[118] The Soviet authorities were ordered to close the offices of their trade mission; and the Soviet diplomatic courier was harrassed, and on one occasion forced to surrender his diplomatic bag. A 'general political line of close friendship', Narkomindel gallantly explained, 'could be combined with disagreements concerning individual special questions'.[119]

Turkish Communists, however, were nevertheless advised to continue to follow the leadership of the Turkish middle class, which was considered still to be progressive in character.[120] Radek conceded at the Fourth Comintern Congress that not only were the eastern peoples not led by communists: in most cases they were not even led by bourgeois revolutionaries, but by 'representatives of the dying feudal cliques, in the person of officers and functionaries'. The first duty of Turkish Communists nevertheless remained the support of the national liberation movement. The 'whole future of the Turkish people is at stake. It is a question of whether the latter can free itself, or whether it will become the slave of world capitalism.' Turkish Communists, notwithstanding the persecution to which they had been subjected, should 'not forget the near future beyond the present. The task of the defence of Turkish independence, which is of great revolutionary importance, is not yet finished. You must defend yourselves against repression . . . but you must also understand that the time has not yet come for the final struggle for emancipation, and that you have still a long road to travel side by side with the revolutionary bourgeois elements'.[121]

Further arrests of Turkish Communists took place in May 1923, on the charge of having 'wished to propagate subversive ideas of communism throughout the land and to modify the form of government'. Two labour organisations were forbidden to carry on agitation or propaganda; May Day demonstrations were prohibited; and the organ of the International Union of Workers was suppressed.[122] Surits, the Soviet envoy, explained to *Izvestiya* at the end of 1923 that Soviet relations with Turkey were 'defined at the present time by the struggle for national independence', which was still being conducted and could not yet be regarded as completed. Kemal's Turkey had still 'objectively speaking' an important revolutionary role to perform.[123] A note of reservation, however, was authoritatively sounded at the Fifth Congress of the Comintern the following summer. Manuilsky, speaking on the national and colonial question on behalf of the executive, noted that the Second Congress had defined the attitude of the eastern Communist parties towards the national liberation movement of a bourgeoisie which was attempting to gain power. In Turkey, however, where the bourgeoisie had now been carried into power by a popular movement, the Turkish Communists were continuing to support native against foreign capital. This, Manuilsky declared, was a 'serious error of tactics'.

No radical change in overall strategy, however, was considered necessary; and Manuilsky went on to condemn 'several deviations', among them that of M. N. Roy, who had 'exaggerated the social movement in the colonies at the expense of the national movement' (Roy had pointed out that the national bourgeoisie in India, alarmed at the intensity of domestic unrest, now supported the Empire and had 'even asked that the army and foreign relations remain the responsibility of the British government'). The class struggle, Manuilsky admitted, was 'relatively advanced' in India; but this was not the case elsewhere.[124] A 'manifesto to the peoples of the East' which was issued by the Congress, while affirming the need for an 'anti-imperialist united front' against the 'rapacious international bourgeoisie', specifically extended greetings to the 'young Communist parties of the East' which, it noted, were 'working and fighting in conditions of extreme difficulty, economic backwardness, feudal survivals, and barbaric torture'. The struggle was one against native feudalists as well as against foreign imperialists; but every 'honest expression' of the national liberation movement, it reminded them, must be supported.[125]

'To those of us who are not capable of a dialectical argument', Chicherin admitted, the 'bourgeois-orientated stand taken by the Workers' and Peasants' Government might appear a betrayal of communist principles'.[126] Soviet and Comintern spokesmen, indeed, did not always succeed in allaying the suspicion that the 'anti-imperialist struggle' might be no more than a convenient means of strengthening the diplomatic position of the Soviet government, at the expense, if necessary, of local radicals. 'The most outright nationalist movement', as Bukharin put it to the RKP's Eighth Congress, 'is only grist to our mill, since it contributes to the destruction of British imperialism'.[127] This argument gradually merged with the more far-reaching proposition that the principal task of the world communist movement must be the defence of Soviet Russia, as the only territorial base which that movement had yet acquired. Kirov made precisely this point to the Baku Propaganda Council in April 1923. Soviet Russia, he explained, was the 'centre of the world revolution, and the position of Soviet Russia must first of all be established if world revolution was to be achieved. If Soviet Russia fails, then world revolution will fail, or at all events will be postponed for many generations'.[128]

This was an argument which was to become exceedingly familiar in later years; and it no doubt reflected, in part, the dominant role which Soviet state interests had come to play in the making of Comintern (as well as Soviet diplomatic) policy. But this should not be allowed to obscure the extent to which the ambiguities of Soviet eastern policy, and of its anti-imperialist strategy generally, reflected the genuinely intractable character of many aspects of the problem which it confronted. Approaching the analysis of the social structure of colonial countries, it has been noted, the Comintern 'confronted problems of enormous complexity. There were extremely few marxist works dealing with the history and the analysis of the social and economic affairs of the countries of the non-Soviet East'. Marxist-Leninist theory could not simply be put into practice: its basic elements required 'further development'.[129] A task stood before them, Lenin pointed out, which had 'not hitherto stood before the Communists of the world': that of applying 'general communist theory and practice' to the 'distinctive conditions' of the countries of the East. This was an 'unusual and difficult task', the solution to which could be found 'in no communist booklet' but only in the course of the struggle itself.[130] The terms of such a solution remained as obscure in 1924 as they had been throughout the preceding years.

The concern of the British government, faced with the expanding influence, in an area of vital interest, of a power professing militantly anti-imperialist objectives, was understandable enough. It was that concern which prompted its repeated attempts to bind the Soviet government with commitments as to its conduct and policy, and which was almost to lead, in the course of 1923, to the breaking-off of diplomatic relations between the two countries. But there seems in retrospect to have been little foundation for the government's alarmism, any more than the Bolsheviks' early and equally ill-founded optimism. The lesson of the imperial confrontation was that local traditions were more recalcitrant, social relations more complex, and governments more shrewd and self-willed than either side was yet prepared to allow.

6 The 'Curzon Note'

The position of the Coalition government steadily worsened throughout 1922. The Genoa Conference, Lloyd George's 'gambler's last throw', failed to improve his political fortunes; its effect, if anything, was the opposite. The negotiation of the Anglo-Irish settlement placed a further strain upon the government's Conservative supporters, especially following the murder of Field-Marshal Sir Henry Wilson in June 1922. The crisis in the Near East three months later gave the impression that Lloyd George's notorious partiality for the Greek cause might again have plunged the country into war had it not been for the presence of mind of the local military commander, General Harington, who had delayed presentation of the government's ultimatum until the situation had eased. Domestically the Coalition continued to lose seats at by-elections, and the sale of political honours was rumoured. The Conservatives, meeting at the Carlton Club on 19 October 1922, accordingly resolved to leave the Coalition; Lloyd George resigned, the King sent for Bonar Law, and Parliament was dissolved on 26 October. In the general election which took place the following month the Conservatives gained an overall majority of seventy-five seats. A new government was thereupon formed; it lacked many senior Conservatives, who had remained loyal to the Coalition, but the presence of Lord Curzon at the Foreign Office suggested an element of continuity in the field of foreign affairs at least.

The appearance of continuity was in fact deceptive: for it had been one of the principal charges against Lloyd George that his exercise of Prime Ministerial powers had verged upon the presidential, and in particular that he had arrogated to himself responsibilities in foreign affairs which belonged more properly to the Foreign Office. Lloyd George's taste for conference diplomacy was partly responsible; and a good deal of attention attached also to the role of the 'garden suburb', a personal staff originally billeted in huts in St James's Park which the Premier had established in 1916. It was this staff which handled all matters connected with international conferences, and also League of Nations business and any other matters with which the Premier entrusted it. The secretariat naturally reflected Lloyd George's political enthusiasms; and where these proved an embarrassment to the government, as in the Near East, the 'garden suburb' inevitably received part of the blame. Much of the criticism of the government's foreign policy in Parliament, Colonel Wedgwood pointed out, was 'not criticism of the Foreign Office so much as criticism of the pseudo-Foreign Office in the Garden City across the road. That is where most of the ground for criticism has been.'¹ Curzon himself found the situation 'painful and even humiliating', and was frequently on the verge of resigning.²

Matters reached the point of a formal debate in the House of Commons in June.³ The 'garden suburb', it was held, was bypassing Parliament and the civil service, and investing the Prime Minister with powers in excess of those he was entitled to discharge. Why, asked Sir Donald Maclean, the Liberal Parliamentary leader, was the 'garden suburb' and not the Foreign Office handling international conference and League of Nations business? Lord Robert Cecil noted that there had been a British delegation of some ninety-one members at the Genoa Conference, but that only three or four of them had been from the Foreign Office. Austen Chamberlain assured the House that the secretariat were 'not themselves authorized to take the initiative in any matters of legislation, or in any matters of executive action'. Over a hundred MPs nevertheless voted against the government on the issue, and the criticism continued. The Conservatives' election manifesto, printed in *The Times* on 27 October 1922, promised that if the party were successful the Cabinet secretariat 'in its present form' would be abolished, and that international conference and League of Nations business, even those which involved the attendance of Bonar Law as Prime Minister, would be handled by the Foreign Office. Following the general election a reduced Cabinet secretariat, under Sir Maurice Hankey, was retained; but the 'garden suburb' was disbanded.⁴ Curzon was left 'very largely . . . to do his own job'.⁵

The change of government, accordingly, implied more than the substitution generally of Conservative policies for those of the Coalition. In the field of foreign affairs it signified more particularly the resumption by the Foreign Office of a central position in the making and implementation of policy, and of its perspectives, more orthodox and 'traditional', in place of those of the Board of Trade and the Prime Minister's secretariat. The dominant influence was no longer Lloyd George, with his penchant for directly negotiated agreements over matters in dispute, but the Foreign Secretary himself. Up to the fall of the Coalition, it was remarked, Curzon had been 'scarcely more than a spectator of events'.[6] With the formation of the Conservative government in November 1922 the Foreign Secretary began to assume a greater degree of control over the making of British policy, and his perspectives in foreign affairs, more inflexible than those of the former Premier and more preoccupied with the fate of British imperial possessions, especially in Asia, began to exert a more direct influence upon the development of British-Soviet relations.

It appears to have been a lecture given by James Fitzjames Stephen, attended by Curzon as a schoolboy at Eton, which first awoke his belief that in India lay the key to a new and dynamic imperial destiny. Stephen had told the boys, Curzon related to an audience of fellow Etonians some time later on his appointment as Viceroy of India, that 'there was in the Asian continent an empire more populous, more amazing, and more beneficent than that of Rome; that the rulers of that great dominion were drawn from the men of our own people; [and] that some of them might perhaps in the future be taken from the ranks of the boys who were listening to his words'. Ever since that day, Curzon recalled, the 'fascination and ... the sacredness of India' had grown upon him.[7] It was a concern which was to provide a fixed point of reference throughout his long and intimate association with the making of British foreign policy. As late as 1923, it was fairly remarked, he remained 'psychologically Vicegerent of India'.[8]

Curzon travelled extensively in the Middle and Far East in his early years, contributing articles to *The Times* and collecting the material for a number of books, which by 1895 had already given him a reputation for knowing more about the East than any living politician. Appointed Viceroy of India in 1898, he defined his mission as one to 'preserve intact and secure, either from internal convulsion or external inroad, the boundaries of that great and Imperial dominion'.[9] His term of office, devoted unswervingly to this end, came to an unhappy conclusion in 1905 when he disagreed with his political superiors in London and was forced to resign. The fortunes of the Empire in the East, and especially of British India, nevertheless remained the dominating concern of his political life; and it was this consideration which, more than any other, underlay his conduct of policy when he became Foreign Secretary after the war. Curzon 'considered English policy and the world position', as Radek put it, 'from the terrace of the Indian Vice-regal palace'.[10]

India provided, as Curzon pointed out, the 'principal, indeed almost the only formidable element in our fighting strength', an army which was 'capable of being hurled at a moment's notice upon any point either of Asia or Africa' (any point, that was, 'where native troops can properly be employed').[11] India represented, moreover, the 'true fulcrum of dominion, the real touchstone of our Imperial greatness or failure'.[12] India was the 'centre and secret of our Imperial dominion': not only was it an important part of any imperial organisation in the future, it was in fact 'so important that without her the Empire could not continue to exist'. India, he noted, had been the determining influence in every considerable movement of British power to the east and south of the Mediterranean. It had been this movement which had 'converted us from a small island with trading and maritime interests into the greatest land Power of the world'.[13]

It was obvious, Curzon considered, that the 'master of India must, under modern conditions, be the greatest power in the Asiatic continent, and therefore, it may be added, in the world' (hence his belief that the 'secret of the mastery of the world' was, 'if they only knew it, in the possession of the British people').[14] The continued existence of Britain, he told his constituents in 1893, was bound up in the maintenance, and even the extension of the British Empire. India was the 'strength and greatness of Britain': 'every nerve a man can strain, every energy he can put forward', could 'not be devoted to a nobler purpose than keeping tight the cords that hold India to ourselves'.[15] As long as Britain ruled India, he wrote to Balfour, she was the 'greatest power in the world'; but should she lose possession of that country, she would 'drop straight away to a 3rd rate power'.[16]

Curzon believed that the imperial connection was of benefit to the Indian population as well. It was, he wrote, the Empire's highest claim to Indian gratitude to have 'educated their character and emancipated their intelligence'. But regrettably, this had been the source of 'many foolish things' and of 'many vain aspirations': for the role of India was 'still, and must for as long as we can foresee, remain in British hands'.[17] The 'advanced natives', he wrote, desired a 'larger control of the executive for which they are as yet profoundly unfitted and which they will never get from me'. He wrote to Balfour about the 'extraordinary inferiority, in character, honesty, and capacity' of the Indians. It was often said that a 'prominent native' should be made a member of the Executive Council. The reason that this was not the case, he told Balfour, was that 'in the whole continent there is not an Indian fit for the post'.[18] The justification of British rule in India was not, in any case, that it was exercised with the consent of the governed; it expressed, simply, the fundamental difference between the economic aptitudes and social and moral concerns of Asiatic races and of communities of European origin. On the whole, his travels around the world had revealed to him a 'satisfied and grateful acquiescence in our domination'.[19] They were 'very strange people, these natives', he ruminated; there was 'scarcely anything that they will not accept from their rulers, however contrary to their own previous utterances or prepossessions'.[20]

To Curzon there was no doubt that the structure of imperial rule was the work of more than human hands. The Empire, he considered, was 'under Providence, the greatest instrument for good that the world has ever seen': it might still remain 'one of the instruments through which He chooses to speak to mankind'.[21] Curzon was not above amending the text of a hymn so as to exclude a verse which made reference to the passing away of earthly empires; and from a comparatively young age he appears to have found himself unable to accept the fundamentals of the Christian faith within which he had been brought up.[22] Yet, speaking at a banquet in February 1903, he declared that if he had 'thought it were all for nothing, and that you and I, Englishmen, Scotchmen and Irishmen in this country, were simply writing inscriptions on the sand to be washed out by the next tide, if I felt that we were not working here for the good of India in obedience to a higher law and a nobler aim, then I would see the link that holds England and India together severed with a sigh. But it is because I believe in the future of this country and the capacity of our own race to guide it to goals that it has never hitherto attained, that I keep courage and press forward.' The Almighty had placed the British hand upon the 'greatest of his ploughs, in whose furrow the nations of the world are germinating and taking shape'.[23] It went without saying that what God had thus joined together, no subject people might break asunder.

Curzon had no doubt that the country against whose influence the British position must be maintained was the 'ever-swelling shadow' of Russia. The Russian presence in Central Asia, he wrote, was a serious menace to India. For a century the possibility of striking at India through Central Asia had been present in the minds of Russian statesmen; they contemplated, indeed, 'the invasion of India, and that with a very definite purpose which many of them are candid enough to avow'. 'Steps, precautionary or otherwise', he was convinced, 'should be taken by this country'. No-one could deny that there was an 'Anglo-Russian question of incalculable seriousness and vast proportions'.[24]

This impression was reinforced in the course of Curzon's travels in the East. In Persia, he found that the Russian presence, 'witnessed with a sort of paralysed quiescence by the native peoples', loomed like a 'thunder-cloud over the land'. Russia had made significant advances in this direction in recent years; and there was every reason to believe that her ambitions fell as yet short of realisation. Those ambitions were, he thought, 'distinctly, and in parts avowedly, hostile'. If the Persians were unwilling or unable to defend themselves, others must clearly do so in their place. There could be no excuse, he thought, for 'any supineness in developing ... Anglo-Indian influence'; the preservation of the integrity of Persia, rather, must be a 'cardinal precept of our Imperial creed'. Persia, he believed, was a country in the shaping of whose future the British nation had it 'in their power to take a highly honourable lead' (Curzon was understandably distressed by the Persians' tendency to 'mistake interest for self-interest in others').[25]

In this period of office as Viceroy Curzon urged a definite policy to check the advance of Russia towards India through Persia and Afghanistan; and he authorised an expedition to Tibet in 1903-4 to assert British interests in the face of what he believed to be a Russian threat.[26] The Anglo-Russian Convention of 1907, dividing Persia into spheres of influence, aroused his deepest misgivings. An agreement with Russia, he had written, was 'one of those sentimental hallucinations that ... it is impossible to remove from the British mind'. The Convention itself, he charged, had 'thrown away to a large extent the efforts of our diplomacy and our trade for more than a century'; nor did he feel at all sure that the treaty in its Persian aspect would 'conduce either to the security of India, to the independence of Persia or to the peace of Asia'.[27]

Harcourt, reading Curzon's 'Russia in Central Asia', wrote to him to beg that the author would 'not make war on Russia in my lifetime'.[28] Curzon was never in fact to do so; but he was among the most vigorous champions of the anti-Bolshevik forces in Russia inside the Cabinet, and he had little sympathy with Lloyd George's subsequent attempts to seek agreement with what he termed 'that deplorable government at Moscow'. H. G. Wells, who had visited Russia in 1920, obtained an interview with Curzon on his return. Wells reported his conviction that, whatever its imperfections, the Soviet government was the only possible government in Russia, and that, whatever the personal feelings of British ministers, it was essential to work out a *modus vivendi* with them. Curzon, Wells later told Maisky, was 'simply unable to understand me. For him, Bolshevik Russia was simply a criminal, which had as quickly as possible to be destroyed.'[29] He consented to the conclusion of the trade agreement only with the greatest reluctance; and not for nothing, perhaps, did Krasin describe it as an 'agreement concluded against Curzon'. The Foreign Secretary, he noted, had been 'unable to prevent its conclusion, but he managed to spoil it [by] inserting the right to break if off on the initiative of either side'. Indeed the undermining of Russia, in Radek's view, was and remained the 'basic idea of Curzon's foreign policy'.[30]

'From the moment of the formation of the new [Conservative] Cabinet', wrote M. N. Pavlovich, 'British policy towards Russia began to be directed by the Minister of Foreign Affairs Curzon, who under Lloyd George's premiership had been unable in the period of the Genoa and Cannes conferences to manifest his bitter hostility towards Soviet Russia, having been restrained in this connection by the Prime Minister, who had not given his Minister of Foreign Affairs an opportunity of initiating a decisive struggle with Russia'. Before Curzon there 'always stood the spectre of a Russian threat upon the approaches to India. This *eastern* policy was the basis of Curzon's hatred of Soviet Russia, which took part in eastern affairs, it is true, not as a competitor to England in a struggle *for the division of the yellow continent*, but, on the contrary, as a good genie, a true friend and *ally* of all the exploited peoples of the East in the struggle with world imperialism and, above all, with England, the main enemy of the emerging East. Bolshevism only multiplied by ten Curzon's hatred of Russia, increasing his Russophobia to extreme bounds.'[31] It was therefore understandable that when Lloyd George's moderating influence was removed in the autumn of 1922, British policy towards the Soviet government became both more sharply hostile and more generally preoccupied with the fate of the British Empire in the East.

Ronald McNeill, Curzon's deputy at the Foreign Office in Bonar Law's administration, was asked in the House of Commons in November 1922 whether the new government intended to continue the policy of its predecessor with regard to Soviet Russia. His response was not a direct one. McNeill noted, however, that the question of diplomatic recognition could not be considered until the Soviet government had adopted a more accommodating attitude on a number of important issues. These, Bonar Law informed the House, were the recognition of debts, the restitution of nationalised property (or at least effective compensation), and the cessation of political propaganda. Failing satisfactory assurances on these points, he went on, it was not proposed to re-open negotiations with a view to the resolution of matters remaining in dispute between the two governments.[32] The Foreign Office was in any case of the opinion that commercial relations with Russia were 'in no way limited by the fact that the Russian government [had] only been recognized "de facto" and not "de jure"'.[33] Even the continuation of relations upon this basis, in fact, began to appear in doubt, as Soviet trade officials found entry visas increasingly difficult to obtain.[34]

In part the change represented a reaction against the over-cordial relations which Lloyd George was believed to have maintained with the Soviet government. In part also it reflected the dissatisfaction of business and trading circles at the pace with which trade between the two countries was developing, and at the failure of negotiations in October 1922 between Leslie Urquhart, a major figure in the mining industry in pre-revolutionary Russia and one of the most prominent private claimants, and the Soviet authorities.[35] Krasin, at his own request, was received by a Foreign Office official; but not, as had previously been the case, by the Prime Minister and his Cabinet colleagues. He wrote to Moscow on 23 January 1923: 'Practically we have no political relations at all with England at the moment, and as I expected, Bonar Law and his Cabinet colleagues display no wish to meet or negotiate with us'.[36]

The new position emerged more clearly in the course of the arrangements which were made for a conference on the Near Eastern question, which was to meet at Lausanne in the late autumn of 1922. Berzin, the deputy official representative in London, reported to Moscow on 27 September 1922 that he had gained the impression that it was not proposed to invite the Soviet government to the conference. Lloyd George, he wrote, was believed to have favoured their invitation, but Curzon had been strongly against it; and no answer had yet been received to the Soviet notes of 12 and 24 September, in which the Soviet government had strongly pressed its claim to participate.[37] In a further communication of 19 October, Chicherin again expressed concern that, despite her special interest in securing a peaceful solution to the Near Eastern problem, no answer had yet been received to the Soviet government's expression of a desire to take part in the conference, which was shortly to begin its work.[38]

On 27 October 1922 a reply was received from the governments of Britain, France and Italy, recognising that the question of the straits required particular consideration and the participation of states which had not been party to the recent Turkish-Greek hostilities. The Soviet government was accordingly invited to send delegates to the conference for the purpose of discussing that part of its proposed agenda. Chicherin in reply declared 'completely improper and in no way justifiable' the exclusion of the Soviet representatives from the discussion of other questions, and he continued to insist upon the participation of Soviet representatives in the work of the conference upon an equal basis with the other participating states.[39] In a further note of 24 November, however, despite the continued refusal of the inviting powers to accept this proposition, Chicherin announced that Russia would after all be represented at Lausanne by a four-man delegation. No official notification of the opening date of the conference had been received; but it was apparent from reports in the press that it had, in fact, already begun its work. The Russian delegation would accordingly depart 'forthwith'.[40]

Curzon explained to the Cabinet that he 'anticipated nothing but hostility' from the Soviet representatives at the conference. Lloyd George had worked 'indefatigably and sincerely' to reach an agreement with Soviet Russia, from the signature of the trade agreement to the conferences at Genoa and The Hague. Curzon nevertheless believed the Soviet government 'still to be in a position of special and inveterate hostility towards the British

Empire', and he expected their representatives at Lausanne strongly to oppose any British initiatives. Their goal, he declared, 'had always been Constantinople'. The Bolsheviks were 'Communists with wide Imperial aspirations', and any solution of the problem of the straits other than a Russian solution would be 'incompatible with Soviet dreams'.[41] Naval intelligence, he told the Cabinet, had already reported a 'close association by the Soviet government with the Turkish nationalists, with strong indications of support'. He now proposed to attempt to 'bring about a break between Turkey and her Soviet allies'.[42]

In this object he was largely successful. The Turkish representatives, despite their obligation under the terms of the 1921 treaty with Russia to consider the question of the straits the proper concern of all the states which bordered upon the Black Sea, accepted the British rather than the Soviet draft convention on the matter and began separate negotiations upon the basis of Curzon's draft. The Soviet delegation, moreover, was not admitted to the second stage of the conference proceedings, which began on 23 April 1923, on the grounds that the question of the straits was not upon the agenda. On 24 July the participating states concluded a peace treaty, and a convention on the straits question, based largely upon Curzon's proposal, was accepted. The Lausanne convention was formally signed in Rome on 14 August 1923. It was not ratified by the Soviet government.[43] Chicherin, who sought and obtained an interview with Curzon during the course of the conference, remarked that the Soviet government 'had the impression that [the present British government] were more hostile than their predecessors'. Curzon agreed that 'no Prime Minister could have been more disposed towards close relations with Russia and certainly none had worked harder to achieve them than Mr Lloyd George, both because of his broad conception of European policy, and because his personal attitude towards the Soviet government had been more elastic than that of some of his colleagues'. Curson added that, for his part, he had been 'primarily responsible for paragraphs in the trade agreement renouncing political propaganda against the British Empire, notably in the East'.[44]

Relations with Soviet Russia had meanwhile become such that Commander Kenworthy thought it necessary to call for a debate in the House of Commons on the 'present policy of this country with regard to Russia'. British interests, he thought, demanded a 'clear, settled and sagacious policy' towards the Soviet government, one which should endeavour to support the moderates, who were becoming more powerful, and avoid 'playing into the hands of the extremists'. The government, however, had 'gone out of its way to pin-prick and annoy the Russian government and people in every possible manner'. In the Near East, the Soviet government had been 'insulted and affronted'; and at Lausanne, Curzon had deliberately attempted to humiliate their representatives. Krasin had requested an interview with the Foreign Secretary or with his Under-Secretary following the recent change of government; but this had been refused. British merchants and business concerns, the government's attitude notwithstanding, were continuing to do business with Russia; but they had found, 'as a rule, that such little attention and assistance as they can look for to our indeterminate mission is diminishing'. Business people, he thought, were suffering from the absence of regular relations between the British and the Soviet governments.

McNeill, replying for the government, expressed a belief that 'one of the most essential necessities of any government' was 'some definite civilized legal system, especially one to which traders can look for the enforcement of contracts, since trade rests upon contracts, and for a definite civilized administration of justice'. Such a system did not exist in Soviet Russia. It was, moreover, the 'greatest possible delusion' to suppose that propaganda had stopped, or that the Soviet government had honoured its promises in this respect. It had, further, been responsible for a series of 'barbarities with which the whole civilized world is at present disgusted and dismayed'. As long as such policies were pursued, the Soviet government could seek no further degree of recognition from the British government than that which it had already obtained.[45]

The succession of events which so distressed McNeill, and which led directly to the presentation of an ultimatum to the Soviet government at the beginning of May 1923, had their origin in the immediately preceding years. The case of Mr C. F. Davison, which the government now espoused, dated in fact from as early as September 1919, when Davison had been arrested and imprisoned by the Soviet authorities. He had been shot four months later. In the absence of a full statement concerning this 'outrageous crime', Curzon wrote to Chicherin on 2 October 1920, the

British government would be forced to conclude that murder in cold blood had been committed, and it would demand 'full compensation'.[46] Chicherin replied that Davison had, in fact, been involved in a 'notorious fuel scandal', part of the proceeds of which he had devoted to counter-revolutionary activity. He had been properly sentenced in accordance with prevailing legislation.[47] Curzon, undaunted, returned to the charge in January 1922. Davison's death, he wrote, represented 'nothing less than the judicial murder of a British subject under revolting circumstances upon trumped-up evidence'. The British government reserved full liberty of action; and should the evidence against Davison, upon examination, prove invalid or insufficient, full compensation would be demanded. Failing this, every publicity would be given to this 'scandalous case'.[48]

The claim to examine the evidence upon which Davison had been convicted was not accepted. The Soviet government, Litvinov pointed out, might equally demand to examine the evidence against Russian citizens who had been executed by the British authorities prior to the signature of the Anglo-Russian Trade Agreement, in particular the 'most scandalous' case of the twenty-six Baku commissars, who had been killed in September 1918 with the complicity of the British military authorities.[49] Litvinov was told in reply that a 'careful examination' of the matter had led the British government to conclude that these charges were 'baseless' and founded upon 'deliberate misstatements'.[50] He continued to maintain, however, that it had been an 'undeniably premeditated crime', and added that in the absence of conclusive evidence the charges would not be withdrawn.[51]

The case of Mrs Stan Harding was raised in the House of Commons on 23 March 1921. A British subject, reportedly 'by no means anti-Soviet' in her views, she had gone to Soviet Russia in June 1920 as a correspondent of the New York *World*.[52] She had subsequently been detained there for five months, and accused of being a member of the British intelligence service. The charge, Harmsworth assured the House of Commons, was completely without foundation.[53] The government did not intend to seek redress, however, Mrs Harding having proceeded to Russia 'on her own responsibility and with a safe conduct from the Bolsheviks at a time when it was known that His Majesty's Government refused to give passport facilities for Russia'. Further Parliamentary pressure followed; and it was eventually agreed that if

Mrs Harding herself lodged a claim for damages, the government would consider it. Representations were meanwhile being made on her behalf.[54]

Curzon raised the matter in a letter to Chicherin on 3 September 1921. Mrs Harding's case, he wrote, was giving rise to 'pressing questions' in the House of Commons; and the government considered that it was of 'such a nature that the Soviet government should meet it by exceptional measures'. Mrs Harding, he noted, had been arrested, placed in solitary confinement, given a 'verminous plank bed', and accused of being the head of the British secret service organisation in Russia. She had been allowed to return to Britain only at the end of November 1920. Hodgson was authorised to endorse Mrs Harding's statement that at no time had she been a member of the secret service; and he was instructed to seek compensation 'commensurate with her sufferings during imprisonment on a false charge whilst visiting Soviet Russia with the explicit approval of that Government'. A 'very unfortunate impression' would be created, in view of the 'wide notoriety' of the affair, were the justice of her case not admitted.[55]

Hodgson was obliged to report in reply that his representations had been to no avail. Litvinov had pointed out that at the time in question a state of war had been in existence between the two countries; and he had added that the Soviet government might wish in its turn to press charges against the British government. Litvinov subsequently quoted the case of Babushkin, a Russian consul in Meshed, Persia, who had been arrested, together with his staff, by the British military authorities on 25 October 1918.[56] Two months later Lloyd-Greame announced in the House of Commons that the government did 'not consider that any useful object would be attained by pursuing this matter further with the Soviet government'. Mrs Harding's claims would be considered together with other private claims when the time came finally to resolve such questions.[57] There, for the time being, the matter rested.

The position of the church in Soviet Russia provided a further source of dispute. Early in 1922 the Soviet government had decreed that the sale of church treasures should be undertaken in order to provide for famine relief. This initiative had been originally proposed by a group of churchmen, noted *Russian Information and Review*, and it had been approved by almost all the clergy,

Patriarch Tikhon among them. There were precedents for such action: bells from certain churches, for instance, had been melted down to make cannon for Peter the Great's army. Local Soviets were to collect the church treasures and hand them over to the Commissariat of Finance, which would accept them on behalf of the Central Commission for Famine Relief. The details were to be published in the local press, and a religious representative was to be included upon the body which was to review and examine the appropriations. Articles of particular religious significance were to be excluded.[58]

In a few places the local clergy had opposed the removal of the treasures; but church sentiment as a whole, according to *Russian Information and Review*, had generally supported the government's decision. Articles to a total value of some twenty million gold roubles had been received by the beginning of April 1922. In some cases, however, church treasures had unaccountably disappeared before the commissions arrived to collect them;[59] and Patriarch Tikhon (a figure, *Pravda* noted, with a counter-revolutionary past) had gone so far as to issue an appeal to remove them from the churches. Following discussion with representatives of the clergy the Patriarch was eventually persuaded to resign.[60] He was brought to trial in May 1922, but discharged following his unconditional disavowal of counter-revolutionary activity.[61]

On 1 June 1922 the Archbishops of York and Canterbury and other British church dignitaries addressed a 'most serious protest' to the Soviet authorities concerning this 'attack upon the Russian church in the person of Patriarch Tikhon'.[62] Karakhan, replying on behalf of the Soviet government, retorted that no attack had been made upon the church as such: charges had simply been preferred against some of its members, the former Patriarch among them, on the grounds that they had opposed government decrees which had themselves been designed to 'save the lives of tens of millions of men and children'. In the dispute only the more privileged sections of the hierarchy of the church, those which had in the past been closely connected with the Tsarist nobility and the capitalist order, had taken the Patriarch's side: and it was precisely this section of the Russian church, rather than the population as a whole or even the majority of the clergy, on whose behalf the British ecclesiastics were now interceding. They had not, he noted, felt it necessary to protest against the blockade, which had been maintained by the British government, and which had brought considerable hardship to Russian workers and peasants and their families.[63]

Matters became worse in March 1923 when Archbishop Cieplak, Monsignor Butkevitch and a number of priests of the Polish Roman Catholic Church were brought to trial on a charge of espionage and other treasonable activities during the civil and Russo-Polish wars.[64] The British agent in Moscow, McNeill told the House of Commons, had 'unofficially represented to the Soviet Government, early in the proceedings, the lamentable impression which would be caused on public opinion abroad by such action'; and he had that day been instructed to continue his efforts. The Russian trade representative had similarly been 'asked in a friendly way to do anything he can to avert a disastrous sentence'. 'Thousands' had been executed in Russia, *The Times* observed, 'simply because they believed in God'.[65]

The trial, Hodgson reported to Curzon, was 'only an incident in a campaign undertaken by the Soviet government which has as its definite object the destruction of religion in Russia'. The clerics, however, were not guiltless in terms of Soviet law (although it could reasonably be argued that that law itself was 'tyrannous and unjust').[66] They had in fact opposed decrees separating church and State, and the appropriation of non-essential church valuables for famine relief; and Monsignor Butkevitch had in addition been in touch with the Polish government during the hostilities of 1920.[67] The trial opened on 21 March 1923, and six days later both men were given death sentences. The Archbishop's sentence was subsequently commuted, but Monsignor Butkevitch's was confirmed. The British agent in Moscow, the House of Commons was informed, had done 'all in his power', under 'repeated instructions' from London, to save the ecclesiastics from these 'barbarities'.[68]

The question of fishing rights and territorial waters further complicated relations between the two governments. In March 1922 a protest was made concerning the arrest of two British-owned vessels, the 'Magneta' and the 'St Hubert', off the northern Russian coast. The owners of the 'Magneta', which sank in a storm while in Soviet custody, subsequently claimed compensation from the Soviet government. The House of Commons was told that the government could not 'assume any special responsibility in this connection',[69] although it did not accept the Soviet authorities' claim, on the basis of which their action had been taken, to a twelve-mile territorial limit.[70] It appeared, however, that the 'St Hubert' had been fourteen miles from shore at the time of its arrest, and further representations were made by the British agent in Moscow.[71] Both cases were taken up in a communication of 15 March 1922. The 'Magneta' had been arrested between nine and ten miles from shore, the Soviet authorities were informed, and it had therefore not infringed the three-mile limit. The Foreign Office was prepared to consider the elaboration of a convention to regulate fishing along the northern coast; but it could not accept a territorial limit greater than three miles, and it could not therefore concede that the ships in question had been fishing in Soviet territorial waters. The 'St Hubert' had to be released forthwith, and compensation paid to its owners and to those of the 'Magneta' and its crew.[72]

The Commissariat for Foreign Affairs, in its reply a week later, pointed out that the position in international law was unclear: a three-mile limit was not universally recognised, and the British government had indeed been willing to review the whole question in conference before the war. The Soviet government, it represented, had been acting within its rights in claiming a twelve-mile limit on the northern coast in its decree of 24 May 1921, thus safeguarding the sole means of livelihood in this area. It had been in accordance with this decree that the British vessels had been arrested.[73] Hodgson's reply continued to dispute the legitimacy of a twelve-mile limit, and refused to accept that the vessels had been fishing illegally. In the absence of an assurance that such a course of action would not be repeated, it was announced that a British naval vessel would be despatched to these waters, the commander of which would be instructed to take such action as might be necessary to protect British fishing boats outside the three-mile limit.[74] This amounted, as Karakhan pointed out, to an attempt forcibly to impose a three-mile limit upon the Soviet government. Retaliation was threatened.[75]

The British government continued to insist that the Soviet authorities bore responsibility for the loss of the 'Magneta': it had been compelled while in custody to remain in dangerous waters, while other ships in the vicinity had been free to proceed elsewhere.[76] The Soviet reply, however, refused to accept either direct or indirect responsibility, and thought further correspondence superfluous.[77] All the British fishermen arrested by the Soviet authorities were in fact released in February 1923; but on

31 March a steam trawler, the 'James Johnson', was arrested off the Murman coast. 'Immediate inquiries' were ordered in Moscow.[78]

It was in fact the religious issue which was taken up in Hodgson's letter to Chicherin of 30 March 1923. It contained an 'earnest and final appeal' for a stay of execution in respect of the sentence passed upon Monsignor Butkevitch. The implementation of the sentence, the letter declared, could 'not fail to produce throughout the civilized world a feeling of horror and indignation'. The reply which was received the following day noted with asperity that Soviet Russia was an 'independent country and a sovereign state', and had the 'undeniable right of passing sentences in conformity with its own legislation on people breaking the law of the country'. Any attempts from outside to interfere with this right or to 'protect spies and traitors in Russia' would be considered an 'unfriendly act and a renewal of the intervention which has successfully been repulsed by the Russian people'. In view of the actions of the British government in Ireland, India and Egypt, moreover, appeals from that quarter in the name of humanity and the sacredness of life were considered particularly unconvincing. Hodgson declined to receive the note. Weinstein, for the Soviet government, nevertheless continued to assert that the original communication had constituted an 'entirely inadmissible attempt at interference in the internal affairs of the independent and sovereign RSFSR'; and he indicated that other means would be found to acquaint the British government with the contents of the note intended for it.[79]

The maintenance of the trade agreement itself now began to appear in doubt. The question of its annulment, Bonar Law assured Arthur Henderson on 19 April 1923, had not yet come before the Cabinet; and the approval of the House of Commons would in any case be sought before action of this kind were undertaken. The prosecution of the Russian ecclesiastics, the arrest of the British trawlers and the violation of the conditions of the trade agreement, he warned, were nevertheless 'serious questions'.[80] The termination of relations with the Soviet government, indeed, was at this time under discussion within the Foreign Office. It was a weapon which could be used only once, Gregory noted, and it should therefore be 'used only if and when there is a reasonable chance of upsetting the Soviet Government or at least of dealing an effective blow at its stability'. That moment, he thought, had not yet arrived.[81] Curzon, however, believed that the British mission in Moscow should be withdrawn, in the event, at least, of members of the Russian trade delegation being asked to leave Britain. Hodgson was asked whether he thought the British mission in the Soviet capital had 'any real justification'.[83]

Relations meanwhile continued to deteriorate. The Cabinet discussed the seizure of the 'James Johnson' on 25 April. It was agreed that the Foreign Secretary should prepare, for the consideration of the Cabinet, a draft despatch to the Soviet government, quoting the 'numerous recent incidents' of an 'unsatisfactory and discourteous attitude' on their part. It should make reference to the arrest of the trawlers, the execution of Mr Davison, and 'propaganda contrary to the Trade Agreement, the studied insolence of the replies of the Russian Soviet government to our representations regarding the trial of Russian ecclesiastics, and any other similar cases'. It should be made clear that if an acceptable reply were not received within a certain period of time, 'our present de facto relations would be severed'.[83] This was a 'great opportunity for us who would like a break anyhow', commented Gregory in a Foreign Office minute; 'I cannot believe that we shall ever get so good a one again'.[84]

The state of relations with Soviet Russia was discussed the same day in the House of Commons. McNeill drew attention to a 'series of acts committed by the Russian Soviet government, of which British subjects have been the victims', which had 'excited the profound indignation' of the government and of the country at large. These incidents testified to a state of affairs which demanded, and which was receiving, the 'earnest attention' of the government. They could not be considered or treated separately, he believed: they were rather 'parts of a whole directly affecting the relations between HMG and the Soviet government'. It was proposed to address a 'serious communication' to the Soviet government dealing with these matters. In the meantime, the British agent in Moscow would 'not cease to exert his influence in the strongest possible manner' in the case of the 'James Johnson', where the action of the Soviet authorities was 'wholly without justification'.[85]

McNeill's 'serious communication' was discussed by the Cabinet on 2 May 1923. The draft of a despatch to the Soviet government was approved, after a number of amendments had been adopted. The advantages of basing the published British case upon 'actual extracts from the despatches which had passed between the Soviet government and its agents' was considered to outweigh the possible disclosure of the secret source from which the despatches had been obtained, 'more especially as this was actually known to the Russian Soviet government'. It was agreed to add to the end of the despatch a passage to the effect that if 'satisfactory treatment was not given to the demands of HMG the Anglo-Russian Trade Agreement would be terminated under Article xiii of the Agreement and that not only would the British Trade Mission be withdrawn from Moscow, but the Russian Trade Mission would have to leave London'. The British agent in Moscow was authorised to 'take such steps as he thought advisable to facilitate the departure of British subjects, and in any event to warn all British subjects in Russia confidentially that within ten days of the receipt of the despatch by the Russian Soviet government it was not improbable that the Anglo-Russian Trade Agreement would come to an end'. The Home Secretary was instructed in the meantime to keep the members of the Russian trade delegation in Britain under observation, 'in order that if any attempt should be made to detain the British Trade Mission in Moscow or other British subjects as hostages, such corresponding actions might be taken here as should prove feasible'.[86]

Curzon on the same day sent a copy of the memorandum to the British agent in Moscow, with instructions to communicate it to the Soviet government. If no reply were received in the following ten days, he was advised to return to Britain with all the members of his staff. He should act in the same sense if a 'clearly unsatisfactory' reply were received.[87] The memorandum itself—the 'Curzon note'—was handed to the Soviet authorities on 8 May. It began by taking exception to the 'tone and character' of the notes recently received by the British agent in Moscow from the Soviet Foreign Affairs Commissariat, and considered it doubtful, with regard to these and a 'large number of similar incidents', whether relations between the two countries could continue upon such a basis. The British government, the note declared, could no longer with 'due self-respect continue to ignore the repeated challenges' which the Soviet government had 'thought it fit with apparent deliberation to throw out', and a 'definite conclusion' was now sought.

A 'series of outrages' had been inflicted upon British subjects in the course of the previous few years, the note continued, for which no apology had been offered and no compensation had been given. The most notable cases were those of Mr Davison and Mrs Harding. The British government was 'unable to allow the matter to be trifled with any longer'; liability must be admitted forthwith and compensation paid accordingly. In contravention of generally accepted conventions of international law, moreover, a series of acts had been perpetrated by the Soviet authorities involving a 'wholly indefensible interference with British shipping and acts of indignity against British subjects'. The cases of the 'Magneta', 'St Hubert' and the 'James Johnson' were recalled; and an assurance was sought that compensation would be paid, and that British fishing vessels would not in future be interfered with outside the three-mile limit.

In the case of the trial of the Soviet ecclesiastics, further, while the British government had refrained from expressing an opinion upon the nature or validity of the charges brought against them, it was bound to take exception to a 'deliberate campaign undertaken by the Soviet government, with the definite object of destroying all religion in Russia, and enthroning the image of godlessness in its place'. This had excited the 'profound consternation and ... provoked the indignant remonstrance of the civilized world'. The correspondence which had ensued, moreover, had been 'not merely inconsistent with that standard of courtesy which ordinarily prevails in the relations between governments' but had actually placed the continuance of those relations in 'grave jeopardy'. The withdrawal of Weinstein's two communications was accordingly demanded.

More important was the question of the observance of the obligation contained in the terms of the trade agreement to 'refrain from hostile action or propaganda', an undertaking which, while 'loyally and scrupulously observed by HMG', had been 'consistently and flagrantly betrayed by the Soviet government'. Following the correspondence which had taken place in the autumn and winter of 1921 there had been 'some slight curtailment' of the activities of Russian agents in Asia, the Soviet authorities 'apparently realising that the Trade Agreement, from which they derived such substantial advantage, might be imperilled by unduly rash conduct'. These 'pernicious activities', however, had recently been 'vigorously resumed', especially in Persia,

Afghanistan and the Indian border areas. The Russian minister at Teheran, for instance, had been 'tireless' in his activities: he had assisted Indian revolutionaries, and had attempted to stir up anti-British movements and rebellion with the sums of money which had been sent to him by the Soviet government for that purpose. In Afghanistan an 'even more favourable base for enterprise' existed, owing to the proximity of the turbulent tribes which inhabited the Indian border areas, and Raskolnikov, the Soviet representative at Kabul, had 'distinguished himself by exceptional zeal' in this connection. Some two-thirds of the spending of the Legation, it was believed, had been devoted to such subversive purposes.

The Soviet government, the note went on, had 'not failed to carry its efforts further into India'. Seven Indians, trained at Tashkent and Moscow as 'Communist agitators', had been arrested in November 1922 on their arrival from Moscow; and a number of one hundred pound banknotes, originally issued to an official of the Russian trade delegation in London, had been cashed in India 'on behalf of a revolutionary Punjabi in touch with other Indian seditionaries who are known to have been closely associated with the Russian representatives in Kabul'. Further funds were believed to have been allocated by the Fourth Congress of the Communist International for the support of the British and Indian Communist parties, and for the despatch to the countries of the East of sixty-two Oriental students 'trained in propaganda schools under the Third International'. These, the note concluded, were 'but a few selected examples among many scores of similar incidents', relating to Egypt, Turkey, the British Dominions, 'and even Great Britain'. Unless such acts were apologised for and repudiated, and the officials responsible for them 'disowned and recalled from the scene of their maleficent labours', it would be impossible to continue with an agreement 'so one-sided in its operation'. Unless within ten days of the receipt of the memorandum the Soviet government 'fully and unconditionally' complied with its terms, the trade agreement would be regarded as terminated.[88]

The terms of the note were warmly commended by the Association of British Creditors of Russia, by religious opinion, and by a large section of the press.[89] The memorandum, the *Economist* noted on 12 May, was 'not a model of moderation'; the Foreign Office, it believed, had now made up its mind to bring the agreement to an end. The *National Review* urged the government to remain firm in 'seeking redress for the outrages in Lord Curzon's powerful indictment'. 'However popular a parliamentary performance', it noted, the 'eating of one's own words is never an effective diplomatic operation'. Once the British government began to discuss the matters at issue with the Soviet authorities, however, J. D. Gregory had noted, they would lose their 'chance of dealing with them in the way we had contemplated, as we can hardly impose a second ultimatum once a discussion has begun'.[90] This weakness in the government's position soon became apparent.

The Soviet response was deliberately conciliatory in tone. The British government, Chicherin told the Moscow Soviet on 12 May, was composed of 'extreme reactionaries' who were badly informed concerning the situation in Russia, and believed that Lenin's recent illness had seriously weakened the Soviet state. Their early hopes that the New Economic Policy represented a capitulation to capitalist forces had been disappointed, and a mood of disenchantment had accordingly set in. Their willingness to contemplate a rift, however, was opposed not only by the workers and by the Liberals, but also by a section of the Conservatives themselves.[91] Litvinov's reply, accordingly, professed to regard with surprise the 'sharp and unjustified hostility' of Curzon's note. Ultimata and threats, he suggested, were not the most appropriate way of dealing with 'private and relatively unimportant misunderstandings between states'. The British government had derived some benefit, as had the Soviet government, from the operation of the trade agreement. The establishment of peaceful relations with Soviet Russia was besides a 'most necessary factor for peace and for the re-establishment of [the] economic well-being of all [the] countries of Europe in which to no small extent Great Britain is interested'.

There had, moreover, been not a few instances in the previous two years of challenges on the part of the British government 'not only to [the] Soviet government, but also to [the] whole Russian people'. These included the disregard for the interests of Soviet Russia in the settlement of a large number of international questions, and the 'intense activity' of British agents in the Caucasus and elsewhere. The accusations contained in Curzon's note were in any case a 'combination of invention, with deciphered parts of telegrams tendentiously manipulated and arbitrarily extended'. The British government must know better than any other, if it was correctly informed, that the Soviet government sought the establishment of friendly relations with the peoples of the East 'not by intrigues and gold, but by measures of real unselfishness and friendly feelings towards them'. The British note appeared to imply that the Soviet government should 'have no policy of its own at all in the East, but should everywhere support English aspirations'. The Soviet government could accept no such obligation.

Apart from the trawlers, Litvinov went on, the infringements of the rights of private citizens which had been quoted in the British note had occurred before the trade agreement had come into force, and before the Soviet government could be considered bound by its provisions. It was nevertheless willing to offer compensation, provided this treatment was extended to analogous Soviet cases. The question of territorial limits should be discussed at an international conference called for this specific purpose. The further charge of the persecution of religion in Russia was baseless; and it had been the British government's apparent desire to interfere in this way in an internal matter which had accounted for the admittedly unusual tone of Weinstein's first letter. It had, however, been returned to him, and might now be regarded, together with his second letter, as 'non-existing'. The matters in dispute were in fact so insignificant in comparison with the possible consequences of a rupture that their settlement might easily be arranged at a bilateral conference, which might also 'regularize Anglo-Soviet relations in their full extent'.[92]

The trade delegation made an effort at the same time to mobilise public opinion in Britain, 'not only in the working class, but even in the liberal-bourgeois trade world', against the inflexible position adopted in Lord Curzon's communication.[93] Krasin, who gave an interview to the press on 13 May 1923, declared that the breaking-off of relations would have 'catastrophic consequences' which it would be 'impossible to foresee'. There could certainly be no doubt that all trade between the two countries would cease, in the absence of a legal basis for commercial transactions; and the Soviet government would no longer be obliged to refrain from anti-British action and propaganda in the East. He pressed these views personally upon Lloyd George, Commander Kenworthy, Alfred Mond and Sir Allen Smith of the

Engineering Employers' Federation.[94] Only the trade agreement, the deputy trade representative, Berzin, told the press, made possible the existence of trade between the two countries. If British businessmen considered that its annulment would not affect that trade, they were making a serious mistake.[95] Such trade as was conducted with Russia, the *Economist* conceded, small though it was, would be made much more difficult if a reversion occurred to the position which had existed before the trade agreement had been concluded. The rupture, it added, would prove 'most acceptable to certain Bolshevik extremists and it would be a definite setback to the N.E.P.' The government should be 'guided in this matter by the realities of the situation rather than by the dictates of passion and righteous indignation'.[96]

On 14 May Curzon informed the Cabinet of the 'general tenor' of the Soviet reply;[97] and the following day he gave the Cabinet a detailed criticism of its contents, 'exposing in each case the weaknesses of the argument and the lack of foundation to each of the counter-accusations against the British government, as well as pointing out that there was only one item in which the demands of the British government had been met, namely, the release of the captured trawlers and their captains and crews'. Curzon was authorised, nevertheless, to grant an interview to Krasin if one were requested. He should continue to insist upon acceptance of the demands contained in the British note as a condition of the continuance of the trade agreement; but Krasin should be allowed at least 'a few days' in order to communicate with the Soviet government.[98]

Replying to Parliamentary criticism later the same day, McNeill pointed out that 'from the very first this question of cessation of propaganda was part and parcel of the Agreement itself'. The Soviet government, however, had never observed its obligations in this regard. It was 'out of the question' to provide proof of origin for the statements quoted in the British note such as would satisfy a court of law; but he insisted upon their 'absolute trustworthiness', and maintained that to withdraw from the demands which had been made was 'impossible'. The Soviet reply on the questions of propaganda, compensation for private citizens, and the trawlers, moreover, had been 'entirely unsatisfactory'. There had been 'instance after instance' of propaganda against British interests, added Lloyd-Greame, in Afghanistan and in India, 'encouraging insurrection against the British

Dominions'. In the meeting with Krasin, arranged for 17 May, the government would require satisfaction in 'all the essential respects'.[99]

Parliamentary support for the government's action was by no means unanimous. Lloyd George urged that 'every caution' be taken lest the 'extremists' in Russia be encouraged. Sir Allen Smith, representing mercantile opinion, noted that the ending of the trade agreement would mean handing over the British position in Russia, both present and potential, to other nations. British traders would be 'entirely separated from what might be our very best and most profitable market'. Other MPs voiced the concern felt by local manufacturers and working people at the possible loss of the Russian trade, and with it the prospect of a significant reduction in the level of unemployment. Stanley Baldwin, Chancellor of the Exchequer, reserved the government's right to act as it saw fit; but he implied that the Cabinet was not unmindful of the considerations suggested by its critics. He hoped, he told the House of Commons, that the government would find that their demands were 'met fairly and reasonably, and that . . . a rupture may not be essential'.[100]

The meeting on 17 May failed to produce a reconciliation; but it was agreed that Krasin should be given time to communicate with his government, and that a further meeting should take place. *The Times* judged that the original time-limit would 'not now be enforced'.[101] A breach became even less likely when on 22 May Baldwin, rather than Lord Curzon, succeeded the ailing Bonar Law as Prime Minister. Baldwin, observed Narkomindel, represented business circles which did not wish to 'complicate their position by a conflict with us'. The assumptions governing the actions of Curzon, on one hand, and of Baldwin, on the other, noted *Izvestiya*, reflected the 'interests of two different sections of British capitalism'. The group behind Curzon's policy was interested primarily in the colonial trade; whereas behind Baldwin stood 'trading and industrial capital, which does not want to lose European markets [and] considers that the markets of the British Empire are insufficient'.[102]

'We must try to avoid a break with Russia', the new Prime Minister told Thomas Jones on 28 May. 'Curzon will see Krasin and try to arrange the withdrawal by the Soviet government of their Afghan propagandist agents'.[103] Two days later he told C. P. Trevelyan that he 'had hopes of avoiding the breach with

Russia'.[104] Baldwin, the *Manchester Guardian Commercial* noted, came to politics 'fortified by long business experience and an uncommon share of the gifts of common sense and shrewdness. His attitude has already been made apparent upon the question of Anglo-Russian trade. Mr Baldwin . . . is alive to the dangers involved for this country in the breaking-off of relations with Russia. His influence may, therefore, be counted upon to combat the possibly unintentional but undoubtedly provocative stiffness of our Foreign Office in its dealings with the Soviet Republics.'[105]

A further conciliatory memorandum followed from Krasin on 23 May 1923. In the interests of avoiding the breaking-off of relations a number of new concessions were offered: a three-mile limit would be observed until a conference had regulated the matter definitively; compensation would be paid to the injured parties as the British government had specified; and Weinstein's two letters would be withdrawn. The question of propaganda in the East, it was suggested, should be discussed independently.[106] These concessions, noted the British reply of 29 May, 'in large measure' satisfied the claims which had originally been made, and no 'insuperable difficulties' appeared to remain. The question of fishing in northern waters appeared to be capable of resolution in the manner proposed; and what were held to be 'moderate claims' of three and ten thousand pounds were advanced on behalf of Mrs Harding and Mr Davison respectively in the interests of a swift settlement. The 'unqualified withdrawal' of Weinstein's letters was noted with satisfaction.

There remained, however, the 'all-important question' of hostile propaganda against the British Empire and British institutions. There had been 'no satisfaction whatever' on this point, upon which the fate of the trade agreement depended. An assurance must be given that the Soviet representatives against whom protests had been lodged, Shumiatsky and Raskolnikov, would 'within a reasonable space of time be transferred to some other areas where their duties will not bring them into contact with British interests' (although their dismissal was not specifically required). A new declaration upon the question of propaganda was attached for the Soviet government's endorsement, reiterating the obligations contained in the trade agreement and undertaking 'not to support with funds or in any other form persons or bodies or agencies or institutions whose aim is to spread discontent or to foment rebellion in any part of the British Empire . . .

and to impress upon its officers and officials the full and continuous observance of these conditions'.[107] This, the Cabinet agreed, was a 'pivotal issue between Great Britain and Soviet Russia'.[108]

The Soviet government expressed its 'entire satisfaction' that a number of points in dispute appeared to have been resolved; and it agreed to pay the sum of compensation which had been suggested by the British government in the cases of Mr Davison and Mrs Harding. It agreed also, in deference to the wishes of the British government, to take the 'extremely major step' of accepting the proposed declaration in regard to propaganda, despite the fact that it altered and extended the obligations originally contained in the trade agreement with regard both to the area to which it applied and to the nature of the undertaking.[109] The Soviet government, Curzon told the Cabinet, had now 'given way on every point with one partial exception'. The wider definition of propaganda, in particular, had been accepted. Agreement had not been reached on the Cabinet's original demand that the Russian representatives at Kabul and Teheran be transferred elsewhere; but it had been learned that the Russian representative at Kabul was in any case in Moscow, and would not be returning to his post. Curzon was asked to note this fact in his reply, and to state that if the Soviet representative in Teheran became involved in further anti-British activity, 'the delinquent should be expelled from the service'.[110]

Curzon communicated a memorandum on these lines to Krasin on 12 June 1923; and with it the correspondence, it was suggested, might be 'brought to a conclusion'. Chicherin continued to insist that the question of the recall of Raskolnikov was an internal matter, which could not be discussed with a foreign government; but it was not denied that he would not, in fact, be returning to Kabul, and Russian diplomatic representatives would be instructed strictly to observe the terms of the understanding which had been reached.[111] This, noted Litvinov, was the 'final chord in all the music about Lord Curzon's "notes"'.[112] While the government did not consider, Baldwin told the House of Commons, that a conference with representatives of the Soviet government could at present usefully be convened, agreement had at least been reached upon certain specific issues. The negotiations with regard to the trade agreement, the Cabinet noted with satisfaction on 20 June, 'were now completed'.[113]

Curzon was congratulated by Baldwin at the Cabinet's meeting on 11 June on the 'highly successful issue of these difficult negotiations'. Curzon himself wrote to Lord Crewe that he thought he could 'claim to have won a considerable victory over the Soviet government'; and he expected them to 'behave with more circumspection for some time to come'.[114] So far as they could be expected to go, noted the *Economist,* 'short of abject humiliation', the Moscow government had gone. *The Times* considered that a 'very satisfactory measure of success' had been achieved. While not wholly breaking with the policy of the Coalition government, the Foreign Office had nevertheless 'shown a refreshing vigour and resolution in dealing with a Government which has displayed special enmity towards the British Empire'.[115]

To a contemporary Soviet observer it appeared, on the contrary, that the cautious and conciliatory policy of the Soviet government had succeeded in averting the danger of a rupture of relations, upon which the British government appeared to have been resolved.[116] Hodgson, moreover, reported from Moscow that it had been decided to recall both Raskolnikov and Shumiatsky even before the ultimatum had been delivered, as a result of complaints regarding their activities from the Afghan government (Bolshevik propaganda, he remarked, was 'a nuisance not only to Great Britain, but to everyone else as well').[117] Raskolnikov, however, remained formally at his post until the end of 1923, and Shumiatsky was still at Teheran the following year. The assumption of the Premiership by Baldwin, Chicherin considered, a representative of business circles interested in the development of trade with Soviet Russia, had forced Curzon to compromise. The Soviet government had yielded on a number of secondary points, but had refused to recall the two diplomatic representatives, as the British government had demanded.[118]

Nor did it appear that the main aim of the ultimatum, the humiliation of the Soviet government in the East, had been accomplished. Soviet relations with Afghanistan were in fact reported to have improved as a result of the ultimatum; and the reaction of Persian public opinion, and of traders and merchants, had been sharply critical of it. Trade negotiations between the Soviet and Persian governments, which were in progress at this time, duly resulted in the conclusion of a treaty the following year.[119] The period following Curzon's ultimatum, Chicherin told

Arthur Ransome, had seen not the deterioration, but the strengthening of relations with other countries, and the conclusion of new and far-reaching agreements.[120]

It was too soon, however, to conclude that the crisis was over. Following the transfer of Krasin to Paris, Christian Rakovsky was appointed to take his place as the head of the Russian trade delegation in Britain. Rakovsky was formally invested with his new responsibilities on 23 July 1923, after the British representative in Moscow had informed the Foreign Affairs Commissariat of the willingness of the British government to receive him.[121] A diplomatic passport was issued in his name and Rakovsky was ready to leave, when on 1 August a polemical attack upon his appointment appeared in the *Morning Post*. Rakovsky was alleged to have declared, in a speech at Kharkov, that the highest point of the revolutionary movement in England was approaching, that the British Empire was on the point of collapsing, and that his official position could be used to spark off a revolution. Reference was also made to a collection of his speeches which had recently appeared, entitled 'England and Russia', which contained a sharp attack upon British imperialism and urged the rejection of Curzon's ultimatum.[122]

A question was asked about his appointment on the same day in the House of Commons; and on 2 August the Foreign Affairs Commissariat was informed that the British government now refused to accept Rakovsky into the country.[123] An urgent telegram was despatched to Hodgson, instructing him to make 'immediate investigations' into the *Morning Post*'s allegations, and, if they proved well-founded, to inform the Soviet government that the British government took so serious a view of the incident that they could not now contemplate receiving in London a person 'so unlikely to conduct the trade relations with their country in a loyal or acceptable manner'. Rakovsky was to be warned not to leave until the matter had been cleared up; and on 3 August the Home Office was advised that he should if necessary be refused permission to disembark at the ports.[124]

Chicherin wrote to the British representative on 9 August to protest against the decision. Rakovsky's speech had been misleadingly quoted, he insisted, and the statements which appeared in the collection of his speeches had been made at a critical moment in Anglo-Soviet relations and before his appointment had been announced.[125] Hodgson, meanwhile, reported that he had examined the papers in question, but that he had found 'no expressions of Rakovsky in the least resembling those quoted by [the] *Morning Post*'. It appeared that Rakovsky had, on the contrary, made clear that he could not, as an official representative of the Soviet Russian government, interfere in British internal affairs. Hodgson had as yet been unable to locate the collection of speeches which the paper had mentioned.[126] Four days later, however, he reported that the pamphlet—which he had now been able to examine—was being withdrawn, and that the Soviet government had in any case been 'really unaware of its existence'.[127] Leeper noted in a minute regarding the booklet, of which the Foreign Office had obtained a copy, that Rakovsky had spoken at a moment of crisis (following the murder of the Soviet diplomat Vorovsky in Switzerland: the pamphlet had black borders), and at a time when he bore no official responsibilities. He concluded that if they really wanted to 'get rid of the very unsatisfactory Trade Agreement, then this incident is not quite big enough to afford the necessary leverage'.[128]

Berzin, the Soviet deputy trade representative in Britain, wrote to the *Morning Post* on 10 August 1923, pointing out that its evidence appeared to have been derived from the Riga *Poslednia Novosti* of 28 July, a publication 'notorious for its unscrupulousness and mendacity'. A Foreign Office representative visited the *Morning Post*'s editor and found the paper's explanation for the whole affair 'very thin'. It was 'difficult to avoid the conclusion', he concluded, that the *Morning Post* had been 'tricked and that they have no corroborating evidence'. Rakovsky's visa, Leeper believed, could now no longer be withheld, notwithstanding the fact that the paper was 'still hopeful' that evidence to sustain its charges would eventually be found.[129] The Foreign Office accordingly informed Peters in Moscow on 30 August that the government was now 'prepared to accept Mr Rakovsky'.[130]

Not once in the three months following, however, was Rakovsky received by the Foreign Secretary, on the tenuous ground that he was not the diplomatic representative of a fully recognised state.[131] The Foreign Office, indeed, found some difficulty even in accepting that Rakovsky ought properly to be adressed as the diplomatic representative of the USSR, following the agreement to form a federal union reached by the RSFSR and three other republican governments of 30 December 1922, communicated to the governments of the world on 13 July 1923.[132] The 'obvious propagandist element' in the change of name was noted, and anxiety was expressed lest its use might appear to legitimate Soviet territorial annexations. It was accordingly proposed to ignore the new development by continuing to address Moscow as the Russian Soviet government, rather than as the government of the USSR, and subsequent communications to Rakovsky were couched in these terms.[133] The Soviet government, moreover, McNeill informed the House of Commons, had 'not yet fully implemented all the undertakings given to it in the course of the correspondence which took place earlier in the year'. The government intended not to relax its efforts to obtain the full satisfaction promised at that time.[134]

Conservative policy was nevertheless not so united in intent as these uncompromising declarations might have suggested. For Curzon, noted Radek, had been unable to bring about a rupture; and this had been 'because the industrialists, forming part of the membership of the English Conservative party, considered to what it might lead. It is sufficient to read the articles of Garvin in the *Observer* [which had opposed the termination of the agreement] to see that in the camp of the Conservatives there is disagreement. Curzon was defeated in his own party, because industrial circles did not want to leap with him into the unknown. From their point of view they were completely right.'[135] These divisions emerged more clearly in the heated discussions which began to take place around the question of the diplomatic recognition of the Soviet government, a proposal first seriously mooted in the latter part of 1923 and canvassed with an increasing degree of energy up to the Labour government's decision to this effect in February 1924. These discussions and the decision to which they led will be considered in the third part of this study, 'Labour, Business and Recognition'.

Part III

LABOUR, BUSINESS AND RECOGNITION

7 'Entente Commerciale'

Curzon's uncompromising attitude towards the Soviet government during the latter part of 1922 and the early part of 1923 found a generally favourable response in business and financial circles. The *Manchester Guardian Commercial*, in a survey of business opinion conducted in May 1923, found only a small (though none the less distinct) body of opinion in favour of the retention of the trade agreement. Businessmen were more inclined to the view that the loss of Russian orders at their existing level would 'make little difference and would certainly not affect employment in this country'. Opinion (the journal added the following month) was 'for the most part, unfavourable to the Anglo-Russian Trade Agreement'.[1] The financial world was no more enthusiastic. The Association of British Creditors of Russia wrote to the Foreign Office that an attempt to secure a *modus vivendi* with the Soviet government was 'quite futile', and urging that the British mission in Moscow be withdrawn forthwith. Its representations were supported by the London Chamber of Commerce.[2] A meeting convened by the Association, at which a representative of the Federation of British Industries was present, was 'unanimous in denouncing the existing agreement with Russia as an agreement which legalized the robbery of British nationals, which action has helped to finance the Bolshevik government since the signing of the agreement'.[3] The attitude of City financial circles towards Russia more generally, the *Westminster Gazette* observed, was 'one of complete aloofness'.[4]

Business opinion, however, was by no means unanimous. At the height of the crisis precipitated by Curzon's ultimatum the 'Becos' group, an amalgamation of engineering firms with a close interest in the Russian trade and a share capital in excess of fifty million pounds, circulated a memorandum among MPs which strongly opposed the threatened rupture in relations. Such a course of action, the group believed, would be to the detriment of British trade generally, and would have a particularly adverse effect upon the shipbuilding industry and shipping (about a hundred British vessels had been engaged by the Soviet authorities in 1922), and upon those factories with which Soviet orders had been placed.[5] Merrifield, Ziegler and Company, a 'leading firm of cotton brokers and merchants' in Liverpool, wrote directly to their MP (who forwarded the letter to the Foreign Office) to inform him that large contracts had been concluded with the Soviet authorities, and asking him to use 'all [his] influence to prevent a commercial rupture between this country and the Soviet Government'.[6] Sir Allen Smith of the Engineering Employers' Federation wrote to Bonar Law in the same sense. He was 'much concerned to hear that there is a proposal to cancel the Russian Trade Agreement', Smith told the Premier. 'In view of the work being done for Russia here and the orders we have recently received for manufactures I hope that we shall not lose the only sheet anchor we have. I say nothing about the political situation in Persia, Afghanistan and the East—my concern at the moment is with trade. I hope my impression is wrong'.[7]

The possible impact of a rupture in relations upon British industry received further consideration in a memorandum prepared by the Board of Trade. It noted that a number of projects which were 'sponsored to the knowledge of the department by first-rate firms' were currently under negotiation, and that they showed 'reasonable chances of success'. Some older firms were interesting themselves again in Russian trade; and there was a 'strong demand for practically all the classes of goods that Russia is likely to be in a position to export in the near future'.[8] A meeting was held in the Foreign Office on 11 May 1923 to consider the implications of a rupture. It was told by the Board of Trade representatives that, if the Russian trade delegation were expelled, it was likely that British firms which had concluded contracts with it would 'in some cases apply for special permission for members of Arcos to remain behind'. The Board of Trade, a minute noted, recognised that 'political considerations must predominate', but it did 'not pretend to like' the possibility that the Russian trade delegation might ultimately be expelled.[9]

The following month the Association of British Chambers of Commerce submitted to the Foreign Office the views of firms and Chambers of Commerce throughout the country upon the question of relations with Russia. Most approved of the government's firm approach. The trade agreement had 'not advanced the interests of British trade in the manner anticipated', the secretary of the Russo-British Chamber of Commerce informed Curzon on 17 May. The Birmingham Chamber was also in 'general agreement with the terms of the Note'.[10] Dundee Chamber of Commerce, however, expressed the view that it 'would give a great fillip to trade' were it found possible to place commercial relations with Russia upon an 'ordinary permanent basis'. Ruston and Hornby, a Lincoln manufacturer of agricultural and other equipment, added that anything which retarded the recovery of trade with Russia would be a 'great deal to our detriment'. They would lose substantial contracts which were 'on the verge of maturity', and their business in general would suffer 'definite and grave injury'.[11]

The major banks were similarly aware of the need to restore European trade, and especially trade with Soviet Russia. Addressing the annual meeting of the Midland Bank at the beginning of the year, Reginald McKenna, himself a former Chancellor of the Exchequer, pointed out that foreign trade had such 'exceptional importance' that anything that inhibited it must 'deeply affect our national prosperity'. The situation in central and eastern Europe, he pointed out, was 'not only destructive of our markets there, but must also hamper our export trade more or less all the world over'. The chairman of Martin's Bank added that the unsettled nature of relations with Soviet Russia was among the factors which had 'greatly interfered with the machine tool industry and with other sections of the engineering industry'. Foreign trade, indeed, commented the chairman of the National Provincial Bank, was the 'very lifeblood of our industries'. No improvement could be expected until some settlement had been effected in the 'distressed countries of Europe'.[12]

These views came to enjoy an increasing degree of support within the commercial and manufacturing world; and it will be suggested that the 'entente commerciale' which thus developed must be considered among the factors which contributed most significantly to the decision to confer diplomatic recognition upon the Soviet government in February 1924. The Conservative Party, traditionally the custodian of business interests of this kind, was not prepared in this instance to accommodate itself to their requirements. Members of the Conservative government such as Baldwin, who had a business background and substantial industrial interests, appear to have been not unsympathetic to the case for improved relations with Soviet Russia. With Curzon at the Foreign Office, however, supported by a substantial section of opinion within the party generally, it proved possible only to secure the retention of the trade agreement, not to advance beyond it and—if commercial considerations thus dictated—to confer full *de jure* recognition upon the Soviet government.

The 'entirely different standards of diplomacy' which appeared to determine relations with the Soviet government, compared with those employed in other cases, impressed the diplomatic correspondent of *Contemporary Review*. The 'City, the industrial North and progressive opinion throughout the country', he noted, supported the government's policy in western Europe, which appeared to aim, as they did, at the restoration of peace-time conditions and the recovery of trade. The same groups, however, were 'perplexed by the inconsistency of the Government in its dealings with Russia', where its policy was the 'despair of all those who realize the importance of the present opportunity for British markets in Russia'.[13] As this and the following chapter will be concerned to demonstrate, it was in fact necessary for a Labour government to be elected before commercial interests of this kind could exert their customarily predominant influence upon British relations with governments abroad, and with the government of the USSR in particular. The Tories were divided on the Russian question by the rival claims of trade and finance; only Labour was able to champion the interests of merchants and manufacturers without equivocation, the more so as the relief of unemployment was held to depend upon their success. The diplomatic recognition of the Soviet government in February 1924 was the product of this incongruous conjunction of interests.

Developments within Soviet Russia at this time afforded some encouragement to those who advocated the extension of commercial and other relations with its government. NEP had been a disappointment, and the conferences of 1922 had found the Russians unwilling to accept economic realities as western governments perceived them. A number of currency and financial reforms which were introduced during 1922 and 1923, however, suggested that the immutability of economic laws might at last be securing a degree of recognition in Moscow. A State Bank had been established in October 1921. During 1922 a number of other banks were set up to assist the development of industry, such as

Prombank and Elektrobank, and a Co-operative Bank was established with the participation of private shareholders as well as of the State Bank. A new currency unit was also introduced, the *chervonets*, backed by gold, as a step towards the creation of a stable currency and a balanced budget.[14] The reforms were a 'great step forward', the *Economist* commented; they showed a 'very strong desire to put the finances on a sound basis, similar to that existing in other countries'. [15] Much of the banking machinery which had earlier been destroyed, commented the *Financial News*, was 'gradually being restored, even though its control is in other hands'. Although much remained to be done, the *Economist* added, it was 'gratifying to note' that the first steps had already been taken towards a 'return to a regime of free enterprise'.[16]

The introduction of the new currency was particularly welcome. This was an 'achievement of the greatest importance', the *Economist*'s Russian correspondent pointed out, indicating as it did that a stable paper standard might be established. The new system was a 'great step forwards' in the direction of a return to normal and stable conditions. *Lloyds Bank Monthly* added that 'for its purpose, the *chervonets* appears to be effective as a currency medium, and is therefore one big step in the direction of Russian economic rehabilitation'.[17] British banks quoted exchange rates with the *chervonets* from the autumn of 1923, and at no time up to the spring of the following year did the rate fall below parity.[18] The new currency had 'achieved some success', commented the *Financial Times*; its performance should be 'followed with close attention by all who look to the effective return of Russia to the markets of the world'. The *Glasgow Herald* concluded that a 'real evolution towards the re-establishment of a normal economic regime', based on 'private initiative', was taking place.[19]

Trade with Soviet Russia, meanwhile, began to assume more considerable proportions. For the year 1921, taken as a whole, imports from Russia were valued at £2,694,674 and exports at £2,181,007. These figures represented almost entirely transactions made after the end of March, upon the basis of the trade agreement. During 1922 a further advance was recorded. Imports from Russia rose by more than three times to a total value of £8,102,829, while exports increased nearly twofold to a figure of £3,640,624.[20] Comparing the first six months of 1922 with the corresponding period of the previous year, imports from Russia had increased more than two times in value; while exports and re-exports had increased by a much greater factor, as much as fourteen times, the trade delegation's journal calculated.[21] In the following year British exports to Russia declined slightly (to £2,491,650), but imports rose by more than a million pounds (to £9,266,100), and the total volume of trade between the two countries was scarcely affected.[22]

British trade with Soviet Russia remained only a small proportion of British foreign trade as a whole. In the year 1923, for instance, imports from Russia amounted to less than 1 per cent by value of total British imports, while exports to Russia represented an even smaller percentage of total British exports.[23] Trade with Britain accounted for a rather larger proportion of total Soviet foreign trade. In 1921, for instance, Britain accounted for nearly half of Soviet Russia's imports, and nearly a third of Soviet exports; and more trade was done with Britain than with any other foreign country.[24] The value of Soviet trade with Britain dropped slightly below that of Soviet trade with Germany in 1922; but in the 1923/24 trading year the value of Soviet trade with Britain again exceeded the value of Soviet trade with any other foreign country, and the same was true of the following year.[25] Soviet exports to Britain, which had originally been exceeded in value by Soviet imports, now constituted the major part of trade between the two countries.[26]

The export of a number of commodities increased markedly during 1923 and 1924. Soviet exports to Britain of wood and wood products, for instance, rose in value from two and a half million pounds in 1922 to three and a half million pounds in 1923 and to nearly five million pounds in 1924, significantly increasing the Russian share of total British imports.[27] The value of Russian barley imported into Britain increased by more than ten times between 1922/23 and 1923/24, and the value of butter imports increased almost in proportion. The export of eggs increased approximately sixfold in value, and the export of Russian wheat to Britain increased in value from a quarter of a million roubles to nearly ten million roubles in the same short period. As a whole, the value of the export of foodstuffs increased from seven to over sixty million roubles.[28] In many cases these figures amounted to only fractions of the corresponding figures for 1913; but they were rapidly increasing, and at least in the case of oil, textiles, wood and foodstuffs, had already come to occupy a significant place in total British imports.

The development of Soviet trade with Britain was paralleled by an expansion in the operations of the Soviet trading apparatus in Britain and in particular of Arcos, the first Soviet export-import organisation to be established and 'practically the only institution' trading in Britain in 1921.[29] It began to make purchases in October 1920, and nearly two million pounds' worth of orders had been placed by the end of the year.[30] The value of purchases the following year amounted to £4,777,918.[31] Sales did not reach these dimensions before the conclusion of the trade agreement, but business steadily increased thereafter and 'substantial sales' were recorded during the last quarter of the year. The most important item of trade was timber.[32] The total turnover of Arcos amounted to over nine million pounds in 1921, nearly fourteen million pounds in 1922, nine and three quarter million pounds in 1923 (sales increased but purchases declined), and to nearly six million pounds in the first half of 1924. This represented an increase in business, compared with the same period of the previous year, of 10.3 per cent.[33]

Arcos swiftly extended its operation beyond the borders of the United Kingdom, opening offices and agencies in Constantinople, Paris, New York, Riga, Moscow, Leningrad, Tiflis, Rostov and elsewhere.[34] A series of more specialised joint-stock companies was also established. Some, such as 'Kniga', established in November 1923 to cater for the import and export of books, were based upon Russian-owned share capital only.[35] Arcos Bank, similarly, was set up on 5 July 1923 with a fully paid-up capital of £250,000, charged with the issuing of travellers' cheques valid for Soviet Russia and generally with facilitating trading operations.[36] 'Rusangloles', however, set up in February 1922 to handle the export of wood, was a 'mixed' company, with a large (minority) British ownership of the share issue. Foreign (non-Russian) capital accounted for 14.5 per cent of the total share capital of the twenty trading companies set up in this and the two following years.[37]

Arcos remained the most important Soviet trading organisation in this period, with sales amounting to 45.2 per cent of the sales of all trading bodies in Britain. A clientele was reported to have been established among the 'oldest, most eminent English firms'.[38] Arcos was refused membership of the London Chamber of Commerce at the beginning of 1923; but indicative of the change in business opinion was the establishment of relations between the Russian State Bank and Lloyds Bank the following October. Moves, moreover, were made to establish an Anglo-Russian Chamber of Commerce,[39] and a meeting was held in Moscow on 25 October which approved the formation of an eight-man organisational bureau.[40] Arcos had itself obtained a trading credit of £875,000 with a number of major British banks by the summer of 1923.[41] Altogether, reported Narkomindel, a 'definite improvement' took place in economic and political relations between the two countries from the summer of 1923 onwards, as British trading and manufacturing circles became 'more and more interested in the USSR'.[42]

A major role in this connection was played by the visit to Moscow in August 1923 of a group of prominent British financiers and industrialists on behalf of Becos Traders Ltd. The delegation was headed by F. L. Baldwin (a cousin of the Prime Minister), the chairman of Becos Ltd. and a director of Kenrick and Sons and of Baldwin and Company. Another leader of the delegation and director of Becos Brothers, A. G. Marshall, had been involved in the organisation of Russian trade in 1918 on behalf of the British government, and was a familiar (if not always a welcome) figure in the Foreign Office.[43] Becos Traders itself was an amalgamation of some eighty-two member firms designed to 'serve its Members as their co-operative selling organization for Russia and the adjacent territories'.[44] The delegation, whose object was to examine the 'conditions in Russia and the possibilities of business between Russia and Great Britain, particularly as regards the Metal, Engineering and Hardware Traders', left London on 9 August and arrived in Moscow on 14 August 1923. It conducted discussions with Krasin regarding Russia's economic needs, and Marshall, in a further interview on 15 August, considered a number of specific business proposals suggested by the Soviet authorities. The delegation also met Chicherin, Dzerzhinsky and the Soviet government's Concessions Committee. Kamenev discussed the reform of the currency with the delegation's members; and further more specific discussions took place with regard to possible orders and business contracts.[45]

The delegation, the *Manchester Guardian Commercial* reported at the end of August, was 'coming back disillusioned'.[46] It soon became clear, however, that this was an unduly hasty verdict. Marshall in fact had already informed a Soviet interviewer that the delegation was returning with 'most favourable impressions';[47] and while the report issued by the delegation on its return did concede that no definite contracts had been signed, it went on to state that the signature of such contracts was imminent and that they might be expected to lead to 'satisfactory business'. The delegation's overall conclusions, moreover, were distinctly favourable ones. The condition of the country, it noted, had been and was 'still being improved very rapidly, and every effort that is possible in this respect is being made by the Government'. State control of industrial activity, it added, had been considerably reduced and would rapidly disappear in all but a number of exceptional cases. The delegation approved the government's policy of balanced budgets, increased taxation and reduced expenditure; and thought the currency reform so far successful.

There was above all 'no question' in the minds of the delegation as to the 'enormous market offered by Russia for British goods of all classes'. Russia, moreover, offered 'very considerable opportunities for the purchase, at reasonably low prices, of raw materials from Russia required for this country's industries'. The development of trade with Russia, the delegation was convinced, should be 'extremely rapid and most advantageous in connection with the unemployment difficulties in this country'. They had themselves discussed proposals of an important nature involving large sums of money, agreement upon which would 'result in considerable benefits to industry in this country'. The delegation recommended the conclusion of a financial agreement between the two countries, and the negotiation of a treaty which would include 'full diplomatic relationships'.[48]

A Foreign Office official commented that the report had been 'given a great deal of publicity in the papers, and [had been] brought personally to the Prime Minister's attention by his cousin Mr F. L. Baldwin'. He now understood how it was, Curzon minuted, 'that the Prime Minister made so enthusiastic a reference to the future of trade with Russia in a recent speech'. Indeed it was precisely the prominence of the delegation's members in British industrial life, Marshall told *Izvestiya*, which guaranteed that the visit would bring about 'more normal relations between Russia and England not only in the field of trade and industry'.[49] The Foreign Office remained unimpressed. Business opinion, however, was more receptive to the delegation's optimistic conclusions, and to the news that it had been thought worthwhile to leave an office staff behind in Moscow. Orders to a total value of some twenty million pounds had been received in Russia, it was later learned, subject only to the availability of credits.[50]

Interviews with individual members of the delegation reinforced this favourable impression. J. M. Denny, the deputy chairman of Denny and Brothers, a Clydebank shipbuilding firm, reported that the Soviet authorities had been 'extremely anxious to do business' with them. He had been 'agreeably surprised . . . to find that all the churches seemed to be well attended'; and generally he had been 'impressed with the great potentialities of Russia'.[51] J. J. Carter, the managing director of Crossley Brothers, told the *Manchester Guardian Commercial* that business would 'be done shortly'. If trade developed with the Soviet authorities, they were 'confident of a straight deal'. The delegation's secretary told a *Daily News* reporter that 'every unbiased person who visits Russia must arrive at a similar conclusion'.[52] Marshall and Baldwin, the delegation's leaders, declared themselves particularly impressed with the efforts which had been made to stabilise the Russian currency and to balance the state budget by cutting expenditure and raising taxes, and they praised the organisation of the State Bank. It had been a 'constant remark' among them that they 'only wished the Germans were handling their currency problems as well'.[53]

Baldwin, at a press conference which the delegation arranged on its return, reported that there was a ready market in Russia for agricultural machinery and for commodities connected with rail or road transport, and also for sawmill plant and mining equipment. A 'tremendous demand' existed besides for the 'ordinary necessities of life', for which the Russians, he thought, were looking 'to this country'.[54] The delegation's members, Marshall added, were 'unanimously optimistic' as to the future; the position was 'distinctly good'. The Russians, he reported, were now making 'every effort . . . to denationalize affairs and return once more to fair methods of international trading'. In the opinion of the British visitors, Russia was 'now shaping her policy much on British lines', and there were 'considerable opportunities' for the development of trade.[55]

Marshall explained his views in more detail to the Sheffield Chamber of Commerce on 24 October 1923. Speaking to a resolution calling upon the government to facilitate the development of trade with Russia, he began by arguing that the Russian government's political views 'had been tried out and failed'. The Bolsheviks had gradually had to abandon the political and social policies adopted during the period of the revolution: 'in other words', he declared, 'Communism was no longer existing in Russia'. Concluding amid cheers, he expressed the hope that 'political matters would not be allowed to interfere with their interests as manufacturers and as traders'.[56] Marshall prepared a 'Memorandum regarding Unemployment and Russia' on 5 November, copies of which he sent to the Prime Minister, Lloyd-Greame, Sir Sidney Chapman and other government ministers, and to the Foreign Office. The memorandum was intended to show that the development of the Russian market offered a 'reasonable substitute' for Germany in foreign trade. Trade with Russia could not be classed as a 'mere palliative', Marshall believed: it was actually 'in the nature of a remedy' for unemployment. No financial arrangements such as those proposed in his memorandum, however, would be possible without the 'full diplomatic recognition' of the Soviet government.[57]

The Becos Traders' report, the Russian trade delegation reported, together with a 'whole series of interviews' given by members of the delegation, had aroused 'exceptional interest in both business and political circles' in Britain.[58] The group's reports upon the economic position of Russia and on the possible acceptance in Russia of British capital had produced a 'great impression in English trading and manufacturing, and financial circles'; it marked a 'definite change in their attitude towards the USSR'.[59] A report of the delegation's conclusions and of an interview with its members appeared in some forty London and provincial papers, many of which commented upon the issues editorially and extended their support to the delegation's call for closer economic relations with Soviet Russia.[60] In the course of only four days in November 1923, no fewer than eighty-five articles devoted to this issue appeared in the British press. The delegation's report, the *Daily News* noted editorially on 5 September, had excited 'extraordinary interest' in commercial circles and beyond them; even the City was 'by no means hostile'. The Becos report, added the *Financial Times*, might be expected considerably to accelerate the development of trading relations between Britain and Soviet Russia. The opinion of the responsible leaders of the business world, in turn, could not fail to have some influence in official circles.[61]

The delegation's formal report was issued on 19 November 1923. The Soviet government, it declared, was 'not only accepted by the people but meets with their approval'. Prospects for the development of trade with Britain, moreover, were 'extremely good', since the goods required by the Soviet authorities were precisely those which Britain was best placed to supply. The only significant obstacle to the development of this trade, Russia's lack of credits, did not appear an insurmountable one.[62] Marshall returned to Russia the following spring to continue discussions on behalf of Becos Traders. The group now embraced more than a hundred and twenty firms and more than two hundred factories and works in Britain. Their visit of the previous summer, he noted, they rightly considered to have 'significantly influenced the recognition of Soviet Russia by England'.[63]

The Becos delegation was present at the opening of the All-Union Agricultural and Handicrafts Exhibition in Moscow on 19 August 1923. If nothing else, they reported, it demonstrated a 'very considerable amount of organization'.[64] Marshall himself thought the significance of the Exhibition 'very great'; it 'showed foreigners how enormous were the natural resources of Russia'.[65] The Exhibition's foreign section was opened on 26 August, in the delegation's presence. Both Marshall and Baldwin declared themselves 'greatly impressed' by it.[66] The Exhibition itself was intended to review the state of Soviet agriculture generally and to promote improved methods of cultivation and husbandry. It was considered essential to have a foreign section at the Exhibition in order that Russians might familiarise themselves with the current state of agricultural science abroad, while foreign exhibitors might have an opportunity to 'evaluate us as a market and as a field for capital investment, of which we are in great need', and to display new types of seed and breeds of animal. The Exhibition, it was hoped, would play an 'enormous role in the strengthening of economic links between the USSR and European countries', whose major industrial concerns appeared not yet to have realised that the Russian market was 'one of the most important factors in the economic stability of Europe'.[67]

The decision to hold the Exhibition was taken by the Presidium of the Central Executive Committee on 20 October 1922.[68] At the beginning of the following year regulations were approved for the participation of foreign exhibitors in the fair. It was decided that they should be accorded all the assistance which was to be available to Russian exhibitors, and provided with transport ahead of turn. Local bureaux were set up in eighteen foreign countries, carrying out their work under the guidance of the Exhibition Committee and of Narkomindel.[69] The regulations for foreign exhibitors were printed in the journal of the trade delegation in Britain in March 1923.[70] Manufacturers of agricultural equipment were urged 'not to miss the opportunity of getting into touch with the Russian markets', for there was an 'immense and growing potential market for western manufactures' among the Russian peasantry.[71] An Exhibition Committee was formed in London in the middle of the same month, consisting of Klishko as chairman, two associates and a secretary. Special cards were inserted into each letter despatched from the trade delegation office, and details were provided for the press.[72]

British industry appears initially to have regarded the project with no great enthusiasm, and the FBI refused to organise a delegation. Attempts were made to get in touch with firms which might be willing to exhibit, but in view of the crisis in relations between the two countries the response was 'not very satisfactory'.[73] In some places, the bulletin of the Central Exhibition Committee noted, the work of local committees had been 'complicated and hindered owing to difficulties in the international position of the USSR'. This had affected work in Britain in particular; orders from this quarter had begun to be received 'only recently'.[74] Following the easing of the diplomatic situation, however, the London committee renewed its contracts with possible exhibitors and made further approaches. Visits were made to firms; an English edition of the Exhibition Almanac was published; and Fridrikhson, the chairman of the Central Exhibition Committee, spent two weeks in Britain at the beginning of July, giving interviews to Reuter and to the Press Association. Segal, a member of the local committee, was interviewed in a number of financial and radical papers, and information was printed in others.[75]

'Some inquiries' had been received from British firms by the middle of April 1923.[76] In July, it was announced that companies intending to take part included Saville and Company, makers of instruments, Turnicraft, and the lorry manufacturing firm of Scammel. The firms of Lowry and Holloway were later added.[77] Reporting the opening of the Exhibition on 19 August,

Ekonomicheskaya Zhizn' noted that British firms represented included Vickers, Portland Cement and Ruston and Hornby, makers of agricultural equipment from Lincoln. The paper exaggerated somewhat in stating that British firms has shown a 'great
interest in the Exhibition'. A total of 401 foreign firms participated in the Exhibition, from some twenty foreign states. Nearly a
hundred of these, however, were from Germany, and there were
more exhibitors from France, Austria, Czechoslovakia, America
and Italy than from Britain, which provided no more than
fourteen; nor were British exhibitors involved in the construction
of any of the fourteen national or other pavilions in the Foreign
Section.[78] Among the British firms represented, moreover, were
many which had already established a close connection with the
trade delegation in London and had supplies orders for Arcos, as
Vickers and Ruston and Hornby, for instance, had done.[79]

The Exhibition was favourably commented upon during July,
nevertheless, by at least twenty major British papers;[80] and there
could be no doubt that the firms which undertook to participate in
the Exhibition, while in many cases renewing long-standing
connections with the Russian market, were present for other than
sentimental reasons.[81] The position of the most significant of
them, for instance, Vickers Metropolitan, was reported to have
been 'very bad' in 1921, essentially as a result of the decline in
foreign trade. In the following year the company's trading profit
was reduced; not one of its departments had a good year; and at
the shipbuilding section in Barrow the commercial position had
never been worse than during 1922 and 1923.[82] International
complications, equally, could 'not fail to affect a firm like Ruston
and Hornby', most of whose raw material came from abroad and
most of whose pre-war trade had been with foreign countries, in
particular with Russia. The immediate post-war years were 'sad
days' for this firm also: machinery had to be sold below cost price
to keep in business at all, and about two-thirds of the staff were
declared redundant.[83]

The representative of one of the British exhibiting firms, quoted
in the *Manchester Guardian* on 27 November 1923, expressed the
view that life in Russia was 'getting on to more normal lines'. As a
businessman, he had become convinced that an extension of trade
with that country was now possible; his own firm, at least, had
done a 'very satisfactory amount of business'. Altogether 456
trade contracts were signed in the Foreign Section in the course of

the Exhibition and immediately after its conclusion; and the Exhibition produced a favourable impression upon the Becos delegation, upon the exhibitors themselves and upon those who visited it, a number of whom were British.[84] In the latter part of July and August, noted the journal of the trade delegation, Moscow had been visited by the Becos delegation, by several merchants and by some members of Parliament. The city, indeed, might be said to have become the 'centre of interest for European and American traders, and for politicians and journalists concerned with economic revival and the renewal of friendly relations between peoples'.[85] As the Petrograd Chamber of Commerce's 'Directory for Russian and Foreign Businessmen' recorded, the mere fact of having attracted such a number of foreign firms to the All-Union Exhibition served as the 'best evidence of a near approaching intensive development of peaceful collaboration and intercourse between the Western Commercial and Industrial Circles and Soviet Russia'.[86]

The Soviet authorities were not unaware of what Krasin called the Exhibition's 'moral effect': the 'great impression which the simple fact of holding the Exhibition had upon all its visitors'.[87] In his speech at the opening of the Foreign Section, Krasin expressed the hope that it might serve as the beginning of 'yet further and closer economic relations' between Soviet Russia and those European countries whose traders were participating in the Exhibition.[86] Speaking on the 'significance of the Exhibition' three days before it opened, Chicherin observed that with every day the 'colossal importance' for the whole international position of Soviet Russia was becoming clearer, and the impression that it was creating abroad was becoming deeper and more distinct. The main cause of the strained relations which had recently existed with the western states, he thought, was their 'economic disenchantment': the feeling in business circles that the development of trading relations was advancing too slowly and was not providing them with the opportunity of 'receiving what they wanted'. The Exhibition, however, was a 'revelation', and the situation had now changed radically: to such an extent, indeed, that it might not be too much to say that it marked the 'beginning of a new period in our international economic relations'. He re-emphasised the point in an interview which was conducted after the Exhibition had closed.[89]

A further manifestation of the change in Anglo-Russian relations in the latter part of 1923 was the formation of the Russo-British Grain Exporting Company on 15 October.[90] The formation of the company was reported to have created a 'great impression, not only in the trading circles in England, but far beyond them',[91] British business, including two well-respected stockbroking firms, had invested fifty thousand pounds, or half its share capital, in the new body; four of its directors were British; and British banks, in an unprecedented gesture, had extended it a credit of some one million pounds.[92] This was reported to have created a 'sensation not only in directly interested circles, but throughout the English press'. Approval of the venture was practically unanimous.[93] Enquiries conducted in the City by the *Pall Mall Gazette* revealed 'tremendous interest' in the announcement, which had brought to an end a 'long series of delicate and intricate negotiations'. It demonstrated, the *Manchester Guardian* commented, that the City, at least, was convinced of the possibility of doing business with Russia. The *Gazette* 'confidently anticipated' that the agreement would have an 'appreciable bearing on the whole course of British trade'.[94]

According to Krasin, the new company's formation was widely considered the most significant new development since the conclusion of the trade agreement. The quality of the Russian bread and grain was considered excellent; and the company 'aroused great interest in European business circles'.[95] By the end of March 1924 over a million pounds' worth of bread and grain had been sold on the British market; and by the end of September a further million and a half pounds' worth had been sold. Sales amounted to 14.5 per cent of the value of all sales in Britain in the 1923/24 trading year. The working masses, Krasin observed, saw before them the fact that the Soviet Union was 'becoming the feeder of Europe'.[96] The business world and the shipping companies had equal reason for satisfaction.

The formation of the new company had more than a commercial significance; in particular, as the *Manchester Guardian Commercial* put it on 25 October, the formation of the new company raised 'in a practical form the question of the present diplomatic relations between Russia and this country'. The *Financial News* in an article published on 7 November entitled 'Trade with Russia: Is it Time for a Change of Policy?', pointed out that the banks were extending credit to the new company on ordinary commercial

lines, a proposition which they had previously refused to enter-
tain. The circumstances, it declared, 'if they have not politically
altered, have, nevertheless, commercially altered'. 'Nobody has a
greater repugnance to the Soviet system of government than we
have', the paper concluded, 'but we would urge, on purely
business reasons, that the facts must be faced. As a country whose
welfare depends on the maintenance of an active export trade, we
can ill afford to allow the Russian market to slip out of our grasp.'

The *Herald* quoted a 'well-known exporter' to the effect that it
was an 'amazing thing that—while everybody is coming to realize
that Russia should be one of our most important markets—the
Government still obstinately refuse to extend to Russian trade the
provisions of the Trade Facilities Act'. The new development, he
hoped, would induce ministers to 'change their minds, for it is
preposterous that their political dislike of the Soviet Government
should be allowed to hamper British trade'. The agreement, the
Observer added, had 'given a lead to the British Foreign Office.
Full commercial relations with the new Russia have now been
established, but full political relations still await establishment.'
The government, the *Spectator* thought, must 'seriously consider
putting the present rather anomalous sate of half-recognition of
the Moscow Government on a more definite basis. After all, the
Bolshevik Government is now the senior Administration of
Europe, and its hold upon the country seems as firm as ever'. The
journal could 'not help feeling that nothing would be lost, and
something might possibly be gained, by the resumption of formal
diplomatic relations'.[97]

Business opinion, in fact, had already sought to bring this point
of view to the attention of the government. Writing to Bonar Law
in December 1922 on behalf of the Industrial Group of the House
of Commons, Sir Allen Smith, of the Engineering Employers'
Federation, complained that the United States had 'to our very
great detriment succeeded in capturing a great deal of the Russian
trade which should have come to us. . . . Whereas with the old
diplomacy the pen was mightier than the sword, with the new
diplomacy we have to recognize that the treasury note is and must
be maintained of greater value than either the pen or the sword.'
The possibility of entering into trading relations with Russia, he
pointed out, depended in great measure upon the state of official
relations with that country. 'While we indulge in the old shib-
boleths of foreign diplomacy', Smith noted, 'other countries are

reducing their employment and I am afraid for some months at least we will increase ours'. Through this 'out-of-date diplomacy', he went on, 'we are cutting our own throats in the matter of present and future trading'. He had 'no doubt these considerations will appeal not in the least degree to the Foreign Office', but he was 'perfectly satisfied ... [that] there is no salvation for this country until the Foreign Office is thoroughly commercialized'. Bonar Law's own business experience, he concluded, should help him to 'appreciate that our diplomacy now must be made subservient to some extent to our commercial requirements'.[98]

Smith returned to the subject in July 1923, following a meeting of the Industrial Group in the House of Commons. In a letter to Baldwin on the Group's behalf, he pointed out that he had heard of no case in which the Soviet authorities had not respected their trading obligations. Orders to a value of between two and three millions pounds were pending, he believed, if the Export Credits Act were extended to trade with Russia. Failure to act, moreover, the Group warned, would 'entail irreparable harm to the "moral" of the workers, and a grave menace to the social and economic stability of the country'. Their views, Smith pointed out in a further letter of 3 August, carried the 'imprimatur of the leading industrial, financial and economic brains of the country'.[99]

Baldwin probably needed little persuasion. Another 'man of affairs', he had drawn attention in a speech the previous month in Glasgow to the fact that 'in Russia, we have one of the largest potential markets in the world'.[100] Sir Robert Horne, the former Chancellor of the Exchequer and still a figure of influence in Conservative circles, had a similar background (he was indeed among other things a director of Baldwins Limited) and appears substantially to have shared the Prime Minister's opinion with regard to relations with Russia. He submitted a memorandum to the Foreign Office in October 1923, for instance, which advocated the extension of the agreement with Russia.[101] Curzon, however, remained departmentally responsible for the conduct of foreign policy, and was considerably Baldwin's senior within the Cabinet; and his uncompromising attitude towards the Soviet government found a considerable degree of support within the Foreign Office, within the Conservative Party as a whole and in the country at large.

Financiers and creditors were also inclined to insist upon the unconditional cessation of propaganda and the acknowledgement of all debts and obligations before the extension of diplomatic relations with the Soviet government was considered. 'Trade between Great Britain and Russia could only be revived', a deputation from the Association of British Creditors of Russia told McNeill at the Foreign Office, 'when property belonging to British firms and individuals had been restored'. The Association sent a memorandum to the government on 17 January 1924 urging that recognition be withheld until satisfactory assurances had been received on this point.[102] While the Soviet government had 'to a certain extent modified some of its extreme views', the Council of Foreign Bondholders added in its Annual Report, 'it has not yet repealed the law repudiating its obligation to repay the money which Russia borrowed from foreign investors who trusted to her honour and good faith'. The Council trusted that no agreement would be entered into which did not provide for the recognition of these claims. The Soviet government must give 'tangible evidence of its honesty of purpose', insisted the *Financier*, 'before it will be entitled to recognition from this country'.[103]

'A million tons of grain', the *Russian Information and Review* commented, was nevertheless a 'powerful argument for converting stubbornly held political convictions';[104] and business opinion, together with the majority even of Conservative papers and journals, appears generally to have come to accept it by the end of the year. There was no sense, Garvin wrote in the *Observer* on 7 October, in the present position. 'We are sacrificing the interests of the Empire to etiquette, and the etiquette is as obsolete as the Bourbons. . . . Words cannot express the fantastic folly of allowing any removable hinderances to stand any longer between our workless masses and the Russian market. . . . We ought to have given full recognition long ago.' Discussions between the City and the Russian trade delegation, the paper noted on 14 October, revealed a 'recognition of mutual interest and a readiness to wipe the slate clean of all past grievances in order the more readily to reach an agreement. The City had been 'impressed partly by the reports of a number of highly competent observers, partly by the success of the revival of the Russian export trade in grain'; it now showed a 'distinct inclination to enlarge the scope of trade with Russia', a development frustrated only by the 'uncertainty of the British government's attitude'. Altogether a most favourable situation had been created in the City, reported a foreign representative of the Russian State Bank, for the renewal of full diplomatic relations with Russia.[105]

A 'new note of friendliness' now appeared in the press. It was

time, wrote the *Manchester Guardian*, for British policy towards
Russia to be 'completely overhauled'. The 'majestic attitude' and
'studied aloofness' which the British Foreign Office had so long
displayed towards the Russian market, argued the paper, was 'no
longer tenable'. Britain must 'abandon its Olympian attitude'.[106]
Reporting negotiations between the Soviet and Italian governments, the *Liverpool Daily Post and Mercury* pointed out that other
countries might be allowed to overtake them in the renewal of
trade with Russia. Britain, the *Daily News* warned, was 'in danger
of being left out in the cold'. The paper had been authoritatively
informed that if the Trade Facilities and Export Credits Acts were
extended to Russia, orders to the extent of 'many millions of
pounds' would be placed by the Russian government with British
manufacturers. The absence of *de jure* relations was already
'retarding the possibility of timber, flax and other trade agreements [being concluded] on the lines of the grain agreement'.
Recognition of Russia, the paper declared, with the 'fullest possible development of trade relations', had become an 'urgent issue'.
Between ninety and a hundred MPs, it added, were now in favour
of it.[107] Indeed during the latter part of December 1923 the British
press was 'almost unanimous' in urging the value of coming to an
agreement, reported *Russian Information and Review*. It was 'naturally enough, the plain feasibility of a rapid extension of Russo-
British trade' which had 'induced this more favourable disposi-
tion in the minds of British writers'.[108]

The autumn of 1923 accordingly saw the conclusion of contracts
on a scale which would have been 'incredible without the fullest
confidence of each of the contracting parties in the other'. The
formation of the grain exporting company, which had caused 'no
little stir in business and political circles', was followed by the
conclusion of contracts with British firms for the supply of timber
to a value of at least three hundred thousand pounds and the
conclusion of agreements with British engineering firms for the
supply of equipment for Soviet power stations.[109] The latter
agreement was entered into by the Metro-Vickers company and
the Soviet government. According to the *Daily Telegraph*'s report
of 15 November, it provided for the building and re-building of
power stations, the Soviet authorities having obtained credit
terms of up to seven years for this purpose. Metro-Vickers, noted
a Foreign Office official, had been 'one of the most enterprising
firms in capturing Russian business'. Yet he could 'hardly believe

it', a colleague commented; and Gregory minuted tetchily that although he had heard that such a contract was being negotiated, he had heard 'nothing about the seven years credit'.[110]

Gregory continued to oppose recognition of the Soviet government, which, he argued in a memorandum of 29 December 1923, would contribute to the 'revival of a force which psychologically, politically and geographically must in the long run become once again a standing menace to our Eastern interests'; and he was sceptical about the possibility of obtaining any more trade as a result.[111] Opinion within the Foreign Office however, was now conspicuously out of step with that within the business and commercial world. During the previous two or three months, the *Glasgow Herald* noted on 26 October, a 'great change has come over the attitude of British traders towards Russia as the result of the reports of several missions made by English and Scottish businessmen to that country recently'. It was obvious, commented the journal of the Birmingham Chamber of Commerce, 'that as in the past, Russia must once more become a valuable market. Her resources, mineral and agricultural, are immense, and her people cannot indefinitely carry on under present conditions'. The London *Chamber of Commerce Journal* agreed that there were signs that the Soviet government 'now take a saner view of things generally, and that an attempt is being made to put the economic state of the country on a more satisfactory basis'. It was likely, the journal added, 'that in the near future a good deal more will be heard about Russia'.[112] There had been 'sweeping modifications of the original Communistic programme' in Russia, commented the *Statist*; present conditions were 'far more favourable to a successful resumption of the negotiations broken off at Cannes than those which rendered futile the Hague discussions'. A settlement of outstanding differences between the two countries would bring 'real and obvious advantages', the paper urged; the time was now ripe for a 'vigorous attack' upon the problem.[113]

Indeed the country's most prominent businessmen, it was remarked, were 'wiser than the Government' in this connection: they realised 'both the opportunities and the importance of Russian trade'. They should get away from the diffidence which had characterised their previous actions, wrote the *Financial News* on 7 November, otherwise traders might discover that they had been 'ousted from a political market of growing wealth'. The possibilities of the Russian market were enormous; and it was 'certainly not in the national interests—financial, commercial or economic—that we should see it fall into other hands'. Even the journal of the Westminster Bank, which had declared in May that the Soviet government had taken 'none of the steps essential to the revival of public confidence in Russia', was now prepared to concede that the situation appeared to be 'undergoing a favourable change'. It was 'permissible to hope', the journal commented, 'that a general settlement to the interest of both parties will not be long delayed'. It might not be long, added *Lloyds Bank Monthly*, before Russia 'again takes her place in the comity of nations'.[114]

These arguments and their diplomatic implications were summed up in a new journal which made its first appearance at this time, the *British-Russian Gazette and Trade Outlook*. Its first issue noted that 'to the surprise, it must be admitted, of all British-Russian business men, the Soviet Government remains in power, and, as cannot be denied, appears now to be displaying a real and not always unpractical desire to maintain order, and to re-establish Russia's economic strength and her credit'. The 'Die-hard' policy, accordingly, was now no longer appropriate, and there was no shortage of evidence to suggest that it was indeed 'rapidly being compelled to yield to the policy of the "get a move on" party of British-Russian traders'.[115]

The journal's second issue in December 1923 returned to the point. It complained of the government's 'purposeless, aimless policy of interminable indecision' with regard to Russia, and noted that the British industrialist and trader was beginning to find himself 'diametrically at variance with the British politicians' on this issue. The wheat agreement, a recent shipping pact, and other understandings, negotiated and concluded with the Soviet government by some of the largest and most significant British business interests, had demonstrated 'beyond all argument . . . that some of our ablest business men differ fundamentally in their views from those members of our recent Governments who have imposed upon us as a nation the same old worn-out policy of "wait and see" in regard to Russia'. The clearly growing determination of the leaders of British trade and industry to 'shake themselves free from the restraining shackles' imposed upon them by successive governments would, it was thought, 'compel a complete change in the British official attitude towards Russia'. 'Full normal relations' must now be resumed.[116]

For it was clear (as the *Financial Times* pointed out) that the extension of trade with Russia was being 'hindered by the lack of

official facilities'.[117] The Russian market was a most important one
for British industry, since its requirements were those which
British industry appeared best placed to supply, while Russia in
return could provide commodities which were urgently needed in
Britain. Commercial relations between the two countries, however, could not develop normally in the absence of political
agreement; and the question of diplomatic recognition accordingly became an issue of 'major importance'.[118] It was impossible to
hope, the *Manchester Guardian* added on 5 December, that normal
trade, even on a small scale, could be established between the two
countries so long as political relations remained on their 'existing
and highly precarious footing'. It was 'time our Russian policy
were completely overhauled, if our traders are not to come into the
field too late'. J. D. Gregory, commenting on the paper's article,
complained that a 'persistent campaign' was being waged against
the Foreign Office on the question of Russian trade.[119] Both sides
evidently appreciated that more was at stake than the development of commerce.

The representative organisations of business now brought these
considerations more directly to the attention of the government.
At the quarterly meeting of the Association of British Chambers of
Commerce on 24 October 1923, a resolution was adopted which
declared 'that this Association, taking into consideration certain
evidence of improvement in the actual economic conditions prevailing in Russia, submits to His Majesty's Government the
advisability of taking such steps as would enable trade between
the two countries to be developed and extended as rapidly as
possible and the advisability of simultaneously making adequate
provision for the recognition of Russia's pre-war indebtedness
and the adjustment of the claims of British Nationals in Russia.
The Association calls the attention of His Majesty's Government
to the fact that the absence of diplomatic relations, consular
services, and a clear statement of liabilities, are all acting as
serious deterrents to the extending of credit facilities, failing
which the growth of trade must be slow.' The resolution was
moved by A. G. Marshall on behalf of the Russo-British Chamber
of Commerce. An amendment was proposed that 'acceptance of
her obligations should precede recognition of the Soviet Government'; but 'the feeling of the meeting being clear', the amendment
was withdrawn and the resolution was thereupon carried
unanimously.[120]

The Russo-British Chamber of Commerce sent a copy of the

resolution to Rakovsky, who replied on 29 October that it 'constituted a very important step towards establishing a better understanding between Russia and this country'. Another copy was sent to the government.[121] The London Chamber of Commerce, at its annual general meeting in January 1924, was also agreed that there was 'very definite evidence' that conditions in Russia were improving. With only one dissentient, it was agreed not to oppose the extension of diplomatic recognition to the Soviet government, and to communicate this view to the government.[122] The Executive Committee of the Association of British Chambers of Commerce sent a further resolution to the Prime Minister, the Secretary of State for Foreign Affairs and the President of the Board of Trade on 10 January 1924, urging that diplomatic recognition be conferred upon the Soviet government without delay. 'In the opinion of the Association', its Secretary was asked to add, 'it is essential, in the interests of the trade of the country, that this matter should have immediate attention, as without some such understanding the efforts at present made to develop trade with Russia can have no permanent result'.[123]

Indeed opinion in the City, the *Daily Herald* noted, was 'swinging very decidedly in favour of recognition'. A few 'die-hards' might protest; but 'the wiser City men will be unfeignedly thankful'. The City, in fact, the deputy Russian trade representative in Britain informed *Izvestiya*, had 'long ago recognized Soviet Russia'. The Foreign Office 'continued its old policy of hostile relations with Soviet Russia', but there was an 'obvious change in English business circles'.[124] Writing to Moscow at the end of November, Rakovsky expressed confidence that, whatever the outcome of the general election of the following month, the state of Anglo-Russian relations would be considered afresh, with particular reference to the question of the extension of the export credits legislation to Soviet Russia.[125] The legislative programme with which the Conservatives met the House of Commons in January 1924, however, following their electoral defeat, made no mention of relations with Russia.[126] The subsequent formation of a Labour government, it appeared, relatively less closely identified with the imperial and financial interests which opposed the extension of diplomatic relations with Russia, was required before beiness and mercantile opinion could resume their normally preponderant position in the making of British foreign policy and secure the full *de jure* recognition, not simply the limited *de facto* recognition conferred by the trade agreement, of the Soviet government in Moscow.[127]

Following Baldwin's unexpected declaration in favour of protection, Parliament was dissolved on 16 November and a general election took place on 6 December 1923. The results left the Conservatives with the largest number of seats (258 as against 346 in the outgoing Parliament); the Liberals had 158 seats; while the Labour Party, with only a few more candidates and 100,000 more votes, increased its representation from 142 seats to 191. Baldwin decided not to resign but to face Parliament when it met on 8 January 1924. A censure motion was moved by the Labour Party on 17 January and Asquith committed the Liberals to its support. The government was defeated on 21 January. The following day Baldwin resigned, and MacDonald was invited to form his party's first administration.[128]

The Labour Party's manifesto in the general election had stated that the party would favour the 'resumption of free economic and diplomatic relations with Russia'; and MacDonald assured the party's victory rally at the Albert Hall on 8 January 1924 that the 'pompous folly of standing aloof from the Russian Government' would be ended.[129] Baldwin's government was subsequently taken to task in the House of Commons by Tom Shaw for the 'very significant omission' from the King's Speech of a proposal for the 'proper recognition' of Russia.[130] It was nevertheless rumoured, following the formation of the new administration, that recognition was to be delayed and—as the *Daily Telegraph* put it—the government's action was to be 'more circumspect'.[131] A committee of inquiry, it appeared, might have to be sent to Russia before recognition was granted; and Russia might first be required to enter the League of Nations. H. N. Brailsford reported that he had officially been assured that recognition would be unconditional; but he was nevertheless 'anxious'.[132]

It has been suggested by some Soviet writers that MacDonald 'by every kind of means obstructed the official recognition of the Soviet government', and that he was ultimately 'compelled' to do so 'only under the strongest pressure of the broad masses of the British proletariat': that he 'hesitated' but that pressure from the masses was 'too strong'.[133] The charge is difficult to sustain. MacDonald had publicly committed the Labour government to recognition; and in a letter transmitted to Rakovsky on 3 January

1924 he had made clear that this would be done immediately, 'without any conditions'.[134] Talk of the despatch of a commission of inquiry, wrote the *Daily Herald*'s correspondent, might be 'dismissed as ridiculous'. No such step was intended, or indeed necessary; the question of recognition was 'already decided'. The short delay before the official announcement of diplomatic recognition of the Soviet government appears, in fact, to have been entirely routine. Labour's supporters, Duff Cooper, Ponsonby's secretary at the Foreign Office, noted in his diary on 29 January, simply appeared unable to 'understand why there should be an hour's delay'.[135]

It is difficult, moreover, to identify the source of that working-class pressure which is supposed to have imposed recognition upon a reluctant government. The National Council of the ILP, certainly, demanded the immediate and unconditional recognition of the Soviet government on 25 January, a step which a contemporary Soviet commentator held to have ended the government's hesitation.[136] This, however, could hardly be considered the authentic voice of working-class opinion; and further pressure appears to have been confined to a couple of letters to the *Daily Herald*. On 29 January Neil Maclean MP wrote to complain about the 'nonsense' which was circulating to the effect that there must be a delay before recognition was accorded to the Soviet government. This had not been thought necessary, he pointed out, in the case of the new Greek government. The following day Duncan Carmichael, the Secretary of the London Trades Council, addressed a further letter to the paper, in which he declared that working people could not understand why a delay should be necessary before the Soviet government was recognised. If the Labour government were to 'adopt the quibbles of the Conservative Cabinet' in such matters, he thought, it would 'disrupt the movement in the country for years'.[137]

The statement that the Trades Council thereupon 'began positive action', moreover, stands in need of correction. Carmichael had done no more, in fact, than provisionally to book a hall in central London for a meeting; and since he was a Vice-President of the National 'Hands off Russia' Committee, a body whose overriding aim was to secure the diplomatic recognition of the Soviet government, his views should not necessarily be taken to represent those of the working class as a whole.[138] It seems unlikely, in any case, that either his action or Maclean's letter could significantly have affected the timing or nature of the formal act of recognition, which took place two days later. MacDonald had in fact instructed the Secretary to the Cabinet to place Russia on a list of questions requiring early consideration on 23 January 1924; and at the following meeting of the Cabinet, before either of the letters had appeared in the *Herald*, he informed ministers that the policy of resuming diplomatic relations with Russia was being 'proceeded with as rapidly as circumstances permitted'. The matter, he indicated, might even be settled before Parliament had assembled.[139]

More important, perhaps, is the objection that to attribute decisive importance to the intervention of the working-class movement is to obscure the extent to which the decision to recognise the Soviet government was one which commanded support not only in the Labour Party, but also among the Liberals (whose election manifesto had similarly advocated recognition), in business and journalistic circles, and beyond them. It was indeed opposition to recognition, not its advocacy, which was the minority opinion. Labour's policy enjoyed the support of both popular and elite consensus; working-class intervention in its support, accordingly, was superfluous. In recognising Russia, Narkomindel noted, MacDonald had the support not only of the Labour Party, but of the Liberals also; so popular had the proposal become by the end of 1923 that 'even several Conservative organs of the press' had declared in its favour. Carmichael, in fact, drew attention to precisely this point in his letter: why should there be a delay, he wrote, when 'both Liberal and Labour candidates were pledged to the policy of recognition' and there was accordingly 'no danger of a defeat in the House of Commons?'[140]

This fact was noted by the Cabinet on 4 February 1924, in approving the decision to extend diplomatic recognition to the Soviet government. He had acted immediately and without calling a special meeting to consider the question, MacDonald stated, 'in accordance with what he knew was the general viewpoint of the Cabinet'. If he had delayed the matter for consultation with other powers (a reference to the negotiations then proceeding between the Soviet and Italian governments) it would have taken three months; whereas by communicating the decision to the Soviet government before the Second Congress of Soviets had ended its meeting it had been possible to secure its endorsement 'not merely by M. Chicherin and the Foreign Office officials in Moscow, but by representatives of the Soviets of all the Russias'. They had now, in fact, sent a 'very cordial telegram of acceptance'. The Cabinet offered its congratulations to Mac-Donald upon the promptitude with which the matter had been expedited.[141] As a general rule, it was agreed, the government should submit large questions of foreign policy to Parliament before taking action. There were special grounds for speed, however, in this instance; and in any case the matter was scarcely one of party politics: 'two political parties out of three had included the *de jure* recognition of Russia in their programme of electoral policy'.[142]

The British note of 1 February 1924 extended recognition to the Soviet government as the *de jure* government 'in the territories of the former Russian Empire which acknowledge its authority'. It remained necessary, however, to secure agreement upon a series of related questions, such as the validity of existing treaties, the claims of the governments and nationals of either state against the other, and propaganda and subversion of institutions. The Soviet government was accordingly requested to send representatives to London as soon as possible to discuss these questions and reach an accommodation upon them.[143]

Recognition was acknowledged by Rakovsky on 8 February 1924, and the invitation to send a delegation to London was accepted.[144] The Cabinet noted warily that Rakovsky's reply defined the territory over which the Soviet government claimed to exercise authority in terms different from those which had been specified in the government's original communication; but it was agreed that 'British recognition was as stated in the British note of February 1st'. MacDonald informed the Cabinet that he intended to send Rakovsky a memorandum covering the outstanding points to be resolved between the two governments, with suggestions as to which should be dealt with by direct negotiation and which should be referred to the joint commission which was to meet in London.[145] He wrote at the same time to Chicherin, expressing satisfaction that in so short a time the Labour government had been able to take the first step towards a resolution of the differences between the two sides, but indicating that for the time being the two countries should establish relations at *chargé d'affaires* rather than ambassadorial level.[146] Chicherin regretted this decision, pointing to the 'moral significance' which would be attached to the appointment of ambassadors, but he agreed with MacDonald that those subsequently appointed in this capacity must be figures of influence who would be acceptable within the receiving country.[147]

Recognition, wrote Krasin, was 'undoubtedly an event of the first political importance'. It would encourage corresponding action on the part of a series of other states; the French government would be obliged to alter its inflexible attitude; the decision might be expected to influence the American government; and it would finally destroy the hopes of the counter-revolutionaries in exile, who would now move off to America, Brazil or elsewhere. Despite unemployment and a depressed foreign trade, Britain remained economically the most important country in Europe, and from the point of view of foreign trade the improvement of relations with that country was of 'major significance'. Even in the unfavourable circumstances which had existed since 1921, he noted, Britain had occupied the first place in Soviet foreign trade.[148] The *de jure* recognition of the Soviet government, however, he added, could certainly not in itself remove all the difficulties and obstacles which served to complicate Soviet economic relations with the capitalist West.[149] This note of caution, as the course of the London negotiations soon made apparent, was a most judicious one.[150]

8 Soviet Russia and Labourism

Labour's decision to extend diplomatic recognition to the Soviet government has variously been interpreted. Perhaps the most influential thesis has been that which has posited a connection between the party's policy and the socialist princcples to which it was—at least ostensibly—committed. The party's foreign policy, in this view, was a 'repudiation of traditional British foreign policy': it was characterised by opposition to the pursuit of national self-interest, and by a hostile attitude to imperialism and colonial exploitation in any (but more especially in its British) variant. The party's 1918 constitution, it has been suggested, 'repudiated capitalism as a system'; after this date the ILP's 'systematic anti-capitalism . . . was incorporated wholesale into Labour's foreign policy pronouncements'.[1]

The decision to confer *de jure* recognition on the Soviet government, in this analysis, was an expression of the party's 'instinctive sympathy with a Workers' government'. The party was motivated by 'ardent pro-Soviet sentiment' and a sense of 'class grievance and solidarity'; and there was an 'assumed identity of common status' with the Soviet government.[2] The ILP executive did indeed welcome the act of recognition, and it looked forward to joint measures to restore the economic life of Europe, to stimulate the development of trade and industry and to lessen the burden of unemployment. The statement explicitly referred to the British and Soviet governments as 'two Labour governments'; and Brailsford, in the *New Leader*, declared that the new Labour Cabinet would stand beside the Soviet executive as 'one of the only two Socialist Governments in the world'.[3] What could be more natural than that one such government should recognise the other?

It will be suggested in what follows that this thesis can scarcely be sustained. Other factors are quite sufficient to account for

Labour's recognition of the Soviet government, in particular the influence of ex-Liberals upon the making of the party's foreign policy and the desire to alleviate unemployment by expanding foreign trade. Nor is the impact of socialism upon the party's policies any easier to discern; cautious moderation was far more apparent, and there was little evidence, at least among the party's more senior spokesmen, of any partiality for Bolshevism. The question, however, cannot quite be left at that point, for the party was (and is) by no means a monolithic one, and some theories have attempted to account for the party's vacillating attitude towards Russia precisely in terms of a notional disjunction between a radical rank and file and a conservative leadership, forced, when pressure from below was sufficiently strong, to accept left-wing policies to which it would not otherwise have consented. This thesis—in our view an unsustainable one—will be examined further in the conclusion of this study, together with other aspects of what may be called the 'sociology of labourism'.

The Conservatives' defeat in the general election of 1923 at once raised the question of the composition of an alternative government. Of its opponents, the Labour Party gained forty-nine seats, securing an altogether more considerable Parliamentary representation than the now-united Liberals. The formation of a Labour government, until this point an unpleasant but remote prospect, now became an immediate and menacing possibility. It was difficult for those who loved England and the British Empire, wrote the *English Review*, to 'regard the prospect . . . with any equanimity'. They now stood 'at a moment when the sun of England seems threatened with final eclipse. For the first time in her history the party of revolution approach their hands to the helm of the state, not only, as in the seventeenth century, for the purpose of overthrowing the Constitution, or of altering the Constitution, but with the design of destroying the very bases of civilized life. These men seek to impose universal slavery on all sections of the nation. . . .'[4]

The *Patriot* warned that the installation of a moderate subversive government had 'always been the prelude to bloody revolution'. A letter to the journal noted that a large number of 'fierce Anarchist aliens' had been active in the campaign. One canvasser, indeed, had had a 'darkskinned fist' shaken in his face, accompanied by threats to destroy existing society.[5] 'Why should the Socialists of Great Britain be differentiated from the Bolsheviks of Russia?' asked a contemporary writer. 'Already the desecration of the churches has begun. The red flag was recently carried into the City Temple by a band of unemployed.'[6] The stock exchange, that sensitive barometer of political change, registered a sharp fall in business. A 'bout of public selling' took place, reported the *Economist*; business 'fell away to a very low ebb', and there was a 'severe depression in prices'. People who 'held perfectly sound stocks and shares grew fidgety, and became increasingly nervous at the constant drop in prices'.[7] The abolition was forecast of the National Anthem, the Boy Scouts, the monarchy and even the institution of marriage.

Reactions to the threat took various forms. One old-established Sussex family, on receiving the news that Labour was to take office, packed all its plate and valuables and headed for the coast, 'before the Bolsheviks close the Channel ports'.[8] Sir Frederick Banbury, formerly MP for the City of London and now elevated to the peerage, was less inclined to run away from the problem. There was a danger, he warned, that MacDonald might refuse to resign if defeated in Parliament. If Mr MacDonald attempted anything of that sort, Banbury informed his audience, he would have 'great pleasure in leading the Coldstream Guards into the House of Commons'. Socialism, he warned in a letter to *The Times*, 'begins moderately—M. Kerensky was not a Bolshevist—but its supporters, once it is started, are unable to control it and anarchy ensues'.[9]

The party leaders shared many of these fears but were more circumspect in their response. The prospect of a Labour government, Davidson recorded, 'threw many Conservatives (and probably the majority) in a panic'.[10] Lord Hunsdon, on behalf of the City of London Conservatives, wrote to Baldwin to inform him that his executive was 'greatly alarmed at the idea that the Labour Party should form a Government both from the point of view of the Conservative Party and that of the Commerce of the Country'.[11] Balfour was also of the opinion that it would be a 'serious danger if the Socialist Party is allowed to assume office at the present time'. 'Every means', if necessary a working arrangement with the Liberals, should be considered in order to avoid a Parliamentary defeat.[12] Asquith recalled that his daily postbag at this time was composed of 'appeals, threats, prayers from all parts, and from all sorts and conditions of men, women and lunatics, to step in and save the country from the horrors of Socialism and Confiscation'. A leading banker came to see him with a message that if he could only set up an Asquith-Grey government, 'all the solid people in the country would support it through thick and thin'.[13] Lord Stamfordham was similarly 'deluged with all manner of bright ideas' to avoid a Labour government, including a proposal, advanced by the editor of the *Spectator*, for a two-year 'Government of National Trustees'.[14]

For various reasons none of these expedients was adopted. In part, at least, this reflected a widespread attachment to the rules of the Parliamentary game more or less regardless of its outcome. The Conservative party, noted a contemporary observer, was 'largely composed of men brought up at public schools' who were 'unable to divest themselves of the idea that Parliament is a political cricket match in which one's side comes in to bat and, being fairly bowled, goes out again to field with great good humour', both sides subsequently shaking hands over drinks and smokes in the pavilion.[15] More important, perhaps, was the fear that a Conservative-Liberal combination to exclude Labour from office might precipitate a polarisation of class forces, thereby placing at risk the institutions of state themselves. Such a combination, Davidson warned, might indeed be the 'first step down the road to revolution'.[16]

These views were echoed in the confidences of an 'eminent Conservative' vouchsafed to a *Manchester Guardian* correspondent on 15 December. An anti-Labour coalition, he felt, would be 'really dangerous': it would be the 'way to revolution'. A Conservative backbencher wrote to Baldwin in the same sense, emphasising the need to avoid a 'bourgeois bloc' which would leave the Socialists as the sole alternative. This, he noted, had been Bonar Law's 'greatest fear'.[17] Asquith also regarded it as the essential point at issue. It would be 'seriously harmful to the national interest and an incitement to class antagonism', he wrote, 'for the two "middle-class" parties to combine together to deprive Labour of an opportunity".[18]

In fact they had little to fear on this occasion. For it was agreed that a Labour government was sooner or later inevitable; and with Labour in a minority in the House of Commons, the experiment could scarcely be made with less risk. Davidson, indeed, expressed the opinion to the King that the election had been a 'blessing in disguise': had the Conservative government carried on for a further eighteen months, he thought, the Labour Party might have been returned with an overwhelming majority. The King agreed. A socialist government in Labour's situation, he thought, might have an 'opportunity of learning their administrative duties and responsibilities under favourable conditions'. The *Economist* agreed that business could contemplate a minority Labour administration 'without misgiving': there was 'no ground for panic'.[19]

Tranquillity returned rather more rapidly following Labour's victory demonstration at the Albert Hall on 8 January 1924. MacDonald, in his speech, emphasised that in agreeing to take office he was 'not thinking of party. I am thinking of the national wellbeing.' Clynes added that Labour would 'not be influenced by any consideration other than that of the national well-being. No class or sect or party could govern the British nation on narrow class lines.' Indeed, it was a 'very tame show', Duff Cooper noted in his diary: 'they sang hymns between the speeches, which were all about God'. Massingham, writing in the *Nation*, concluded that the new government would base itself 'not on the class-war, but on the co-operative and even the religious instincts of the whole nation'.[20]

MacDonald's Cabinet offered further reassurance. Lord Haldane, an eminent Liberal, became Lord Chancellor; Major C. B. Thomson, MacDonald's golfing companion at Lossiemouth, became Air Secretary; Lord Parmoor, formerly a Conservative, became Lord President of the Council; and Lord Chelmsford, a life-long Tory and Viceroy of India at the time of the Amritsar shootings, was appointed to the Admiralty. Chelmsford had never previously been associated in any way with the Labour Party; nor, it appears, did he even trouble to become a member during his period of office.[21] Indeed if there was a doubt about the Cabinet, wrote the *Review of Reviews*, it was less about its acceptability to Liberal and Conservative opponents than to some of the government's own supporters. The City, the *Economist* reported, was 'visibly impressed'. The Stock Exchange enjoyed a 'sustained rally'; and 'sweeping rises' occurred in practically all markets on the day the new Cabinet was announced.[22]

The King told his new ministers that he 'was himself rather anxious' about entrusting government to the Labour Party. Clynes assured him, however, that they 'were not cranks' (a crank, he noted, was 'a little thing that makes revolutions').[23] The

King mentioned an incident which had distressed him, the singing of the 'Red Flag' and the 'Marseillaise' at the victory demonstration in the Albert Hall. MacDonald asked the King to bear in mind the 'very difficult position he was in vis à vis his own extremists'. Had he attempted to prevent the singing of the Red Flag at that meeting, a riot, he thought, would certainly have taken place. It might even be sung in the House of Commons. They had, he explained, 'got into the way of singing this song', and only by degrees could the habit be broken down.[24]

For much of its earlier history the Labour Party had been a junior partner to the Liberals in government, and in all but trade union questions had been virtually indistinguishable from it. The new constitution which was adopted in 1918, however, bound the party to attempt to secure the 'common ownership of the means of production', and appeared to commit it, for the first time, to an explicitly socialist position. A new statement of party policy. 'Labour and the New Social Order', was adopted later in the same year. The document, an outline of Labour's 'House of Tomorrow', specified a reasonably far-reaching programme of nationalisation, and made provision for a capital levy, high levels of income tax, and heavy death duties. By this means, it was thought, private concentrations of wealth would become more equitably distributed throughout society, and a minimum standard of living for all might be guaranteed. It was emphasised, however, that these were 'not "class" measures', but ones which would promote the interests equally of the 'clerk, the teacher, the doctor, the minister of religion, the average retail shopkeeper and trader'.[25]

In the case of the coalmines and the railways, Henderson explained, it had been 'accidental circumstances and not abstract theory' which had led the party to conclude that they could not be organised as public services other than under national ownership.[26] Common ownership of the means of production meant no more than resistance to the proposal to hand back to private capitalists the industries and services which had come under government control during the war.[27] The strain of the war, the party's executive noted, had broken down the competitive industrial system and led to national organisation to a degree that had appeared 'practically impossible in the days of peace'. The 'more thoughtful of the community', it considered, were now considering proposals for national reorganisation on lines which had been popular only in Labour circles before the war.[28] Most of these proposals, in fact, had already been approved as resolutions at previous party conferences. The 1914 conference, for instance, had called for the 'abolition of capitalism' and for the introduction of a minimum wage; and the 1917 conference had opposed the return of the mines or railways to private hands after the war. It was a question not of the introduction, but of the retention and codification of such policies.[29]

If the party conferences of 1918 did mark a significant turn in the party's development, it was less in the adoption of a new and socialist programme than in a number of other decisions less obviously related to that objective. These decisions—notably that to open the party to individual membership without requiring prior membership of an affiliated trade union or socialist society—were designed, in Henderson's words, to 'remove the idea that the party is the party of the manual wage earners merely, and that its politics are the politics of the trade unions': a 'purely class-conscious demand for specific improvements in wages, hours, conditions of employment'.[30] A place, it was felt, must be found in the party's ranks, and especially among its parliamentary candidates, for women (who were to receive voting rights for the first time) and for the middle class in general. The party, Henderson, explained, must transform itself from a federation of societies into a 'national popular party'. It must constitute itself so as to be able to include within its ranks 'unattached democrats with no acknowledged allegiance to any industrial or political movement'. 'Real political democracy', he declared, could 'not be organized on the basis of class interest'.

Henderson's aim, in fact, was to change the 'old conditions' in which the party had 'seemed to be, although it never actually was, a class party'.[31] W. F. Purdy, the chairman of the party's conference in the summer of 1918, told delegates that with the new programme the party had adopted a 'claim to be a National Party in its broadest and widest sense'. Their aim should be 'not to serve sectional interests alone, or to get class against class, but rather to secure that all classes, as far as possible, shall come together'.[32] The party's new constitution, Webb wrote, might well prove to be an event of far-reaching importance. Instead of a 'sectional and somewhat narrow group', a party was now established into which it was hoped to attract many men and women of the shopkeeping, manufacturing and professional classes who were 'dissatisfied with the old political parties'.[33]

Some concern was voiced at the party conference of January 1918 that Labour should grow 'not by attracting every disgruntled Liberal and Tory they could find, but by attracting men and women who really believed in the Party'.[34] Henderson's criteria were somewhat more accommodating. The distinction between those who lived by working and those who lived from the proceeds of ownership, he wrote, did 'not exclude the so-called capitalist from membership of the Party';[35] and the adoption of the new constitution did indeed lead to a sharp rise in recruitment, if not of capitalists, at least of members of the professional and middle classes. A significant change came about in the social composition of the party's parliamentary candidates. Several Liberal MPs, Henderson informed C. P. Scott, had given notice to their constituents that they intended to stand as independents at the forthcoming elections. This meant, he thought, that they would probably join the Labour Party. His own policy, he added, was 'to enlarge the bounds of the Labour Party and bring the intellectuals in as candidates'.[36] In the 1918 election, the *New Statesman* reported, 'something like a fourth of the Labour candidates' were 'from the professional and property-owning classes'.[37]

A year later the same journal noted that the new Labour representatives on local authorities were a 'sufficient indication of the change which is coming about' in the party. 'Doctors, architects, lawyers—professional men of every type' had been returned, side by side with trade union representatives as in the past. In the new Parliament, it was expected, there would be a 'respectable muster of the professionals and the business men, who have thrown in their lot with Labour'.[38] The party's elected representatives at the general election of 1922 did indeed contain a larger element of middle class people and professional men. The party, wrote Snowden, now embraced 'doctors, lawyers and a parson!' By the general election of December 1923 it was clear, wrote MacDonald, that the Labour Party had 'gained the trust of many of the middle and professional classes'. A 'considerable proportion' of the party's members now belonged to the middle classes (it had enrolled 'manufacturers . . . and even landed proprietors'); and it was made clear that a Labour government would 'certainly contain many men of this type'.[39]

It could not reasonably be maintained that these groups had

been won over to socialist policies. On the contrary, the necessity of contesting and winning parliamentary seats in socially heterogeneous or even middle class areas, if a parliamentary majority were to be attained, effectively constrained the party's articulation of a socialist programme: for middle class voters, however enlightened, were hardly likely to wish to accord their support to a party which proposed to launch a determined assault upon their material position. This point was not lost upon the Labour leaders; and many of them, no doubt, found it highly congenial. Now was the time, declared the *Socialist Review*, for a 'bold and clear lead' to the middle class, and for an attempt to explain the party's policy 'in terms which will appeal to them'.[40] To a 'host of middle class minds', added the *Labour Magazine*, '"Labour" is synonymous with "strikes", and while this impression remains the possibility of progress is and will be very limited'. Labour's case for seeking middle class support, the paper remarked, was 'overwhelming'. Its attempt to do so would have every prospect of success, provided the party's policy were simply 'presented with greater regard for the instincts and traditions of those classes'.[41]

It was indeed the weakness of the Labour Party, MacDonald believed, that it represented a '"Red Terror" to the minds of large masses of people who know little about it'.[42] The party accordingly lost no opportunity—indeed, given its chosen strategy, it could not afford to do so—of reassuring middle class voters. Its general election manifesto in 1918 boldly declared that Labour's objective was to 'build a New World', but stressed at the same time that it would be built only 'by constitutional means'. The 1922 manifesto went further. Labour's proposal to bring about a more equitable distribution of the nation's wealth by constitutional means, it declared, was 'neither Bolshevism or Communism, but common sense and justice': 'Labour's alternative', in fact, 'to Reaction and Revolution'. It represented the 'best bulwark against violent upheaval and class wars'.[43]

Militant socialists were not infrequently elected as Labour MPs, usually for traditionally dissident working-class constituencies. The ten Glasgow ILP members elected in 1922—the 'Clydesiders'—appeared to be one group of such representatives. Behind the front benches, the *Review of Reviews* correspondent wrote, now lay 'the Mountain, mostly from the submerged regions of Glasgow, who interject guttural expletives or make explosive speeches in a language which no man can understand'.[44] These 'Wild Men' from the north, the *National Review* observed, had 'little respect for Parliamentary game as understood and played by older Parties, and none for Parliamentary decorum'. It thought that they would learn conduct, however, before they could hope to serve their cause.[45] Mills, for instance, a Labour MP, had 'toned down not a little since he entered the House'.[46] David Kirkwood, one of the Clydeside rebels, promised the House of Commons shortly after his election that he would 'create a new atmosphere in this building'. If the Prime Minister or anyone else thought that there would be 'tranquillity in this House', or that he would 'kow-tow and bow down to all the symbols of this awful accursed system', they had, he assured them, 'never made a bigger mistake in their lives'.[47] He later recalled that he had to shake himself as he found himself 'moving about and talking with men whose names were household words'. It was more strange to 'find them all so simple and unaffected and friendly'. In the end, he added, he 'learned to understand' the House's conventions.[48] A few Labour MPs—Maxton perhaps—remained recalcitrant to the end; but most required less conversion.

If there was little foundation for the fear that Labour rule heralded the 'expropriation of the expropriators', there was even less for the belief that the party was indifferent to the fate of British colonial possessions in Asia or to the Soviet and radical nationalist threat which confronted them. Labour, Clynes insisted, had 'never said or done anything which can be construed into lack of support to Empire maintenance and development'.[49] Indeed Empire, the *New Leader* wrote on 5 October 1923, was an 'unhappy word' for the 'freest Commonwealth in the world'. The party did favour colonial reform, and in some cases even ultimate self-government; but this was because (as the *Labour Speakers Handbook* put it) 'unless there is a radical change in our attitudes and policy', India (and much else besides) would be 'lost to the British Commonwealth'.[50] It was a question, J. C. Wedgwood, the party's colonial spokesman and joint vice-chairman, told the House of Commons, 'of security for a great amount of British capital'. He believed that 'British capitalists themselves ... would say that their capital was going to be more secure under a self-governing India than it is under an India in which race hatred is going on boiling up, in which the only policy of every Indian is to get rid of the English. As long as you have the struggle for independence, there is a risk to capital. When once India ceases to see that her principal business is to get rid of the English, they will be able to work with the English'.[51] So far from threatening the Empire, the reforms which the party promoted were held to represent the best—indeed perhaps the only—means of preserving it.

Party spokesmen were similarly aware of the threat which Soviet Russian policy (and radical political movements generally) represented to British possessions in Asia. The 'great Socialist Russian State', wrote Morel, 'half European, half Asiatic, the focus of a thought revolution', was a 'deadly foe to the continuance of a British Empire in the Far East and the Middle East'.[52] The party opposed the threatened rupture in official relations with Russia in the spring of 1923; but the activities of the Russian consul at Kabul, wrote MacDonald, 'concealed acts of war done against us', which were 'designed to promote civil war in India'. A Labour Foreign Minister, he declared, would object to such propaganda 'just as much as Lord Curzon'. It was 'absolutely impossible for us to take no notice'.[53] Russian agents in Afghanistan, added Brailsford, did appear to be 'plotting against us'. If the charges of Bolshevik plotting in the East were confirmed, he considered, the situation would require an 'apology and . . . the dismissal of all the guilty agents'.[54]

To tear up the trade agreement, however, MacDonald told the House of Commons, was no solution at all. It would simply revive the 'old revolutionary animus' in Russia, while it would make no contribution at all to the resolution of the matters in dispute and would have a bad effect on British trade.[55] On 24 May 1923, accordingly, the Assistant Secretary of the Labour Party submitted a resolution to local party branches, calling upon the government to accord full diplomatic recognition to the Russian government as the 'best means of ensuring good relations between the two countries'. Local branches were requested to approve the resolution and send it on to the government;[56] and a number of them did so.[57] MacDonald also wrote directly to Baldwin, pointing out that the Labour Party took the 'keenest interest in the re-establishment of trade with Russia in the interests of our own country and of the workmen affected', and expressing the hope that the government was not 'banging the door' on further negotiation. The 'saner sections of the country', he believed, wished for a 'policy of patient peace-making and rebuilding'.[58]

Henderson, writing to Bonar Law on 17 April, added that the party was convinced that the termination of the trade agreement would seriously affect trade between the two countries, and that British would suffer more than Soviet interests thereby.[59]

The industrial section of the movement did not differ significantly in its reaction. The General Council of the TUC expressed concern lest the crisis lead to any reduction in the volume of trade with Russia, 'in view of the abnormal unemployment prevailing for a long period'. Trade with Russia, it thought, should be extended, and the Soviet government recognised. The Scottish TUC pressed the same point of view upon Scottish MPs in a communication of 12 June 1923. The executive council of the miners' union was also opposed to the breaking-off of relations. 'The coal trade of this country is directly affected by Russian commerce', it pointed out, 'and any interference with existing relations would involve the mining industry in still further poverty'. A resolution to this effect was carried unanimously at a special conference of the union on 30 May 1923.[60]

There was no suggestion in any of this that Labour's response derived from a feeling of political community with the Soviet government. The party, on the contrary, was at the same time conducting a vigorous and largely successful campaign against Communist influence within its own ranks. The Communist Party's application for membership of the Labour Party was turned down by the 1921 party conference, and again in 1922 and 1924, when the decision was reaffirmed by a majority of over sixteen to one.[61] Communists were also barred as representatives to national or local Labour Party conferences, and in 1924 it was agreed to forbid their nomination as either local or national Labour Party candidates and their membership of the party on an individual basis. The following year it was resolved that no Communist could become or remain a member of any affiliated section of the party.[62] Internationally, British Labour was the mainstay of the reconstituted Second International, an organisation which vigorously opposed the 'terroristic party dictatorship' in Russia and supported its moderate opponents.[63] British Labour, far from manifesting any sympathy for Bolshevism, was among its most determined and vigorous opponents on both the national and international arenas.

This was clear in Soviet Russia, at least, if not always on the Conservative backbenches. The Labour Party, the Comintern

executive declared, more closely represented a 'bourgeois group-
ing than a party of proletarian class struggle'. The government
which it formed in 1924 was designed to 'strengthen the bourgeois
state by means of reforms and class harmony rather than to
develop the class struggle'.[64] The only satisfaction that Zinoviev
could glean from its formation was that 'the longer it stays in
power, the less will it create illusions in the British working
class'.[65] There would certainly have been no reason, if political
principle were alone involved, for such a government to reverse
the policy of its predecessor and extend diplomatic recognition to
the Soviet government in Moscow. To account for that decision
we shall have to consider the nature of the making of Labour
foreign policy, and the influence upon that policy of the growing
crisis of unemployment.

It was a source of some satisfaction to the Foreign Office, when the
possibility of the breaking-off of relations with the Soviet government was being considered in the spring of 1923, that an adverse
public reaction was not among the factors which needed seriously
to be taken into consideration. The 'normal apathy in the country
in the matter of foreign affairs', J. D. Gregory observed, made it
unlikely that there would be much response from the public,
whatever the government decided. Curzon was substantially in
agreement. The public showed 'amazing apathy', he thought,
about anything apart from a 'murder, a divorce case or a football
match'.[66] Within the labour movement more particularly, recalled
Leonard Woolf, there was a 'profound and almost universal
ignorance of international and imperial facts and problems'.
Woolf's own efforts, as an advisor to the party in this field, were
devoted to an attempt to get its members and their leaders to
understand the 'complications and urgency of what was happen-
ing in remote places and among strange peoples about whom they
were profoundly and complacently ignorant'.[67]

Labour, J. H. Thomas admitted to the House of Commons, had
'never yet been trained in foreign politics'; and it was widely
believed that the party would find difficulty in filling the Foreign
Secretaryship in any government it might form.[68] Non-Labour
people, wrote Leonard Woolf, always maintained that a Labour
government would be unable to deal with foreign affairs, the party
having no leaders who would be able to control the Foreign Office
and deal with negotiations, and 'understand the direct movement

of foreign relations'.[69] This criticism lost some of its force after the war, when many union leaders became involved in the work of international trade union federations and in other activities of this kind;[70] but a good many people, the *Review of Reviews* commented, nevertheless believed that this 'recently acquired and fragmentary information' could 'hardly take the place of a comprehensive grasp of foreign policy'. It was in this area that the party's qualifications were thought to be particularly deficient.[71]

Henderson, writing to C. P. Scott in February 1922, nevertheless felt able to assure him that the party's resources in the field of foreign affairs were 'much greater than was commonly supposed'.[72] Indeed there was no party in the country. Snowden wrote in 1923, which was so well informed on foreign affairs as the Labour Party. Since the end of the war in particular, added Clynes, there had been no party which had taken a greater interest in this field.[73] Their confidence was based less upon the recent acquisition of this expertise by long-standing members of the party than upon the adhesion to its ranks, in the immediate post-war period, of a group of former Radicals and Liberals whose interests and qualifications were concentrated in the field of foreign affairs. The contribution of the members of this group to the making of Labour foreign policy in the period under review can scarcely be exaggerated; and it is in their liberal perspective on foreign affairs that part of the explanation of Labour's recognition of the Soviet Russian government must be sought.

Most of the former Liberals had joined the Labour Party during or immediately after the First World War. The Liberal Party's wholehearted commitment to a 'fight to a finish' distressed them; only the Labour Party, it appeared, was willing to discuss a negotiated conclusion. Many became Labour parliamentary candidates in the general election of 1918. Together with others who had opposed the war, their fate was almost uniformly unsuccessful. This was 'on the whole ... as it should be', the *Workers' Dreadnought* commented on 4 January 1919; for although some of them had a higher standard of morality than many who had belonged only to the Labour Party, it was not the mission of Labour to 'provide a refuge for men who are neither workers nor Socialists, but who happen to have disagreed with the majority of the capitalist party to which they had hitherto been content to belong'. The Liberal converts nevertheless succeeded in making their influence felt outside Parliament. As the 1921 party conference was told, the party's expertise in foreign affairs was 'confined practically to two or three people who were in the nature of advisers to the Labour Party, people like Roden Buxton or Brailsford, who contributed tremendously to their knowledge of foreign affairs'.[74]

The following year most of the group were successfully returned to Parliament, where they immediately began to dominate the party's contribution to debates on foreign affairs. A 'striking transformation' had been brought about in Labour's representation in Parliament, it was noted, with the arrival of this 'highly cultivated intelligentsia' of which there had been only two or three representatives in the previous Parliament.[75] In particular, it was noted, the party could now claim 'three or four specialists in foreign policy'.[76] These were Liberal converts in every case. Their contribution to Labour's foreign policy was the greater because not simply were they able and experienced politicians: they were also as a rule preoccupied precisely with those questions of foreign policy and international affairs which the existing party leadership had hitherto neglected. It was their belief that the Liberal Party had abandoned traditional Liberal principles in foreign affairs which was in almost every case responsible for their move into the ranks of Labour; as Shinwell recalled, it could 'hardly be said that they had accepted the Socialist faith'.[77]

Charles Roden Buxton, for instance, who was dropped by Central Hackney Liberals because of his advocacy of a negotiated peace, gave as his main reason for severing the Liberal connection the fact that he 'could no longer agree with the party over the conduct of foreign affairs'. He joined the ILP in 1917. According to his biographer, however, he 'never rejected the Liberal ideal of freedom'.[78] H. B. Lees-Smith, who followed Buxton into the ranks of Labour, explicitly declared that his principles had 'in no way changed': he had simply been forced to the conclusion that, especially so far as foreign affairs were concerned, he could 'not look to any section of the Liberal Party to carry them into effect'. He had been attracted first of all towards the ILP, he added, because it was the 'only powerful party . . . that took a close and continuous interest in foreign policy'.[79] J. C. Wedgwood insisted that his admission into the Labour Party would 'involve no change in my Parliamentary activities, nor even in those colleagues with whom I work in the House of Commons'.[80] Buxton's brother Noel came to the similar conclusion that the 'Radical point of view, particularly on peace and war, was better represented by the Labour Party than by the Official Liberals'. Buxton declared in a letter written jointly with Lees-Smith that 'the leading men who dare to utter truly Liberal views and are ready to fight for them with enthusiasm are in the ranks of Labour'.[81]

Charles Trevelyan had resigned from the pre-war Liberal government on learning of its secret treaty commitments. He thought the Liberals' policy on the war and on Ireland 'indistinguishable from that of the imperialists and reactionaries'. But Labour, he believed, was the 'saviour of Europe'; and in the ILP it had the 'one organized body with which [he could] cooperate in the struggle against the fatal and disastrous policy of the "knockout blow"'.[82] Joseph King also left the Liberal Party in consequence of what he considered to be the 'insincerity and even treachery towards Liberal principles' of its leaders. He joined the ILP, whose attitude to the Russian Revolution and to the League of Nations he professed to find congenial.[83] Norman Angell similarly turned, after the outbreak of the world war, to 'co-operation with men whose bent was towards an internationalist policy. They happened to be men prominent in the politics of the Left'.[84]

The most outstanding member of the group was undoubtedly E. D. Morel, the campaigner for colonial justice and prime mover of the Union of Democratic Control. In July 1917 he wrote to Arthur Ponsonby (another prominent Liberal who was shortly to join the ILP) that he had formerly believed that 'Liberalism was a force, a real tangible force making for righteousness in public affairs. Since then I have discovered that it is a fraud. . . . Nothing would induce me to stand in with any members of the gang which have brought the country to its present pass.'[85] The following year Morel left the Liberal Party, in whose interest he had stood for Parliament at Birkenhead, and joined the ILP.[86]

Morel's pamphlet *Morocco in Diplomacy*, later reissued as *Ten Years of Secret Diplomacy*, made a strong impression upon Ramsay MacDonald. He professed to remember it well two years afterwards. He 'did not want to believe it', he wrote, yet 'its facts were so authoritative and its conclusions so logical that I had to believe it'. The 'most strikingly dramatic part of its revelation', he considered, was the demonstration that agreements publicly concluded were good and made for peace, while those made secretly were the 'cause of trouble, illfeeling and war'. From that time, MacDonald declared, he 'suspected our diplomacy, and ceased to believe the assurances given by ministers in parliament or out of it'.[87] Snowden was similarly impressed with what he described, in his introduction to Morel's pamphlet *Truth and the War*, as Morel's 'great knowledge of and authority on international questions'. Indeed Morel's exposure of Liberal policy before the war, declared a speaker at the 1923 party conference, had 'placed the whole of humanity in his debt'.[88]

Lenin was understandably less impressed. In an article entitled 'English Pacifism and English Dislike of Theory', he congratulated Morel for 'turning from the chauvinist bourgeoisie to the pacifist bourgeoisie'. His policies stood no chance of success, however, 'without revolutionary action on the part of the proletariat'; and Morel remained bourgeois in all other economic and political questions.[89] In spite of this (or, perhaps more accurately, because of it) the influence of Morel and of the former Liberals upon Labour foreign policy was a major one, and virtually all sections of the party welcomed the accession of the new members with (as one writer put it) their money—'not unneeded'—and their 'different and wider experience of life, particularly foreign affairs and finance'.[90]

Their influence was exerted at at least three levels. In the first place, the ex-Liberals had a considerable influence as individuals upon thinking about foreign relations within the ranks of the labour movement (the influence of Morel, indeed, extended far beyond them). More important, perhaps, was the influence of the ex-Liberals through the organisations which they set up and controlled, many of which included established leaders of the labour movement among their membership, and whose statements had a direct influence upon those issued in the name of the Labour Party. There were several such bodies, most of them aggregating Liberal and Labour opposition to the conduct of the war: the No Conscription Fellowship, the Bryce Group, the 1917 Club, the Lansdowne Committee, the Women's International League and the Peace Negotiations Committee. The most important of them, however, was the Union of Democratic Control.

The signatories of the UDC's inaugural circular were MacDonald, Trevelyan, Angell and Morel.[91] The group which formed around them, Brockway recalled, were 'bourgeois to their fingertips. They were suave, gracious, cultured. They might have been lifted out of any gathering of the gentlemen of England.' The UDC nevertheless devoted a considerable amount of effort to recruitment within the labour movement, in the belief, as the Union's historian has put it, that 'the Labour Party as a whole must be won for a distinctly international Labour foreign policy'. Three labour organisers were appointed; and at the end of the war the total membership of Labour bodies affiliated to the Union was estimated to be 650,000. Five members of its executive committee had by this time joined the Labour Party; the other six did so subsequently.[92] Indeed, as Trevelyan noted, the UDC was 'in effect a link between the large volume of Radical opinion which no longer found guidance from the Liberal leaders, and the ILP. . . . Here was laid the foundation of the coalition between Radicalism and Labour which is now rapidly becoming a complete amalgamation'.[93]

The close personal and organisational link which existed between the Union and the labour movement established a basis for the adoption by the Labour Party, virtually *in toto*, of the Union's foreign policy programme. The Labour Party 'turned to Morel when it began to have doubts about the war', it has been noted; 'in fact no member of the Labour movement troubled to work out a socialist foreign policy . . . so long as Morel was alive'.[94] The Labour Party's War Aims manifesto of December 1917 closely resembled peace terms which the UDC had suggested the previous June; and Labour and the UDC condemned the Versailles treaty in May 1919 in exactly the same terms (the hand, it has been remarked, was Henderson's, but the voice was that of E. D. Morel).[95] Not all the elements of Labour's foreign policy in the early post-war years originated with the UDC: support for the abolition of secret diplomacy, for instance, was of considerably longer standing. But it was the advocacy of the UDC which now secured the adoption of these and other points of the UDC programme, and their incorporation in 'Labour's foreign policy'.

The ex-Liberals also played a prominent role in the party's foreign policy-making machinery and within the House of Commons on the party's behalf. C. R. Buxton, for instance, became Parliamentary Adviser to the Labour Party on Foreign Affairs and Imperial Questions, with a private room in the House of Commons.[96] Buxton was also by 1924 acting as chairman of the party's Advisory Committee on International Questions.[97] The Committee had been set up in 1918 with the task of furnishing information to the Parliamentary Party, and its initiatives gave rise to many Parliamentary questions. The Committee also gave advice and information to the party executive and provided many memoranda on questions of fact, a number of which were published as Labour Party pamphlets. Among the Committee's most notable characteristics was its high proportion of ex-Liberal members. It has, indeed, been described as 'almost a continuation of the UDC'.[98] Among the prominent recruits who served upon it were the Buxtons, Angell, Trevelyan, Ponsonby, Morel, Bertrand Russell and Helena Swanwick. If the main spokesmen for the party, on foreign affairs and other matters, remained the established leadership, the ex-Liberal recruits 'very much dominated the positions of second rank'.[99]

It was not altogether surprising, therefore, that Palme Dutt should have had occasion to denounce Labour's foreign policy in the *Communist* as a 'middle class Liberal and not a working-class Socialist policy'. Nowhere, he charged, did the present Labour leadership show such an 'intellectual slavery to middle class views' as in international affairs, where Labour had 'no policy of its own', being content to leave such matters 'in the hands of a group of Liberal-minded intellectuals' whose policy was 'based on Liberal-Capitalist ideas'. Indeed in actual practice, he added in January 1924, 'Labour and Liberal policy on immediate issues represent a single force. . . . Nowhere is this more clearly the case than in the most typical expression of capitalist policy, the sphere of foreign affairs'.[100]

It is important for our purpose to note that the ex-Liberals exerted this considerable and even dominating influence in favour of the *de jure* recognition of the Soviet government. The ex-Liberals persuaded the 1922 ILP annual conference to adopt by a narrow majority (and despite MacDonald's opposition) a resolution expressing the party's 'intense sympathy with the Bolsheviks in their anti-Imperialism', and its approval of their publication of the secret treaties. Trevelyan proposed a four-point plan to the conference, to be implemented if Labour won the succeeding general election. Its first point was the 'immediate recognition of the Russian government without asking the leave of France'.[101] He later proposed an eight-point plan for a Labour foreign policy, the first point of which again envisaged the 'immediate recognition of the Soviet government of Russia and the granting of credits to it'.[102]

Trevelyan's proposal was contrasted by the *Communist Review* with 'malignant hysteria which overwhelms Mr J. R. MacDonald whenever Bolshevism is mentioned'. Indeed one of the more ironic aspects of the ILP's policy at this time, it was noted, was that its 'most courageous expounders of real internationalism' were the 'sincere middle-class politicians who recently left the Liberal Party'.[103] J. R. Clynes, for instance, for all his faults, had been 'no hypocrite in his attitude towards Russia': he had always been a 'straightforward, honest and consistent opponent' of the Soviet government. Were it not for 'one of two honest Liberals in the ILP', the journal concluded, men like Trevelyan, Buxton, Ponsonby and Brailsford, it would be 'difficult to convince many people that the old ILP leaders, like Snowden and MacDonald, were not mere pedlars of the anti-Bolshevik dope that appears in the *Morning Post*'.[104]

The point was not lost upon Theodore Rothstein, who appears to have envisaged Morel as the Foreign Secretary of a post-revolutionary Britain as he was 'better than all the Socialists'.[105] Morel was in fact passed over for this position in the first Labour Cabinet; but the UDC as a whole contributed no fewer than nine ministers to the government, and within it they were generally the most enthusiastic supporters of the diplomatic recognition of the Soviet government. Snowden, for instance, commented with regard to the government's proposed note of recognition that 'some preliminary understanding on the matter of trade debts and confiscated properties would have been desirable'. His attitude was in marked contrast to that of Trevelyan, who urged that the note be 'sent and published with the least possible delay. The quicker our action the finer the gesture.' He proposed the omission of a referance to propaganda, of which there had been no 'reasonable proof . . . for a long time past'. Arthur Ponsonby, another ex-Liberal, wrote directly to Rakovsky to congratulate him on the recognition of his government. He received a reply which noted the 'prominent part' which Ponsonby had himself played in its negotiation, and conveyed Rakovsky's thanks 'personally and in the name of the workers of our Soviet Union, for your sympathy and your efforts'.[106] To the influence of the ex-Liberals, then, must in large part be attributed Labour's prompt and *de jure* recognition of the Soviet Russian government. It was a proposal which evidently need have little to do with socialism.

It remains necessary to account for the adoption by the established Labour leadership of a policy with which few of them—its
impeccably liberal credentials notwithstanding—had any instinctive sympathy. That explanation, it will be suggested, lies
essentially in the connection which was believed to exist between
the reduction of unemployment and the revival of foreign trade.
The level of unemployment had been relatively low during the
immediate post-war period; but by the end of 1920 it had exceeded 10 per cent of the insured labour force, and not until 1924
was a lower monthly figure again recorded. In certain industries,
moreover, even these levels were considerably exceeded. Unemployment among trade union members in the engineering, shipbuilding and metal industries, for instance, ranged between 20
and 30 per cent over this period, considerably above the average
for the insured population as a whole, and in the mining iron ore
and quarrying industry a figure of no less than 50 per cent was
recorded during 1921.[107]

The Labour Party, largely composed of, voted for and financed
by such trade unionists and their families, could scarcely fail to be
affected by this problem, and an increasing amount of effort was
devoted to the search for an effective solution. The policy which
appeared to hold out the greatest prospect of success was the
expansion of foreign trade, in particular trade with Soviet Russia.
The Russian market, it was widely believed, offered limitless
opportunities for the sale of British goods, while the import of
Russian raw materials seemed likely in turn to reduce the cost of
living in Britain. Trade between the two countries, however,
could prosper only upon a firm juridical basis; and this in turn
required the establishment of diplomatic relations between the
two governments concerned. This, then, was the second factor
accounting for Labour's decision to extend diplomatic recognition to the Soviet government: it was the price which had to be
paid if the volume of trade with Russia was to be increased, and
the level of unemployment in Britain thereby reduced.

The connection between trade with Soviet Russia and the relief
of unemployment began to receive serious attention in Labour
circles from about the end of 1920. In view of the sharp increase in
the number of unemployed, the Labour Party executive agreed to
allow an emergency resolution on this subject to be discussed at a
special party conference on Ireland on 29 December 1920. The
resolution, which was adopted unanimously, noted that the grow-

ing volume of unemployment and underemployment was 'due in
. . . large measure to the interruption in world trading following on
the war and defective peace treaties, in addition to the folly of
British and Allied policy in relation to the Soviet government of
Russia'. The conference condemned the government for its 'un-
warrantable delay in securing peace and opening trade relations
with the Russian government'.[108]

It was agreed that the Labour Party executive and the Parliamentary Committee of the TUC should set up a Joint Committee of Inquiry into Unemployment. The Committee prepared a
report, 'Unemployment—a Labour Policy', which was presented
to a Special National Joint Conference in London on 27 January
1921. The conference adopted the Joint Committee's report and
reaffirmed the resolution which had been agreed the previous
month, adding that the growing volume of unemployment was
'largely due to the failure of the government to secure the resumption of trade with Russia and central Europe' and calling for the
'immediate adoption of a policy of unobstructed trade' with the
countries concerned.[109] A joint Labour Party–TUC manifesto
was issued on 17 February 1921. It declared that the causes of the
industrial crisis through which Britain was passing lay 'for the
most part, abroad', and that unemployment was the 'direct
outcome of a suicidal foreign policy'. The manifesto called for a
'reversal of the whole line of the Allies' conduct towards Central
Europe and Russia', and for the 'conclusion of a sincere peace
with Russia'.[110]

The Anglo-Russian Trade Agreement, which was signed the
following month, was warmly received in labour circles. The
modest improvement in Anglo-Russian relations which it appeared to presage, however, was felt to be insufficient. A National
Conference on Unemployment and the International Situation,
held under Labour Party and TUC auspices on 8 December 1921,
explored the possibility of the further development of trading
relations between the two countries, and advocated the diplomatic recognition of the Soviet government toward this end. The
party's International Advisory Committee prepared a memorandum which guided the conference in its work. It was 'universally
admitted', the memorandum noted, 'that the foreign situation,
due in large measure to the Government's policy, is the main
cause of the trade depression and unemployment from which our
people are suffering. The tragedy of unemployment in our midst

has at last brought home the fatal errors of our Government's policy abroad.' Britain's exports to Russia could be increased tenfold if credits were made available, the Committee reported, and the import of food could swiftly be resumed.

The 'crucial importance to ourselves of the fullest possible resumption of trade with Russia', the memorandum went on, 'can indeed only be gauged if one realises that Russia offers by far the best—if not the only—alternative to America as a market for our manufactures (which America no longer requires) and also as a source of supply for the food we require (which America is ceasing to grow, and which exchange difficulties are putting out of our reach)'. Russia should be 'enabled to become, as of old, a vast granary for the nations of Europe and a boundless market for their manufactures'. It concluded by recommending the diplomatic recognition of the Soviet government and the provision of credits.¹¹¹ The National Conference, echoing this proposal, agreed that the country's 'present industrial misfortunes' were largely the result of the government's international policy, 'particularly as regards Russia and Central Europe'. It called for a 'reversal of that policy, so as to include the recognition of the Russian Government . . . in the interests of the wage earners of this country'.¹¹²

The resolution was submitted to the Prime Minister on 15 December 1921. At his request it was followed by a lengthier memorandum, 'Unemployment and the International Situation, Reparations and Russia', which described Russia as 'potentially Europe's largest granary and the greatest market in Europe for the purchase of manufactured articles', and argued that the maintenance of a regular and sufficient food supply to the United Kingdom would 'depend more and more upon the prosperity of Russian agriculture'. Since the Soviet government played a central role in commercial relations with the outside world, trade with Russia would depend upon the 'credit of the Russian government, and therefore upon recognition of the Russian government by other governments and upon free and unrestricted cooperation and consultation with it'. In the interests of British trade, the memorandum went on, it was essential that normal relations should be 'fully restored, both diplomatic and otherwise', with the Soviet government, and that credits should be extended to it. Some risk might be involved in doing so, but this had to be accepted in the interests of the development of trade (credits, it suggested, might even prove to be the 'cheapest form of unemployment relief'). Action, moreover, must be taken 'immediately'; the pressure of unemployment was 'dangerously insistent'.[113]

This, then, was the substance of Labour's argument. Unemployment was alarmingly high; it was high because foreign trade had collapsed, in particular trade with Central Europe and Russia; and it might be reduced if that trade were revived. Towards this end the party advocated, in the first place, the extension of credits to the Soviet government. The Russian market, Clynes told the House of Commons, offered 'great opportunities' for the sale of agricultural implements and machinery; but trade of such a kind would be 'impossible without adequate credit arrangements'. Shipping orders to a value of fifteen million pounds, added another Labour member, would have been placed with British dockyards had credit facilities been available: and this would have 'absorbed a considerable amount of unemployment'.[114] O'Grady informed the House that he had seen Krupps locomotives in Russia; and Krupps, he pointed out, was 'not a sympathetic or philanthropic association'. In fact it might be wiser and cheaper and better for Britain and the world, Brailsford wrote, to 'use our resources in paying men to make ploughs and locomotives for Russia, instead of keeping them idle and half alive on doles'.[115]

It was in the second place necessary, if trade were to develop as swiftly as Labour spokesmen desired, that full diplomatic recognition should be extended to the Soviet Russian government. The case was stated most compellingly by Morel. Any businessman, he told the House of Commons, would confirm his statement that the absence of normal diplomatic relations was a 'great stumbling block to the granting of trade facilities'. Merchants, bankers and shipowners were 'naturally shy at doing business, although they are doing business, to a considerable extent, with a country where we have no Embassy and no consulates to look after their interests'.[116] Merchants, he wrote, were disinclined to risk their goods; shipowners were reluctant to sent their ships to Russian ports; crippling rates of insurance were exacted; bankers were unwilling to make advances; credit facilities and transactions were hampered; there was no Embassy or consulate to protect national interests; 'in short, the whole machinery of commerce is semi-paralysed'. Some business could take place upon the basis of short-term credits; but not the 'very much bigger thing of great capital works', such as railways, transport in general, and power stations, in which Britain could have a 'very large share if only there were normal diplomatic relations established'.[117]

Morel argued the case further in correspondence with Robert McNeill, the Under-Secretary of State at the Foreign Office. The absence of normal diplomatic relations, he insisted, was 'in itself a palpable trade deterrent'. The government's continued refusal to extend *de jure* recognition to the Soviet Russian government was a 'serious impediment to the development of commercial relations', and it helped, therefore, to 'aggravate the volume of unemployment in this country'. McNeill declined to 'enter fully into these general considerations'. As Morel noted in a letter to the Secretary of the Fabian Society, enclosing the text of the correspondence, 'the real gist of the matter viz.: the difficulties which the absence of normal diplomatic relations with Russia puts in the way of a full resumption of general Anglo-Russian trade *is not dealt with by the Under-Secretary of State*'.[118]

There was no necessary connection between the advocacy of closer relations with the Soviet government and support for the principles of the system over which it presided. The policy, indeed, might recommend itself in an entirely opposite sense: for, as Snowden explained to the House of Commons, the more Russia traded with other countries, the more it would 'approximate the Russian system to that of other countries with whom they were having commercial relations'. The development of trade with Russia, he noted, might be used as a device to compel the Soviet government to 'throw away the last shreds of Bolshevism and Communism by which it is at present fettered' (there were, moreover, 'great possibilities for the profitable employment of capital').[119] The opening up of trade with Russia, in this view, was the 'best way to kill Bolshevism': even if the men in power survived, their methods would not outlast the 'opening up of intercourse with the rest of the world'. The Russian peasant, Clynes noted, was turning away from the Soviet government; 'he is the man we ought to encourage'.[120]

There were still further considerations. The rise in the level of unemployment meant a reduction in trade union membership and in the affiliated union membership of the Labour Party (which dropped by over a million between 1921 and 1924). This was a serious matter for Labour parliamentarians, many of whom were union officials, and for the party's finances, which derived overwhelmingly from union sources.[121] The party was compelled to announce the end of grants to local agents: and local parties began to experience financial difficulties.[122] The previous year, the ILP's National Administrative Council reported to the party's conference in 1922, had been one of 'great difficulty for all political organizations. . . . The widespread unemployment which has prevailed during the year has seriously affected our income.' As many as one-third of the party's members had at some time been unemployed; and affiliation fees were down by one-quarter.[123] 'If only for the most selfish of reasons (i.e. self-preservation)', Birmingham Trades Council's executive reported in 1924, 'as workers we must think and act internationally'.[124]

As MacDonald observed, moreover, as the unemployed man's 'membership of thrift club lapses, he acquires bad habits'. He might even follow 'allurements of intemperance or . . . the temple of Fortune'. Gambling, he warned, led to 'moral and intellectual unsettlement . . ., an impatience against the slow process of legitimate accumulation, a revolt against the discipline of . . . sustained action'.[125] Capitalism, he conceded, was ultimately to blame; but unlike G. D. H. Cole, who professed to see no solution within its bounds, MacDonald argued that the 'only way to deal with the problem at its roots' was to support the parliamentary work of the Labour Party.[126] He deplored 'vain and futile demonstrations'. The ILP, MacDonald warned, must not let the leadership of the unemployed pass out of its hands, nor must the Labour Party allow itself to be 'stampeded into demands which have no relation to sound policy'.[127]

'One of the most marvellous things in the world', MacDonald remarked, was the 'docility' of the unemployed. One could not, however, rely indefinitely upon their forbearance. The unemployed of London, warned the *British Trades Union Review*, had 'already taken drastic action'. Unless steps of an effective kind were taken to deal with the problem of unemployment, 'serious trouble will arise such as we have never known'. The workers were 'becoming more bitter and desperate daily'.[128] To reduce unemployment, accordingly, was to reduce the political influence of the Communist Party, into whose hands the leadership of the unemployed workers' movement had largely fallen, and to undermine the position of militants within the labour and trade union movement generally. It was an additional ground for the adoption and promotion of the party's policy of the development of trading relations with and the diplomatic recognition of the Soviet Russian government.

The overriding consideration, however, remained the belief that diplomatic recognition would materially assist the development of British–Soviet trade and thus contribute to the reduction of unemployment and to industrial recovery, a prospect which appealed to traders and manufacturers as much as it did to Labour Party leaders. 'Those who could not respond to the moral appeal, that Russia should be allowed, undisturbed by outside interference, to work out her salvation for herself—her own way', Ponsonby noted, could 'now be rallied by the practical, though more sordid consideration, that trading with Russia is good business. Therefore, in the business world there is a change of opinion, and consequently', he added, 'a step in the right direction becomes possible'.[129] The party's major spokesman, indeed, pressed the interests of business in this connection with little sign of diffidence. Henderson wrote to Baldwin to express the party's regret at the delay in granting a visa to Rakovsky, the newly-appointed Soviet representative. The hitch was most unfortunate, he felt, 'especially in view of the effort now being made by the British Trade Delegation to do business in that country'.[130] The immense Russian population, Clynes pointed out, offered a 'fine field for British trade if our commercial and political leaders face the problem with courage'.[131]

The termination of the trade agreement, added MacDonald, representing what he thought to be majority opinion among businessmen interested in the Russian trade, would be a 'serious handicap to British traders'. He quoted to the House of Commons from a letter written to him by Ruston and Hornby Limited, makers of agricultural implements and oil and gas engines. In the previous year, 1922, he reported, the firm had done over a hundred thousand pounds' worth of business with the Soviet authorities, and it hoped to increase this trade 'greatly' in the current year. In general, the business outlook was 'distinctly hopeful'. Every firm which could do so, MacDonald urged, 'ought to be encouraged to do business with Russia'.[132] At any time during the previous twelve months, he told the House of Commons in November 1923, 'any businessman who knew the situation of Russia from the inside could have told us that if [the Expor

Credit] Act was used for the purpose of backing trade with Russia to a reasonable extent, that trade would be very safe and would enable hundreds and thousands of our workmen to be put into work'.[133]

Defending recognition in the House, Clynes quoted authoritative business opinion to the effect that not a single instance had occurred in which the Russian government had failed to honour any arrangement of a commercial or financial nature. The Soviet authorities' reputation in this respect was 'without reproach'. Labour was in no sense in agreement with the Soviet government in political outlook, method or principle: indeed the Diehards could scarcely say things more extreme or more hostile against the Labour Party than the leaders of that party expressed daily against the Soviet government. 'So far as British employers, British trading companies and British commercial men could be assisted through the agency of the government in relations with Russia', however, Labour's view was that such support 'should not be withheld from any who are anxious or willing to deal either with the Russian government or with the Russian employers of labour'.[134]

This was, on the whole, the opinion of the business community also. The opinion of 'business interests generally', Sir A. Balfour, the chairman and managing director of a Sheffield steelworks and the President of the Association of British Chambers of Commerce, informed a meeting of the Board of Trade Advisory Council, was that 'recognition of the Russian government was one step forward'. He himself 'welcomed the *de jure* recognition of Russia'.[135] There were 'very many influential people associated with trade and commerce', Henderson noted, who were 'exceedingly anxious that Russia should be recognized'. Recognition, the *Fortnightly Review* pointed out, had 'met with considerable approval even in circles which have no connection with the Labour Party'. The 'commercial aspect of recognition', in particular, appealed to the businessmen of the country, who hoped to find a market for their goods in Russia. The new government, commented the *Economist*, appeared at least to have 'started in the right direction'.[136]

MacDonald summed up the party's policy in the field of foreign affairs in a short book, *The Foreign Policy of the Labour Party*, which appeared in the autumn of 1923. A Labour government, he wrote, would consider its own world policy 'essentially akin to the spirit and purposes of America'; and it would pursue a policy of 'consistent friendship and co-operation with the people of America'. The influence of the UDC and of the Liberal recruits was evident in the statements that the League of Nations would form the 'focus of our contacts with Europe', that the government would support the principles of free trade, that it would modify its diplomatic style, and that it would bear in mind 'our responsibility to Germany'.

Regarding Russia more specifically, MacDonald made it clear that Bolshevik methods were 'not ours'. Labour disagreed profoundly with Bolshevist methods, and with their adherence to 'abstract book theories and dogmas' such as the nationalisation of the property and investments of foreign nationals. A Labour government, nevertheless, would recognise the Soviet government without delay. Existing policy, he thought, was 'foredoomed to failure', and in addition it had been 'very damaging to our interests'. Only in August 1923 a 'responsible body of traders' had been compelled to go to Moscow to make their own arrangements. A Labour government, MacDonald promised, would take 'immediate steps' to develop trade with Russia by direct communication with Moscow and by granting what assistance was legitimate, including export guarantees. This, it was thought, would facilitate the subsequent conclusion of a treaty dealing with the question of confiscated property.

In the second place, there was a need to guard against the possibility that Russia might unite with Germany in order to subvert the Versailles settlement. The victors in the world war had failed to make a real peace, MacDonald argued, and Russia was of all powers the most likely to upset their arrangements, for it had enormous reserves of power and could undermine treaties and conventions to which its government had not been a signatory. 'Nobody but a madman', wrote MacDonald, could 'contemplate without horror a combination of revengeful German economic power and hostile Russia material and human resources against the rest of Europe'.

Thirdly, Labour's policy of diplomatic relations was likely to prove a more effective anti-Bolshevik policy than that of the previous and preceding governments. Boycott, forgery and faked evidence had formed nine-tenths of the propaganda which had been directed against the Bolsheviks in both Britain and America;

but this, MacDonald warned, was the 'very worst defence'. The firm and well-informed opposition of the Second International between 1919 and 1922, in contrast, inspired mainly by British Labour and its colleagues in Germany and Scandinavia, had 'borne the brunt of the fight against Bolshevism in its young vigorous days'. Only by a continuation of the same policy, he believed, could the 'noxious weed ... be cleaned out'.

Recognition, MacDonald emphasised in conclusion, 'in no way meant that our Labour movement agreed with [the Soviet] Government'. Diplomatic relations were 'in no sense a partnership'; they were simply a channel for diplomatic communications, the need for which could hardly be disputed. A Labour government, moreover, would 'stand no nonsense and no monkey tricks from Russian diplomatic representatives', who would be compelled to observe the 'most scrupulously correct behaviour'.[137] The Soviet government had in fact been recognised, he told the 1924 Labour Party conference, 'for exactly the same reason that Christian Foreign Secretaries have recognized Mohammedans and people whose religious persuasions were of somewhat more doubtful quality even than that'.[138] As a summary of the party's policy toward the Soviet government this could scarcely be improved.

Conclusion: Class, Party and Foreign Policy

This study has sought to demonstrate that an adequate account of the development of British-Soviet relations over the period under consideration cannot confine itself simply to a description of the process by which that policy was formulated within government. Individual decisions were, of course, powerfully influenced by the advice of the government's representatives abroad, the recommendations of the Foreign Office, the predilections of the Foreign Secretary of the day and the views of the Cabinet as a whole. At a more fundamental level, however, British policy was shaped by a number of factors which together constituted the structural environment within which the makers of policy had necessarily to work. The most important of these factors, so far as relations with the Soviet government were concerned, were the fluctuating levels of unemployment and foreign trade, the strength and political orientation of colonial nationalism and the extent and degree of militancy of labour solidarity with the Russian workers' state. It is in the interaction between these factors and British governing circles, we have suggested, that an explanation of the course of British-Soviet relations must ultimately be located. Those relations, that is to say, were an expression, in the last resort, of relations between classes.

This is not necessarily to suggest that the Conservative Party, as the traditional custodian of the interests of big business, was engaged in a policy of consistent and uncompromising hostility towards the Soviet government, while Labour, as a party at least ostensibly representing the different and opposed interests of working people, aimed rather at the establishment of closer and more fraternal relations with that government. In fact no categorisation of this kind can reasonably be sustained. Both the Labour and Conservative parties, as we have seen, were deeply divided on the Russian question; and even the business world, while presumably united so far as the defence of capitalist interests in the abstract was concerned, was by no means agreed about the policy towards the Soviet government by which those interests might best be promoted. A closer study of the historical mediation of class forces, in fact, suggests that rather more significant than the ostensible contest between a 'Labour' and a 'Conservative' Russian policy was a debate which took place within these parties, and which divided the business community also. This was a debate, not between supporters and opponents of the Soviet regime (for the former were at no time a considerable quantity), but between those who believed that the Soviet government might most effectively be undermined by a policy of hostile confrontation, and those who inclined to the view that the same object might more readily be attained through negotiation and the development of trade and commerce between the two countries—a policy which had the additional merit of promising to rescue British trade and unemployment from their post-war depression.

The House of Commons elected in 1918 had become known as a 'lot of hard-faced men who looked as if they had done well out of the war'. The prevailing type, Baldwin observed, was a 'rather successful looking business type' which was 'not very attractive'.[1] Lord Davidson drew attention, in a letter to Lord Stamfordham, to the 'high percentage of hard-headed men, mostly on the make, who fill up the ranks of the Unionist Party. The old-fashioned country gentlemen, and even the higher ranks of the learned professions, are scarcely represented at all.' He had, indeed, the impression, Lloyd George remarked on one occasion, that he was addressing not the House of Commons, but the TUC on one side and the Associated Chambers of Commerce on the other.[2]

So far as the Conservatives were concerned, at least, there was some substance in this observation. About two hundred and sixty businessmen were elected to the House of Commons in 1918, a figure considerably in excess of the average for the post-war years as a whole.[3] It was established five years later that as many as two hundred and fifty-five directors of public companies or landowners were represented in the House of Commons, with a further two hundred and seventy-seven in the House of Lords. About one-fifth of the former represented firms involved in the engineering, shipbuilding and metal industries, and a further fifth came from the world of finance, land and investment. Lloyd George's supporters in the House of Commons, the *New Statesman* calculated, represented capital to an average value to fifty-one million pounds a head. Another detailed investigation concluded that the opposition to the Labour Party in Parliament represented nothing so much as a 'mass meeting of employers and shareholders, assisted by their legal representatives'.[4]

The employers' organisation itself, the Federation of British Industries, maintained a Parliamentary Department, and a Liaison Department was set up in 1918. In fact it was hardly necessary to provide for communication between the two bodies in this formal manner, for the connection was scarcely at risk: at least sixty-six MPs, and seventy members of the House of Lords, were at this time directors of companies which belonged to the Federation. Directors of such firms, moreover, were in many cases prominently represented in government, Horne, Chamberlain and Lloyd-Greame among them. A reciprocal link was established when Sir Eric Geddes, a former Minister of Transport, became President of the Federation in November 1922.[5]

Bonar Law's accession to the party leadership, indeed, has been described as the 'final open assumption of power by the party's capitalist wing'.[6] Bonar Law, noted Amery, had few interests outside business, 'and politics when they became his business'. Within the Cabinet he was a business man for whom an agenda was something to which decisions were to be got as quickly as possible. In Lord Davidson's view, he regarded himself as a 'man at the head of a big business who allowed the work to be done by others and gives it general supervision'.[7] With the subsequent accession of Baldwin to the Premiership in the spring of 1923, commented the *New Leader*, the Federation of British Industries had 'definitely assumed the reins of power'.[8] It had, indeed, been partly upon this basis that Davidson had recommended Baldwin's candidature in a memorandum written after Bonar Law had resigned. Baldwin, Davidson noted, had 'the confidence of the City and the commercial world generally'.[9]

Baldwin had followed his father into the old-established family business and into the House of Commons (his father had been responsible, among other things, for the introduction of cider into the Members' Bar).[10] The operations of Baldwins Ltd. were on a major scale even before the war, and Baldwin left its administration very largely in the hands of subordinates. He did become vice-chairman of the company upon the death of his father, however, and he was also a director of Great Western Railways and of Lloyds Bank.[11] In Parliament he gravitated naturally towards the Business Committee of Conservative MPs and to a series of related positions in government, becoming in turn President of the Board of Trade and Chancellor of the Exchequer. He brought to his stewardship of the nation's affairs a consciousness of the family business, a place, as he described it, 'where I knew and had known from childhood every man on the ground . . . where I was able to talk with the men not only about the troubles in the works, but troubles at home and their wives'; a place, moreover, where 'strikes and lock-outs were unknown'. His policy in social matters, it has been remarked, was the 'straightforward expression of the benevolent but firm philosophy of the West Country employer, now translated to the supreme charge of the country's economy'.[12]

Curzon's background and attitudes were clearly rather different from those of Bonar Law and Baldwin, although it would be wrong to suppose that he had had no experience at all of the business world. He had, in fact, been for a year a member of the board of the Persian Bank Mining Rights Corporation Limited; and he was also for some time the chairman of the Imperial Bank of Persia.[13] His business involvements, however, were clearly subordinate to the imperial perspective to which his life had been dedicated and which informed his whole conduct of foreign affairs. The *Socialist Review* described Curzon as an 'Elder Statesman . . . whose feet are washed by the Persian Gulf, while his head is still in the Pamirs'. All his life, Newbold observed, he had been 'representative of the those interests which looked away from the Dominions and the Democracy of the US to the autocratic Empire in India'.[14]

Commander Kenworthy MP, on a visit to Russia in 1923, identified these interests as 'very influential circles, mainly [composed of] landowners and the aristocracy'. Phillips Price, writing in the *Communist*, described them as 'outspoken militarists elements and . . . certain powerful families of the aristocracy which have regarded the War Office, the Admiralty and the India Office for years past as their special preserve'.[15] These 'reactionaries of an older period, guarding the property of the landed proprietors and the credit manipulators—expressing the point of view of the Court and the Services', were held to be the 'strongest section of

the capitalist class' early in 1922. It was these groups, together
with 'powerful interests in the City', which provided the main
substance of Lord Curzon's support.[16]

Their uncompromising attitude towards the Soviet government found enthusiastic support among the firms and individuals
whose property in Russia had been nationalised. Investors and
creditors, even distressed gentlefolk of good position who might
now be 'compelled to enter the workhouses',[17] were initially
inclined to regard their misfortunes with some fortitude, believing
that the nationalisation of private property could be no more than
a temporary aberration from the universal principles of political
economy. By September 1921, however, as patience and good
humour began to exhaust themselves, an Association of British
Creditors of Russia was formed.[18] The Association represented
some 350,000 British investors, traders and industrialists, whose
total claims against the Soviet government amounted to some
three hundred million pounds. It proposed to bring its influence
to bear in appropriate quarters, thus compelling the recognition
of British claims and the resumption of commercial relations
between the two countries on the 'right lines'.[19] The Association's
president, Leslie Urquhart, was present at the Genoa Conference
at the British government's invitation, and was a member of its
delegation to the Hague Conference. He informed a Belgian
interviewer at the time that the Russian delegation's concessions
were 'quite illusory', and that the 'only solution' was the 're-
establishment of a system of private property without
restrictions'.[20]

The Association wrote to the Foreign Office in the spring of
1923 to express its 'warm appreciation' of the government's
decisive action. Meetings were organised in the City of London,
and the Association canvassed MPs in support of its claims.[21]
Izvestiya, indeed, saw the British creditors as 'undoubtedly the
main instigators of [this attempt to] break off relations between
England and Russia'.[22] British investment in Tsarist Russia,
however, had always been less than of France (which accounted
for some 32.6 per cent of total foreign investment),[23] and British
creditors exercised an altogether less considerable influence over
the making of government policy than did their French counterparts. The influence of the 'traditional' section of the Conservative Party, moreover, that section whose position rested upon
colonial and landed possessions and whose interests, at least as far

as Russia was concerned, had much in common with those of the investors and creditors, was in relative decline within the party.

Aristocrats and members of the landed gentry, it has been established, together accounted for some thirty-three members of the Conservative government of 1902 (62.3 per cent), but for only twenty-eight (41.1 per cent) of that of 1924. Within the Cabinet itself the relative decline of the more traditional sections of the party was even more pronounced, aristocrats and the landed gentry together accounting for 61.1 per cent of the Conservative Cabinet of 1902 but for only 28.5 per cent of that of 1924. Landowning was the occupation of half of the members of the 1902 Conservative Cabinet, but only of 14.5 per cent of those of 1924; while members with a background in industry and commerce had increased from about a quarter to a third of the total.[24] Curzon himself, Lord Davidson remarked, was an 'ancient monument and constructed like one'.[25] The Conservatives were now a businessmen's party, under the leadership successively of a Glasgow-Canadian iron merchant (Bonar Law) and two Midland industrialists (Baldwin and Neville Chamberlain).[26] It was the perspectives of manufacturing industry and commerce, rather than those of imperial and colonial wealth, which came increasingly to inform their policy in government.

It is important for our purposes to note that the relative position of these groups exercised a very direct influence upon the course of British diplomatic relations with the Soviet government. To Curzon and those who shared his views, to accept that even the most minimal relations should be maintained with 'this deplorable government at Moscow' was a major concession; while the best response to the Bolsheviks' nefarious designs upon British colonial possessions in the East, it was thought, was to issue a series of firm and sharply-worded ultimata. At least in the earlier part of 1923, Kenworthy told *Izvestiya*, it had been this group which exercised a dominant influence within the Cabinet; and it had been these 'Conservative, mainly agrarian circles', in the view of the Soviet deputy trade representative in Britain, which had played the major role in the threatened rupture of relations of the spring of that year.[27]

Their action, however, had compelled 'liberal circles of the industrial bourgeoisie' to come to the defence of commercial relations with Soviet Russia, in whose development they were now agreed in seeing the prospect of considerable gain; and these views found some response in governing quarters. Bonar Law, in Kenworthy's view, personally favoured the diplomatic recognition of the Soviet government: he was a 'practical man, who understood the advantages for Britain of such recognition'.[28] Baldwin was also believed to take a 'rather more moderate line than Lord Curzon's on the Russian question', which he saw from a 'rather different angle after his long experience of trade affairs'.[29] With the accession of Baldwin to the Premiership, and later of Austen Chamberlain to the Foreign Secretaryship, the influence of pragmatic business opinion within the Cabinet appeared to have become a preponderant one.

It was, however, by no means an assured or undisputed predominance. For while the 'businessmen' were able to prevent the implementation of Curzon's ultimatum in the spring of 1923, they were not sufficiently powerful (nor, perhaps, convinced) to take the logical next step and confer diplomatic recognition upon the Soviet government. The 'colonial-agrarian-finance' group, for their part, succeeded in preventing the ratification of the treaties with the Soviet government which had been signed by the Labour government in the summer of 1924, but they proved unable to secure the revocation of the diplomatic recognition of the Soviet government, as Churchill urged Baldwin to do immediately after the new administration had been formed.[30] It was a division which recalled the earlier cleavage in ruling circles between 'doctrinaire' and 'circumspect interventionists'; and it goes far to explain the apparent ambiguity which would characterise the next phase of the Conservatives' attempt to 'solve the Russian problem'.[31]

Labour's policy was no less ambivalent. The party was also a divided one: but these divisions (or so, at least, it has been argued) were less between sections of its leadership than between that leadership as a whole and a more radically-disposed rank and file. Only the intervention of the working-class movement, it has been suggested, brought about the diplomatic recognition of the Soviet government by a reluctant Labour Cabinet; and that intervention, it is further argued, was inspired by sentiments of class solidarity with the Russian workers' state.[32] We have sought to demonstrate above that this thesis—generally, although not universally deployed by Soviet scholars[33]—is a mistaken and misconceived one. There is in fact no good evidence that it was working-class intervention which led the Labour government to implement its election promise to confer diplomatic recognition upon the Soviet government; equally, it is not difficult to account for the party's advocacy of recognition in terms which owe nothing to hypothetical sentiments of solidarity. The influence of the ex-Liberals upon the making of the party's foreign policy and the pressing need to reduce the level of unemployment, we have suggested, were rather more salient considerations.

Indeed it is the episode of the Council of Action, so often cited as evidence of the readiness of the working class to defy even the constitution in order to 'save the Soviet republic', which in many ways provides the clearest demonstration that working people conceived of their dispute with government policy in no such terms. Rank and file opposition was overwhelmingly to the threat of war rather than to the possibility of an attack upon Soviet Russia, whose government, when intervention had been at its most determined during the previous year, they had taken few effective steps to defend. As soon as the threat of war had receded, moreover, the Councils movement lost most of its momentum, and no efforts which the 'Hands off Russia' Committee could undertake proved capable of restoring the determination which the movement had once manifested, even when it became clear that British military assistance to the Polish forces had not in fact been ended. There was no greater response when the formation of Councils of Action was urged in the spring of 1923 to protest against the possible break-off of diplomatic relations with Russia.[34] The Councils of Action episode demonstrated that Labour leaders, however moderate their inclinations, could be induced to undertake 'direct action' against the government of the day if the rank and file of the movement were resolved upon it. The party's failure to adopt a consistent policy of class solidarity with the Soviet state, conversely, must largely be explained in terms of the absence of support for such a policy among the mass of working people themselves.

It would be too much to deny altogether the existence within the labour movement of some degree of amorphous sympathy with the new Soviet government.[35] More tangible evidence of support, however, is remarkably difficult to find. Membership of the Communist Party, for instance, was one of the ways in which working-class support for the principles of the Soviet state might be expected to have found expression. According to official figures, however, the party had four thousand members in August

1920, at the time of its foundation, but only three thousand by May 1924; and numbers had declined still further by the end of the decade. Membership fell, in other words, at a time when other left-wing groups, such as the ILP, were rapidly increasing in size.[36] It would be difficult, moreover, to argue that the party's political influence had recorded a compensating advance. The party was refused representation upon the National Council of Action, and upon all but a few local Councils; and its attempts to affiliate to the Labour Party were defeated by margins which varied only in their degree of comprehensiveness. The rejection of the party's application to affiliate by the Labour Party conference in 1924, by a majority of more than sixteen to one, was by a margin so humiliating that it could not seriously be argued that the manipulation of the Labour leadership was alone responsible for it. Considering the level of unemployment and of the suffering of the British proletariat, Zinoviev remarked with understandable impatience, 'the slow growth of Communism in Britain is remarkable'.[37]

Another way in which this amorphous sympathy with the Soviet regime might have found expression was in the form of contributions to the Russian famine relief fund which the TUC inaugurated in 1921. The TUC General Council itself opened the fund on 29 August 1921 with a donation of a thousand pounds. By the following November, however, only a further £1,548/4/10 had been received. This surely did not 'fairly represent the degree of goodwill towards Russia existing in trade union organizations', commented the *British Trades Union Review*; 'a little sacrifice on the part of the rank and file of the trade union movement could safely be made'. The time had come, urged the *Herald*, to show 'to whom international working class solidarity is a mere phrase and to whom it is deed and truth'.[38]

British workers, however, showed some reluctance to demonstrate their attachment to the latter rather than the former interpretation; and the *British Trades Union Review* was obliged to report the following March that the response to its appeal had been 'far from satisfactory'. But neither the TUC nor the Labour Party undertook any further action beyond an (unavailing) appeal to the government to make a generous contribution to the relief fund and to receive a deputation,[39] and the response of local labour bodies was scarcely more gratifying. Liverpool Trades Council, for instance, sent a 'strong resolution' on famine relief to the Prime Minister in February 1922, but appears to have declined to make any more tangible contribution. Glasgow Trades Council decided that in view of the unemployment in Britain it was 'not practicable to render support', and recommended instead that an appeal be made to the government.[40] Edgar Whitehead, the British representative on the Central Workers' International Relief Committee, was compelled to report that the total relief which the Committee had received amounted to no more than a farthing per organised worker per six months, a result which revealed a 'total indifference as damning alike to leaders of various sections of the working class of this country as to the rank and file'. British workers had contributed, not, as their numbers might have suggested, the second largest amount of famine relief, but the ninth largest; less than a third, in fact, of the amount collected by Dutch workers. This was not, he concluded, 'an enviable result for the workers of the proudest and richest country in the world'.[41]

It proved remarkably difficult, in fact, to detach party members from their traditionally distant and somewhat patronising attitude to foreign affairs in general, and towards the Soviet government in particular. This was not simply a matter of the attitude of the party in general towards the movement for colonial independence (and on this point even Communist Party policies were not without ambiguity). More important for our purposes was the attitude adopted, even by those whose record in terms of domestic questions was an uncompromisingly militant one, towards the Soviet government in Moscow. Frank Hodges, for instance, the miners' general secretary, informed the 1922 Labour Party conference that the Communists were the 'intellectual slaves of Moscow . . . taking orders from the Asiatic mind'. Two years later one of the party's MPs went so far as to object to the dictation of British policy by a 'certain number of gentlemen in Moscow, with unpronounceable names, and of very dubious nationality'.[42] Working people who regarded other members of their own class in this manner could scarcely be expected to conceive that they might have political interests in common.

This was a verdict, essentially, upon the structure and political consciousness of the British working class movement. Even at this time it was a source of some exasperation in left-wing circles. As the *Communist* put it, 'four generations of industrial capitalism have bred a class so pathetically loyal to existing institutions that almost any crime is regarded with less abhorrence than attacks upon the framework of society. Every thinking capitalist is amazed at this stolid conservatism, however much he secretly rejoices. It is worth battalions of riflemen and parks of artillery to a governing class otherwise very shaky about its future prospects'.[43] There was no use, wrote the *Communist Review*, in disguising the 'melancholy fact that British Labour today is impotent and apathetic'. A year later the journal conceded that 'from the International Labour standpoint, the British masses are the most apathetic at the moment'.[44] It was, ironically, the least proletarian section of the party, the influential but numerically insignificant ex-Liberals, which was typically most favourably disposed towards closer relations with the Soviet government for their own sake. To the party's working-class majority, more concerned with unemployment than with the principles of the international political order, closer relations with the Soviet government were simply the price which had to be paid for the alleviation of their local economic difficulties.

It was in many ways incongruous that the government's Russian policy should have been opposed so diffidently and ineffectively at a time when labour militancy—as reflected, for instance, in the number and intensity of industrial disputes—was otherwise at an unusually high level. Even the most radical sections of the movement, however, consistently failed to discern a connection between the Russian workers' attempt to establish a socialist state and their own domestic objectives; and Labour's policy towards Russia, in the absence of a political commitment of this kind, was in the end determined by more mundane considerations of trade and unemployment. There were many who regarded Labour's recognition of the Soviet government, motivated thought it might have been by such essentiallly 'economistic' sentiments, as a defeat for capitalist interests. Business opinion, however, was generally favourably disposed towards recognition, and regarded it as a measure which was likely if anything to weaken the influence of socialism within both Soviet Russia and the labour movement in Britain. It might be more accurate to conclude that Labour, precisely by basing its decision to recognise the Soviet government upon utilitarian considerations of the kind which have been indicated, was in fact conceding its capitalist opponent an altogether more crucial—ideological—victory.

Notes

1 THE TRADE AGREEMENT (pp. 3–26)

1. Lord Riddell, *Intimate Diary of the Peace Conference and After* (London 1923), p. 161.
2. F.O. 371/4032/179078 and 179079.
3. The best accounts of the preceding period are Richard H. Ullman, *Intervention and the War* (London 1961) and *Britain and the Russian Civil War* (London 1968).
4. Birse memorandum, 21 January 1920, F.O. 371/4032/172292.
5. 125 *H.C.Debs.* col. 43, 10 February 1920; *DBFP*, vol. 2, no. 71, p. 874.
6. To Derby (Paris) for Curzon, 20 January 1920, F.O. 371/4032/172293.
7. Tsentrosoyuz to Paris, 2 February 1920, *DVP*, vol. 2, no. 231, p. 358.
8. Tsentrosoyuz to Paris, 25 February 1920, *DVP*, vol, 2, no. 255, pp. 391–92. The co-operatives had been nationalised on 27 January 1920; Lenin appears to have been aware that it was intended to use them as a 'mechanism for the restoration of capitalism' (Lenin, *PSS*, vol. 40, p. 53).
9. L. B. Krasin, *Vneshtorg i Vneshnyaya Ekonomicheskaya Politika Sovetskogo Pravitel'stva* (Petrograd 1921), pp. 5–6.
10. Riddell, *Intimate Diary*, p. 175.
11. Telegram for M. Krasin, 25 April 1920, *DBFP*, vol. 8, no. 20, pp. 230–31.
12. L. B. Krasin, *Voprosy Vneshnei Torgovli* (Moscow 1928), pp. 249 and 250.
13. I. M. Maisky, 'Anglo-sovetskoe torgovoe soglashenie 1921 goda', *Voprosy Istorii*, 1957, no. 5, p. 77.
14. Memorandum, 11 May 1920, Cabinet Paper CP 1309, Cab 24/106; Lord Beaverbrook, *The Decline and Fall of Lloyd George* (London 1963), p. 292.
15. Conference of British Ministers with the Head of the Russian Trade Delegation, 10 Downing Street, 31 May 1920, *DBFP* vol. 8, no. 24, pp. 281–92. The records of the negotiations are included in this volume of the British Documents; a detailed narrative account is available in Richard H. Ullman, *The Anglo-Soviet Accord* (London 1972).
16. *DBFP*, vol. 8, no. 37, pp. 380–8.
17. Memorandum, 30 June 1920, F.O. 371/4036/207569.
18. F.O. 371/4036/207602 (Russian text in *DVP*, vol. 3, no. 6, pp. 16–17).
19. 131 *H.C.Debs.* col. 1950, 12 July 1920.
20. Rumbold (Warsaw), 23 January 1920, *DBFP*, vol. 3, no. 651, pp. 765–6.
21. Notes of a Conversation at the Villa Fraineuse, Spa, 10 July 1920, *DBFP*, vol. 8, no. 57, p. 515, and no. 59, Appendix 1, p. 530.
22. Curzon to Chicherin, 11 July 1920, F.O. 371/4058/207846.
23. Curzon to Chicherin, 20 July 1920, F.O. 371/4058/208802.

24. Notes of a Conference held at 10 Downing Street, *DBFP*, vol. 8, no. 81, pp. 670–80; *ibid.*, 6 August 1920, no. 82, pp. 681–708.
25. Lloyd George to Kamenev, 8 August 1920, *DVP*, vol. 3, p. 98.
26. Notes of an Anglo-French Conference, Lympne, 8 August 1920, *DBFP*, vol. 8, no. 83, pp. 709–23; no. 84, pp. 724–30; and no. 85, Appendix 3, pp. 747–8.
27. Conference of Ministers, 10 August 1920, Cab 49(20) Appendix 2, Cab 23/22.
28. 133 *H.C.Debs.* cols. 351–3, 10 August 1920.
29. Notes of a Conversation at the Villa Haslihorn, Lucerne, ICP 143, Cab 29/87.
30. Curzon to Chicherin, 24 August 1920, in F.O. 371/5434/N4512.
31. 25 August 1920, *DVP*, vol. 3, no. 72, pp. 144–47; Balfour to Chicherin, 1 September 1920, *ibid.*, p. 171.
32. Balfour to Kamenev, 23 August 1920, *DVP*, vol. 3, pp. 147–9.
33. Conference of Ministers, 10 September 1920, Cab 51(20) Appendix 4(2), Cab 23/22.
34. Notes of a Conference with the Russian Trade Delegation, 10 Downing Street, 10 September 1920, *DBFP*, vol. 8, no. 90, pp. 783–91.
35. Conference of Ministers, 15 September 1920, Cab 51(20) Appendix 4 minute 2 (a), Cab 23/22; Cabinet minutes, 30 September 1920, Cab 53(20)2, Cab 23/22.
36. Curzon to Chicherin, 1 October 1920, in F.O. 371/5434/N4512.
37. Curzon to Chicherin, 9 October 1920, in F.O. 371/5431/N1118.
38. Chicherin to Curzon, 13 October 1920, *DVP*, vol. 3, no. 133, pp. 258–29.
39. *Ibid.*, no. 167, p. 313, 1 November 1920.
40. 133 *H.C.Debs.* col 918, 20 October 1920.
41. *Dokumenty i Materialy po Istorii Sovetsko-Pol'skikh Otnoshenii* vol. 3 (Moscow 1965), nos. 236 and 275, pp. 428–36 and 520–552.
42. Cabinet minutes, 11 November 1920, Cab 60(20) 1, Cab 23/23.
43. Curzon to Sir H. Dering (Bucharest), 21 October 1920, Curzon Papers F112/302.
44. Received 14 February 1920, Lloyd George Papers F/95/2/9; George Lansbury, *What I Saw in Russia* (London 1920), pp. 22 and 27.
45. W. T. Goode, *Bolshevism at Work* (London 1920), pp. 121, 123, 139 and 140.
46. H. G. Wells, *Russia in the Shadows* (London 1920), p. 64; Curzon to Sir H. Dering (Bucharest), 21 October 1920, Curzon Papers F112/302. Other contemporary accounts include Col l'E. Malone, *The Russian Republic* (London 1920); Arthur Ransome, *Six Weeks in Russia in 1919* (London 1919); and Sylvia Pankhurst, *Soviet Russia as I Saw It* (London 1921).
47. *British Labour Delegation to Russia, 1920, Report* (London 1920), pp. 6–29.
48. 'What we saw in Russia', *Labour Leader*, 27 June 1920.
49. *The Times*, 8 July and 10 June 1920.
50. *Labour Leader*, 29 July 1920, and *Pioneer* (Merthyr Tydfil), 31 July 1920.
51. Cmd. 1041, Parliamentary Papers 1920, pp. 2, 11 and 17.
52. *18th Abstract of Labour Statistics of the United Kingdom*, Cmd. 2740, Parliamentary Papers 1926, p. 50.
53. Conference of Ministers, 24 January 1921, Cab 4(21) Appendix 2(3), Cab 23/24.

54. Cabinet minutes, 24 December 1920, Cab 77(20)2 and 3, Cab 23/23.
55. 134 *H.C.Debs.* col 1521, 15 November 1920.
56. 134 *H.C.Debs.* cols. 2116–17, 18 November 1920, and 135 *H.C.Debs.* cols. 897 and 954, 29 November 1920.
57. 133 *H.C.Debs.* col. 1516, 20 October 1920.
58. Krasin, *Voprosy Vneshnei Torgovli*, pp. 251–2; Soviet archival source quoted in V. A. Shishkin, *Sovetskoe Gosudarstvo i Strany Zapada v 1917–1923 gg.* (Leningrad 1969), p. 186.
59. *The Times*, 29 September 1920; Shishkin, *Sovetskoe Gosudarstvo*, p. 187.
60. Lloyd George Papers F/58/2/1 (Russian text in *DVP*, vol. 3, no. 123, pp. 228–32).
61. Krasin, *Voprosy Vneshnei Torgovli*, pp. 279–80.
62. *Sunday Times*, 19 December 1920, in F.O. 371/5434/N4547.
63. Indian Tea Association to the F.O., 6 December 1920, F.O. 371/5434/N4637.
64. F.O. 371/5434/N4645, 22 December 1920.
65. F.O. 371/5431/N2218 (Russian text in *DVP*, vol. 3, no. 170, pp. 314–16); Chicherin to Curzon, 9 November 1920, F.O. 371/5431/N2266 (Russian text in *DVP*, vol. 3, no. 171, pp. 320–4).
66. *Godovoi Otchet NKID k IX S"ezdu Sovetov, 1920–21gg.* (Moscow 1922), p. 136.
67. Krasin, *Voprosy Vneshnei Torgovli*, p. 280.
68. F.O. 371/5434/N3804, 6 December 1920; F.O. 371/5434/N3741, 4 December 1920.
69. Krasin, *Voprosy Vneshnei Torgovli*, p. 280.
70. Cabinet minutes, 17 November 1920, Cab 61(20)6, Cab 23/23.
71. Cabinet minutes, 18 November 1920, Cab 62(20)4, Cab 23/23.
72. Cabinet minutes, 26 November 1920, Cab 64(20)3, Cab 23/23. Chamberlain, Churchill, Curzon and Montagu recorded their dissent from part of the conclusions.
73. Minutes of a meeting at the Board of Trade, 29 November 1920, F.O. 371/5434/N4655. On 1 December 1920 a draft Soviet text was handed to the British negotiators (both texts are contained in *ibid.*; printed versions are in *DBFP*, vol. 8, pp. 869–78).
74. Krasin to Wise, 30 November 1920, *DVP*, vol. 3, no. 196, pp. 351–3.
75. Krasin, *Voprosy Vneshnei Torgovli*, p. 282; Maxse, 'Summary of Relations between HMG and the Soviet Government from September 12 1920, to December 22 1920', 30 December 1920, F.O. 371/5435/N4997.
76. Meeting of British Ministers and the Russian Trade Delegation, 21 December 1920, F.O. 371/5435/N4777.
77. 139 *H.C.Debs.* col. 476, 9 March 1921; *Izvestiya*, 11 March 1921.
78. The Revolutionary Committee, it was reported, described themselves as 'true upholders of the Soviet system'. The feeling, according to another report, was 'very confident, but anti-White' (received 14 March 1921, F.O. 371/6847/N3223; Secret Intelligence Service report no. 86, 14 March 1921, F.O. 371/6847/N3296).
79. Cabinet minutes 14 March 1921, Cab 13(21)1, Cab 23/24.
80. 136 *H.C.Debs.* cols. 1866–67, 22 December 1920.
81. 138 *H.C.Debs.* col. 419, 17 February 1921.
82. Krasin, *Voprosy Vneshnei Torgovli*, pp. 248–9.

83. 138 *H.C.Debs.* cols. 780 and 1391, 22 and 28 February 1921.
84. Krasin, *Voprosy Vneshnei Torgovli*, p. 249.
85. Trade Agreement between HMG and the RSFSR, 16 March 1921, Cmd. 1207, Parliamentary Papers 1921; Russian text in *DVP*, vol. 3, no. 344, pp. 607–14.
86. *Ibid.* Postal and telegraphic communications with the RSFSR were renewed at the beginning of April, and in May 1921 the Soviet trade delegation was granted the right to issue visas to travellers to Russia (*Godovoi Otchet NKID k IX S"ezdu Sovetov*, p. 63).
87. 140 *H.C.Debs.* cols. 111 and 709, 5 and 11 April 1921.
88. A satisfactory legal ruling was eventually obtained when the earlier decision in the case of Luther v. Sagor was reversed in the Court of Appeals, followed by a ruling in the case of Marshall v. Grinbaum which established that gold imported into Britain by the Soviet government was not attachable in respect of the obligations of its predecessors (reported in *The Times*, 13 May and 14 July 1921). Both judgements hinged upon statements from the Foreign Office to the effect that the Soviet government was now recognised *de facto* by HMG (F.O. 371/6895/N4495, 13 April 1921; F.O. 371/6895/N5441, 6 May 1921).
89. 139 *H.C.Debs.* col. 2506, 22 March 1921, and col. 2198, 21 March 1921.
90. 139 *H.C.Debs.* cols. 2506–8, 22 March 1921.
91. 139 *H.C.Debs.* cols. 537 and 538, 9 March 1921; 136 *H.C.Debs.* col. 1867, 22 December 1920.
92. 'The Political Aspect of Trading with Russia', 22 November 1920, F.O. 371/5434/N2966.
93. 139 *H.C.Debs.* cols. 2508–11, 22 March 1921.
94. K. Radek, *Vneshnyaya Politika Sovetskoi Rossii* (Moscow 1923), pp. 77–8.

2   LABOUR AND SOVIET RUSSIA (pp. 27–54)

1.   Cabinet minutes, 4 November 1919, Cab 1(19)5, Cab 23/18.
2.   Cabinet minutes, 25 July 1919, WC 599(3), Cab 23/11.
3.   104 *H.C.Debs.* col. 513, 14 March 1918 (Lees-Smith was shortly to join the ILP).
4.   107 *H.C.Debs.* cols. 775 and 770, 24 June 1918.
5.   The description of the *Workers' Dreadnought*, 6 July 1918, p. 1033.
6.   Labour Party, Annual Conference Report, 1918, pp. 34–35; *Herald*, 27 July 1918.
7.   *Labour Leader*, 1 August 1918; *Foward*, 3 August 1918.
8.   Labour Party, Annual Conference Report, 1918, p. 10.
9.   P. U. Kellogg and A. Gleason, *British Labour and the War* (New York 1919), pp. 293–6; meeting of the Parliamentary Committee of the TUC and the Labour Party Executive, 18 September 1918, Labour Party National Executive Committee minutes, vol. 15.
10. James Hinton, *The First Shop Stewards' Movement* (London 1973), p. 269; quoted in *Industrial Peace*, September 1918, p. 28.
11. *Herald*, 23 November 1918; *Call*, 7 November 1918.
12. *New Statesman*, 21 December 1918, pp. 231 and 232.

13. Cabinet Paper GT 5986, 12 October 1918, Cab 24/66.
14. Labour Party, Annual Conference Report, 1919, Appendix V.
15. *Ibid.*, pp. 25 and 26; Labour Party, National Executive Committee minutes, 18 December 1918, vol. 14, and 3 January 1919, vol. 16.
16. *Labour Leader*, 9 January 1919; see also Glasgow Trades Council minutes, 19 March 1919; East Ham ILP minutes, 1 December 1918; Glasgow ILP executive committee minutes, 15 November 1918.
17. 30 April 1919, Cabinet Paper GT 7196, Cab 24/76.
18. *Labour Leader*, 3 April 1919.
19. *The Times*, 4 April 1919; B. C. Roberts, *The Trades Union Congress 1868–1921* (London 1958), pp. 319–20.
20. Labour Party, National Executive Committee minutes, 9 and 10 April 1919, vol. 16; Triple Alliance Conference Report, London, 23 July 1919, p. 6.
21. *The Times*, 17 April 1919. The Triple Alliance had been formed by the railwaymen, miners and transport workers in 1914; it lasted until 1921.
22. Triple Alliance Conference Report, London, 23 July 1919, p. 6; TUC Parliamentary Committee minutes, 28 May 1919.
23. *Herald*, 31 May and 8 April 1919; *Worker*, 7 June 1919.
24. Labour Party, Annual Conference Report, 1919, pp. 113, 118 and 156.
25. *Fortnightly Review*, August 1919, p. 106; *The Times*, 8 July 1919.
26. Pankhurst Papers, item 51A.
27. *The Times*, 27 and 28 July 1919. For a general account, see Arno J. Mayer, *The Politics and Diplomacy of Peacemaking* (London 1968), pp. 853–73.
28. Glasgow Trades Council minutes, 8 and 16 July 1919; Harry Pollitt, *Serving My Time* (London 1950), p. 97.
29. 'Report on Revolutionary Organizations in the UK', 24 July 1919, Cabinet Paper GT 7790, Cab 24/84.
30. Sunderland Trades Council and Labour Party, 26 July 1919, and F.O. minute, 1 August 1919, F.O. 371/3960/109019, and Woolwich and District Trades and Labour Council, 1 August 1919, F.O. 371/3960/111805.
31. Triple Alliance Conference Report, 23 July 1919, p. 53.
32. *Call*, 31 July 1919; *The Times*, 13 August and 5 September 1919.
33. *The Times*, 13 September 1919; *Forward*, 13 September 1919.
34. Cabinet Paper CP 462, 15 January 1920, Cab 24/96.
35. Labour Party, National Executive Committee minutes, 7 October 1919, vol. 18; 13 October 1919, and reply, 5 November 1919, F.O. 371/3961/141106.
36. 18 December 1919, F.O. 371/3961/162909.
37. *The Times*, 11 December 1919.
38. Hands off Russia Committee, *Peace with Soviet Russia* (London 1920), p. 5.
39. W. P. and Z. Coates, *A History of Anglo-Soviet Relations* (London 1945), p. 141.
40. *Workers' Dreadnought*, 25 January 1919; Pollitt, *Serving My Time*, pp. 94–5.
41. Professor Simpson, memorandum, 11 February 1919, F.O. 371/4377/PID 115.
42. *The Times*, 10 February 1919; J. M. Kenworthy, *Soldiers, Sailors and Others* (London 1933), p. 182; *Manifesto of the Woolwich Hands off Russia Committee* (n.d.), p. 3.

43. *The Times*, 23 June 1919.
44. *Call*, 25 September 1919.
45. *Zarya Vostoka*, 31 July 1923, mimeo translation (n.d.), p. 1.
46. Pollitt, *Serving My Time*, p. 95.
47. *New Statesman*, 12 June 1920, p. 266.
48. Lord Curzon, memorandum, 2 September 1920, Curzon Collection Mss. Eur. F112/236.
49. See for instance Clynes's contribution to the adjournment debate on Russia on 16 April 1919, 114 *H.C.Debs.* cols. 2998–3004.
50. 114 *H.C.Debs.* col. 3001, 16 April 1919; *New Statesman*, 26 April 1919, p. 85.
51. Labour Party, *Labour's Russian Policy* (London 1920), p. 4.
52. 121 *H.C.Debs.* col. 766, 17 November 1919.
53. *Labour Leader*, 13 November 1919.
54. See, for example, V. G. Trukhanovskii, *Uinston Cherchill': politicheskaya biografiya* (Moscow 1968), pp. 206–8.
55. Cabinet Paper GT 7196, 30 April 1919, Cab 24/76; Cabinet Paper GT 8400, 23 October 1919, Cab 24/90.
56. Cabinet Paper GT 6713, 28 January 1919, Cab 24/74.
57. Cabinet Paper GT 6976, 10 March 1919, Cab 24/76.
58. J. T. Murphy, *New Horizons* (London 1941), p. 203.
59. Pankhurst Papers, item 32E, pp. x and xxii.
60. See, for examples of local indifference, East Ham ILP minutes, 26 November 1919; and Liverpool Trades Council minutes, 14 May, 2 July and 8 October 1919.
61. *New Statesman*, 8 May 1920, p. 117, and 15 May 1920, p. 149.
62. *The Times*, 14 May 1920; Alan Bullock, *The Life and Times of Ernest Bevin* vol. 1 (London 1960), pp. 133–4; Pollitt, *Serving My Time*, pp. 115–16.
63. Coates, *Anglo-Soviet Relations*, p. 150; Pollitt, *Serving My Time*, p. 117.
64. Pollitt, *Serving My Time*, pp. 113–14; Cabinet Paper GT 1328, 20 May 1920, Cab 24/106.
65. Bullock, *Life and Times of Ernest Bevin*, p. 134.
66. *Forward*, 15 and 22 May 1920.
67. Labour Party, Annual Conference Report, 1920, pp. 132, 133 and 138.
68. James Klugmann, *History of the Communist Party of Great Britain* vol. 1 (London 1968), p. 80.
69. See above, pp. 7–12.
70. GEN/9, Council of Action archive. A more detailed account is available in Stephen White, 'Labour's Council of Action 1920', *Journal of Contemporary History*, vol. 9, no. 4, October 1974, pp. 99–122.
71. ADM/1–13 and 15, Council of Action archive.
72. FOR/5, Council of Action archive.
73. ADM/53, Council of Action archive.
74. Labour Party, Annual Conference Report, 1921, p. 13.
75. References to the proceedings of the Conference are taken from the published proceedings: Council of Action, *Report on the Special Conference on Labour and the Russo-Polish War in the Central Hall, Westminster, on 13 August 1920* (London 1920).
76. PRI/55ff, Council of Action archive.
1977. ADM/23, Council of Action archive.

78. PRI/46, Council of Action archive.
79. PRI/64, Council of Action archive.
80. ADM/16, Council of Action archive.
81. Copies of the three Reports issued are in MEM/31–35, 42–44 and ADM/29, Council of Action archive.
82. *Pioneer* (Merthyr Tydfil), 4 September 1920.
83. Home Office Intelligence Department, 9 September 1920, Cabinet Paper CP 1848, Cab 24/111.
84. Birmingham Trades Council minutes, 17 August 1920.
85. GEN/757, Council of Action archive; Birmingham *Town Crier*, 20 November 1920.
86. Birmingham Trades Council, Annual Report, 1920, p. 10.
87. ADM/42, Council of Action archive.
88. GEN/542, Council of Action archive.
89. GEN/1114 and 1115, November 1920 and January 1921, Council of Action archive.
90. GEN/711, 837 and 767, Council of action archive.
91. GEN/894, Council of Action archive.
92. Lenin, for instance, regarded the situation as one of 'dual power' and thought that the Councils (which were Soviets in all but name) would point the way to Bolshevik revolution (*PSS*, vol. 41, pp. 283 and 327).
93. *Communist*, 19 August 1920.
94. Sidney and Beatrice Webb, *A History of Trade Unionism* (London 1920), p. 669.
95. Cabinet Paper CP 1793, 19 August 1920, Cab 24/110.
96. 'For Litvinov and Lenin', p. 9, typescript autobiography, Newbold Papers.
97. Intelligence Report, Cabinet Paper CP 1793, 19 August 1920, Cab 24/110.
98. GEN/164 and 40, Council of Action archive.
99. *Communist*, 26 August 1920.
100. *The Diaries of Beatrice Webb 1912–1924* (London 1952), p. 187; *New Statesman*, 14 August 1920, p. 517.
101. On this point see particularly L. J. MacFarlane, 'Hands off Russia in 1920', *Past and Present*, No. 38, December 1967, pp. 126–252.
102. MEM/44, Council of Action archive.
103. GEN/1116, Council of Action archive.
104. GEN/756, Council of Action archive.
105. Labour Party, Annual Conference Report, 1921, p. 18.
106. *Labour International Handbook*, 1921, p. 164.
107. *Review of Reviews*, September 1920, pp. 169–70.
108. *Worker*, 3 October 1920; *International*, 11 September 1920.
109. 127 *H.C.Debs.* col. 702, 25 March 1920, and 129 *H.C.Debs.* col. 1708, 20 May 1920.
110. 126 *H.C.Debs.* col. 1168, 9 March 1920.
111. 136 *H.C.Debs.* cols. 1852–7, 22 December 1920.
112. *Ibid.*, cols. 1859–65, 22 December 1920.
113. *Ibid.*, cols. 47 and 16, 13 December 1920, col. 485, 15 December 1920, and col. 1260, 20 December 1920.
114. *Daily Herald*, 7 December 1920.

115. Labour Party, *Unemployment: a Labour Policy* (London 1921), p. 28.
116. *Labour Leader*, 24 March 1921; Labour Party, Annual Conference Report, 1921, p. 208.
117. 139 *H.C.Debs.* col. 550, 9 March 1921; 136 *H.C.Debs.* col. 1853, 22 December 1920; 139 *H.C.Debs.* col. 587, 9 March 1921; 133 *H.C.Debs.* col. 498, 11 August 1920.

3   CONFERENCES (pp. 55–78)

1.   A phrase employed by Lloyd George at his meeting with Clemenceau on 12 December 1919: 'the Bolsheviks had talked much of propaganda', he had told the French Premier, 'but civilisation might also undertake its peaceful penetration' (I.C.P. 2, Cab 29/81).
2.   *Review of Reviews*, April 1921, p. 268; *New Statesman*, 5 November 1921, p. 126.
3.   *Spectator*, 19 November 1921, p. 659; *Economist*, 5 November 1921, p. 809 and 15 April 1922, p. 722.
4.   Lyubov Krassin, *Leonid Krassin: His Life and Work* (London 1929), p. 156; *The Times*, 19 November 1921.
5.   Memorandum, 28 May 1921, F.O. 371/6878/N6216; *Chamber of Commerce Journal*, vol. 41, 8 April 1921, p. 234.
6.   A typescript copy of Lenin's speech is in Lloyd George Papers F/149/2/12; the Premier, Lloyd Graeme recalled, 'placed an exaggerated faith' in it (*I Remember* [London 1948] p. 17).
7.   152 *H.C.Debs.* col. 1900, 3 April 1922.
8.   Thomas Jones, *Whitehall Diary* vol. 1 (London 1969), p. 196.
9.   *DVP*, vol. 4, nos. 193, 201 and 202, pp. 281–6 and 294–8.
10. J. D. Gregory, minute, 12 September 1921, F.O. 371/6851/N10364.
11. Churchill to Curzon, 21 December 1921, quoted in Martin Gilbert, *Winston Churchill, vol. 4 (1917–1922)* (London 1974), pp. 760–1.
12. 146 *H.C.Debs.* cols. 1240–41, 16 August 1921.
13. Note of an interview (manuscript), 5 August 1921, Lloyd George Papers F/203/3/7.
14. British Secretary's Notes of an Allied Conference, Paris, 10 August 1921, I.C.P. 205, Cab 29/93; *ibid.*, 13 August 1921, I.C.P. 207, Cab 29/93.
15. International Commission, 30 August 1921, Report, Cabinet Paper CP 3283, Cab 24/127; Chicherin to the governments of Britain, France, Italy and Belgium, 7 September 1921, *DVP*, vol. 4, no. 209, pp. 307–11.
16. Report on a Meeting of the International Commission, 11 October 1921, Cabinet Papers CP 3398, Cab 24/128.
17. 149 *H.C.Debs.* col. 289, 16 December 1921; 147 *H.C.Debs.* col. 7, 18 October 1921.
18. *Leninskii Sbornik* vol. 36 (Moscow 1959), pp. 338–9.
19. *Pravda*, 29 October 1921, and in F.O. 371/6933/N12085, 31 October 1921.
20. L. S. O'Malley and J. D. Gregory, minutes, and Curzon to Chicherin, 1 November 1921, in F.O. 371/6933/N12085 (the note was also printed in *Pravda* on 15 November 1921).
21. Chicherin to Curzon 12 November 1921, *DVP* vol. 4, no. 301, pp. 492–93.

22. A good general discussion is provided in V. A. Shishkin, *Sovetskoe Gosudarstvo i Strany Zapada v 1917–1923 gg.* (Leningrad 1969), pp. 302–12.
23. Cabinet minutes, 16 December 1921, Cab 93(21)2, Cab 23/27.
24. Krasin to Chicherin, 17 December 1921, *DVP*, vol. 4, no. 330, pp. 579–81.
25. Anglo-French Conference, London, 19–22 December 1921, ICP 209–213, Cab 29/94.
26. Paris Meeting of the Allied Experts, 29–31 December 1921, ICP 214–220, Cab 29/94 (the text of the final agreement is in ICP 220, App. III).
27. The resolution is contained in ICP 230, App. II, Cab 29/94.
28. 'Propositions en vue de rétablir en Europe de meilleures conditions économiques', 31 December 1921, ICP 220, Cab 24/94.
29. Shishkin, *Sovetskoe Gosudarstvo*, p. 305; *The Times*, 2 January 1922.
30. Shishkin, *Sovetskoe Gosudarstvo*, pp. 306–7.
31. The proceeding of the Cannes conference are in ICP 221–35, Cab 29/94 and 95; the resolution adopted on 6 January 1922 is in ICP 222, Cab 29/94.
32. *Economist*, 28 January 1922, pp. 148–51, and 4 February 1922, pp. 193–95.
33. *Ibid.*, 22 April 1922, p. 755.
34. Curzon to Tom Jones, 16 December 1921, Curzon Papers F112/232; Curzon to Churchill, 30 December 1921, *ibid.*
35. Curzon to Chamberlain, 13 May 1922, Chamberlain Papers AC 23/6/34.
36. Churchill to Curzon, 26 April 1922, in *The Aftermath* (London 1929), pp. 414–15.
37. Chamberlain to Lloyd George, 21 and 23 March 1922, Chamberlain Papers AC 23/6/18 and 20.
38. Letter of 22 March 1922, quoted in *My Darling Pussy: the Letters of Lloyd George and Frances Stevenson 1913–1941* (ed.) A. J. P. Taylor (London 1975), p. 40.
39. Lloyd George to Chamberlain, 24 March 1922, Lloyd George Papers F/7/5/23.
40. Lloyd George to Chamberlain, 22 March 1922, Lloyd George Papers F/7/5/21.
41. Conference of Ministers, 27 March 1922, Cab 21(22) Appendix I (3), Cab 23/29.
42. Conference of Ministers, 28 March 1922, Cab 21(22) Appendix II, Cab 23/29.
43. Memorandum of a meeting at 10 Downing St, 20 February 1922, Cabinet Paper S-46, Cab 23/36.
44. Cabinet minutes, 28 March 1922, Cab 21(22)3, Cab 23/29.
45. 152 *H.C.Debs.* cols. 1900–2, 3 April 1922.
46. The text as communicated to the Soviet government is in *Materialy Genuezskoi Konferentsii: polnyi stenograficheskii otchet* (Moscow 1922), p. 5 (hereinafter *Materialy*).
47. Krasin to Chicherin, 13 February 1922, *DVP*, vol. 5, no. 56, pp. 102–3.
48. Memorandum of a Conversation at 10 Downing Street, 10 February 1922, Cabinet Papers S-39, Cab 23/35.

49. 150 *H.C.Debs.* col. 578, 13 February 1922.
50. Chicherin at a meeting of the All-Russian Central Executive Committee, 27 January 1922, *Materialy*, p. 17.
51. Lenin, *PSS*, vol. 44, pp. 371 and 376.
52. *DVP*, vol. 5, no. 80, p. 739; *Vneshnyaya Torgovlya*, no. 13(43), 2 April 1922.
53. Trotsky archives T726, quoted in Louis Fischer, *Russia's Road from Peace to War* (New York 1969), p. 95.
54. Louis Fischer, *The Soviets in World Affairs* (London 1930), vol. 1, p. 332; Chicherin to NKID, *DVP*, vol. 5, no. 101, p. 181, 4 April 1922.
55. The account which follows is necessarily restricted to those aspects of the Conference which affected British-Soviet relations most directly. See further, for a detailed contemporary account, J. Saxon Mills, *The Genoa Conference* (London 1922), and for an authoritative Soviet discussion, A. A. Gromyko et al. (eds.), *Istoriya Diplomatii* vol. 3 (Moscow 1965), pp. 249–94.
56. B. Shtein, *Geneuzskaya Konferentsiya* (Moscow 1922), p. 35.
57. Litvinov to Chicherin, 5 April 1922, *DVP.* vol. 5, no. 103, p. 184.
58. Shtein, *Geneuzskaya Konferentsiya*, p. 36; Chicherin to NKID, 15 April 1922, *DVP*, vol. 5, no. 119, p. 217.
59. Shtein, *Genuezskaya Konferentsiya*, p. 12.
60. Cabinet paper CP 3902, Cab 24/136; Russian text in *Materialy*, pp. 92–114.
61. Memorandum of the Russian Delegation, 20 April 1922, *Materialy*, pp. 127–39.
62. Fischer, *Soviets in World Affairs*, vol. 1, p. 355.
63. British Secretary's Notes of an Informal Meeting held at the Villa d'Albertis, Genoa, 14 April 1922, and 15 April 1922, ICP 238B and D, Cab 29/95.
64. *Materialy*, pp. 168–9; English text in ICP 244 Appendix II, Cab 31/11.
65. Shtein, *Genuezskaya Konferentsiya*, pp. 62–3; Lenin, *PSS*, vol. 45, pp. 163–4.
66. *Materialy*, pp. 148–9.
67. Cabinet minutes, 27 April 1922, Cab 25(22)1, Cab 23/30.
68. Shtein, *Genuezskaya Konferentsiya*, p. 75.
69. *Materialy*, pp. 216–24; English text in *DBFP*, vol. 19, pp. 694–702.
70. L. S. O'Malley, memorandum of 8 May 1922, *DBFP*, vol. 19, pp. 702–3.
71. Shtein, *Genuezskaya Konferentsiya*, p. 53; the text is printed in *Materialy*, pp. 303–4.
72. Gregory to Curzon, 17 April 1922, F.O. 418/57 no. 86; *ibid.*, no. 90, 19 April 1922.
73. *Materialy*, p. 171; Shtein, *Genuezskaya Konferentsiya*, p. 53.
74. Gregory, *On the Edge of Diplomacy* (London 1928), p. 214; M. Tanin (Litvinov), *Desiat' Let Vneshnei Politiki SSSR 1917–1927* (Moscow 1927), p. 109.
75. Shtein, *Genuezskaya Konferentsiya*, p. 69.
76. *Mezhdunarodnaya Zhizn'*, no. 7 (125), 22 May 1922, pp. 1 and 3–4.
77. *Economist*, 13 May 1922, p. 890.
78. 154 *H.C.Debs.* cols. 1463–66, 25 May 1922.
79. Shtein, who was again secretary to the Russian delegation, provides a

detailed contemporary account (B. E. Shtein, *Gaagskaya Konferentsiya* [Moscow 1922]). The proceedings were published in NKID, *Gaagskaya Konferentsiya: polnyi stenograficheskii otchet (Materialy i Dokumenty)* (Moscow 1922) (hereinafter *Materialy i Dokumenty*).

80. I. M. Maisky, *Sovetskaya Rossiya i Kapitalisticheskii Mir* (Moscow 1922), pp. 32–3.
81. *Ibid.*, pp. 32–3: Shtein, *Gaagskaya Konferentsiya*, p. 15.
82. *Ibid.*, col. 492, 26 July 1922, Philip Lloyd-Greame.
83. Shtein, *Gaagskaya Konferentsiya*, p. 12; *Ekonomicheskaya Zhizn'*, 7 July 1922.
84. *Materialy i Dokumenty*, pp. 157, 161, 164, 165 and 168.
85. *Ibid.*, pp. 7–14.
86. *Ibid.*, pp. 81, 112, 114 and 117.
87. Shtein, *Gaagskaya Konferentsiya*, p. 25.
88. *Ibid.*, pp. 50 and 52.
89. *Ibid.*, pp. 62, 63 and 70–71.
90. *DVP*, vol. 5, no. 216, pp. 511–12 and 514.
91. *Materialy i Dokumenty*, p. 199.
92. 157 *H.C.Debs.* cols. 491–504, 26 July 1922.
93. *Ibid.*, cols. 550 and 554.
94. Report of the Credits Sub-commission, Cmd. 1724, Parliamentary Papers 1922, p. 14.
95. Notes of a Meeting held at the Villa Raggi, Genoa, 18 April 1922, ICP 241, Cab 29/96.

4 IMPERIAL CRISIS AND SOVIET RUSSIA (pp. 81–109)

1. Lord d'Abernon, *An Ambassador of Peace* (London 1929–30), vol. 1, pp. 19–20 and 22.
2. Cabinet Minutes, W.C. 599 (3), Cab 23/11.
3. Cabinet Minutes, 25 September 1919, W.C. 624A, Cab 23/15.
4. Conference of Ministers, Cab 18(19) Appendix 3 (1), Cab 23/18.
5. Wardrop to Curzon, received 4 October 1919, *DBFP*, vol. 3, no. 453, pp. 575 and 576.
6. Received 4 January 1920, *DBFP*, vol. 3, no. 622, pp. 741–2.
7. Received 8 January 1920, *DBPF*, vol. 3, no. 631, pp. 747–8; *ibid.*, no. 635, note 3, p. 751.
8. Note prepared by the British Delegation, Paris, 12 January 1920, *DBFP*, vol. 2, no. 77, section 2, p. 925; and document 2, pp. 926–7.
9. *The Times*, 5 January 1920.
10. 13 February 1920, to Sir W. Goode, *DBFP*, vol. 12, no. 500, p. 562.
11. C. E. Callwell, *Field-Marshal Sir Henry Wilson: His Life and Diaries* (London 1927), vol. 2, pp. 221–2, entry for 12 January 1920.
12. Conference of Ministers, Paris, 16 January 1920, S-10, Cab 23/35.
13. Conference of Ministers, Paris, 18 January 1920, S-11, Cab 23/35.
14. F.O. 371/4032/179080, 19 January 1920. Georgia and Azerbaidzhan were granted *de facto* recognition on 10 January 1920 (*DBFP*, vol. 12, no. 500, p. 599).
15. Curzon to Wardrop, 3 March 1920, *DBFP*, vol. 12, no. 512, p. 572.

16. Curzon to Wardrop, 27 April 1919, *DBFP*, vol. 12, no. 547, p. 599.
17. Curzon to Colonel Stokes, 15 December 1920, *DBFP*, vol. 12, no. 642, p. 659.
18. Colonel Stokes to Curzon, *DBFP*, vol. 12, no. 662, p. 678. The most satisfactory general account of this period is Richard Pipes, *The Formation of the Soviet Union*, rev. ed. (Camb., Mass. 1964).
19. Cabinet minutes, 21 May 1920, Cab 30(30)3, Cab 23/21.
20. Conference of Ministers, Cab 33 (20), Cab 23/21.
21. 'Negotiations with M. Krassin', 27 May 1920, Cabinet Paper CP 1350, Cab 24/106.
22. See above, pp. 6–24.
23. F.O. 371/4036/207569; see further above, p. 7.
24. Curzon to Chicherin, 1 October 1920, F.O. 371/5435/N4512.
25. Curzon to Chicherin, 9 October 1920, F.O. 371/5431/N118.
26. Cabinet minutes, 18 November, Cab 62(20)4, Cab 23/23; for the exchange of notes of June and July see above, pp. 6–7.
27. Meeting of British Ministers and the Russian Trade Delegation, 21 December 1920, F.O. 371/5435/N4777.
28. 136 *H.C.Debs.* cols. 1872–5, 22 December 1920.
29. Cmd. 1207, Parliamentary Papers 1921; Russian text in *DVP*, vol. 3, no. 344, pp. 607–14.
30. 139 *H.C.Debs.* col. 2336, 22 March 1921.
31. Lord Robert Cecil, in *ibid.*, col. 1696, 17 March 1921.
32. The letter was handed to Krasin by Sir Sidney Chapman on 16 March 1921, at the same time as the Agreement was signed; it 'drew the attention of the Soviet government to events whose continuance would be regarded as a breach of the understandings and which required the Soviet Government to give immediate attention to them' (16th meeting of British and Russian representatives, 16 March 1921, F.O. 371/6878/N4032). The text of the letter is in Cabinet Paper CP 2724, Cab 24/121, and in F.O. 371/6854/N3438; it was printed in *The Times* on 17 March 1921, and a text in Russian is printed in *Anglo-Sovetskie Otnosheniya: Noty i Dokumenty 1921–1927* (Moscow 1927), pp. 8–11 (but not in *DVP*).
33. R. A. Leeper, minute, 23 April 1921, in F.O. 371/6854/N4823.
34. 'Short Memorandum', 13 December 1917, Cabinet Paper GT 2959, Cab 23/35 (the manifesto is printed in *DVP*, vol. 1, no. 18, pp. 34–5); National Archives of India, quoted in D. Kaushik and L. Mitroalum (eds.), *Lenin: His Image in India* (Delhi 1970), p. ix.
35. K. M. Troyanovsky (ed.), *Sinyaya Kniga* (Moscow 1918); Wardrop to London, 17 June 1918, F.O. 371/3999/140052.
36. Sir C. Marling, Copenhagen, to London, received 31 March 1919, F.O. 371/3951/50116.
37. *The Times*, 20 and 27 November 1919.
38. *Ibid.*, 15 January 1920.
39. *Ibid.*, 16 February 1920.
40. 23 June 1920, F.O. 371/3951/207541.
41. F.O. 371/6895/N1181, 25 January 1921; Secret Report, 2 June 1920, F.O. 371/4057/202035.
42. Minute, on Tallents to Curzon, 11 August 1920, F.O. 371/3951/212499.

43. On F.O. 371/3951/207541, 6 July 1920; Political Department, India Office, 'Bolsheviks in Central Asia and Afghanistan', 30 March 1920, F.O. 371/3991/19128.

44. C. S. Samra, *India and Anglo-Soviet Relations* (Bombay 1959), pp. 37–8. See further 'Papers regarding Hostilities in Afghanistan', Cmd. 324, Parliamentary Papers 1919; L. B. Poullada, *Reform and Rebellion in Afghanistan 1919–1929* (London 1973); and, for a contemporary Soviet account, A. E. Snesarev, *Afghanistan* (Moscow 1921).

45. Cabinet minutes, 6 May 1919, W.C.563, Cab 23/10; Samra, *India and Anglo-Soviet Relations*, p. 39.

46. Cabinet minutes, 6 December 1920, Cab 65(20)3, Cab 23/13; for the Horne letter, see above, pp. 88–9.

47. Cabinet minutes, 3 March 1921, Cab 10(21)2, Cab 23/24, and message to the Government of India, *ibid.*, Appendix 1, 4 March 1921.

48. Cabinet minutes, 10 May 1921, Cab 27(21)3, Cab 23/25.

49. Cabinet minutes, 5 August 1921, Cab 63(21)1, Cab 23/26.

50. Anglo-Persian Treaty, 9 August 1919, Cmd. 300, Parliamentary Papers 1919.

51. 132 *H.C.Debs.* cols. 2080 and 2082, 2 August 1920. For contemporary accounts of developments in Persia at this time, see J. M. Balfour, *Recent Happenings in Persia* (Edinburgh 1922) and M. N. Pavlovich, *Persiya v Bor'be za Nezavisimost'* (Moscow 1925).

52. Cabinet minutes, 3 November 1920, Cab 59(20)4, Cab 23/23.

53. 140 *H.C.Debs.* col. 89, 5 April 1921; *The Times*, 2 August 1923.

54. 150 *H.C.Debs.* col. 46, 7 February 1922; see, for developments in Egypt at this time, John Marlowe, *Arab Nationalism and British Imperialism* (London 1961), and P. J. Vatikiotis, *The Modern History of Egypt* (London 1969).

55. Conference of Ministers, 1 November 1920, Cab 62(20) Appendix 1, Cab 23/23.

56. Allenby to London, 17 November 1921, Cab 92(21) Appendix 3(5), Cab 23/27.

57. Conference of Ministers, 18 November 1921, Cab 93(21) Appendix 3(5), Cab 23/27.

58. Vatikiotis, *Modern History of Egypt*, pp. 264–7.

59. *Near East*, 18 July 1919, p. 63; *United Empire*, May 1919, p. 218.

60. See F.O. 371/3720/147429 and 136445.

61. Allenby to London, received 23 February 1920, F.O. 371/5005/E511.

62. Foreign Office to Allenby, 19 March 1920, F.O. 371/5005/E1519.

63. *Mezhdunarodnaya Politika v 1922g. Otchet NKID* (Moscow 1923), p. 25; Vatikiotis, *Modern History of Egypt*, pp. 336–7.

64. 136 *H.C.Debs.* col. 536, 15 December 1920.

65. 138 *H.C.Debs.* cols. 647–8, 21 February 1921. For events in Ireland, at this time, see Allison Phillips, *The Revolution in Ireland 1906–1923* (London 1923) and a contemporary Soviet account, a copy of which was in Lenin's personal library, V. Kerzhentsev, *Revolyutsionnaya Irlandiya* (Moscow 1918, new eds. 1922 and 1923).

66. 129 *H.C.Debs.* col. 1719, 1 June 1920.

67. Cabinet minutes, 16 May 1922, Cab 27(22)3, Cab 23/30; 150 *H.C.Debs.* col. 1265, 16 February 1922.

68. 134 *H.C.Debs.* cols. 1351–2, 11 November 1920.
69. Russell (Berne) to London, received 8 March 1921, F.O. 371/7142/N2542; Report on Bolshevik Propaganda no. 153, 15 April 1921, F.O. 371/6844/N4709.
70. 'Intercourse between Bolshevism and Sinn Fein', Cmd. 1326, Parliamentary Papers 1921.
71. The House of Commons was informed that he was at this time already acting as a representative of the Sinn Fein republic in Russia (143 *H.C.Debs.* col. 36, 13 June 1921).
72. Special Branch, Report no. 206, 12 May 1923, Cabinet Paper CP 249(23), Cab 24/160.
73. *Irish Times*, 17 February 1923 (cited, with a denial on the part of the Russian mission in Britain, in *Russian Information and Review* vol. 2, no. 21, 24 February 1923, p. 322).
74. W. K. Hancock, *Survey of British Commonwealth Affairs* vol. 1 (London 1937), p. 169.
75. The offence was compounded, in Indian eyes, by the defence of Dyer's actions which was mounted in Parliament and by the well-established public collection which was taken up after his dismissal. The non-cooperation movement was launched in August 1920, and the following month a special session of the Indian National Congress approved and adopted Gandhi's programme.
76. Memorandum, 22 May 1917, Cabinet Paper GT 822, Cab 24/14.
77. Cabinet minutes, 5 July 1917, WC 176(13), Cab 23/3.
78. Cabinet minutes, 14 August 1917, WC 214(11), Cab 23/3.
79. Conference of Ministers, 9 February 1922, Cab 12(22) Appendix 1, Cab 23/29.
80. Conferences of Ministers, 19 February 1922, *ibid.*, Appendix 3.
81. Cabinet minutes, 14 August 1917, WC 214(11), Cab 23/3. See further S. R. Mehrotra, 'The Politics behind the Montagu Declaration', *Politics and Society in India*, (ed.) C. R. Phillips (London 1963), pp. 71–96.
82. 'Moral and Material Report for India, 1920', Cmd. 950, Parliamentary Papers 1920, p. 6.
83. 132 *H.C.Debs.* col. 403, 21 July 1920, and 123 *H.C.Debs.* col. 374, 17 December 1919.
84. *The Times*, 16 January 1920.
85. *Review of Reviews*, vol. 63, February 1921, pp. 107ff.
86. 135 *H.C.Debs.* col. 1719, 6 December 1920.
87. *The Times*, 7 April 1920, 16 May and 17 August 1922.
88. 14 February and received 2 February 1920, F.O. 371/4028/177199.
89. 'Summary of the Bolshevik Situation', 18 March 1920, F.O. 371/4028/186084. Copies of the 'Weekly Report' of the Special Bureau of Investigation are in F.O. 371/4028/193237, 22 April 1920 (nos. 1 and 2), and following.
90. Viceroy to London, received 14 October 1920, F.O. 371/5383/N614.
91. Memorandum 171, Delhi, 16 December 1920, Section 3, file 1229/1920 part 1, India Office Papers L/P and S/10/886.
92. Memorandum 163, Delhi, 3 February 1921, file 1339, *ibid.*
93. 139 *H.C.Debs.* col. 2545, 23 March 1921; 150 *H.C.Debs.* cols. 895–6, 14 February 1922.

94. India Office Papers L/P and S/10/886, papers P3378/1921, 4 August 1921, and P2956/1921, Indian Office Papers L/P and S/10/886.
95. *Ibid.*, paper 2094, circulated 14 June 1921.
96. Montagu to Reading, 15 December 1921, Montagu Collection, India Office Library.
97. A series of reports on 'Violations of the Trade Agreement' was maintained by the Foreign Office; no. 16, for instance, based upon Secret Report no. 181 of 30 April 1921, is in F.O. 371/6844/N5434.
98. Received 28 December 1922, F.O. 371/8171/N11298; Report 898, 6 December 1922, F.O. 371/8171/N10823.
99. 167 *H.C.Debs.* col. 8, 23 July 1923; *The Times*, 16 May 1923.
100. Imperial Conference Committee, 3 May 1921, Cabinet Paper CP 218(23), Cab 24/140.
101. Imperial Conference Proceedings, part 1, pp. 7, 8 and 17, Cab 32/2.
102. Cabinet minutes, 9 May 1923, Cab 25(23) 3, Cab 23/45.
103. Memorandum, 8 November 1923, F.O. 371/9373/N8795.
104. Imperial Conference Proceedings, Fifth Meeting, pp. 16–17 and 20, Cab 32/9.
105. 129 *H.C.Debs.* col. 1729, 1 June 1920, and 141 *H.C.Debs.* col. 2364, 13 May 1921.
106. *Glasgow Herald*, 2 March 1921; *National Review*, February 1922, p. 782.
107. Cabinet minutes, 5 August 1921, Cab 63(21)2, Cab 23/26.
108. Cabinet minutes, 15 August 1921, Cab 67(21)8, Cab 23/26.
109. Cabinet minutes, 17 August 1921, Cab 69(21)5, Cab 23/26; Cabinet minutes, 19 August 1921, Cab 71(29)9, Cab 23/26.
110. Curzon to Hodgson, 7 September 1921, F.O. 371/6855/N10221.
111. Berzin to F.O., 26 September 1921, F.O. 371/6855/N10849 (not printed in *DVP*).
112. Copies of the instructions sent to the Soviet representatives in the East are printed in *DVP*, vol. 4, nos. 112 and 251; the instructions to Raskolnikov in Kabul, dated 3 June 1921, are in Cabinet Paper CP 3201. Cab 24/127.
113. Litvinov to Curzon, 27 September 1921, *DVP*, vol. 4, no. 240, pp. 374–80; communicated to London by Hodgson, 7 October 1921, F.O. 371/6855/N11283.
114. Memorandum, 14 October 1921, Cabinet Paper CP 3411, Cab 24/129.
115. Hodgson to F.O., received 1 November 1921, F.O. 371/6856/N1212.
116. Received 3 November 1921, F.O. 371/6856/N12208.
117. Curzon minute, in F.O. 371/6855/N11337, 11 October 1921.
118. Curzon minute, in F.O. 371/6856/N12040, 29 October 1921.
119. Curzon to Chicherin, 2 November 1921, F.O. 371/6856/N10240.
120. *Pravda*, 24, 25 and 27 September 1921.
121. *Pravda*, 18 November 1921, Radek's original article, communicated to the Foreign Office by Hodgson, was described in a minute as 'scandalous'; but Radek, it was noted, was 'not popular with Chicherin, and the Soviet Foreign Office, who regard him as a meddler' (F.O. 371/6855/N11138, 5 October 1921; a further despatch contained translations of Radek's articles, together with photocopies of *Ostinformation* [F.O. 371/6855/N11336, received 11 October 1921]).

5 SOVIET RUSSIA AND REVOLUTION (pp. 110–40)

1. See, for instance, *DVP*, vol. 1, nos. 13, 32 and 38.
2. L. Trotsky, *Moya Zhizn'* (Berlin 1930), vol. 2, p. 64.
3. V. A. Bystriansky, *Imperialisticheskaya Angliya protiv Sotsialisticheskoi Rossii* (Petrograd 1919), pp. 7–8; M. N. Pavlovich, *Sovetskaya Rossiya i Kapitalisticheskaya Angliya* (Moscow 1925), p. 3.
4. M. N. Roy, *Memoirs* (Bombay 1964), p. 305.
5. G. V. Chicherin, *Vneshnyaya Politika Sovetskoi Rossii za Dva Goda* (Moscow 1920), p. 29; L. B. Kamenev, *Tretii Internatsional: popularnyi ocherk* (Prague 1920), p. 27; *Izvestiya*, 7 November 1922.
6. *Devyatyi S"ezd RKP: stenograficheskii otchet* (Moscow 1920), p. 9.
7. G. Z. Besedovsky, *Na Putiakh k Termidoru* (Paris 1931), p. 48.
8. I. M. Maisky, 'G. V. Chicherin', *Novaya i Noveishaya Istoriya*, 1972, no. 6, pp. 122–5.
9. 'Who's Who in Soviet Russia', received 9 April 1923, F.O. 418/59, no. 39.
10. *Odinnadtsatyi S"ezd RKP(B). Stenograficheskii otchet* (Moscow 1922), p. 532.
11. *Compte Rendu de la Conférence Elargi de l'Internationale Communiste* (Paris 1922), pp. 255–6; E. K. Poretsky, *Our Own People* (Oxford 1969), p. 79.
12. G. Zinoviev, *Tretii Kommunisticheskii Internatsional* (Petrograd 1919), p. 17; *Odinnadtsatyi S"ezd RKP*, p. 186.
13. G. Zinoviev, *Report to the Second World Congress* (Amsterdam 1920), p. 376.
14. Treaty of Friendship with the Finnish Socialist Workers' Republic, 1 March 1918, in Yu. V. Klyuchnikov and A. Sabanin, (eds.), *Mezhdunarodnaya Politika Noveishego Vremeni v Dogovorakh, Notakh i Deklaratsiakh* (Moscow 1925–8), vol. 2, p. 120 (not printed in *DVP*).
15. P. Stuchka, *Konstitutsiya Rossiiskoi Sotsialisticheskoi Federativnoi Sovetskoi Respubliki v Voprosakh i Otvetakh* (Moscow 1919), pp. 74–5, 89 and 19.
16. V. I. Lenin, *PSS*, vol. 35, pp. 170, 247, 271 and 279, December 1917 and January 1918.
17. Lenin, *PSS*, vol. 37, p. 440.
18. *VIII S"ezd RKP(B): stenograficheskii otchet* (Moscow 1919), p. 7; Lenin, *PSS*, vol. 38, p. 262, 3 April 1919.
19. Lenin, *PSS*, vol. 37, pp. 511 and 520, and vol. 39, p. 89.
20. *Kommunisticheskii Internatsional*, no. 1, 1 May 1919, cols. 28, 38 and 42–4.
21. Lenin, *PSS*, vol. 40, p. 31.
22. Kommunisticheskii Internatsional, *Vtoroi Kongress: stenograficheskii otchet* (Moscow 1934) p. 11; G. Zinoviev, *Kommunisticheskii Internatsional* (Petrograd 1920), p. 38.
23. *Kommunisticheskii Internatsional*, 1920, no. 10, col. 1445.
24. *Ibid.*, 1924, no. 1, cols. 142–7.
25. *Trinadtsatyi S"ezd RKP(B): stenograficheskii otchet* (Moscow 1924), p. 42.
26. Developments in Germany during the autumn of 1923, in particular, aroused considerable (short-lived) optimism. Germany was 'on the eve of revolution', declared *Izvestiya* (14 August 1923); Zinoviev, who declared that the proletarian revolution was 'knocking at the door', thought that a turning-point might be reached 'in the history not only of Germany, but in that of mankind as a whole' (*Pravda*, 12 October 1923).
27. Quoted in Jane Degras, 'United Front Tactics in the Comintern', *St Antony's Papers*, no. 9, (London 1960), p. 10.

28. *Pravda*, 13 November 1921.
29. Lenin, *PSS*, vol. 43, p. 19, 8 March 1921.
30. *Kommunisticheskii Internatsional*, 1922, no. 20, col. 5149.
31. *Mezhdunarodnaya Zhizn'*, no. 15 (133), 7 November 1922, pp. 3–4.
32. Lenin, *PSS*, vol. 17, pp. 174–83; *ibid.*, vol. 23, p. 167.
33. *Ibid.*, vol. 27, pp. 252–66 and p. 51.
34. *DVP*, vol. 1, no. 3, pp. 14–15, 15 November 1917, and no. 18, pp. 34–5, 3 December 1917.
35. Roy, *Memoirs*, p. 515.
36. N. Bukharin, *Ekonomika Perekhodnogo Perioda* (Moscow 1920), ch. 1, p. 155.
37. *VIII S"ezd RKP(B)*, p. 123; *VII Vserossiiskii S"ezd Sovetov: stenograficheskii otchet* (Moscow 1920), p. 116; G. Zinoviev, *Nabolevshie Voprosy Mezhdunarodnogo Rabochego Dvizheniya* (Petrograd 1920), p. 125.
38. *Zhizn' Natsional'nostei*, 26 May 1919; Soviet archival source, quoted in *Narody Afriki i Azii*, 1974, no. 5, p. 45.
39. *Communist International*, June–July 1920, col. 2316.
40. Kommunisticheskii Internatsional, *Vtoroi Kongress*, p. 28.
41. *Ibid.*, pp. 101 and 27; Lenin, *PSS*, vol. 41, p. 247. The debate on the national and colonial question is considered in detail in A. S. Whiting, *Soviet Policies in China 1917–1924* (Stanford 1954), ch. 3; J. P. Haithcox, 'The Roy-Lenin debate on colonial policy', *Journal of Asian Studies*, vol. 23, no. 1, November 1962, pp. 93–101; and in N. E. Korolev, 'Razrabotka Leninym politiki Kominterna po natsional'nomu i kolonial'nomu voprosam', in K. E. Shirinya, (ed.), *Vtoroi Kongress Kominterna* (Moscow 1972), pp. 152–93.
42. Kommunisticheskii Internatsional, *Vtoroi Kongress*, pp. 106 and 498.
43. *Ibid.*, pp. 155 and 161.
44. *Ibid.*, pp. 492–3 and 139.
45. *Ibid.*, pp. 458 and 114.
46. *Narody Dal'nego Vostoka*, no. 2, June 1921, col. 113; *Novyi Vostok*, 1924, no. 5, p. 3.
47. Lenin, *PSS*, vol. 42, pp. 71–72, 6 December 1920; *ibid.*, vol. 41, p. 133, 4 June 1920.
48. G. Z. Sorkin, *Pervyi S"ezd Narodov Vostoka* (Moscow 1961), p. 15; A. I. Mikoyan, *Dorogoi Bor'by* (Moscow 1971) p. 581; A. Rosmer, *Moscou sous Lénine* (Paris 1970), vol. 1, p. 144.
49. *Kommunisticheskii Internatsional*, 1920, no. 12, cols. 2259–64.
50. The number of delegates given in the official protocol (*Pervyi S"ezd Narodov Vostoka: stenograficheskie otchety* [Petrograd 1920] p. 5) is 1891, a figure which has widely been regarded as definitive. A study of the lists of delegates and of delegates' mandates, however, reveals that 'not fewer than 2050' delegates were present (Sorkin, *Pervyi S"ezd*, p. 21). For a more detailed account, see the present author's 'Communism and the East: Baku 1920', *Slavic Review*, vol. 33, no. 3, September 1974, pp. 492–514.
51. *Pervyi S"ezd Narodov Vostoka*, pp. 31, 45 and 48.
52. *Ibid.*, p. 70.
53. *Ibid.*, pp. 80, 211–13 and 219–20.
54. *Narody Vostoka*, 1920, no. 1, pp. 57–61.
55. *Narody Vostoka*, 1920, no. 1, pp. 9–10; *Kommunist* (Baku), 12 September 1920, p. 1.

56. *The Times*, 23 September 1920; *Near East*, vol. 18, 5 August 1920, p. 199.
57. Curzon to Chicherin, F.O. 371/5434/N4512 and F.O. 371/5431/N118.
58. *Kommunist* (Baku), 30 August 1920, p. 1.
59. Sorkin, *Pervyi S"ezd*, p. 21; *Pravda*, 16 September 1920.
60. *Trotsky Papers*, vol. 2 (The Hague 1971), no. 556, p. 509.
61. Political Report, Copenhagen, 8 June 1920, F.O. 371/4036/205118.
62. M. N. Pavlovich, *Sovetskaya Rossiya i Kapitalisticheskaya Angliya*, p. 37.
63. Roy, *Memoirs*, pp. 461, 470 and 471.
64. *DVP*, vol. 4, no. 112, pp. 165–8, and no. 251, p. 394.
65. Secret Report no. 233, 2 June 1921, F.O. 371/6844/N6733.
66. Hélène Carrère d'Encausse and Stuart Schram, *Marxism and Asia* (London 1969), p. 41; Roy, *Memoirs*, p. 482.
67. Secret Political Report, 25 October 1920, F.O. 371/5178/E13412.
68. *Pervyi S"ezd Narodov Vostoka*, pp. 87–90 and *passim*.
69. Detailed accounts are available in M. N. Ivanova, *Natsional'no-osvoboditel'noe Dvizhenie v Irane v 1918–22 gg.* (Moscow 1961) and A. N. Kheifets, *Sovetskaya Rossiya i Sopredel'nye Strany Vostoka 1918–20* (Moscow 1964).
70. *Godovoi Otchet NKID VIII S"ezdu Sovetov (1919–20)* (Moscow 1921), p. 72; M. N. Pavlovich, *Ekonomicheskoe Razvitie i Agrarnyi Vopros v Persii XX Veka* (Moscow 1921), p. 30.
71. *Godovoi Otchet*, p. 73 (this and the passage quoted above are omitted from the version reprinted in *DVP*).
72. *Zhizn' Natsional'nostei*, no. 7(105), 17 March 1921. There was an analogous experience in Turkey, where an attempt was made to establish Soviets; they soon collapsed, and the Turkish Communist Party modified its policy to one of support for democratic and agrarian reforms (A. M. Shamsutdinov, *Natsional'no-osvoboditel'naya Bor'ba v Turtsii 1918–1923 gg.* (Moscow 1966), pp. 162–3).
73. G. Safarov, *Problemy Vostoka* (Petrograd 1922), pp. 171 and 176.
74. *Novyi Vostok*, 1927, no. 2, p. 286; A. G. Park, *Bolshevism in Turkestan 1917–1927* (New York 1957), pp. 52–4; I. V. Stalin, *Sochineniya*, vol. 5, (Moscow 1947), p. 41.
75. *Pervyi S"ezd Narodov Vostoka*, pp. 88 and 90.
76. G. Safarov, *Kolonial'naya Revolyutsiya* (Moscow 1921), p. 97; *Desyatyi S"ezd RKP(B)*. *Stenograficheskii otchet* (Moscow 1921), p. 105.
77. *Dvenadtsatyi S"ezd RKP(B)*. *Stenograficheskii otchet* (Moscow 1923), p. 169.
78. *Desyatyi S"ezd*, p. 105; *Pervyi S"ezd Narodov Vostoka*, pp. 227–9.
79. S. Usmani, *From Peshawar to Moscow* (Benares 1927), p. 168; Jawaharlal Nehru, *An Autobiography* (London 1942), p. 363. See also more generally Zafar Iman, 'The effects of the Russian revolution in India, 1917–1920', *St Antony's Papers*, no. 9 (London 1960) and 'The rise of Soviet Russia and socialism in India', in B. R. Nanda, (ed.), *Socialism in India* (Delhi 1972).
80. L. P. Sinha, *The Left-Wing in India, 1919–1947* (Muzaffarpur 1965), p. 58; M. Ahmad, *Myself and the Communist Party of India* (Calcutta 1970), p. 81.
81. Roy, *Memoirs*, p. 489; A. Gupta, (ed.), *Lenin and India* (Delhi 1960), pp. 28–30.
82. Gene Windmiller and Marshall Overstreet, *Communism in India* (Berkeley 1960), chs. 2–4.

83. Communist International, *Fourth Congress: abridged report* (London 1923), pp. 222 and 224; *Ezhegodnik Kominterna* (Moscow–Petrograd 1923), p. 682.
84. Philip Spratt, *Blowing up India* (Calcutta 1955), pp. 34 and 37; Zafar Iman, *Colonialism in East-West Relations* (Delhi 1969), p. 190.
85. Windmiller and Overstreet, *Communism in India*, pp. 42, 43 and 66.
86. Government of India, Home Department, *Communism in India 1924–27* (Calcutta 1927), pp. 51, 58 and 63.
87. Windmiller and Overstreet, *Communism in India*, p. 68.
88. G. Zinoviev, *Kommunisticheskii Internatsional za Rabotoi* (Moscow 1922), p. 66.
89. Kommunisticheskii Internatsional, *Tretii Vsemirnyi Kongress: stenograficheskii otchet* (Petrograd 1922), p. 6; *Zhizn' Natsional'nostei*, no. 12(147), 15 June 1922.
90. *V Vsemirnyi Kongress Kommunisticheskii Internatsionala. Stenograficheskii Otchet* (Moscow 1925), vol. 1, p. 591.
91. *Ezhegodnik Kominterna*, pp. 54–5.
92. S. Zabih, *The Communist Movement in Iran* (Berkeley 1966), p. 52.
93. *Kommunisticheskii Internatsional*, 1924, no. 4, cols. 158 and 174.
94. *Vestnik NKID*, no. 8, 15 October 1920, p. 116.
95. The texts of these agreements are in *DVP*, vol. 3, nos. 305 (26 February 1921), 309 (28 February 1921) and 342 (16 March 1921) respectively.
96. *Ibid.*, vol. 4, pp. 168, 167 and 394.
97. *Ibid.*, no. 166, pp. 247–48.
98. M. N. Pavlovich, *Revolyutsionnaya Turtsiya* (Moscow 1921), p. 90; *Mezhdunarodnaya Zhizn'*, no. 15(133), 7 November 1922, p. 15.
99. Kommunisticheskii Internatsional, *Vtoroi Kongress*, pp. 99 and 498.
100. *Zhizn' Natsional'nostei*, no. 41(97), 24 December 1920; *Kommunisticheskii Internatsional*, 1920, no. 15, col. 3368.
101. Quoted in B. Lazitch and M. Drachkovitch, *Lenin and the Comintern*, vol. 1 (Stanford 1972), p. 411.
102. Zinoviev, *Kommunisticheskii Internatsional za Rabotoi*, p. 74; I. V. Stalin, *Sochineniya*, vol. 6 (Moscow 1947), p. 144.
103. *Vestnik Sotsialisticheskoi Akademii*, vol. 1, 1922, p. 163; V. Osetrov, *Mezhdunarodnaya Zhizn'*, no. 15 (133), 7 November 1922, pp. 35 and 36; Yu. Tivel', *Novyi Vostok*, 1922, no. 1, p. 118.
104. A. Gol'farb, *Mezhdunarodnaya Zhizn'*, no. 6(124), 10 May 1922, p. 12.
105. *Pod Znamenem Marksizma*, 1922, no. 1–2, p. 65.
106. Kommunisticheskii Internatsional, *IV Vsemirnyi Kongress: Izbrannye Doklady, Rech'i i Rezolyutsii* (Moscow 1923), pp. 263–7.
107. *Pyatyi Vsemirnyi Kongress*, p. 615.
108. *Mezhdunarodnaya Politika v 1922g. Otchet NKID* (Moscow 1923), p. 65.
109. Soviet archival source, cited in A. N. Kheifets, *Sovetskaya Diplomatiya i Strany Vostoka 1921–1927* (Moscow 1968), p. 229. See further I. A. Yusupov, *Ustanovlenie i Razvitie Sovetsko-Iranskikh Otnoshenii 1917–1927* (Tashkent 1969) and R. A. Tuzmukhamedov, *Sovetsko-Iranskie Otnosheniya (1917–1921)* (Moscow 1960).
110. *Mezhdunarodnaya Politika v 1922g.*, p. 61; Kheifets, *Sovetskaya Diplomatiya*, pp. 235 and 252–3.

111.   B. Z. Shumiatsky, *Na Postu Sovetskoi Diplomatii* (Moscow 1960), pp. 40–1.
112.   L. B. Teplinsky, *50 Let Sovetsko-Afghanskikh Otnoshenii 1919–1969* (Moscow 1971), p. 41.
113.   Soviet archival source, cited in A. N. Kheifets, *Velikii Oktyabr' i Ugnetennye Narody Vostoka* (Moscow 1959), pp. 51–2.
114.   3 January 1921, quoted in *Kommunisticheskii Internatsional*, 1927, no. 24, p. 34. See further P. Moiseev and Yu. Rozaliev, *K Istorii Sovetsko-Turetskikh Otnoshenii* (Moscow 1958) and S. E. Kuznetsova, *Istoriya Sovetsko-Turetskikh Otnoshenii* (Moscow 1961).
115.   *Zhizn' Natsional' nostei*, 14 May 1921; G. S. Harris, *The Origins of Communism in Turkey* (Stanford 1967), p. 91.
116.   G. Safarov, *Natsional'nyi Vopros i Proletariat*, p. 196.
117.   Kommunisticheskii Internatsional, *Tretii Vsemirnyi Kongress*, p. 464.
118.   R. P. Kornienko, *Rabochee Dvizhenie v Turtsii 1918–1963 gg.* (Moscow 1965), pp. 40–3.
119.   *DVP*, vol. 5, pp. 635 and 650, and vol. 4, p. 706.
120.   *Izvestiya*, 21 November 1922.
121.   *Fourth Congress: abridged report*, pp. 221–2.
122.   *Inprecorr*, vol. 3, nos. 28 and 47(27), 5 July and 8 June 1923, pp. 430 and 461.
123.   *Izvestiya*, 25 December 1923; *Pod Znamenem Marksizma*, 1924, no. 1, p. 187.
124.   *V Congrès: compte rendu analytique* (Paris 1924), pp. 213, 222 and 327.
125.   Jane Degras, (ed.), *The Communist International 1919–1943*, vol. 2 (London 1960), p. 159.
126.   *Kommunisticheskaya Revolutyutsiya*, no. 13–14, July–August 1923, p. 28.
127.   *VIII S"ezd RKP(B): stenograficheskii otchet* (Moscow–Petrograd 1919), p. 128.
128.   Secret Intelligence Report No. 1189, 27 June 1923, F.O. 371/9369/N5849.
129.   M. A. Cheshkov, 'Analiz sotsial'noi struktury kolonial'nkh obshchestv v dokumentakh Kominterna (1920–1927)', in R. A. Ulyanovsky et al., (eds.), *Komintern i Vostok* (Moscow 1969), p. 193.
130.   Lenin, *PSS*, vol. 39, pp. 329–30.

6   THE 'CURZON NOTE' (pp. 141–71)

1.   152 *H.C.Debs.* col. 1054, 27 March 1922.
2.   Memorandum, November 1924, Curzon Collection Mss. Eur. F112/319.
3.   155 *H.C.Debs.* col. 213ff, 13 June 1922.
4.   Stephen W. Roskill, *Hankey: Man of Secrets*, vol. 2 (London 1972), pp. 304–20.
5.   John Barnes and Keith Middlemas, *Baldwin* (London 1969), p. 178.
6.   Harold Spender, *Fortnightly Review*, 1 March 1924, p. 322.
7.   G. N. Curzon, 'James Stephen', in *Speeches on India* (London 1904), vol. 1, p. iv.
8.   Chicherin, speech to the Moscow Soviet, 12 May 1923, *Izvestiya*, 13 May 1923.
9.   Quoted in Michael Edwardes, *High Noon of Empire* (London 1965), p. 64.
10.   K. Radek, *Vneshnyaya Politika Sovetskoi Rossii* (Moscow 1923), p. 57.

11. G. N. Curzon, *The Place of India in the Empire* (London 1909), pp. 13, 12 and 27.
12. Quoted in L. J. Dundas, *Life of Lord Curzon* (London 1928), vol. 1, p. 315.
13. Curzon, *Place of India*, pp. 9–11.
14. *Ibid.*, p. 12; G. N. Curzon, *Problems of the Far East* (London 1894), p. xii.
15. Quoted in Dundas, *Curzon*, vol. 1, p. 192.
16. Curzon to Balfour, 31 March 1901, B.M.Add.Mss.49732.
17. Curzon, *The Place of India in the Empire*, pp. 37, 38 and 39.
18. Curzon to Godley, 9 April 1901, quoted in David Dilks, *Curzon in India* vol. 1 (London 1969), p. 105; Curzon to Balfour, 31 March 1901, B.M.Add.Mss.49732.
19. Curzon, *The Place of India in the Empire*, p. 44; Dundas, *Curzon*, vol. 1, p. 133.
20. Quoted by S. Gopal, *St Antony's Papers*, no. 18 (London 1966), p. 68.
21. Curzon, *Problems of the Far East*, p.v; quoted in Eric Stokes, *The English Utilitarians and India* (London 1959), p. 311.
22. Dundas, *Curzon*, vol. 2, p. 230 and vol. 3, p. 390.
23. *Ibid.*, vol. 2, pp. 418 and 424.
24. G. N. Curzon, *Russia in Central Asia and the Anglo-Russian Question* (London 1889), pp. 319–23, 333 and 370.
25. G. N. Curzon, *Persia and the Persian Question* (London 1892), vol. 1, pp. 84, 171 and 216, and vol. 2, pp. 589, 605 and 631–4.
26. Dundas, *Curzon*, vol. 2, p. 114.
27. *Ibid.*, vol. 2, pp. 312–13 and vol. 3, p. 43.
28. *Ibid.*, vol. 1, p. 296.
29. I. M. Maisky, *B.Shou i Drugie* (Moscow 1967), p. 74 (and see above p. 14).
30. Memorandum, 16 March 1921, Krasin Archive document 2(c); Radek, *Vneshnyaya Politika*, p. 57.
31. M. N. Pavlovich, *'Russkii Vopros' v Angliiskoi Vneshnei Politiki (1922–1924)* (Moscow 1924), pp. 4–5 (emphasis in original).
32. 159 *H.C.Debs.* col. 254, 29 November 1922; *ibid.*, cols. 674 and 3136, 14 December 1922.
33. O'Malley minute, 24 November 1922, F.O. 371/7147/N10623.
34. Soviet archival source, quoted in V. A. Shishkin, *Sovetskoe Gosudarstvo i Strany Zapada v 1917–1923gg.* (Leningrad 1969), p. 340.
35. A preliminary agreement which was signed by Urquhart and Krasin on 9 September was revoked by the Politbureau on 5 October 1922 (DVP, vol.5, no. 273, pp. 608–9).
36. Soviet archival source, quoted in R. F. Karpova, *L. B. Krasin – Sovetskii Diplomat* (Moscow 1962), p. 148.
37. Berzin to Karakhan, 27 September 1922, *DVP*, vol. 5, no. 267, p. 598 (the Soviet notes are in *ibid.*, nos. 249 and 264, pp. 574–7 and 593–5).
38. *Ibid.*, no. 283, pp. 621–3.
39. *Ibid.*, no. 301, p. 653, and no. 301, pp. 650–3, 2 November 1922.
40. *Ibid.*, vol. 6, no. 7, p. 18.
41. Cabinet minutes, 1 November 1922, Cab 64(22), Annex iv, Cab 23/32.
42. Conference of Ministers, 29 September 1922, Cab 52(22) Appendix vi, Cab 23/31; Cabinet minutes, 1 November 1922, Cab 64(22) Annex iv, Cab 23/32. For an account of the Lausanne Conference, see A. Gromyko

et al., (eds.), *Istoriya Diplomatii* vol. 3 (Moscow 1965), ch. 12; and Harold Nicolson, *Curzon: The Last Phase* (London 1934), chs. 10 and 11. A lengthy 'Record of Proceedings' was published as Cmd. 1814, Parliamentary Papers 1923.

43. *Istoriya Vneshnei Politiki SSSR* vol. 1 (Moscow 1966), pp. 175–6.
44. Curzon to London, received 19 December 1922, F.O. 371/8147/N11110.
45. 162 *H.C.Debs.* cols. 813–22, 844 and 848, 29 March 1923.
46. Cmd. 1846, Parliamentary Papers 1923, p. 3.
46. Chicherin to Curzon, 26 December 1920, F.O. 371/5433/N4801.
48. Curzon to Chicherin, 3 January 1922, Cmd. 1846, Parliamentary Papers 1923, pp. 5–6.
49. Litvinov to Curzon, 7 March 1922, *ibid.*, p. 7.
50. Curzon to Litvinov, 20 December 1922, *ibid.*, p. 11.
51. Litvinov to Curzon, 12 January 1923, *ibid.*, p. 12.
52. *Nineteenth Century and After*, July 1922, p. 3.
53. 139 *H.C.Debs.* cols. 2602–3, 23 March 1921.
54. 144 *H.C.Debs.* cols. 1515 and 1759, 14 and 18 July 1921; 146 *H.C.Debs.* col. 1628, 18 August 1921.
55. Curzon to Chicherin, 3 September 1921, Cmd. 1602, Parliamentary Papers 1922, pp. 3–6.
56. Hodgson to Curzon, 29 September 1921 and 10 January 1922, *ibid.*, pp. 6–10.
57. 151 *H.C.Debs.* col. 2154, 15 March 1922.
58. *Russian Information and Review*, vol. 1, no. 16, 15 May 1922, pp. 364–5. There is an authoritative general discussion of church-state relations at this time in J. S. Curtiss, *The Russian Church and the Soviet State 1917–50* (Boston 1953); see also R. Yu. Plaskin, *Krakh Tserkovnoi Kontrrevolyutsii 1917–1923gg.* (Moscow 1968).
59. *Russian Information and Review*, vol. 1, no. 16, 15 May 1922, pp. 364–5.
60. *Pravda*, 12 and 17 May 1922.
61. *DVP*, vol. 5, note 108, p. 747.
62. *Ibid.*, vol. 5, p. 441.
63. Telegram of 4 June 1922, *ibid.*, no. 179, pp. 440–1.
64. *The Times*, 28 March 1923.
65. 161 *H.C.Debs*, col. 1756, 15 March 1923 (Hodgson was urged: 'Please do what you can to save the lives of the arrested ecclesiastics . . .' (15 March 1923, F.O. 371/9341/N2372)); *The Times*, 4 April 1923.
66. Received 9 April 1923, F.O. 371/9365/N3177.
67. *Russian Information and Review*, vol. 2, no. 26, 7 April 1923, p. 403.
68. Hodgson to Curzon, received 9 April 1923, F.O. 371/9365/N3177; 162 *H.C.Debs.* col. 270, 27 March 1923.
69. *DVP*, vol. 5, note 49, p. 727; 152 *H.C.Debs*, col. 1880, 3 April 1922.
70. 151 *H.C.Debs.* col. 1754, 13 March 1922; 152 *H.C.Debs.* col. 429–30, 22 March 1922.
71. 153 *H.C.Debs.* col. 67, 10 April 1922; 153 *H.C.Debs.* col. 960, 1 May 1922.
72. Grove to NKID, 15 March 1922, *DVP*, vol. 5, pp. 165–6.
73. NKID to Grove, 22 March 1922, *ibid.*, no. 90, pp. 163–5.
74. Hodgson to NKID, 4 April 1922, *ibid.*, no. 115, p. 213.
75. Karakhan to Hodgson, 13 April 1922, *DVP*, vol. 5, no. 115, pp. 212–13.

Further correspondence is in *ibid.*, no. 278, pp. 615–6, 14 October 1922.
76. Peters to NKID, 19 December 1922, in F.O. 371/9332/N7848.
77. NKID to Peters, 26 December 1922, *DVP*, vol. 6, no. 54, pp. 113–4.
78. 161 *H.C.Debs.* col. 462, 7 March 1923, and 162 *H.C.Debs.* col. 876, 9 April 1923.
79. Hodgson to Chicherin, 30 March 1923, Weinstein to Hodgson, 31 March 1923, and Hodgson to Weinstein, 1 April 1923, in F.O. 371/9365/N3177; Weinstein to Hodgson, 4 April 1923, F.O. 371/9365/N3402 (not printed in *DVP*).
80. Bonar Law to Henderson, 19 April 1923, MacDonald Papers, F.O. 800/219.
81. J. D. Gregory, memorandum, 31 March 1923, F.O. 371/9341/N2950.
82. Curzon to Hodgson, 10 April 1923, F.O. 371/9365/N3228. Hodgson suggested in reply that a rupture would 'tend for a time to throw power more completely into extremist hands'. The balance of argument, he thought, was against withdrawing the British mission (received 14 April, F.O. 371/9365/N3334).
83. Cabinet minutes, 25 April 1923, Cab 21(23)2, Cab 23/45.
84. Minute, 15 April 1923, on F.O. 371/9365/N3334.
85. 163 *H.C.Debs.* col. 424, 25 April 1923.
86. Cabinet minutes, 2 May 1923, Cab 23(23)2, Cab 23/45. Steps were also to be taken to provide for the return of the captain and crew of the 'James Johnson'.
87. Curzon to Hodgson, 2 May 1923, F.O. 371/9365/N3948 ('Very Secret').
88. Curzon to Hodgson, 2 May 1923, F.O. 371/9365/N3948; reprinted, together with other correspondence, in Cmd. 1890, Parliamentary Papers 1923, pp. 6–13.
89. Association of British Creditors of Russia to the F.O., 9 May 1923, F.O. 371/9366/N4175; Rev. G. B. Piper to McNeill, 2 May 1923, McNeill Papers, F.O. 800/227.
90. *National Review*, June 1923, p. 506; Gregory minute, 7 May 1923, F.O. 371/9366/N4012.
91. *Izvestiya*, 13 May 1923. Chicherin had been advised by Arthur Ransome, who had arrived in Moscow four days earlier, that the majority of the Cabinet would like to avoid a break if they could; he also arranged a meeting between Litvinov and Hodgson, in a wood outside Moscow, at which the British government's position was more fully explained (*The Autobiography of Arthur Ransome*, (ed.) R. Hart-Davis (London 1976), pp. 309–11).
92. Litvinov to Hodgson, 11 May 1923, F.O. 371/9369/N4526 (Russian text in *DVP*, vol. 6, no. 172, pp. 288–96).
93. NKID, *Godovoi Otchet za 1923g. ko II S"ezdu Sovetov* (Moscow 1924), p. 37.
94. *Russian Information and Review*, vol. 2, no. 32, 19 May 1923, pp. 505–6; Memorandum, Krasin Archive, document 2(c).
95. *Rosta* interview, in F.O. 371/9352/N4340, 15 May 1923.
96. *Economist*, 19 May 1923, p. 1042.
97. Cabinet minutes, 14 May 1923, Cab 26(23)2, Cab 23/45.
98. Cabinet minutes, 15 May 1923, Cab 27(23)1, Cab 23/45.
99. 164 *H.C.Debs.* cols. 299–319 and 374–7, 15 May 1923.

100. 164 *H.C.Debs.* cols. 320, 323, 364, 772 and 811, 17 May 1923.
101. Notes of a Meeting, 17 May 1923, F.O. 371/9367/N4501; *The Times*, 18 May 1923.
102. NKID, *Godovoi Otchet za 1923g.*, p. 38; *Izvestiya*, 1 August 1923.
103. Thomas Jones's diary, quoted in Barnes and Middlemas, *Baldwin*, p. 207.
104. Trevelyan to Ponsonby, 30 May 1923, Ponsonby Papers.
105. *Manchester Guardian Commercial*, 24 May 1923.
106. Memorandum, 23 May 1923, *Izvestiya*, 25 May 1923 (and in F.O. 371/9369/N4675).
107. Curzon to Chicherin, 29 May 1923, F.O. 371/9369/N4839.
108. Conference of Ministers, 24 May 1923, Cab 29(23) Appendix, Cab 23/46.
109. Memorandum, 4 June 1923, communicated by Krasin on 9 June with a covering letter for Curzon, *DVP*, vol. 6, no. 194, pp. 334–8 (and in F.O. 371/9368/N5244).
110. Cabinet minutes, 11 June 1923, Cab 30(23)2, Cab 23/46.
111. Curzon to Krasin, 12 June 1923, F.O. 371/9368/N5244; Chicherin to Curzon, 18 June 1923, *DVP*, vol. 6, no. 202, pp. 353–4.
112. M. Tanin (Litvinov), *Mezhdunarodnaya Politika SSSR (1917–1924)* (Moscow 1925), p. 16.
113. 165 *H.C.Debs.* cols. 969 and 970, 18 June 1923; Cabinet minutes, 20 June 1923, Cab 32(23)7, Cab 23/46.
114. Cabinet minutes, 11 June 1923, Cab 30(23)2, Cab 23/46; Curzon to Crewe, 13 June 1923, quoted in Dundas, *Life of Lord Curzon*, vol. 3, p. 356.
115. *Economist*, 16 June 1923, p. 1334; *The Times*, 14 June 1923.
116. Tanin, *Mezhdunarodnaya Politika SSSR*, pp. 15–6.
117. Hodgson to Curzon, 7 June 1923, F.O. 371/9368/N5132; Hodgson to Curzon, received 18 June 1923, F.O. 481/59, no. 83.
118. NKID, *Godovoi Otchet za 1923 g.*, p. 41; *Kratkii Obzor Vneshnei Politiki za 1923g.*, 14 January 1924, *DVP*, vol. 6, p. 592.
119. NKID, *Godovoi Otchet za 1923 g.*, p. 74; I. A. Yusupov, *Ustanovlenie i Razvitie Sovetsko-Iranskikh Otnoshenii* (Tashkent 1969), p. 171.
120. Interview between Chicherin and Ransome, 20 June 1923, *DVP*, vol. 6, no. 206, pp. 357–8.
121. NKID, *Godovoi Otchet za 1923 g.*, pp. 134 and 100.
122. *Morning Post*, 1 August 1923, in F.O. 371/9356/N6617.
123. NKID, *Godovoi Otchet za 1923 g.*, p. 101; Tanin, *Mezhdunarodnaya Politika SSSR*, p. 27.
124. F.O. to Peters, 1 August 1923, F.O. 371/9356/N6617, and to the Home Office, 3 August 1923, F.O. 371/9356/N6617.
125. NKID, *Godovoi Otchet za 1923 g.*, p. 101 (omitted from the version printed in *DVP*, vol. 6).
126. Hodgson to F.O., received 3 August 1923, F.O. 371/9356/N6669.
127. Hodgson to F.O., received 7 August 1923, F.O. 371/9356/N6697.
128. A copy of Rakovsky, *Angliya i Rossiya* (Gos. Izd. Ukrainy 1923, 40pp) is in F.O. 371/9356/N6767; Leeper's minute, 11 August 1923, is in *ibid.*
129. Berzin to the Editor, *Morning Post*, 10 August 1923, in F.O. 371/9356/N7013; Ovey minute, 22 August, and Leeper minute, 28 August 1923, in *ibid.*
130. F.O. to Peters, 30 August 1923, F.O. 371/9356/N7013.

131. NKID, *Godovoi Otchet za 1923g.*, pp. 101–2; Tanin, *op. cit.*, pp. 27–8.
132. Dekret Ts.I.K.SSSR, 13 July 1923, *DVP*, vol. 6, no, 218, pp. 382–5.
133. Ovey to Hodgson, 19 October 1923, F.O. 371/9366/N7652; F.O. to Rakovsky, 27 October 1923, F.O. 371/9356/N8202.
134. 168 *H.C.Debs.*, col. 181, 14 November 1923 (McNeill referred to Rakovsky as the 'chief official agent appointed in succession to M. Krasin for the purpose of Anglo–Russian Trade Agreement').
135. Kommunisticheskii Internatsional, *Rasshirennyi Plenum Ispolnitel'nogo Komiteta (12–23 Iyunya 1923 g.)* (Moscow 1923), p. 109.

7 'ENTENTE COMMERCIALE' (pp. 175–203)

1. *Manchester Guardian Commercial*, 17 May and 14 June 1923.
2. Chairman, Association of British Creditors in Russia, to the Foreign Office, 10 April 1923, F.O. 371/9365/N3254; Secretary, London Chamber of Commerce, to the Foreign Office, F.O. 371/9365/N3243.
3. Federation of British Industries, Organisation and Management Committee minutes, 4 June 1923, F.B.I. Papers.
4. *Westminster Gazette*, 8 February 1923.
5. Soviet archival source, cited in V. A. Shishkin, *Sovetskoe Gosudarstvo i Strany Zapada v 1917–1923 gg.* (Leningrad 1969), p. 352.
6. Letter forwarded to the Foreign Office, 11 May 1923, F.O. 371/9366/N4334.
7. Sir Allen Smith to Bonar Law, 18 April 1923, Baldwin Papers.
8. Board of Trade memorandum, received 17 April 1923, F.O. 371/9365/N3456 (a further memorandum was received on 24 April, F.O. 371/9365/N3860).
9. O'Malley, report of meeting, and Leeper, minute, 11 May 1923, F.O. 371/9366/N4253.
10. Secretary, Russo-British Chamber of Commerce, to Curzon, 17 May 1923, Steel-Maitland Papers GD 193/335; *Birmingham Chamber of Commerce Journal*, 15 June 1923, p. 372.
11. A.B.C.C. to Foreign Office, 12 June 1923, F.O. 371/9368/N5314.
12. *Economist*, 27 January 1923, pp. 158–164, and 3 February 1923, p. 229.
13. *Contemporary Review*, June 1923, p. 777, and September 1923, pp. 384–5.
14. Alec Nove, *An Economic History of the USSR* (London 1969), pp. 91–2.
15. *Economist*, 12 August 1922, p. 277.
16. *Financial News*, 17 November 1923; *Economist*, 24 March 1923, p. 633.
17. *Economist*, 9 December 1922, p. 1076, and 24 November 1923, p. 916; *Lloyds Bank Monthly*, November 1923, p. 401.
18. *Bankers' Magazine*, September 1923, p. 309; *Gosudarstvennyi Bank SSSR, 1923–1924 gg.* (Moscow 1925), p. 65.
19. *Financial Times*, 11 August 1923; *Glasgow Herald*, 4 December 1923.
20. *Statistical Abstract for 1912–1926*, Cmd. 3084, Parliamentary Papers 1928, pp. 290–9.
21. 155 *H.C.Debs.*, col. 8, 12 June 1922; *Russian Information and Review*, vol. 1, no. 23, 1 September 1922, p. 545.
22. *Statistical Abstract for 1912–1926*, pp. 290–9.

23. *Ibid.* Trade with Finland and the Baltic States was excluded from figures relating to trade with Soviet Russia from 1922 onwards; the direct trade of the Irish Free State was excluded as from April 1923.
24. A. I. Kutuzov (ed.), *Vneshnyaya Torgovlya Soyuza SSR za X Let: Sbornik Materialov* (Moscow 1928), pp. 302–7; V. I. Frolova, *Statistika Vneshnego Tovarobmena Rossii za 1921–23 gg.* (Moscow 1923), p. 62.
25. Kutuzov, *Vneshnyaya Torgovlya*, pp. 306–7.
26. *Vneshnyaya Torgovlya SSSR za 1918–40 gg.* (Moscow 1960), p. 13.
27. *Entsiklopediya Russkogo Eksporta* (Berlin 1924–5), vol. 3, p. 484.
28. *Vneshnyaya Torgovlya SSSR za 1918–40 gg.*, pp. 451, 456 and 455 (1913 prices).
29. *Entsiklopediya Russkogo Eksporta*, vol. 3, p. 467. For a general account of the operations of Arcos, see *Bol'shaya Sovetskaya Entsiklopediya*, 1st ed., vol. 3 (Moscow 1930), p. 354.
30. *Russian Information and Review*, vol. 1, no. 1, 1 October 1921, p. 19.
31. *Russian Information and Review*, vol. 1, no. 8, 15 January 1922, p. 186.
32. *Ibid.*, vol. 1, no. 5, 1 December 1921, p. 112.
33. *Inostrannoe Torgovoe Obozrenie*, no. 18, 1 September 1924, p. 27.
34. *Entsiklopediya Russkogo Eksporta*, vol. 3, p. 465 (the Paris office was closed in February 1924; the New York office became 'Amtorg', an independent body, in June 1924).
35. *Ibid.*, vol. 3, p. 466.
36. *Inostrannoe Torgovoe Obozrenie*, no. 23, 5 November 1923, pp. 5–6; Arcos Banking Corporation Ltd., *Balance Sheet 1923–24* (London 1924).
37. *Entsiklopediya Russkogo Eksporta*, vol. 3, p. 466.
38. *Ibid.*, vol. 3, p. 468; *Arkos Kommercheskii Byulleten'*, no. 15, 15 December 1922.
39. *Russian Information and Review*, vol. 2, no. 21, 24 February 1923, p. 324, vol. 3, no. 14, 6 October 1923, p. 210, and vol. 3, no. 20, 17 November 1923, p. 317.
40. *Ekonomicheskaya Zhizn'*, 25 and 26 October 1923.
41. Soviet archival source, quoted in Shishkin, *Sovetskoe Gosudarstvo*, p. 354.
42. NKID, *Godovoi Otchet za 1923 g. ko II S"ezdu Sovetov* (Moscow 1924), p. 105.
43. *Ekonomicheskaya Zhizn'*, 12 August 1923. The other members of the delegation were Sir Charles Wright of Baldwins Ltd.; Mr J. Carter of Crossley Brothers Ltd.; Mr J. M. Denny of Denny and Co., Dumbarton; Major Barley of Nobel Industries Ltd; and a staff of four (a Soviet source erroneously states that the delegation was led by the Prime Minister himself (*Istoriya Vneshnei Politiki SSSR*, vol. 1 (Moscow 1966), p. 183). Marshall's activities in 1918 are referred to in a letter from Gregory to Marshall of 19 November 1920 (F.O. 371/5446/N2032). Marshall submitted memoranda dealing with trade with Russia to the Foreign Office in February 1919 and in December 1920. Gregory, however, minuted on the second; 'For Goodness's Sake stave off this bore. He is intolerable!' (F.O. 371/3956/27348 and F.O. 371/5434/3980 respectively.)
44. *F.B.I. Year Book and Export Register*, 1922, pp. 272–3.
45. Becos Traders, *Report of the Visit to Russia of the Becos Mission* ('strictly private and confidential') (London 1923), pp. 2–6.
46. *Manchester Guardian Commercial*, 30 August 1923, p. 232.

47. *Izvestiya,* 21 August 1923.
48. Becos Traders, *Report,* pp. 7–8.
49. O'Malley minute, 19 October 1923, in F.O. 371/9353/N9234; Curzon minute, 6 September 1923, in F.O. 371/9352/N7387; *Izvestiya,* 21 August 1923.
50. *Daily Herald,* 23 August 1923; *Manchester Guardian Commercial,* 20 December 1923.
51. *Glasgow Herald,* 3 September 1923.
52. *Manchester Guardian Commercial,* 6 September 1923; *Daily News,* 5 September 1923.
53. *Arkos Kommercheskii Byulleten',* no. 20, 24 September 1923, pp. 6–7; *Economic Review,* vol. 8, 28 September 1923, p. 273.
54. *Glasgow Herald,* 4 September 1923; *Manchester Guardian,* 3 September 1923.
55. *Evening Standard,* 3 September 1923; *Financial News,* 4 September 1923; *Financier,* 4 September 1923; *The Times,* 4 September 1923.
56. *Sheffield Chamber of Commerce Journal,* November 1923, pp. 99–100.
57. A. G. Marshall, *Memorandum regarding Unemployment and Russia* ('private and confidential'), pp. 1-3, in Marshall to the Foreign Office, 14 November 1923, F. O. 371/9353/N8955.
58. *Arkos Kommercheskii Byulleten',* no. 20, 24 September 1923, p. 6.
59. NKID, *Godovoi Otchet za 1923 g.,*p. 106.
60. Soviet archival source, quoted in Shishkin, *Sovetskoe Gosudarstvo,* p. 353.
61. *Vneshnyaya Torgovlya,* 1923, no. 37-8, p. 20; *Financial Times,* 4 September 1923.
62. *Manchester Guardian,* 20 November 1923.
63. *Ekonomicheskaya Zhizn',* 11 March 1924.
64. Becos Traders, *Report,* p. 5. For an account of the Exhibition, see *Sel'skhokhozyaistvennaya Entsiklopediya,* 3rd ed., vol. 4 (Moscow 1955), p. 438.
65. *Arkos Kommercheskii Byulleten',* no. 20, 24 September 1923, pp. 6 – 7.
66. *Russian Information and Review,* vol. 3, no. 9, 1 September 1923, p. 130.
67. Vserossiiskaya Sel'skokhozyaistvennaya i Kustarno-promyshlennaya Vystavka, *Materialy i Dokumenty* (Moscow 1922), p. 9; *Ekonomicheskaya Zhizn',* 31 July 1923.
68. Vserossiiskaya Vystavka, *Materialy i Dokumenty,* p. 5.
69. Decree of 23 January 1923, *Byulleten' Glavnogo Komiteta Vsesoyuznoi .. Vystavki,* no. 1, 10 February 1923, pp. 14 – 16; *ibid.,* no. 17, 5 July 1923, p. 13.
70. *Russian Information and Review,* vol. 2, 17 March 1923, pp. 381 – 3.
71. *Ibid.,* p. 370; *ibid.,* vol. 2, no. 26, 7 April 1923, p. 404.
72. *Arkos Kommercheskii Byulleten',* no. 16, 30 July 1923, pp. 10 – 11.
73. *Russian Information and Review,* vol. 3, no. 6, 11 August 1923, p. 86.
74. *Byulleten' Glavnogo Komiteta Vsesoyuznoi .. Vystavki,* no. 17, 5 July 1923, p. 14.
75. *Arkos Kommercheskii Byulleten',* no. 16, 30 July 1923, p. 11 (an article by Segal dealing with the Exhibition appeared, for instance, in the *Westminster Gazette* on 12 July 1923).
76. *Russian Information and Review,* vol. 2, no. 27, 14 April 1923, p. 418.
77. *Byulleten' Glavnogo Komiteta Vsesoyuznoi .. Vystavki,* no. 17, 5 July 1923,

p. 23, and no. 20, 13 August 1923, p. 12.

78. Soviet archival source, quoted in Shishkin, *Sovetskoe Gosudarstvo*, p. 349. A partial list of British exhibiting firms is in *Russian Information and Review*, vol. 3, no. 6, 11 August 1923, p. 87.

79. *Ibid.*, vol. 2, no. 32, 19 May 1923, p. 508.

80. *Ibid.*, vol. 3 no. 6, 11 August 1923, p. 83.

81. Soviet archival source, quoted in Shishkin, *Sovetskoe Gosudarstvo*, p. 352.

82. J. D. Scott, *Vickers* (London 1962), pp. 144 – 5.

83. Bernard Newman, *100 Years of Good Company* (London 1957), pp. 115 – 16.

84. Soviet archival source, quoted in Shishkin, *Sovetskoe Gosudarstvo*, p. 350. According to *Vneshnyaya Torgovlya*, no. 37 – 8 (67 – 8), 13 October 1923, p. 28, there had been ten British visitors to the Exhibition by 20 September 1923.

85. *Russian Information and Review*, vol. 3, no. 9, 1 September 1923, p. 130.

86. Chamber of Commerce for North-West Russia, *Directory for Russian and Foreign Businessmen* (Petrograd 1924), p. 151.

87. *Ekonomicheskaya Zhizn'*, 30 November 1923.

88. *Ekonomicheskaya Zhizn'*, 28 August 1923.

89. G. V. Chicherin, *Znachenie Vystavki* (Moscow 1923), pp. 3 – 5; *Ekonomicheskaya Zhizn'*, 7 November 1923.

90. NKID, *Godovoi Otchet za 1923 g.*, p. 106.

91. M. Tanin, *Mezhdunarodnaya Politika SSSR (1917 – 1924)* (Moscow 1925), p. 28.

92. *Ekonomicheskaya Zhizn'*, 23 October 1923; *Entsiklopediya Russkogo Eksporta*, vol. 3, p. 466.

93. *Vneshnyaya Torgovlya*, no. 44(74), 25 November 1923, p. 13.

94. *Pall Mall Gazette*, 18 October 1923; *Manchester Guardian*, 18 October 1923.

95. *Ekonomicheskaya Zhizn'*, 30 November 1923.

96. *Entsiklopediya Russkogo Eksporta*, vol. 3, p. 469; *Ekonomicheskaya Zhizn'*, 1 January 1924.

97. *Herald*, 18 October 1923; *Observer*, 21 October 1923; *Spectator*, 27 October 1923, p. 583.

98. Sir Allen Smith to Bonar Law, 22 December 1922, Bonar Law Papers 112/40/1 – 4.

99. Sir Allen Smith to the Prime Minister, 24 July and 3 August 1923, correspondence between the Prime Minister and the Industrial Group, House of Commons, Prem. 1/30.

100. *Glasgow Herald*, 27 July 1923.

101. O'Malley minute, 24 October 1923, F.O. 371/9353/N8234.

102. Notes respecting an interview, 26 July 1923, F.O. 371/9352/N6561; *Mezhdunarodnaya Zhizn'*, 1924, no. 2 – 3, p. 195.

103. Council of Foreign Bondholders, *Fiftieth Annual Report for the Year 1923* (London 1924), pp. 29 – 30; *Financier*, 21 December 1923.

104. *Russian Information and Review*, vol. 3, no. 25, 22 December 1923, p. 386.

105. *Observer*, 7 and 14 October 1923; *Pravda*, 23 December 1923.

106. *Russian Information and Review*, vol. 3, no. 19, 3 November 1923, p. 275; *Manchester Guardian*, 5 December 1923.

107. Quoted in *Vneshnyaya Torgovlya*, no. 1 (79), 9 January 1924, p. 20; *Daily News*, 13 December 1923.

108. *Russian Information and Review*, vol. 4, no. 1, 5 January 1924, p. 2.
109. *Russian Information and Review*, vol. 3, no. 17, 27 October 1923, p. 258; *ibid.*, no. 16, 20 October 1923, p. 242.
110. Minutes, 21 November 1923, F.O. 371/9349/N9116.
111. J. D. Gregory, memorandum, 29 December 1923, F.O. 371/9373/N10123.
112. *Birmingham Chamber of Commerce Journal*, December 1923, p. 807; *Chamber of Commerce Journal*, vol. 46, 30 November 1923, p. 277.
113. *Statist*, 29 December 1923, p. 1077.
114. *Westminster Bank Monthly Review*, May 1923, p. 4, and November 1923, p. 6; *Lloyds Bank Monthly*, January 1924, p. 47.
115. *British-Russian Gazette and Trade Outlook*, October 1923, pp. 4 – 5.
116. *Ibid.*, December 1923, pp. 33 – 4.
117. Quoted in *Russian Information and Review*, vol. 4, no. 1, 5 January 1924, p. 3.
118. *Financial Times*, 26 December 1923, quoted in Shishkin, *Sovetskoe Gosudarstvo*, p. 355.
119. Minute, 19 December 1923, F.O. 371/9353/N9988.
120. *Chamber of Commerce Journal*, vol. 46, 2 November 1923, p. 224.
121. Russo-British Chamber of Commerce, *Report of the Executive Committee*, June 1924 (mimeo), Steel-Maitland Papers, GD 193/335.
122. London Chamber of Commerce, *Annual Report*, 1923, pp. 119 – 20.
123. Executive Committee minutes, 9 January 1924, Association of British Chambers of Commerce Papers, MS 14,476.
124. *Daily Herald*, 25 and 21 January 1924; *Izvestiya*, 11 November 1923; *Vneshnyaya Torgovlya*, no. 44 (74), 25 November 1923, p. 1.
125. Rakovsky to NKID, 27 November 1923, *DVP*, vol. 6, no. 309, pp. 522 – 3.
126. 169 *H.C.Debs*. cols. 77 – 81, 15 January 1924.
127. The conferment of *de facto* rather than *de jure* recognition is strictly speaking a matter of domestic rather than international law; the term is conventionally held to reflect doubts as to the stability or political acceptability of the goverment in question (D. W. Greig, *International Law*, 2nd ed. (London 1976), pp. 127 – 9).
128. Charles. L. Mowat, *Britain between the Wars* (London 1968), pp. 168 – 71.
129. *The Times*, 5 December 1923; *Herald*, 9 January 1924.
130. 169 *H.C.Debs.*, col. 159, 15 January 1924.
131. *Daily Telegraph*, 29 January 1924.
132. *New Leader*, 1 February 1924.
133. I. M. Maisky, *Puteshchestive v Proshloe* (Moscow 1960), p. 279; I. Taigin (Maisky), *Angliya i SSSR* (Leningrad 1926), p. 28.
134. Soviet archival source, quoted in *Istoriya Vneshnei Politiki SSSR*, vol. 1, pp. 183 – 4. MacDonald pointed out that it would nonetheless facilitate his task if agreement on a number of contentious issues could be anounced at the same time as recognition was conferred (*DVP*, vol. 7, pp. 33 – 4).
135. *Herald*, 30 January 1924; A. Duff Cooper, *Old Men Forget* (London 1953), p. 123.
136. ILP, Annual Conference Report, 1924, p. 68; *Mezhdunarodnaya Zhizn'*, no. 2 – 3, 1924, p. 195.
137. *Herald*, 29 and 30 January 1924.
138. W. P. and Z. Coates, *A History of Anglo-Soviet Relations* (London 1945), p.

123, London Trades Council, *Sixty-fourth Annual Report*, 1923, p. 9 (it is not the case that the meeting actually took place, as stated in *Istoriya Vneshnei Politiki SSSR*, vol. 1, p. 184).

139. Cabinet minutes, 23 and 28 January 1924, Cab 7 (24) 19 and 8 (24) 10, Cab 23/47.
140. NKID, *Godovoi Otchet za 1923 g.*, pp. 106 and 6; *Herald*, 30 January 1924.
141. Cabinet minutes, 4 February 1924, Cab 9(24)1, Cab 23/47.
142. Cabinet minutes, 4 February 1924, Cab 9(24)2, Cab 23/47.
143. Foreign Office to NKID, 1 February 1924, F.O. 371/10465/N902.
144. Rakovsky to Foreign Office, 8 February 1924, F.O. 371/10465/N1093 (Russian text in *DVP*, vol. 7, no. 30, pp. 54 – 5). The resolution adopted by the Second Congress of Soviets on 2 February 1924 was remitted to the Foreign Office by Hodgson (received 4 February 1924, F.O. 371/10465/N911), and by Rakovsky (received 4 February 1924, F.O. 371/10465/N978) (Russian text in *DVP*, vol. 7, no. 32, pp. 58 – 9); it was printed in the *Herald* on 4 February 1924.
145. Cabinet minutes, 8 February 1924, Cab 11(24)1, Cab 23/47.
146. MacDonald to Chicherin, 1 February 1924, MacDonald Papers, F.O. 800/219.
147. Chicherin to MacDonald, 13 February 1924, *ibid.* (Russian text in *DVP* vol. 7, no. 47, pp. 98 – 9).
148. *Vneshnyaya Torgovlya*, no. 4 – 5 (82 – 3), 10 February 1924.
149. *Ibid.*, no. 8 (86), 2 March 1924, p. 8.
150. The Anglo-Soviet conference of the summer of 1924 falls outside the period with which this volume is concerned. Contemporary Soviet accounts may be found in *Mezhdunarodnaya Letopis'*, 1925, nos. 1 and 2, *Sotsialisticheskoe Khozyaistvo*, 1924, kn. 4, pp. 5 – 23, and in *Godovoi Otchet NKID za 1924 g. k III S''ezdu Sovetov SSSR* (Moscow 1925), pp. 25 – 40; two more modern discussions are in F. D. Volkov, *Anglo-Sovetskie Otnosheniya (1924 – 1929 gg.)* (Moscow 1958), which is based in part upon Soviet archives, and Gabriel Gorodetsky, *The Precarious Truce: Anglo-Soviet Relations 1924 – 27* (Cambridge 1977), pp. 13 – 35.

8 SOVIET RUSSIA AND LABOURISM (pp. 204–33)

1. Michael R. Gordon, *Conflict and Consensus in Labour's Foreign Policy* (Stanford 1969), pp. 1, 13, 18, 32 and 24.
2. *Ibid.*, p.27. See also Stephen R. Graubard, *British Labour and the Russian Revolution* (Camb. Mass. 1956), pp. 242 – 3.
3. *New Leader*, 18 April and 11 January 1924.
4. *English Review*, December 1923, pp. 782 – 3, and January 1924, pp. 3 – 4.
5. *Patriot*, January 1924, pp. 341 and 349.
6. Nesta H. Webster, *Secret Societies and Subversive Movements* (London 1924), pp. 339 and 343.
7. *Economist*, 15 December 1923, p. 1061, and 21 December 1923, pp. 1090 and 1097.
8. Lewis Chester et al., *The Zinoviev Letter* (London 1967), p. 17.
9. *Economist*, 12 January 1924, p. 49; *The Times*, 12 December 1923.

10. J. C. C. Davidson, *Memoirs of a Conservative* (London 1969), p. 189.
11. Hunsdon to Baldwin,18 December 1923, Baldwin Papers.
12. J. S. Horne to Baldwin, 10 December 1923, *ibid.*
13. J. Spender and C. Asquith, *Life of H. H. Asquith* (London 1932), vol. 2, p. 343.
14. H. Nicolson, *King George V* (London 1953), p. 383.
15. Nesta H. Webster, *Surrender of an Empire* (London 1931), p. 209.
16. Davidson, *Memoirs of a Conservative*, p. 189.
17. John Barnes and Keith Middlemas, *Baldwin* (London1969), p. 252.
18. Spender and Asquith, *H. H. Asquith*, p. 373.
19. Davidson, *Memoirs of a Conservative*, p. 189; *Economist*, 15 December 1923, p. 1040.
20. *The Times,* 9 January 1924; A. Duff Cooper, *Old Men Forget* (London 1953), p. 122; *Nation,* 6 February 1924.
21. Philip Snowden, *An Autobiography* (London 1934), vol. 2, p. 607.
22. *Review of Reviews*, February 1924, p. 103; *Economist*, 26 January 1924, pp. 128 and 137.
23. J. R. Clynes, *Memoirs* (London 1937 – 8), vol. 1, p. 344 and vol. 2, p. 19.
24. Nicolson, *King George V*, p. 384.
25. Labour Party, *Labour and the New Social Order* (London 1918), *passim.*
26. *International Journal of Ethics*, January 1922, p. 122.
27. Arthur Henderson, *The Aims of Labour* (London 1918), p. 24.
28. Labour Party, Annual Conference Report, January 1918, p. 15.
29. Frank Bealey (ed.), *The Social and Political Thought of the British Labour Party* (London 1970), pp. 10 and 13.
30. *Contemporary Review*, February 1918, p. 122.
31. Henderson, *Aims of Labour*, pp. 16 and 21.
32. Labour Party, Annual Conference Report, June 1918, p. 25.
33. Sidney Webb, *The New Constitution of the Labour Party* (London 1918), pp. 1 – 2.
34. Labour Party, Annual Conference Report, January 1918, p. 104.
35. *International Journal of Ethics*, January 1922, p. 120.
36. Entry for 11 December 1917, Scott Papers, B.M.Add.Mss. 50904.
37. *New Statesman*, 4 January 1919, p. 273.
38 *Ibid.*, 17 January 1920, pp. 425 – 6.
39. Snowden, *Autobiography*, vol. 2, p. 572; *Socialist Review*, January 1924, p. 2; Philip Snowden, *If Labour Rules* (London 1923), p. 12.
40. *Socialist Review*, April 1923, p. 165.
41. *Labour Magazine*, November 1922, p. 331.
42. *Socialist Review*, June 1923, p. 242.
43. Labour Party, Annual Conference Report, 1919, Appendix v, and 1923, Appendix iii.
44. *Review of Reviews*, December 1922, p. 567.
45. *National Review*, January 1923, p. 667.
46. *Fortnightly Review*, July 1921, p. 51.
47. 159 *H.C.Debs.* cols. 133 – 4, 23 November 1922.
48. David Kirkwood, *My Life of Revolt* (London 1936), pp. 201 – 3.
49. *United Empire*, January 1923, p. 16.
50. *Labour Speakers Handbook* (London 1922), p. 130.

51. 155 *H.C.Debs*. col. 652, 12 June 1922.

52. *Labour Leader*, 19 August 1920.

53. *New Leader*, 8 June 1923; 164 *H.C.Debs*. col. 283, 15 May 1923.

54. *New Leader*, 11 May 1923.

55. 164 *H.C.Debs*. cols. 292 – 4, 15 May 1923.

56. Circular, 24 May 1923, NEC minutes vol. 27, Labour Party Archives. The action was reported to and endorsed by the party's executive on 5 June (*ibid*).

57. 'We have to date about two hundred resolutions of a similar nature', William Strang noted on a resolution submitted to the Foreign Office by a Yorkshire ILP branch, 'as well as about fifty communications from private persons. More than half of the resolutions come from local branches of the ILP; the bulk of the remainder from branches of the Labour Party or trade unions' (24 May 1923, F.O. 371/9366/N4157).

58. MacDonald to Baldwin, 4 May 1923, Baldwin Papers.

59. Henderson to Bonar Law, 17 April 1923, MacDonald Papers, F.O. 800/219. Henderson's information on the value and prospects of trade with Russia derived from a communication which he received from the Russian Trade Delegation (*DVP*, vol. 6, no. 148, pp. 252 – 4).

60. *The Times*, 25 May 1923; STUC, Annual Conference Report, 1924, pp. 56 – 7; MFGB. Executive Council meeting, 29 May 1923, p. 16 and Special Conference Report, 30 May 1923, p. 2.

61. Labour Party, Annual Conference Report, 1921, p. 167; *ibid*., 1922, p. 179; *ibid*., 1924, p, 131.

62. *Ibid*., 1922, p. 109; *ibid*., 1924, p. 128; *ibid*., 1925, p. 181.

63. *Ibid*., 1923, p. 15.

64. *Kommunisticheskii Internatsional*, 1924, no. 1, col. 571.

65. Kommunisticheskii Internatsional, *Pyatyi Vsemirnyi Kongress: stenograficheskii otchet* (Moscow-Leningrad 1925), vol. 1, p. 59 (Trotsky similarly believed that MacDonald was 'pushing the British workers onto the revolutionary road': *Zapad i Vostok* [Moscow 1924] p. 22).

66. J. D. Gregory, minute, 15 April 1923, on F.O. 371/9365/N3334; Curzon minute, 12 April 1923, on F.O. 371/9365/N3360.

67. Leonard Woolf, *Downhill All the Way* (London 1967), pp. 219 and 223.

68. 121 *H.C.Debs*. col. 759, 17 November 1919; *Nineteenth Century and After*, January 1920, p. 24.

69. Leonard Woolf, 'Labour and Foreign Affairs', in R. W. Hogue (ed.), *British Labour Speaks* (New York 1924), p. 124.

70. A new body, the Workers' Travel Association, was set up in 1922. It catered for the study of the languages and culture of foreign countries, and arranged group travel for some two thousand members. A tour of Russia was organised in 1924, the 'first organized group', it was noted, 'to visit Russia since the Revolution' (Workers' Travel Association, *Annual Report*, 1924, pp. 1 –5).

71. *Review of Reviews*, July 1920, p. 4.

72. Trevor Wilson (ed.), *The Political Diaries of C. P. Scott 1911 – 1928* (London 1970), p. 418.

73. Snowden, *If Labour Rules*, p. 52; *Forward*, 19 May 1923.

74. Labour Party Annual Conference Report, 1921, p. 172.

75. *Fortnightly Review*, 1 January 1923, p. 3.
76. *Review of Reviews*, December 1922, p. 567.
77. Emmanuel Shinwell, *The Labour Story* (London 1963), p. 111.
78. V. de Bunsen, *Charles Roden Buxton. A Memoir* (London 1948), pp. 76–8.
79. *Herald*, 25 June 1919; *Forward,* 21 February 1920.
80. *Herald*, 17 April 1919.
81. Mosa Anderson, *Noel Buxton* (London 1952), pp. 103 and 105.
82. Charles P. Trevelyan *From Liberalism to Labour* (London 1921), pp. 29–77; *New Leader*, 23 May 1924.
83. *Leeds Weekly Citizen*, 5 March 1920; *Labour Who's Who* (London 1927), p. 123.
84. Norman Angell, *After All* (London 1951), p. 227.
85. Morel to Ponsonby, undated (c. July 1917), Morel Papers.
86. Herbert Tracey, *The Book of the Labour Party* (London 1925), vol. 3, pp. 326–8; *Forward,* 20 April 1918.
87. E. M. Morel, *Ten Years of Secret Diplomacy* (London 1915), pp. xiii-xiv; quoted in A. J. P. Taylor, *The Troublemakers* (London 1957), p. 120.
88. E. D. Morel, *Truth and the War* (London 1916), p. ix; Labour Party, Annual Conference Report, 1923, p. 227.
89. Lenin, *PSS*, vol. 26, pp. 268–9.
90. *Labour Leader*, 22 September 1921.
91. Inaugural circular, August 1914, Morel Papers.
92. Fenner Brockway, *Inside the Left* (London 1942), p. 54; Helena M. Swanwick, *Builders of Peace* (London 1924), pp. 51–2.
93. Charles P. Trevelyan, *The Union for Democratic Control* (London 1919), p. 8.
94. Taylor, *The Troublemakers*, p. 135.
95. Marvin Swartz, *The Union of Democratic Control in British Politics during the First World War* (Oxford 1971), p. 147; Taylor, *The Troublemakers*, p. 160.
96. V. de Bunsen, *C. R. Buxton. A Memoir*, p. 82.
97. Labour Party, Annual Conference Report, 1924, p. 52.
98. Kenneth E. Miller, *Socialism and Foreign Policy* (The Hague 1967), p. 83.
99. Catherine A. Cline, *Recruits to Labour* (Syracuse 1963), pp. 69–70.
100. *Communist*, 22 July 1922; *Labour Monthly*, January 1924, p. 26.
101. ILP, Annual Conference Report, 1922, pp. 80–1 and 75.
102. *Socialist Review*, July 1922, p. 17.
103. *Communist Review*, October 1922, p. 270.
104. *Ibid.*, June 1923, p. 57.
105. Walter Kendall, *The Revolutionary Movement in Britain, 1900–21* (London 1969), p. 416.
106. Snowden and Trevelyan, minutes, 31 and 30 January 1924; Ponsonby to Rakovsky, 1 February 1924, and Rakovsky to Ponsonby, 2 February 1924, F.O. 371/10465/N902.
107. *Eighteenth Abstract of Labour Statistics of the United Kingdom*, Cmd. 2740, Parliamentary Papers 1926, pp. 56, 62 and 94.
108. Labour Party, Annual Conference Report, 1921, p. 26. See also above, pp. 51–3.
109. *Ibid.*, pp. 27–8.
110. Labour Party, Annual Conference Report, 1921, Appendix v.
111. Draft Memorandum on Labour's Foreign Policy, November 1921, Advis-

ory Committee memorandum, No. 226, Labour Party Archives.

112. Labour Party, Annual Conference Report, 1922, p. 5. Krasin, in an interview with British labour leaders on 29 November 1921, told them that Russia's need of all kinds of agricultural machinery was 'practically unlimited', and 'capable of immediately creating a large market for Western industry'. Equipment was needed also for the restoration of mining and of industry generally. Russian orders, he assured them, would whenever possible be placed in Britain (National 'Hands off Russia' Committee, *Trade with Russia: the Facts* (London 1921); see also *Labour Leader*, 22 December 1921).

113. Labour Party, *Memorandum on Unemployment and the International Situation, Reparations and Russia* (London 1921).

114. 150 *H.C.Debs.* cols. 381 and 353–4, 9 February 1922.

115. 164 *H.C.Debs.* col. 793, 17 May 1923; *New Leader*, 3 November 1922.

116. 162 *H.C.Debs.* cols. 826–7, 21 March 1923.

117. *Forward*, 27 January 1923; 162 *H.C.Debs.* col. 827, 29 March 1923.

118. Morel-McNeill correspodence, December 1922–January 1923, B.L.P.E.S.

119. 159 *H.C.Debs*, cols. 1084–5, 1 December 1922.

120. *Labour Leader*, 11 and 25 November 1920; *Forward*, 19 May 1923.

121. Labour Party, Annual Conference Report, 1925, pp. 42 and 78–9.

122. See for instance Birmingham Borough Labour Party, *Annual Report and Yearbook*, 1922–23, pp. 9–10; and Glasgow ILP Federation, *Annual Report*, 1921–2, p. 18.

123. ILP, Annual Conference Report, 1922, p. 91.

124. Birmingham Trades Council, *Annual Report*, 1923–24, p. 7.

125. J. R. MacDonald, *The Socialist Movement* (London 1911), p. 71; *Socialism and Society* (London 1905), p. 4; Benjamin Sacks, *J. Ramsay MacDonald in Thought and Action* (Albuquerque 1952), p. 154.

126. *Socialist Review*, October–December 1921, p. 300; G. D. H. Cole, *Out of Work* (London 1923), pp. 87 and 91; *Socialist Review*, December 1922, p. 246.

127. *Socialist Review*, December 1922, p. 245; *ibid.*, October–December 1921, p. 300.

128. *Ibid.*; *British Trades Union Review*, January 1921, p. 2.

129. Arthur Ponsonby, preface to W. P. Coates, *Export Credit Schemes and Anglo–Russian Trade* (London 1923), p. 5.

130. Henderson to the Prime Minister, 17 August 1923, F.O. 371/9356/N7123.

131. *Forward*, 8 September 1923.

132. *Socialist Review*, June 1923, p. 249; 164 *H.C.Debs.* col. 293, 15 May 1923.

133. 168 *H.C.Debs.* col. 466, 15 November 1923.

134. 169 *H.C.Debs.* cols. 272–3, 13 February 1924.

135. Meeting of 6 February 1924, Cabinet Paper CP 101, Cab 24/165; *The Times*, 4 March 1924.

136. *The Times*, 11 February 1924; *Fortnightly Review*, 1 May 1924, pp. 629 and 635; *Economist*, 16 February 1924, p. 281.

137. J. R. MacDonald, *The Foreign Policy of the Labour Party* (London 1923), *passim*.

138. Labour Party, Annual Conference Report, 1924, p. 109.

CONCLUSION: CLASS, PARTY AND FOREIGN POLICY (pp. 234–44)

1. John Barnes and Keith Middlemas, *Baldwin* (London 1969), p.72 (Sir Leo Chiozza Money calculated that the number of people with incomes in excess of five thousand pounds had 'rather more than doubled between 1913 and 1920', largely as a result of wartime profiteering [*New Leader*, 4 January 1923]).
2. Harold Nicolson, *King George V* (London 1953), p. 333; Lord Riddell, *Intimate Diary of Peace Conference and After* (London 1933), p. 22.
3. A. J. P. Taylor, *English History 1914–1945* (Oxford 1965), p. 129.
4. Labour Research Department, *Labour and Capital in Parliament* (London 1923), pp. 8 and 10; *New Statesman*, 12 June 1920, p. 268; *Labour Party Local Government Parliamentary and International Bulletin*, vol. 1, no. 12 (1920), p. 149.
5. Labour Research Department, *The F.B.I.* (London 1923), pp. 12–17; *Labour and Capital in Parliament*, p. 17.
6. Walter Kendall, *The Revolutionary Movement in Britain, 1900–1921* (London 1969), p. 24.
7. Leopold S. Amery, *My Political Life* (London 1953), vol. 2, pp. 262 and 246; Lord Davidson, *Memoirs of a Conservative* (London 1969), p. 139.
8. *New Leader*, 25 May 1923.
9. *Memoirs of a Conservative*, p. 154.
10. Barnes and Middlemas, *Baldwin*, p. 9.
11. *Ibid.*, pp. 55 and 43; *Communist Review*, July 1923, p. 111. Walton Newbold, in an article on 'Baldwin of Baldwins Limited' in the *Workers Weekly* on 5 October 1923, noted that Baldwin held 191,558 one pound shares in his own name in the company.
12. Barnes and Middlemas, *Baldwin*, pp. 9 and 209.
13. Kenneth Rose, *Superior Person* (London 1969), pp. 232–3; *Communist Review*, July 1923, p. 109.
14. *Socialist Review*, July 1923, p. 24; typescript autobiography, p. 28, Newbold Papers.
15. *Izvestiya*, 27 February 1923; *Communist*, 6 May 1922.
16. *Communist*, 27 May 1922.
17. Sir H. Cowan, 147 *H.C.Debs.* col. 1543, 1 November 1921.
18. *The Times*, 27 September 1921.
19. *The Times*, 5 April 1922.
20. *Indépendance Belge*, 5 July 1922, quoted in F.O. 371/8195/N6511, 6 July 1922.
21. A.B.C.R. to the Foreign Office, 9 May 1923, F.O. 371/9366/N4175; *The Times*, 1 June and 24 July 1923.
22. *Izvestiya*, 12 May 1923.
23. P.V.Ol', *Inostrannye Kapitaly v Rossii* (Petrograd 1922), p. 9.
24. Hugh Stirk, *The Leadership of the Conservative Party, 1902–1951* (B.A. thesis, Manchester, 1958), pp. 11, 12, 16 and 49.
25. *Memoirs of a Conservative*, p. 148.
26. E. J. Hobsbawm, *Industry and Empire* (London 1968), p. 171.
27. *Izvestiya*, 27 February and 11 November 1923.
28. *Izvestiya*, 11 November 1923.

29. *Manchester Guardian*, 23 May 1923.

30. Chamberlain's letter to Rakovsky of 21 November, informing him that the government did not intend to recommend ratification, is in Cab 61(24) Appendix II, Cab 23/49; Churchill to Baldwin, 14 November 1924, Baldwin Papers.

31. The fullest accounts are F. D. Volkov, *Anglo–Sovetskie Otnosheniya 1924–29gg.* (Moscow 1958), S. V. Nikonova, *Anti-Sovetskaya Vneshnyaya Politika Angliiskikh Konservatorov 1924–1927gg.* (Moscow 1963) and G. Gorodetsky, *The Precarious Truce: Anglo–Soviet Relations 1924–1927* (Cambridge 1977).

32. See above, pp. 199–201.

33. See for instance, F. M. Burlatsky, *Lenin, Gosudarstvo, Politika* (Moscow 1970), p. 51.

34. Communist Party circular to all party committees, 9 May 1923, in Curzon Collection Mss. Eur. F112/236.

35. An impression based upon conversation and correspondence with contemporaries, the details of which are recorded in the Bibliography to this study.

36. L. J. Macfarlane, *The British Communist Party* (London 1966), p. 302; ILP membership, in contrast, almost doubled between 1918 and 1924, when it amounted to 56,000 (ILP, Annual Conference Report, 1925, p. 97).

37. *Communist Review*, vol. 3, no. 8–9 (1923), p. 489.

38. TUC, Parliamentary Committee minutes, 29 August 1921; *British Trades Union Review*, vol. 3, 4 November 1921, p. 1; *Herald*, 3 August 1921.

39. *British Trades Union Review*, vol. 3, 8 March 1922, p. 5; Labour Party and TUC, Joint International Committee minutes, 1 and 15 February 1922.

40. Liverpool Trades Council and Labour Party, 1st Annual Report, 1922, n.p.; Glasgow Trades and Labour Council, Executive Committee minutes, 4 October 1921.

41. *Worker*, 11 March 1922.

42. Labour Party, Annual Conference Report, 1922, p. 198, and 1924, p. 128.

43. *Communist*, 17 June 1922.

44. *Communist Review*, June 1922, p. 63 and August 1923, p. 172.

Select Bibliography

UNPUBLISHED SOURCES

1. *Private papers*

Asquith Papers, Bodleian Library, Oxford
Baldwin Papers, Cambridge University Library
Balfour Papers, British Library, London, and Public Record Office, London
R. D. Blumenfeld Papers, House of Lords Record Office, London
Bonar Law Papers, House of Lords Record Office, London
John Braddock Papers, Liverpool Public Library
W. C. Bridgeman Diary, courtesy of Viscount Bridgeman, Minsterley, Salop
Broady Collection, Glasgow University Library
C. R. Buxton Papers, Rhodes House Library, Oxford
Lord Robert Cecil Papers, Public Record Office, London
Austen Chamberlain Papers, Birmingham University Library, and Public Record Office, London
Chelmsford Collection, India Office Library, London
Eyre Crowe Papers, Public Record Office, London
Curzon Collection, India Office Library, London, and Curzon Papers, Public Record Office, London
D'Abernon Papers, British Library, London
Darling Collection, Hoover Institution, California, USA
H. A. L. Fisher Papers, Bodleian Library, Oxford
Golovin Collection, Hoover Institution, California, USA
Haldane Papers, National Library of Scotland, Edinburgh
Harmsworth Papers, Public Record Office, London
G. A. Hill Transcripts, Hoover Institution, California, USA
Janin Collection, Hoover Institution, California, USA
Kennet Papers, Cambridge University Library
Krasin Archive, Internationaal Instituut voor Sociale Geschiedenis, Amsterdam
Lansbury Papers, British Library of Political and Economic Science, London

Lloyd George Papers, House of Lords Record Office, London
Lothian Papers, Scottish Public Record Office, Edinburgh
MacDonald Papers, Public Record Office, London, and Mac-
    Donald Collection, British Library of Political and
    Economic Science, London
Halford Mackinder Papers, Public Record Office, London
John Maclean Papers, National Library of Scotland, Edinburgh
MacNeill Papers, Public Record Office, London
Maklakov Collection, Hoover Institution, California, USA
Alfred Mattison Collection, Brotherton Collection, Leeds Uni-
    versity Library
Miller Collection, Hoover Institution, California, USA
Milner Papers, Bodleian Library, Oxford
Montagu Papers, India Office Library, London
Morel Papers, British Library of Political and Economic Science,
    London
Newbold Papers, Manchester University Library
Pankhurst Papers, Internationaal Instituut voor Sociale Ges-
    chiedenis, Amsterdam
Passfield Papers, British Library of Political and Economic Sci-
    ence, London
Peel Collection, India Office Library, London
Ponsonby Papers, Public Record Office, London, and Bodleian
    Library, Oxford, and Diary, by courtesy of Lord Ponsonby
    of Shulbrede
Reading Collection, India Office Library, London
Runciman Papers, Newcastle University Library
Scott Papers, British Library, London
Steel-Maitland Papers, Scottish Public Record Office, Edinburgh
Strachey Papers, House of Lords Record Office, London
Templewood Papers, Cambridge University Library
C. P. Trevelyan Papers, Newcastle University Library
Leslie Urquhart, typescript letter, Hoover Institution, California,
    USA
Harold Williams Papers, British Library, London
Worthington-Evans Papers, Bodleian Library, Oxford
Zetland Collection, India Office Library, London

2. *Records of Organisations*

Association of British Chambers of Commerce:
    Executive Committee minutes, 1917–24;
    Foreign and Colonial Affairs Committee minutes;

President's Advisory Committee minutes (Guildhall Library, London)

Birmingham District Trades and Labour Council: Minutes of Council and Executive Committee meetings (Birmingham Public Library)

Birmingham Labour Representation Committee minutes (Birmingham Public Library)

Council of Foreign Bondholders:
Russian Committee minutes;
Correspondence: Russia (Council of Foreign Bondholders, London)

Communist Party:
Dalmuir branch minutes;
Dundee branch minutes;
Sheffield branch minutes (Communist Party, London)

Edinburgh Trades Council minutes (Trades Council, Edinburgh)

Engineering Employers' Federation: Executive Committee minutes; National and Central Conference reports (EEF, London)

Fabian Society:
Executive Committee minute books;
Local Fabian Society minutes (Nuffield College, Oxford)

Federation of British Industries:
Directors' Committee minutes;
Employers' Advisory Council minutes;
Executive Council (later Committee) minutes;
Grand Council minutes;
Organisation and Management Committee minutes (Confederation of British Industry, London).

Glasgow Central Labour Party minutes (Mitchell Library, Glasgow)

Glasgow ILP Federation:
Executive Council minutes;
Minutes of Bi-monthly and Special Aggregate meetings;
Organising Committee minutes;
Rough minute book (Mitchell Library, Glasgow)

Glasgow Trades and Labour Council minutes (Mitchell Library, Glasgow)

Independent Labour Party:
Attercliffe branch minutes (Sheffield Public Library);
Bristol branch minutes (BLPES [microfilm]);

East Ham branch minutes (BLPES);
Edinburgh Central branch papers (National Library of Scotland, Edinburgh);
Minutes etc. of Watford and City of London branches, North London and District Federation and no. 6 Divisional Council (BLPES);
National Administrative Council minutes (BLPES and Brynmor Jones University Library, Hull [microfilm]);
Sheffield Federal Council minutes (Sheffield Public Library)
Labour Party:
Advisory International Committee memoranda (Labour Party, London);
Council of Action archive (Labour Party, London);
Hawick branch papers (National Library of Scotland, Edinburgh);
Joint International Committee minutes (Labour Party, London);
Minutes, Letters and Other Papers of the Labour Party Executive (BLPES);
National Executive Committee minutes (Labour Party, London)
Liverpool Chamber of Commerce: Executive Committee minutes; Russian Trade Section minutes (Liverpool Public Library)
Liverpool Labour Representation Committee, Labour Party, and Labour Party and Trades Council minutes (Liverpool Public Library)
Liverpool Trades Council minutes (Liverpool Public Library)
London Chamber of Commerce:
Council minutes;
Russian Section minutes (Guildhall Library, London)
London Trades Council minutes and papers (Warwick University Library, Coventry [microfilm])
Manchester Association of Importers and Exporters minutes (Manchester Public Library).
Manchester Central ILP minutes (Manchester Public Library)
Manchester Chamber of Commerce minutes (Manchester Public Library)
National Unionist Association: Executive Committee minutes (Conservative Party Research Department, London)
Russo–British Chamber of Commerce: Reports of Proceedings at

Annual General Meetings (Russo-British Chamber of Commerce, London)

Scottish Trades Union Congress: Parliamentary Committee minutes (STUC, Glasgow)

Sheffield Trades and Labour Council:
Delegate Meeting minutes;
Executive Committee minutes (Trades and Labour Council, Sheffield)

Society for Cultural Relations with the USSR: Press cutting book (Society for Cultural Relations, London)

Trades Union Congress: Parliamentary Committee minutes (TUC, London [microfilm])

3. *Government Records* (Public Record Office, London)

Board of Trade: Advisory Committee to the Department of Overseas Trade (BT 90);
Commercial Department (BT 11);
Department of Overseas Trade (BT 60);
Minutes (BT 5).

Cabinet Office: Allied and Imperial Conferences (Cab 29);
Cabinet Minutes (Cab 23);
Cabinet Papers (Cab 24);
Committees: General Series (Cab 27);
Genoa (International Economic) Conference (Cab 31);
Imperial Conferences (Cab 32)

Export Credits Advisory Committee minutes (ECG 1)

Foreign Office: Confidential Prints (F.O. 418);
General Political Correspondence (F.O. 371);
'Green' (Secret) Papers;
Peace Conference Correspondence (F.O. 608).

Home Office: Correspondence and Papers (H.O. 45)

India Office: Political and Secret Department (India Office Library, London)

Prime Minister's Papers (PREM 1)

PUBLISHED SOURCES

1. *Collections of Documents*

Anglo-Sovetskie Otnosheniya 1921–1927: Noty i Dokumenty (Moscow 1927)

Degras, J. (ed.): *Soviet Documents on Foreign Policy*, vol. 1 (London 1951)

The Communist International 1919–43: Documents, vols. 1–2 (London 1956–60)

Dekrety Sovetskoi Vlasti, vols. 1–7 (Moscow: 1957–75; in progress)

Desiat' Let Sovetskoi Diplomatii (akty i dokumenty) (Moscow 1927)

Documents of the History of the Communist Party of India, (ed.) G. Adhikari, vols. 1–2 (Delhi, 1971–4; in progress)

Documents on British Foreign Policy (eds.) E. L. Woodward and R. Butler, First Series, vol. 1–19 (London, 1947–74; in progress)

Dokumenty i Materialy po Istorii Sovetsko-Pol'skikh Otnoshenii, (ed.) I. A. Khrenov et al., vols. 1–4 (Moscow 1963–6; in progress)

Dokumenty Vneshnei Politiki SSSR, (eds.) A. A. Gromyko et al., vols. 1–7 (Moscow 1957–63; in progress)

Eudin, X. Y. and Fisher, H. H. (eds.): *Soviet Russia and the West, 1920–1927* (Stanford 1957)

Eudin, X. Y. and North, R. C. (eds.): *Soviet Russia and the East, 1920–1927* (Stanford 1957)

Klyuchnikov, Yu. V. and Sabanin, A. (eds.): *Mezhdunarodnaya Politika Noveishego Vremeni v Dogovorakh, Notakh i Deklaratsiakh* (3 vols., Moscow 1925–8)

KPSS v Rezolyutsiakh i Resheniakh S"ezdov, Konferentsii i Plenumov Ts. K. (eds.) P. N. Fedoseev and K. U. Chernenko (10 vols., Moscow 1970–2)

Kun, B. (ed.): *Kommunisticheskii Internatsional v Dokumentakh* (Moscow 1933)

Markin, N. (ed.): *Sbornik Sekretnykh Dokumentov iz Arkhiva Byvshego Ministerstva Inostrannykh Del* (3 vols., Petrograd 1917–18)

Sovetsko-Afganskie Otnosheniya 1919–1969, (eds.) V. M. Vinogradov et al. (Moscow 1971)

Sovetsko-Germanskiye Otnosheniya, vols. 1–2 (Moscow 1968–71; in progress)

Tivel', A. and Kheimo, N. (eds.): *Desiat' Let Kominterna v Resheniakh i Tsifrakh* (Moscow-Leningrad 1929)

2. *Reports and Documents of Organisations*

Amalgamated Society of Engineers: *Annual Report* (London 1917–19)

Arcos Banking Corporation Ltd.: *Balance Sheet: December 1923–24* (London 1924)

Association of British Chambers of Commerce: *Monthly Proceedings* (London 1917–24)
  Report of the Executive Council, 1919–21, 1924–25 (London 1920–5)
Becos Traders Ltd.: *Report on the Visit to Russia of the Becos Mission* (London 1923)
Birmingham Chamber of Commerce: *Reports and Bulletins* (Birmingham 1917–24)
Birmingham Trades Council: *Annual Report, 1917–1923/4* (Birmingham 1917–24)
Communist International: *Pervyi Kongress Kominterna Mart 1919g.* (Moscow 1933)
  Vtoroi Kongress Kominterna Iyul' – Avgust 1920g. (Moscow 1934)
  Der Zweite Kongress der Kommunist. Internationale (Hamburg 1921)
  Tretii Kongress Kominterna (Petrograd 1922)
  Protokoll des III Kongresses der Kommunistischen Internationale (Hamburg 1921)
  Fourth Congress of the Communist International: Abridged Report (London 1923)
  IV Kongress Kominterna: Izbrannye Doklady, Rech'i i Rezolyutsii (Moscow 1923)
  Pyatyi Vsemirnyi Kongress: stenograficheskii otchet (2 vols., Moscow 1925)
  Vème Congrès de l'Internationale Communiste: compte rendu analytique (Paris 1924)
  Pervyi S"ezd Narodov Vostoka: stenograficheskie otchety (Petrograd 1920)
  Pervyi S"ezd Revolyutsionnykh Organizatsii Dal'nego Vostoka (Petrograd 1922)
  Executive Committee: *Compte Rendu de la Conférence de l'Executif Elargi* (Paris 1922)
  Rasshirennyi Plenum Ispolnitel'nogo Komiteta (12–13 Iyunya 1923g.) (Moscow 1923)
Council of Action: *Special Conference on Labour and the Russo-Polish War* (London 1920)
  Declaration of the Russian Soviet Government on Polish Independence (London 1920)
  Russia and Poland (London, 10 August 1920)
  Peace with Soviet Russia (London, 17 August 1920)
  Form Your Councils of Action (London n.d.)

Report to the Local Councils of Action, Executives of Trades Councils etc., nos. 1–3 (London, 26 August, 10 September and 1 October 1920)

Council of Foreign Bondholders: *Annual Report* (London 1917–24)

Federation of British Industries: *Annual Report*, 1918/19, 1921/22, 1922/23 (London 1919–23)
    What it Is and What it Does (London 1922)

Glasgow Trades Council: *Annual Report*, 1916/17–1924/25 (Glasgow 1917–25).

Independent Labour Party: *Annual Conference Report* (London 1917–24)
    The Communist International (London 1920)
    The ILP and the Third International (London 1920)
    Glasgow Federation: *Annual Report* (Glasgow 1918–24)
    Left Wing Group: *Moscow's Reply to the ILP* (Glasgow 1920)
    National Administrative Council: *Russia and Britain: Give Work to our People and Peace to the World* (London 1923)

India, Government of: *India in 1920* (Calcutta 1920)
    Indian Politics 1921–1922 (Calcutta 1922)
    India in 1923–1924 (Calcutta 1924)
    Home Department: *Communism in India* (Delhi 1926)
    Communism in India 1924–1927 (Delhi 1927)

Labour Party: *Annual Conference Report* (London 1914–1925)
    Appeal to the British Nation (London 1920)
    Control of Foreign Policy (London 1921)
    Labour and the European Situation (London 1923)
    Labour and the National 'Economy' (London 1922)
    Labour and the New Social Order (London 1918)
    Labour and the Unemployment Crisis (London 1921)
    Labour's Russian Policy: Peace with Soviet Russia (London 1920)
    Memorandum on Unemployment and the International Situation, Reparations and Russia (London 1921)
    Report of the British Labour Delegation to Russia, 1920 (London 1921)
    Report of the British Trades Union Delegation to Russia in November and December, 1924 (London 1925)
    Unemployment: a Labour Policy (London 1921)
    Unemployment, Peace and the Indemnity (London 1921)

Labour Research Department: *Annual Report* (London 1917–24)
    Federation of British Industries (London 1923)
    Labour and Capital in Parliament (London 1923)

Liverpool Chamber of Commerce: *Annual Report* (Liverpool 1920–4)

Liverpool Trades and Labour Council: *1st Annual Report* (Liverpool 1922)

London Chamber of Commerce: *Annual Report* (London 1917–24)

London Trades Council: *Annual Report* (London 1918, 1919, 1923)

Manchester and Salford Trades Council: *Annual Report* (Manchester 1917–22)

Miners' Federation of Great Britain: *Annual Report and Documents* (London 1917–24)

Narodnyi Kommissariat po Inostrannym Delam:

    Gaagskaya Konferentsiya, Iyun'-Iyul' 1922. Sbornik Dokumentov (Moscow 1922)

    Genuezskaya Konferentsiya: Materialy i Dokumenty, vyp. 1 (Moscow 1922)

    Godovoi Otchet NKID Sed'momu S"ezdu Sovetov (1918–1919) (Moscow 1919)

    Godovoi Otchet NKID k VIII S"ezdu Sovetov, 1919–1920gg. (Moscow 1921)

    Godovoi Otchet NKID k IX S"ezdu Sovetov (1920–1921gg.) (Moscow 1922)

    Godovoi Otchet za 1923g. ko II S"ezdu Sovetov (Moscow 1924)

    Godovoi Otchet za 1924g. k III S"ezdu Sovetov (Moscow 1925)

    Krasnaya Kniga (Moscow 1920)

    Livre Rouge: Receuil de Documents Diplomatiques relatifs aux Relations entre la Russie et la Pologne 1918–1920 (Moscow 1920)

    Materialy Genuezskoi Konferentsii (Moscow 1922)

    Mezhdunarodnaya Politika RSFSR v 1922g. Otchet NKID (Moscow 1923)

    Sinyaya Kniga, (ed.) K. M. Troyanovsky (Moscow 1918)

    Sovetskaya Rossiya i Pol'sha (Moscow 1921)

Narodnyi Kommissariat Vneshnei Torgovli:

    Vneshnyaya Torgovlya Rossii za Pervuyu Tret' 1922g. (Moscow 1922)

    Vneshnyaya Torgovlya RSFSR (s Dek. 1920g. po Dek. 1921g.) Otchet k IX Vseros. S"ezdu Sovetov (Moscow 1921)

National 'Hands off Russia' Committee:

    Attacks on Russia during 1921 (London 1922)

    Manifesto of the Woolwich 'Hands off Russia' Committee (London n.d.)

    Peace with Russia: Organized Labour's Demand (London 1920)

Russia's Protest against the British Government's Unwarranted Interference in the Republic's Internal Affairs (mimeo., London 1923)

The Arrest of British Trawlers (mimeo., London 1923)

The British Ultimatum to Russia (London 1923)

The Hague Conference: Interview with the Russian Delegation (London 1922)

Trade with Russia: the Facts (London 1921)

National Unionist Association: *Annual Conference Reports, 1917–1924* (microfilm)

Rossiiskaya Kommunisticheskaya Partiya (Bol'shevikov):

Sed'moi S"ezd R.K.P. (6–8 Marta 1918g.): sten. otchet (Moscow 1923)

VIII S"ezd R.K.P. (B.) 18–23 Marta 1919g.: sten. otchet (Moscow 1919)

Devyatyi S"ezd R.K.P. (29 Marta–14 Aprelya 1920g.): sten. otchet (Moscow 1920)

Desyatyi S"ezd R.K.P. (8–16 Marta 1921g.): sten. otchet (Moscow 1921)

Odinnadtsatyi S"ezd R.K.P. (B.) (27 Marta–2 Aprelya 1922g.): sten. otchet (Moscow 1922)

Dvenadtsatyi S"ezd R.K.P.(B.) (17–23 Aprelya 1923g.): sten. otchet (Moscow 1923)

Trinnadtsatyi S"ezd R.K.P.(B.) (23–31 Maya 1924g.): sten. otchet (Moscow 1924)

Vos'maya Konferentsiya R.K.P.(B.) Dekabr' 1919g. Protokoly (Moscow 1961)

Devyataya Konferentsiya R.K.P.(B.) Sentyabr' 1920g. Protokoly (Moscow 1972)

Proekt Ustava (Moscow 1920)

Programma R.K.P.(B.) prinyata VIII S"ezdom Partii (Moscow 1919)

Russian Trade Delegation Information Department:

Famine in Russia: Documents and Statistics presented to the Brussels Conference (London 1921)

Nailed to the Counter (London 1923)

Restoration of Agriculture in the Famine Areas of Russia (London 1922)

Russian Soviet Federal Socialist Republic: Congresses of Soviets:

Pyatyi S"ezd Sovetov (4–10 Iyulya 1918g.): sten. otchet (Moscow 1918)

Shestoi S"ezd Sovetov (6—9 Noyabrya 1918g.): sten. otchet (Moscow 1919)

Sed'moi S"ezd Sovetov (5—9 Dekabrya 1919g.) : sten. otchet (Moscow 1920)

Vos'moi S"ezd Sovetov (22—29 Dekabrya 1920g.): sten. otchet (Moscow 1921)

Devyatyi S"ezd Sovetov (22—27 Dek. 1921g.): sten. otchet (Moscow 1922)

Desyatyi S"ezd Sovetov (22—27 Dekabrya 1922g.): sten. otchet (Moscow 1923)

Scottish Trades Union Congress: *Annual Report* (Glasgow 1917—24)

Sheffield Chamber of Commerce: *Annual Report* (Sheffield 1920, 1923)

Sheffield Trades and Labour Council: *Annual Report* (Sheffield 1917—24)

Society for Cultural Relations with the USSR: *1st Annual Report* (London 1925)

State Bank of the USSR:
  Gosudarstvennyi Bank SSSR: 1923—1924 god (Moscow 1925)
  The State Bank Note 1923—1924 (Moscow 1924)

Trade Union Congress: *Annual Report* (London 1915—24)
  General Council: *Deputations to the Prime Minister, September 1922* (London 1922)
  Deputations to Ministers, February 1923 (London 1923)
  Parliamentary Committee: Joint Committee on the Cost of Living: *Final Report* (London 1921)

Union of Soviet Socialist Republics: Congresses of Soviets:
  Pervyi S"ezd Sovetov Soyuza SSR (30 Dek. 1922g.): sten. otchet (Moscow 1922)
  Vtoroi S"ezd Sovetov Soyuza SSR (26 Yan.—2 Fevr. 1924g.): sten. otchet (Moscow 1924)

Vserossiiskaya Sel'skokhozyaistvennaya i Kustarno-promyshlennaya Vystavka:
  Byulleten' (Moscow 1922—3)
  Materialy i Dokumenty (Moscow 1922)
  Materialy i Dokumenty, vyp. 2 (Moscow 1923)
  Obshchii Katalog (Moscow 1923)
  Sputnik po Vystavke, kn. 1—2 (Moscow 1923)

Workers' Travel Association: *Annual Report* (London 1924)

3. Government (Parliamentary) Publications

Parliamentary Debates (Hansard): House of Commons (1917–24)
  House of Lords (1917–24)
Parliamentary Papers (1917–24; as indicated)

INTERVIEWS AND CORRESPONDENCE

Rajani Palme Dutt (prominent Communist, editor of *Labour Monthly* from 1921)
Morgan Phillips Price (*Manchester Guardian* correspondent in Russia, left-wing MP for Forest of Dean from 1922)
Tom Reed (ILP member, in Russia 1921–3; correspondence)
Andrew Rothstein (Information Department, Russian Trade, Delegation, from 1920; son of Theodore Rothstein, Soviet diplomat; correspondence)

THESES AND DISSERTATIONS (Unpublished)

Aziz, K. K., *Britain and Muslim India* (Manchester Ph.D, 1959–60)
Bather, L., *A History of Manchester and Salford Trades Council* (Manchester Ph.D, 1956)
McEwen, J. E., *Unionist and Conservative Members of Parliament, 1914–1939* (London Ph.D, 1959)
Meynell, H., *The Second International 1914–1923* (Oxford B.Litt., 1958)
Ritter, G. A., *The British Labour Movement and Russia from the Revolution to Locarno* (Oxford B.Litt., 1959)
Schinness, R., *The Tories and the Soviets: the British Conservative Reaction to Russia, 1917–1927* (SUNY at Binghampton Ph.D, 1972)
Stirk, H., *The Leadership of the Conservative Party, 1902–1951* (B.A. thesis, Manchester 1958; copy in Conservative Research Department, London)

CONTEMPORARY WORKS OF REFERENCE

Anglo-Soviet Trade 1920–1927 (London 1927)
Annual Register
Bracher, S. V. (ed.): *The Herald Book of Labour Members* (London 1923)

Business Prospects Yearbook (London 1923)

Chamber of Commerce for North-West Russia: *Directory for Russian and Foreign Businessmen* (Petrograd 1924)

Directory of Directors (London 1922)

Dod's Parliamentary Companion

Dutt, R. P. (ed.): *Labour International Handbook* (London 1921)

Employer's Year Book (London 1920)

Entsiklopediya Russkogo Eksporta (3 vols., Berlin 1924–5)

Ezhegodnik Kominterna (Moscow-Petrograd 1923)

Ezhegodnik N.K.I.D. (Moscow 1925)

F.B.I. Yearbook and Export Register (London 1922, 1924)

Financial Times Investor's Guide (London 1923)

Foreign Office List

Frolova, V. A. (ed.): *Statistika Vneshnego Tovarobmena Rossii 1921–1923gg.* (Moscow 1923)

Indian Yearbook, (ed.) Sir S. Reed (London 1921–4)

Industrial Yearbook, (ed.) P. Gee (London 1922)

Kutuzov, A. I. (ed.): *Vneshnyaya Torgovlya Soyuza SSR za X Let* (Moscow 1928)

Labour Party: *Labour Speaker's Handbook* (London 1922)

Labour Research Department: *Labour International Year Book* (London 1923)

Labour Who's Who (London 1924, 1927)

Labour Year Book (London 1916, 1919, 1924)

Lees-Smith, H. B. (ed.): *Encyclopedia of the Labour Movement* (3 vols., London 1928)

Peacock, N. (ed.): *Russian Almanac* (London 1919)

Santalov, A. A. (ed.): *SSSR na Angliiskom Rynke*, vyp. 1 (Moscow 1926)

Santalov, A. A. and Segal, L. (eds.): *Commercial Yearbook of the Soviet Union* (London 1925)

Statisticheskii Ezhegodnik (Moscow 1918–24)

Stock Exchange Year Book (London 1923)

Thornsby, F. (ed.): *Who's Who in the Labour and Co-operative Movement* (London 1924)

Tracey, H. (ed.): *The Book of the Labour Party* (3 vols., London 1925)

Vaks, B. (ed.): *Ot Oktyabrya do Genui. Mezhdunarodnye Otnosheniya RSFSR. Spravochnik* (Moscow 1922)

Vinokura, A. P. and Sakulin, S. N. (eds.): *Vnezhnyaya Torgovlya SSSR za period 1918–1927/28* (Moscow 1931)

CONTEMPORARY NEWSPAPERS AND JOURNALS
(all issues for the period consulted unless otherwise indicated)

Amalgamated Engineering Union *Monthly Journal and Report*
Arkos Kommercheskii Byulleten'
Bankers' Magazine (1922–1923)
Birmingham Chamber of Commerce *Journal and Monthly Record*
Board of Trade Journal (1922–1924)
Bol'shevik
Bradford Pioneer (1917, 1919, 1920)
British-Russian Gazette and Trade Outlook (1923–1924)
British Trades Union Review
Bulletin of the Federation of British Industries (1923–1924)
Byulleten' N.K.I.D.
The Call (London)
Chamber of Commerce Journal (London)
The Communist
Contemporary Review
Daily Chronicle (individual issues)
Economist
Edinburgh Review
Ekonomicheskaya Zhizn'
Ekonomicheskoe Obozrenie
Empire Review
The Employer
English Review
Fabian News
Financial News (1923)
Financial Review of Reviews
Financial Times (1923)
Financier (1923)
Fortnightly Review
Forward (Glasgow)
Glasgow Chamber of Commerce *Monthly Journal*
Glasgow Herald
Gleanings and Memoranda (1919, 1921, 1923)
The Herald (later the *Daily Herald*)
Inostrannoe Torgovoe Obozrenie
International Press Correspondence (*Inprecorr*)
Izvestiya (1920–1924)

Journal of the Institute of Bankers (1923)
Kommunisticheskii International
Labour Leader
Labour Magazine
Labour Monthly
Labour Party Local Government, Parliamentary and International Bulletin
Leeds Weekly Citizen (1917, 1919, 1920)
Leicester Pioneer (1917, 1919, 1920)
Liverpool Pioneer (November 1919)
Lloyds' Bank Monthly (1921–1924)
Manchester Chamber of Commerce *Monthly Record*
Manchester Guardian (individual issues)
Manchester Guardian Commercial (1923)
Mezhdunarodnaya Zhizn'
Midland Bank *Monthly Review*
Monthly Journal of the Liverpool Incorporated Chamber of Commerce (1920, 1923)
Narody Vostoka
Narodnoe Khozyaistvo (1920–1924)
The Nation (individual issues)
National Review
Near East and India
New Leader
New Russia
New Statesman
Nineteenth Century and After
Novyi Vostok
Observer (1923)
Pioneer (Merthyr Tydfil) (1917, 1919, 1920)
Pod Znamenem Marksizma
Proletarskaya Revolyutsiya
Pravda (1920–1924)
Quarterly Review
Review of Reviews
Round Table
Russia
Russian Economist
Russian Information and Review
Russian Life
Russian Outlook
Russo-British Chamber of Commerce Journal

Sheffield Chamber of Commerce Journal (1920–1924)
Sheffield Forward (1921–1922)
The Socialist
Socialist Review
Sotsialisticheskoe Khozyaistvo
The Spectator
The Statist
The Times
The Town Crier (Birmingham) (1917, 1919, 1920)
United Empire
Vestnik N.K.I.D.
Vestnik N.K.V.T.
Vestnik Sotsialisticheskoi (later *Kommunisticheskoi*) *Akademii*
Vestnik Statistiki
Vneshnyaya Torgovlya
Westminster Bank Review (1923–1924)
Woman's (later *Workers'*) *Dreadnought*
Woolwich Pioneer and Labour Journal (1917–1920)
The Worker
Workers' Weekly
Yorkshire Factory Times and Workers' Weekly Record (1917, 1919, 1920)
Zhizn' Natsional'nostei

SELECTED MEMOIRS AND BIOGRAPHIES

Agabekov, G., *G.P.U.: Zapiski Chekista* (Berlin 1930)
√Allen, C., *Plough My Own Furrow*, (ed.) M. Gilbert (London 1965)
√Amery, L. S., *My Political Life*, vol. 2 (London 1953)
Anderson, M., *Noel Buxton* (London 1951)
Angell, N., *After All* (London 1951)
Aralov, S., *Vospominaniya Sovetskogo Diplomata* (Moscow 1960)
√Asquith, H. H., *Memories and Reflections* (2 vols., London 1928)
Attlee, C., *As It Happened* (London 1954)
Bailey, F. M., *Mission to Tashkent* (London 1946)
Besedovsky, G. Z., *Na Putiakh k Termidoru* (Paris 1931)
Bell, T., *Pioneering Days* (London 1941)
Blake, R., *The Unknown Prime Minister* (London 1935)
Brockway, A. F., *Inside the Left* (London 1942)
Buchanan, Sir G., *My Mission to Russia* (2 vols., London 1923)
Bullock, A., *The Life and Times of Ernest Bevin*, vol. 1 (London 1960)

Bunsen, V. de, *C. R. Buxton. A Memoir* (London 1948)

Clynes, J. R., *Memoirs* (2 vols., London 1937–8)

Cole, M., ed., *The Diaries of Beatrice Webb 1912–1924* (London 1952)

✗ Cooper, D., *Old Men Forget* (London 1953)

✗ Cunliffe-Lister, P., *I Remember* (London 1948)

D'Abernon, Viscount, *An Ambassador of Peace* (3 vols., London 1929–30)

Dugdale, B., *Arthur James Balfour* (2 vols., London 1939)

Dundas, L. J., *The Life of Lord Curzon* (3 vols., London 1928)

Elton, G., *The Life of James Ramsay MacDonald* (London 1939)

Feiling, K., *The Life of Neville Chamberlain* (London 1946)

Fischer, L., *Men and Politics* (London 1941)

Fry, A. R., *Three Visits to Russia* (London 1942)

Gallacher, W., *Revolt on the Clyde* (London 1936)

Gandhi, M. K., *An Autobiography* (London 1949)

Gilbert, M., *Winston S. Churchill, vol. 4: 1917–1922* (London 1974)
   Winston S. Churchill, vol. 5: 1922–1939 (London 1976)

Gorokhov, I. M. et al., *Chicherin* (2nd ed., Moscow 1973)

✗ Gregory, J. D., *On the Edge of Diplomacy* (London 1928)

Haldane, Lord, *Autobiography* (London 1929)

Hamilton, M. A., *Arthur Henderson* (London 1938)
   J. Ramsay MacDonald (London 1925)
   The Man of Tomorrow: J. Ramsay MacDonald (London 1923)
   Remembering My Good Friends (London 1944)

Hannington, W., *Unemployed Struggles 1919–1936* (London 1936)

Hodges, F., *My Adventures as a Labour Leader* (London 1925)

Humbert-Droz, J., *De Lénine à Staline* (Neuchâtel 1971)
   Mon Evolution du Tolstoïsme au Communisme (Neuchâtel 1969)

James, R. R., (ed.), *Memoirs of a Conservative: J. C. C. Davidson's Memoirs and Papers 1910–1937* (London 1969)

Johnston, T., *Memories* (London 1952)

Jones, T., *Whitehall Diary*, (ed.) K. Middlemas, vol. 1 (London 1969)

Karpova, R. F., *L. B. Krasin—Sovetskii Diplomat* (Moscow 1962)

Kenworthy, J. M., *Soldiers, Statesmen—and Others* (London 1933)

Kirkwood, D., *My Life of Revolt* (London 1936)

L. B. Krasin. Sbornik Vospominanii (Moscow–Leningrad 1926)

Krassin, L., *Leonid Krassin: his Life and Work* (London 1929)

Kremnev, B. G., *Krasin* (Moscow 1968)

Lansbury, G., *My Life* (London 1928)
   What I Saw in Russia (London 1920)

Lloyd George, D., *The Truth about the Peace Treaties* (2 vols., London 1938)
    War Memoirs (2 vols., London 1938)
✕ Long, W., *Memories* (London 1923)
Lyubimov, N. N. and Erlich, G. K., *Genuezskaya Konferentsiya* (Moscow 1963)
Maisky, I. M., *B. Shou i Drugie* (Moscow 1967)
    Lyudi, Sobytiya, Fakty (Moscow 1973)
    Puteshchestvie v Proshloe (Moscow 1960)
    Vospominaniya Sovetskogo Posla (2 vols., Moscow 1964)
    Vospominaniya Sovetskogo Posla v Anglii (Moscow 1960)
Middlemas, K. and Barnes, J., *Baldwin* (London 1969)
Mogilevich, B. L., *Nikitin* (Moscow 1963)
Montagu, E. S., *An Indian Diary* (London 1930)
Morrison, H., *An Autobiography* (London 1960)
Mosley, L., *Curzon, the End of an Epoch* (London 1960)
Murphy, J. T., *New Horizons* (London 1941)
    Preparing for Power (London 1934)
Nabokov, K., *Ispytaniya Diplomata* (Stockholm 1921)
Nehru, J., *An Autobiography* (London 1936)
Nicolson, H., *Curzon: the Last Phase* (London 1934)
Pares, B., *My Russian Memoirs* (London 1931)
Parmoor, Lord, *A Retrospect* (London 1936)
Petrie, Sir C., *Austen Chamberlain*, vol. 2 (London 1940)
Pollitt, H., *Serving My Time* (London 1940)
Postgate, R., *Life of George Lansbury* (London 1951)
Radek, K., *Portrety i Pamflety* (Moscow–Leningrad 1927)
✳ Ransome, A., *The Autobiography of Arthur Ransome*, (ed.) R. Hart-Davis (London 1976)
Riddell, Lord, *Intimate Diary of the Peace Conference and After* (London 1933)
    Lord Riddell's War Diary (London 1933)
Roskill, S., *Hankey, Man of Secrets*, vol. 2 (London 1972)
Roy, M. N., *Memoirs* (Bombay 1964)
Russell, B., *An Autobiography*, vol. 2 (London 1968)
Sacks, B., *J. Ramsay MacDonald: in Thought and Action* (Albuquerque 1952)
Shinwell, E., *Conflict without Malice* (London 1955)
Shumiatsky, B. Z., *Na Postu Sovetskoi Diplomatii* (2nd ed., Moscow 1969)
Smillie, R., *My Life for Labour* (London 1924)

Snowden, P., *An Autobiography* (2 vols., London 1934)
Spratt, P., *Blowing up India* (Calcutta 1955)
Stasova, E. D., *Stranitsy Zhizni i Bor'by* (Moscow 1957)
Stewart, B., *Breaking the Fetters* (London 1967)
Stevenson, F., *Lloyd George: A Diary* (ed.) A. J. P. Taylor (London 1971)
Thomas, J. H., *My Story* (London 1937)
Thomson, B., *Queer People* (London 1922)
 The Scene Changes (London 1939)
Thorne, W., *My Life's Battles* (London 1923)
Trotsky, L. D., *Moya Zhizn'* (2 vols., Berlin 1930)
 Lenin (London 1925)
Trukhanovsky, V. G., *Uinston Cherchill': politicheskaya biografiya* (Moscow 1968)
Turner, B., *About Myself* (London 1930)
Usmani, S., *From Peshawar to Moscow* (Benares 1927)
Vinogradov, K. B., *Devid Lloid Dzhordzh* (Moscow 1970)
Wedgwood, J. C., *Memoirs* (London 1941)
Wilson, T., (ed.) *The Political Diaries of C. P. Scott, 1911–1928* (London 1970)
Woolf, L., *Downhill All The Way* (London 1967)
Woodman, D. (ed.), *Nehru: the First Sixty Years* (2 vols., London 1960)
Zarnitsky, S. and Trofimov, L., *Sovetskoi Strany Diplomat* (Moscow 1968)
Zarnitsky, S. and Sergeev, A., *Chicherin* (Moscow 1967)

CONTEMPORARY PAMPHLETS AND OTHER WRITINGS

Anderson, W. C., *The Profiteers' Parliament* (London 1919)
Anstey, F., *Red Europe* (Glasgow 1921)
Attlee, C., *The Labour Party in Perspective* (London 1937)
Beaverbrook, Lord, *Men and Power 1917–1918* (London 1956)
Bell, T., *The British Communist Party* (London 1937)
Berlovich, E., *Angliya i SSSR* (Leningrad 1927)
Brailsford, H. N., *The Russian Workers' Republic* (London 1921)
Branley, F. and Middleton, J. S., *The Anglo-Russian Treaties* (London 1924)
Bukharin, N., *Ekonomika Perekhodnogo Perioda*, ch. 1 (Moscow 1920)

Bukharin, N. and Preobrazhensky, E. A., *Azbuka Kommunizma* (Moscow 1920)

Bundock, C. J., *Direct Action and the Constitution* (London 1920)

Buxton, C. R., *In a Russian Village* (London 1922)

Bystriansky, V. A., *Imperialisticheskaya Angliya protiv Sotsialisticheskoi Rossii* (Petrograd 1919)

Chicherin, G. V., *Doklady i Noty* (Saratov 1920)
   Stat'i i Rechi po Voprosam Mezhdunarodnoi Politiki (Moscow 1961)
   Vneshnyaya Politika Sovetskoi Rossii za Dva Goda (Moscow 1920)
   Znachenie Vystavki (Moscow 1923)

Churchill, W. S., *The Aftermath* (London 1929)

Coates, W. P., *The Anglo-Russian Treaties* (London 1924)
   Export Credit Schemes and Anglo-Russian Trade (London 1923)
   The Present Position of Anglo-Russian Relations (London 1923)
   Russia's Counter-claims (London 1924)
   Why Russia should be Recognized (London 1924)

Coates, W. P. and Z., *Armed Intervention in Russia, 1918-1922* (London 1935)
   A History of Anglo-Russian Relations (London 1944)

Cole, G. D. H., *Out of Work* (London 1923)

Curzon, G. N., *Persia and the Persian Question* (2 vols., London 1892)
   The Place of India in the Empire (London 1909)
   Problems of the Far East (London 1894)
   Russia in Central Asia and the Anglo-Russian Question (London 1889)

Dutt, R. P., *The Two Internationals* (London 1920)

Farbman, M., *Bolshevism in Retreat* (London 1923)

Fisher, A., *V Rossii i v Anglii* (Moscow 1922)

Fisher, H. H. (ed.), *The Famine in Soviet Russia* (Stanford 1927)

Gallacher, W. and Campbell, J. R., *Direct Action* (London 1919)

Ganetsky, Ya., *Angliiskii Imperializm i SSSR* (Moscow 1927)

Garratt, G. T., *The Mugwumps and the Labour Party* (London 1932)

Glasgow, G., *MacDonald as Diplomatist* (London 1924)

Goode, W. T., *Bolshevism at Work* (London 1920)

Gould, G., *The Coming Revolution in Great Britain* (London 1920)

Groman, V. G. et al., *Vneshnyaya Torgovlya Rossii v 1922-1923 Khozyaistvennom Godu* (Moscow 1923)

Groman, V. G., (ed.), *Vneshnyaya Torgovlya SSSR (za 1923g.) Sbornik* (Moscow 1924)

Guest, L. H., *The Labour Party and the Empire* (London 1926)

Henderson, A., *A World Safe for Democracy* (London 1917)
  Labour and Foreign Affairs (London 1922)
  The Aims of Labour (London 1918)
Hobson, J. A., *The Economics of Unemployment* (London 1922)
Hogue, R. W. (ed.), *British Labour Speaks* (New York 1924)
Ioffe, A. A., *Mirnoe Nastuplenie* (Petrograd 1921)
  Ot Genui do Gaagi: sbornik statei (Moscow 1923)
Kamenev, L. B., *O Vnutrennem i Mezhdunarodnom Polozhenii v Svyazi
  s Novoi Ekonomicheskoi Politikoi* (Moscow 1921)
  Tretii Internatsional: populyarnyi ocherk (Prague 1920)
  Vtoroi S"ezd III Internatsionala (Moscow 1920)
Kerzhentsev, P. M., *Angliiskii Imperializm* (Moscow 1919)
  Revolyutsionnaya Irlandiya (Moscow 1918; 2nd. ed. 1922)
Khinchuk, A., *K Istorii Anglo-Sovetskikh Otnoshenii* (Moscow 1928)
King, J., *Bolshevism and the Bolsheviks* (London 1919)
  A Brace of — (Glasgow 1920)
  Our Policy towards Russia (London 1919)
Krasin, L. B., *Blizhaishie Perspektivy Russkogo Eksporta* (Moscow
  1923)
  Delo Davno Minuvshikh Dnei (Moscow 1925)
  *Kak Raboche-Krest'yanskaya Vlast' vosstnavlivaet Vyvoz Zagranitsu
  Khleba* (Moscow 1924)
  Priznanie de-Iure; Lenin i Vneshnyaya Torgovlya (Khar'kov 1924)
  *Vneshtorg i Vneshnyaya Ekonomicheskaya Politika Sovetskogo
  Pravitel'stva* (Petrograd 1921)
  Voprosy Vneshnei Torgovli (Moscow 1928; rev. ed. 1970)
Kurella, A., *Itogy Genui i Gaagi* (Moscow-Leningrad 1927)
Lenin, V. I., *O Vneshnei Politike Sovetskogo Gosudarstva* (Moscow
  1960)
  Polnoe Sobranie Sochinenii (55 vols., Moscow 1958–65)
Lenin i Vostok: Sbornik Statei (Moscow 1925)
Leninskii Sbornik, vols. 36 (Moscow 1959), 37 (Moscow 1970) and
  38 (Moscow 1975)
Litvinov, M. M., *The Bolshevik Revolution, its Rise and Meaning*
  (London 1918)
Lovat-Fraser, J. A., *Why a Tory joined the Labour Party* (London
  1921)
Lunacharsky, A. V., *Rechi i Stat'i po Mezhdunarodnam Politicheskam
  Voprosam* (Moscow 1959)
MacDonald, J. R., *The Awakening of India* (London 1910)
  The Foreign Policy of the Labour Party (London 1923)

The Government of India (London 1919)
Labour and the Empire (London 1907)
Parliament and Democracy (London 1920)
Parliament and Revolution (Manchester 1919)
The Real Issues of the General Election (London 1923)
Socialism (London 1907)
Socialism for Businessmen (London 1925)
Socialism, Critical and Constructive (London 1924)
Socialism and Society (London 1905)
The Story of the ILP; and What it Stands For (London 1924)
Why Socialism Must Come (London 1924)
Maisky, I. M., *Ekonomicheskaya Politika Sovetskoi Respubliki* (Irkutsk 1920)
 Sovetskaya Rossiya i Kapitalisticheskii Mir (Moscow 1922)
 Vneshnyaya Politika RSFSR 1917–1922 (Moscow 1922)
Malone, Col. C. l'E., *The Russian Republic* (London 1920)
Marshall, A. G., *A Short Memorandum on the Difficulties in the Way of Re-Opening Trade with Russia* (London n.d.)
 Memorandum regarding Unemployment and Russia (Becos Traders, 'private and confidential', London 5 November 1923)
 The Re-Opening of Trade with Russia (London n.d.)
Meijer, J. M., (ed.), *The Trotsky Papers*, vols. 1–2 (The Hague 1964–71)
Mellor, W., *Direct Action* (London 1920)
Mikhailovich, A., *Krushenie Kapitalizma* (Moscow 1918)
Mills, J. S., *The Genoa Conference* (London 1922)
Milyukov, P., *Russia and England* (London 1919)
Morel, E. D., *Labour's National Ideal* (London 1921)
 McNeill correspondence, with covering letter to F. W. Galton (mimeo., 1923) (B.L.P.E.S.)
 The Poison That Destroys (London 1923)
 Ten Years of Secret Diplomacy (London 1915)
 Truth and the War, pref. P. Snowden (London 1916)
Nehru, J., *Soviet Russia* (Allahadbad 1928)
Mstislavsky, S., *Rabochaya Angliya* (Moscow 1924)
Newbold, J. T. W., *Bankers, Bondholders and Bolsheviks* (Glasgow 1919)
Ol', P. V., *Inostrannye Kapitaly v Rossii* (Petrograd 1922)
Orton, W., *Labour in Transition* (London 1921)
Paul, W., *Hands off Russia!* (Glasgow 1919)
 Labour and Empire: a Study in Imperialism (Glasgow 1917)

Pavlovich, M.P., *Osnovy Imperialisticheskoi Politiki* (Moscow 1921)
    'Russkii Vopros' v Angliiskoi Vneshnei Politiki (1922–24) (Moscow 1924)
    Sovetskaya Rossiya i Kapitalisticheskaya Angliya (Moscow 1925)
    Voprosy Kolonial'noi i Natsional'noi Politiki i Tretii Internatsional (Moscow 1920)
Pethick-Lawrence, F. W., *The Labour Party: What it Is, What it Wants, and How it Means to Get It* (London 1922)
Ponsonby, A., intr., *The Anglo-Soviet Treaties* (London 1924)
Postgate, R., *The Workers' International* (London 1920)
Preobrazhensky, E. A., *Itogy Genuezskoi Konferentsii* (Moscow 1922)
    Ot NEPa k Sotsializmu (Moscow 1922)
Price, M. P., *Capitalist Europe and Socialist Russia* (London 1919)
    The Origins and Growth of the Russian Soviets (London 1919)
    The Truth about Allied Intervention in Russia (Moscow 1918)
Radek, K., *Golod v Rossii i Kapitalisticheskii Mir* (Moscow 1921)
    Likvidatsiya Versal'skogo Mira (Moscow 1922)
    Mezhdunarodnaya Politika SSSR (Moscow-Leningrad 1925)
    Put' Kommunisticheskogo Internatsionala (Petrograd 1921)
    Vneshnyaya Politika Sovetskoi Rossii (Moscow 1923)
Rafail, A., *Anglo-Sovetskii Dogovor* (Moscow 1924)
Rakovsky, Kh. G., *Angliya i Rossiya* (Khar'kov 1923)
    Nakanune Genui (Moscow 1922)
Ransome, A., *Six Weeks in Russia in 1919* (London 1919)
    The Crisis in Russia (London 1921)
    The Truth about Russia (London 1918)
Reading, Lord, *Speeches . . . from 1st April 1921 to 1st April 1926* (Simla 1926)
Rotshstein, F. A. (ed.), *Mirovaya Politika v 1924g. Sbornik Statei* (Moscow 1925)
Russell, B., *The Theory and Practice of Bolshevism* (London 1920)
Safarov, G., *Kolonial'naya Revolyutsiya* (Moscow 1921)
    Natsional'nyi Vopros i Proletariat (Petrograd 1922)
    Problemy Vostoka (Petrograd 1922)
Seven Members of the Labour Party, *The Labour Party's Aims: a Criticism and a Re-statement* (London 1923)
Shtein, B., *Gaagskaya Konferentsiya* (Moscow 1922)
    Genuezskaya Konferentsiya (Moscow 1922)
    'Russkii Vopros' na Parizhskoi Mirnoi Konferentsii (Moscow 1949)
    'Russkii Vopros' v 1920–1921gg. (Moscow 1958)

Sovetskaya Rossiya v Kapitalisticheskom Okruzhenii (Moscow 1921)
Torgovaya Politika i Torgovye Dogovory Sovetskoi Rossii 1917–1922gg. (Moscow 1923)
Stalin, J. V., *Sochineniya*, vols. 4–6 (Moscow 1946–55)
Snowden, E., *Through Bolshevik Russia* (London 1920)
Snowden, P., *If Labour Rules* (London 1923)
Labour and the New World (London 1921)
Socialism Made Plain (London 1920)
Stuchka, P., *Konstitutsiya RSFSR v Voprosakh i Otvetakh* (Moscow 1919)
Sultan Zade, A., *Ekonomika i Problemy Natsional'nykh Revolyutsii v Stranakh Blizhnego i Dal'nego Vostoka* (Moscow-Leningrad 1922)
Sverdlov, V., *K Voprosu o Kontsessii Urkarta* (Moscow 1923)
Swanwick, H. M., *Builders of Peace* (London 1924)
Taigin, I. (Maisky), *Angliya i SSSR* (Leningrad 1926)
Tanin, M., *Desiat' Let Vneshnei Politiki SSSR* (Moscow 1927)
Mezhdunarodnaya Politika SSSR (1917–1924) (Moscow 1925)
Thomas, J. H., *When Labour Rules* (London 1920)
Trevelyan, C. P., *From Liberalism to Labour* (London 1921)
The U.D.C. (London 1919; 3rd ed. 1921)
Trotsky, L. D., *The Bolsheviki and World Peace* (New York 1918)
Novyi Etap (Moscow 1921)
Pyat' Let Kominterna (Moscow-Leningrad n.d.)
Sochineniya (11 vols., Moscow-Leningrad 1925–7)
Where is Britain Going? (London 1926)
Zapad i Vostok (Moscow 1924)
Troyanovsky, K., *Vostok i Revolyutsiya* (Moscow 1918)
Vasil'ev, M. I., *Put' k Kommunizmu* (Petrograd 1920)
Vorovsky, V. V., *Stat'i i Materialy po Voprosam Vneshnei Politiki* (Moscow 1959)
Vospominaniya o V. I. Lenine (5 vols., Moscow 1968–9)
Wauters, A., *Les Travaillistes dirigent l'Empire Britannique* (Brussels 1924)
Webb, S., *The New Constitution of the Labour Party* (London 1918)
Principles of the Labour Party (London 1919)
Webb, S. and B., *A History of Trade Unionism* (London 1926)
Wells, H. G., *Russia in the Shadows* (London 1920)
Williams, R., *The New Labour Outlook* (London 1920)
Zangwill, I., *Hands off Russia* (London 1919)
Zinoviev, G., *Doklad o Deyatel'nosti Ispolkoma Kommunisticheskogo Internatsionala za 1920–1921gg.* (Moscow 1921)

Glavnye Etapy v Razvitii Kominterna (Moscow 1922)

Istoriya R.K.P.(B.): populyarnyi ocherk (Petrograd 1924)

Kommunisticheskii Internatsional: doklad na Vos'mom S"ezde R.K.P. (Petrograd 1920)

Kommunisticheskii Internatsional za Rabotoi (Moscow-Petrograd 1922)

Mirovaya Revolyutsiya i Kommunisticheskii Internatsional (Petrograd 1920)

Nabolevshie Voprosy Mezhdunarodnogo Rabochego Dvizheniya (Moscow 1920)

Sochineniya (10 vols., Leningrad 1925–7)

Taktika Kominterna: posleslovie k rabotam III Vsemirnogo Kongressa (Petrograd 1921)

Tretii Kommunisticheskii Internatsional (Petrograd 1921)

Vtoroi Kongress Kommunisticheskogo Internatsionala i ego Znacheniya (Moscow 1920)

Zolotar'ev, A. I., *Priznanie De-Iure i Zadachi Vneshnei Politiki* (Khar'kov 1924)

Index